Participant Observers

BERKELEY SERIES IN BRITISH STUDIES

Edited by James Vernon

1. *The Peculiarities of Liberal Modernity in Imperial Britain*, edited by Simon Gunn and James Vernon
2. *Dilemmas of Decline: British Intellectuals and World Politics, 1945–1975*, by Ian Hall
3. *The Savage Visit: New World People and Popular Imperial Culture in Britain, 1710–1795*, by Kate Fullagar
4. *The Afterlife of Empire*, by Jordanna Bailkin
5. *Smyrna's Ashes: Humanitarianism, Genocide, and the Birth of the Middle East*, by Michelle Tusan
6. *Pathological Bodies: Medicine and Political Culture*, by Corinna Wagner
7. *A Problem of Great Importance: Population, Race, and Power in the British Empire, 1918–1973*, by Karl Ittmann
8. *Liberalism in Empire: An Alternative History*, by Andrew Sartori
9. *Distant Strangers: How Britain Became Modern*, by James Vernon
10. *Edmund Burke and the Conservative Logic of Empire*, by Daniel I. O'Neill
11. *Governing Systems: Modernity and the Making of Public Health in England, 1830–1910*, by Tom Crook
12. *Barbed-Wire Imperialism: Britain's Empire of Camps, 1876–1903*, by Aidan Forth
13. *Aging in Twentieth-Century Britain*, by Charlotte Greenhalgh
14. *Thinking Black: Britain, 1964–1985*, by Rob Waters
15. *Black Handsworth: Race in 1980s Britain*, by Kieran Connell
16. *Last Weapons: Hunger Strikes and Fasts in the British Empire, 1890–1948*, by Kevin Grant
17. *Serving a Wired World: London's Telecommunications Workers and the Making of an Information Capital*, by Katie Hindmarch-Watson
18. *Imperial Encore: The Cultural Project of the Late British Empire*, by Caroline Ritter
19. *Saving the Children: Humanitarianism, Internationalism, and Empire*, by Emily Baughan
20. *Cooperative Rule: Community Development in Britain's Late Empire*, by Aaron Windel
21. *Are We Rich Yet? The Rise of Mass Investment Culture in Britain*, by Amy Edwards
22. *Participant Observers: Anthropology, Colonial Development, and the Reinvention of Society in Britain*, by Freddy Foks

Participant Observers

*Anthropology, Colonial Development,
and the Reinvention of Society in Britain*

Freddy Foks

UNIVERSITY OF CALIFORNIA PRESS

University of California Press
Oakland, California

© 2023 by Freddy Foks

Library of Congress Cataloging-in-Publication Data

Names: Foks, Freddy, 1989– author.
Title: Participant observers : anthropology, colonial development, and the reinvention of society in Britain / Freddy Foks.
Description: Oakland, California : University of California Press, [2023] | Series: Berkeley series in British studies ; 22 | Includes bibliographical references and index.
Identifiers: LCCN 2022027199 (print) | LCCN 2022027200 (ebook) | ISBN 9780520390324 (cloth) | ISBN 9780520390331 (paperback) | ISBN 9780520390348 (ebook)
Subjects: LCSH: Ethnology—Great Britain—History—20th century. | Economic development—Great Britain—20th century. | National characteristics, British. | Great Britain—Colonies—History—20th century.
Classification: LCC GN308.3.G7 F65 2023 (print) | LCC GN308.3.G7 (ebook) | DDC 306.0941/0904—dc23/eng/20220714
LC record available at https://lccn.loc.gov/2022027199
LC ebook record available at https://lccn.loc.gov/2022027200

32 31 30 29 28 27 26 25 24 23
10 9 8 7 6 5 4 3 2 1

Contents

Map	*vii*
Acknowledgments	*ix*
Abbreviations	*xiii*
Introduction	1
1. Islands and Institutions	
Anthropology in Britain and the British Empire in the First Decades of the Twentieth Century	9
2. Philanthropists and Imperialists	
Indirect Rule, the Rockefeller Foundation and the Rise of LSE Anthropology	32
3. Pencils, Schemes and Letters	
Fieldwork and Pedagogy in 1930s Social Anthropology	58
4. Popularising the Field	
Interwar Anthropologists on the Radio and in Literary Culture	80
5. From Kinship Studies to Community Studies	
'Race Relations', the 'Traditional Working-Class Neighbourhood' and the 'Social Network' in Post-war British Sociology	102

6. The Development Decades
   The African Survey, *the CSSRC and Three Approaches
   to Social Anthropology in the British Empire, 1935–1955*   130

7. From Development Economics to the 'Moral Economy'
   *At the Margins of Anthropology, Economics and Social History
   in the 1950s and 1960s*   152

Epilogue   175

Notes   183
Bibliography   229
Index   257

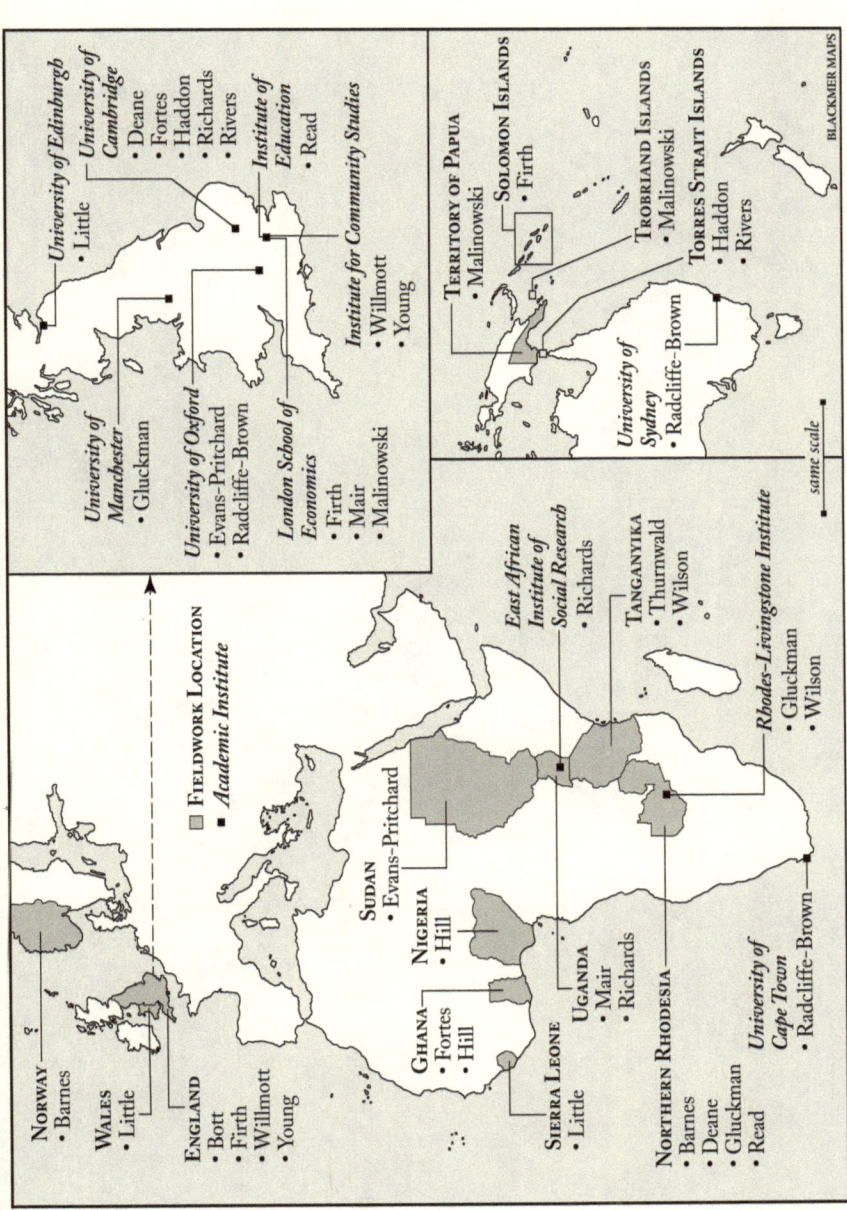

Map showing where the anthropologists mentioned in this book did their fieldwork and the higher education institutions where they subsequently taught.

Acknowledgments

This book argues that academics' ideas are nurtured by patrons, funders and colleagues. I could not have written what follows without the labour of others.

Peter Mandler's advice and encouragement guided this project from a vague research proposal into the PhD dissertation that formed the first draft of this book. Over many years he has answered panicked emails, written endless references, read terrible drafts and suggested refinements, and has done so with kindness and gentle encouragement. Thank you Peter. I wrote my PhD dissertation often with my examiners, Susan Pedersen and Joel Isaac, in mind. Their combined knowledge and close reading during my viva prompted me to write what I hope is a much better book. James Vernon has been a constant source of enthusiasm and intellectual inspiration throughout that process of revision and has kept me on track and open to new ideas. The two reviewers for the University of California Press were a dream. They both offered ways to improve the text and a much-needed confidence boost in the final stretch of writing up. At the Press I would like to thank Niels Hooper and Naja Pulliam Collins for shepherding the manuscript through the editing process, and my thanks to Jon Dertien and Sharon Langworthy for their help in preparing the book for publication.

I owe my friends and colleagues so much. Every idea and every word has been run past multiple people multiple times. My interest in social anthropology was sparked by Rev. Rupert Demery, who showed some sceptical teens a video of the Zande chicken oracle during an AS-level RS class. Anne Goldgar unknowingly provided the subsequent impetus by assigning works of social anthropology alongside historiography in her undergraduate class on early modern European cultural history at King's College, London.

To Tom Arnold-Forster, Laura Carter, Brendan Downey, Merve Fejzula, Hester Van Hensbergen, Mimi Howard, Max Long, George Moore, Tom Pye and Emily Rutherford, and to all my friends who have been members of the NYCTC group, especially those who read an early draft of chapter 4 back in 2016: thank you. Roseanna Webster cast a critical and constructive eye over chapter 4 when it was a PhD chapter and made suggestions that greatly improved it and for which I am very grateful. Early versions of all these chapters were workshopped variously at Cambridge, Columbia, Princeton and NACBS 2016 and 2018. My thanks to the organisers of those events and to the audiences. Parts of what became chapters 6 and 7 were presented at a workshop organised by Anna Alexandrova at King's College, Cambridge, and I am very grateful to Anna, Federico Brandmayr and Tejas Parasher for their feedback. Lorraine Daston was a visiting fellow at King's during that time, and I would like to thank her for her comments on what would become chapter 3. Alma Igra organised a book workshop during which Taylor Moore suggested I start the book with Barbara Pym: thank you, Taylor. Robin Osborne organised a manuscript workshop at King's in May 2021 for the almost-final versions of chapters 3, 4 and 5. John Arnold, Lise Butler, Cléo Chassonnery-Zaïgouche, Matei Candea, Stefan Collini, Simon Goldhill, David Good, Peter Mandler, Helen McCarthy, Basim Musallam, Michael Sonenscher and Richard Staley all took part and helped me sharpen my arguments over three (sometimes gruelling) days on Zoom. I am grateful for their close engagement with my ideas.

Lise Butler and Roslyn Dubler generously shared their unpublished work when I was researching chapter 5: huge thanks to both of them. Grahame Foreman responded to emails about the Rhodes-Livingstone Institute, and his ground-breaking Berkeley PhD dissertation (available open access online) was a great help when researching this book. Katherine Ambler shared unpublished work on the Rhodes-Livingstone Institute and on Raymond Firth. John Lonsdale and Bruce Berman also shared forthcoming work and met with me to discuss Malinowski and Kenyatta. Ray Abrahams and John Pilgrim offered their recollections about post-war social anthropology and suggested ideas that helped researching that topic. Keith Thomas was a gracious host and an informative interview subject when I went to talk to him at All Souls, Oxford, in May 2016. I am grateful to Carrie Humphrey, who lent me a book and suggested citations for my conclusion. My thanks to Alan Macfarlane for our conversations about this book and for the books he has given me. Adam Kuper has been an encouraging and inspiring reader and interlocutor throughout the process of writing and researching this monograph; I owe him a huge debt of gratitude.

I would like to thank all the archivists whose expertise I have relied on. Special thanks to Emma Pizarro at the LSE for helping me source images at very late notice. I would like to acknowledge Elaine Anderson and the Geographical Association for permission to reproduce the map in chapter 1, SAGE Publishing (and the journal *Human Relations*) for the diagram in chapter 4, and Hugh Firth for permission to reproduce the diagram of kinship relations from his father's papers at the LSE. Kate Blackmer made the brilliant map of anthropologists, academic institutions and field sites.

Parts of chapters 1 and 2 have appeared as Freddy Foks, 'Bronislaw Malinowski, "Indirect Rule," and the Colonial Politics of Functionalist Anthropology, ca. 1925–1940', *Comparative Studies in Society and History*, 60.1 (2018), 35–57 (copyright Society for the Comparative Study of Society and History). Parts of chapter 3 have been published as 'Constructing the Field in Inter-war Social Anthropology: Power, Personae and Paper Technology', *Isis*, 111/4 (2020), 717–39 (copyright History of Science Society). I wish to thank the reviewers for their comments on those articles and the editors of both journals for their permission to republish here.

Part of the funding to write and research this book was provided by the Arts and Humanities Research Council. I also wish to thank the trustees of the Henry Fund for awarding me a Procter Fellowship at Princeton University and to acknowledge the support of my advisor there, Robert Tignor. Without that year at Princeton and the support of David Cannadine, Linda Colley and Susan Pedersen, who all let me sit in on their graduate classes, it would have been impossible to range over the topics I planned to tackle. I wrote up this book at King's College, Cambridge. I wish to thank the Provost and Fellows for financially supporting my research and for providing such a wonderful environment in which to work.

Finally, thanks to Charlie, to my family and to my non-academic friends whose eyes (I notice) often glaze over when I try to explain what I spend my days writing about. Their polite lack of interest in social anthropology and their good sense about what really matters in life kept me suitably distracted from the otherwise solitary act of writing this book. Finally, I would like to thank my grandmother and my aunt, who always supported my research and who were both so proud of my achievements. I dedicate this book to their memory.

Abbreviations

ASA   Association of Social Anthropologists
CSSRC   Colonial Social Science Research Council
EAISR   East African Institute of Social Research
IIALC   International Institute of African Languages and Cultures
LSE   London School of Economics and Political Science
RLI   Rhodes-Livingstone Institute

Introduction

This book is about the place of social anthropology in Britain's intellectual culture. Barbara Pym captured the mood of this culture in her novel *Less Than Angels* (1955). Pym's plot turns on an attempt by a group of social anthropologists to lobby a rich American for fieldwork funding. But *Less Than Angels* is also about love, class and urban change, literature, youth and suburbia. On buses, in country houses and in restaurants, the book's characters describe themselves and their society using terms of anthropological art such as 'social structure' and 'joking relationships'.[1] Like *Less Than Angels*, this book also follows the money (often to rich Americans), and it shows, too, how society and social change were re-imagined in an anthropological idiom in mid-century Britain.

The year Pym's novel was published, 1955, saw social anthropology at the apex of its intellectual prestige, both as an academic discipline and, as the literary critic Raymond Williams explained, as a source for thinking of culture as a 'whole way of life'.[2] Over the course of seven chapters this book sets out the various forces that propelled anthropologists into such a position of influence and the field's subsequent decline in the policy sphere. In brief, government funding in the 1940s allowed anthropologists to study development projects in the British Empire, and their work then began to be read by a wide range of scholars creating new ways to imagine 'the social' in Britain.[3] Soon, however, things began to change. Only a few years after Pym's book was published, the rise of development economics and the growth of anticolonial politics challenged the anthropologists' intellectual authority in the British Empire and its former colonies. The 1960s was a time of transition in the history of the discipline: in the United Kingdom (UK), academics continued to emulate anthropologists' holistic social analyses; in Britain's former colonies, social anthropology was often criticised as conservative, irrelevant or imperialist. This is therefore a story of rise and a fall, from one point of view, and rise and diffusion, from another.

Setting the history of anthropology in its wider cultural, political and intellectual contexts is a more familiar move across the Atlantic, where Franz Boas, Margaret Mead and Ruth Benedict have long figured in histories of racism, science and cultural relativism.[4] By contrast, when most historians think about British anthropology, they tend to imagine a rather dry and dull discipline that was more obviously compromised by the colonial context of its research. While it is always dangerous to generalise, historians tend to think of American anthropologists in the first half of the twentieth century as studying the formation of 'personality' in cross-cultural contexts, whereas British anthropologists tended to analyse 'social structures'.[5] When comparing these national traditions, the British are often found wanting. For instance, according to one of the discipline's preeminent historians, it was their production of intensive field studies after the 1920s that led to the 'decline of anthropology's popular relevance' in Britain; another summed up decades of research on the history of social anthropology by lamenting: 'How could so many intelligent anthropologists have been so long infected by such a sterile and/or derivative viewpoint?'[6]

But these arguments present us with a quandary. For if social anthropology was really so 'sterile' and 'derivative', why was it so influential? From Aldous Huxley's speculative fiction, to the community studies of Elizabeth Bott and Michael Young, to the social histories of Keith Thomas and E. P. Thompson, British writers and academics found value and inspiration in works of social anthropology. This reception history has yet to be told, perhaps because so many of social anthropology's historians have been so negative about its theories and methods.[7] By contrast, we now have a good sense of the impact of literary criticism (especially the writings of F. R. Leavis) in mid-century Britain: a discipline that was influentially described by Wolf Lepenies as Britain's 'concealed sociology'.[8] Since Lepenies made this argument, sociologists have been busy 'unconcealing' their past, either by ignoring social anthropologists or by patronising them as 'gentlemanly social scientists'.[9]

The history of twentieth-century anthropology has thus been squeezed between histories of sociology and histories of literary criticism; it has been left largely to disciplinary historians, often themselves anthropologists, to unearth.[10] So while we possess a number of what Stefan Collini calls 'discipline' histories, which seek to bore a '"vertical" hole in the past' in order to unearth 'the concerns of the current practitioners', what we lack is an 'intellectual' history of social anthropology that would 'excavate a "lateral" site, to explore the presuppositions, ramifications, and resonances of ideas, which may often involve pursuing them into neighbouring fields.'[11]

This book offers one such 'lateral' history by tracking the formation of anthropology across the boundaries that have sprung up around anthropology, economics and sociology. By excavating this broader intellectual history, I tell a different tale to the one heard by generations of undergraduates. Traditionally, the story goes, British anthropology underwent a methodological 'revolution' when the Polish-born ethnographer Bronislaw Malinowski did his fieldwork in the Trobriand Islands and wrote about these experiences in *Argonauts of the Western Pacific* (1922).[12] The lasting importance of *Argonauts*, it is often explained, resides in the fact that Malinowski asked his readers to adopt the 'native's point of view, his relation to life, to realise *his* vision of *his* world.'[13] To do this, anthropologists were told to live for an extended period of time amongst the community they wanted to study. Then, what may seem to the outsider to be mystifying behaviours would condense into a kind of order, as patterns and regularities emerged. In Malinowski's day this approach to patient, intense participant observation went along with a kind of sociological 'functionalism': the idea that each society functioned as a social whole. To give another famous example of this kind of approach, Edward Evans-Pritchard argued that a belief in magic and witchcraft was not 'irrational' but functioned as a way to make sense of the world and of society, in his important book *Witchcraft, Oracles, and Magic among the Azande* (1937).[14] This turn to fieldwork in British anthropology has been the source of methodological inspiration and debate ever since.

This well-worn historical sketch emphasises individual anthropologists and their genius. The turn to fieldwork and functionalism is the result of the power and persuasion of ideas alone. It leaves underexplained how theories changed, which methods were discarded and why the turn to fieldwork became so influential. Rather than presume that Malinowski and Evans-Pritchard had some power to compel their readers to adopt a 'methodological revolution' through their prose, this book shows how anthropologists transformed their discipline in dialogue with one other and with colonial administrators, their research assistants, the subjects of their ethnographies and philanthropic funders. To reconstruct this more richly contextual account of anthropology's history, we need to look beyond anthropologists' published ethnographies and dig into their archives. This allows us to understand these men and women in much the same way that they wrote about their own subjects – as 'others' situated in cultures formed by institutions, exchanges, feuds and rituals – and to centre the specific places where anthropological knowledge was constructed, from the South Pacific to Bermondsey, from the classrooms of the London School of Economics (LSE) to the printed pages of journals and ethnographic monographs.[15]

The archives left by social anthropologists are exceptionally rich and have been surprisingly underexplored by historians. Of necessity, I have had to be selective about exactly which topics to focus on. I have chosen to dwell on questions of particular contemporary salience: expertise, ideas about 'race', economics, kinship and community. I have also had to be selective about where I start my tale. It would be possible to begin a book on the history of social anthropology back during the Enlightenment or even in the Renaissance.[16] Thematically, it would be possible to frame many of the discipline's concerns in the wake of the great intellectual debates of the Victorian era: about Christianity, the Bible and evolution.[17] I have not followed either of these paths. Nor have I written a history of social anthropology solely as a professional organisation.[18] Rather, I pose a set of connected questions: How did anthropology come to be so marked by the 'social' in twentieth-century Britain (rather than by anatomy or museology or archaeology), and why did anthropologists' theories and methods come to have such a great deal of influence on neighbouring disciplines at mid-century? Both of these questions respond to Collini's demand for 'lateral' intellectual history, and I hope that answering them will appeal to readers in anthropology departments, historians studying modern Britain and all those interested in the question of how social research influences discourses of social change.[19]

In sum, my aim is to show that social anthropology had a far wider intellectual reach in Britain than has hitherto been appreciated. I have tried to achieve this aim by constructing two narrative arcs. The first narrative begins with the professionalising culture of early twentieth-century anthropology in Britain and the British Empire. The opening chapters argue that colonial politics, Rockefeller Foundation funding and sheer good fortune led to the concentration of an intense anthropological research seminar at the LSE during the 1930s. I explain how the discipline's focus on fieldwork and the intricacies of social life rather than on anatomy and museology was reproduced at the LSE not merely via the force of Malinowski's ideas, but because he secured funding from the Rockefeller Foundation and patronage via alliances with prominent colonial grandees. I describe how these ties between anthropologists and their patrons can explain social anthropology's rise in the 1930s and also how the vicissitudes of patronage made anthropology vulnerable to criticism in the 1950s and 1960s, when the discipline's financial backers shifted their interests towards economics. This narrative encompasses the rise and fall of social anthropology as a prop to colonial development.

The book's second narrative focuses on the dispersion of anthropological ideas and methods in mid-century Britain. By the 1950s social anthropology was increasingly perceived as a valuable body of theory that could explain 'the social' in a non-Marxist, non-economically determinist fashion: as a 'whole way of life', as Raymond Williams put it. The post-war decades stand, then, as an inflection point in the discipline's history and also in the narrative arc of this book. Whereas in the post-war British Empire, economics was muscling social anthropology out of the field by the mid-1950s, it was anthropologists' functionalist desire to connect together kinship, economics, law and religion – to reconstruct the 'native's point of view' – that made their ideas so appealing to writers, academics and social scientists studying Britain's present and its past. Telling these twin narratives – of social anthropology's rise and fall as a prop to colonial development and rise and afterlife in Britain's intellectual culture – bridges the colonial and metropolitan histories of social anthropology.[20]

This immediately raises a question about the 'Britishness' of British social anthropology. After all, Malinowski was born in Poland, and the other pioneering anthropologist of his generation, Alfred Radcliffe-Brown, spent much of his career outside the UK (in South Africa, then Australia and then the USA). Furthermore, several of the key figures discussed in this book – Meyer Fortes and Max Gluckman most prominently – owed a great deal to the teaching, mentorship and theories of the South African anthropologist Winnifred Hoernlé.[21] Nevertheless, the professionalisation of this generation of Hoernlé's students flowed ultimately in one direction: from South Africa to Britain, and then on into university posts from there. It was Malinowski's seminar that formed what sociologists of science would call the 'obligatory passage point' in their disciplinary formation.[22] This is why this book is framed in an overwhelmingly national and imperial context, introducing some South African and Australian institutions but placing French, American and German ideas at the margins.[23] Choosing to centre different locations within these transnational histories, most importantly South Africa and Australia, would have meant writing a very different book.[24] A global history of social anthropology still waits to be written.

I justify using an imperial rather than a global or comparative lens because it was in the British Empire that British social anthropology came of age, and it was in British universities that what Alfred Gell called its 'seminar culture' reproduced itself.[25] To be sure, the history of British anthropology cannot be explained in a hermetically sealed national container. Thus, even though this book is about British anthropology and is aimed at an audience of scholars mostly in British studies, a national frame is insufficient, as so much of social anthropology's history was transnational, imperial and international. To give only one example taken from chapter 2, British imperial policy began to be associated with the League of Nations and with 'indirect rule' in the 1920s, which in turn influenced the discipline's fortunes and explains its contemporary appeal. Only by interlacing anthropology's colonial and metropolitan histories together can we explain how overlapping networks of patronage and funding concentrated and narrowed a wider 'community of inquiry' into a well-financed and productive disciplinary project with a common set of protocols and research questions by the 1940s.[26]

The result (from the outside looking in) was a narrow intellectual outlook, remarked upon by the American anthropologist George Peter Murdock in 1951. 'British social anthropology', he wrote, was a paradigm marked by an interest in kinship and the practice of intensive fieldwork, whose members tended to ignore theoretical influences from outside their own in-group.[27] Scholars writing in the critical spirit of post-1960s disciplinary history have tended to agree with that assessment, taking issue with the British anthropologists' penchant for positivism and their proximity to colonial politics.[28] While these arguments clearly have some purchase, they have led historians to underestimate or simply ignore how influential social anthropologists' ideas and methods were in the 1950s and 1960s. One writer who did appreciate how important social anthropology had been to Britain's intellectual culture was thirty-year-old Perry Anderson. Looking back over the recent past in 1968, Anderson suggested that British social anthropology, unlike British sociology, had been a truly innovative and pathbreaking field. Anthropology had achieved this status, he argued, because it had been 'useful to colonial administration and dangerous to no domestic prejudice', concluding that 'these were the twin conditions of existence of British anthropology, as it developed.'[29] Anderson argued influentially that it was only outside the empiricist and positivist culture of metropolitan Britain that such a flourishing research program could have survived in an otherwise barren wasteland of anti-intellectualism.

Since Anderson made this argument, we now know a great deal more about the extent of anthropology's entanglements with colonial rule. At its most ambitious, this history has been set in a genealogy running from John and J. S. Mill in the British Raj, via interwar social anthropology, to the Cold War and Central Intelligence Agency (CIA)-sponsored social science.[30] There is a risk, however, in writing about the history of social anthropology in this fashion. As Talal Asad explained in the often-cited introduction to *Anthropology & the Colonial Encounter* (1973), 'it is a mistake to view social anthropology in the colonial era as primarily an aid to colonial administration, or as the simple reflection of colonial ideology ... bourgeois consciousness has always contained within itself profound contradictions and ambiguities.'[31] Archie Mafeje made a similar point four years later. The fact that anthropology was a colonial science was not particularly interesting; how could it not have been? The important thing was to link social anthropology to a particular ideology of colonial control, to a bourgeois, liberal sensibility that aimed at 'reformism', both in Europe and in the European empires.[32] This diminishment of anthropology's ideological power and its subaltern status with respect to the state has been summed up by one commentator: 'Anthropology needed empires far more than empires needed anthropologists.'[33]

This book carries this conversation about anthropology and empire forward by centring what Asad called the discipline's 'contradictions and ambiguities', explaining how the changing contours of imperial power, especially in Africa, warped and guided anthropology's institutionalisation, first by competition between policies of indirect rule and settler colonialism, then by colonial development and finally by decolonisation. The second way this book contributes to histories of anthropology and empire is to bring metropolitan histories together with imperial histories, in ways that Mafeje urged. For if we now know more about anthropology's entanglements with empire, we know far less about its metropolitan contexts. This book argues that anthropological knowledge and the colonial fieldwork encounters from which it was constructed came to have their greatest impact in informing intellectual debate about Britain, influencing new studies of community and culture. Adopting Collini's 'lateral view' results in some surprising conclusions about the wide-ranging and long-lasting influences of anthropological ideas in twentieth-century Britain. As we wind from metropole to colony and back again, we will come to the surprising conclusion that Perry Anderson's thesis needs to be turned on its head: the discipline was mostly useless to colonial administrators; instead, its lasting legacy lay in shaping debates about social change in Britain.

What follows is, to this extent, a story of spectacular and surprising success. Between the 1920s and the 1960s a number of British anthropologists leveraged their academic credentials and political alliances to transform their discipline away from the study of bones and biology towards an analysis of 'the social', which in turn spilled over into neighbouring disciplines. Telling this story as part of a narrative that encompasses anthropology's rise and fall in the policy sphere and its rise and dispersion across the social sciences offers a new appreciation of the discipline's place at the heart of the intellectual, political and cultural history of modern Britain and its empire.

CHAPTER 1

Islands and Institutions

*Anthropology in Britain and the British
Empire in the First Decades of the
Twentieth Century*

The 1908 *Chambers* dictionary defined anthropology as 'the science of man, more especially considered as a social animal: the natural history of man in its widest sense, treating of his relation to the brutes, his evolution, the different races.'[1] But this definition raises more questions than it answers. What is the 'natural history of man'? How does it relate to 'social' life? What does evolution have to do with 'the different races'? Which 'brutes' should be compared with which?

These questions may seem vague, problematic and even dangerous to us now, but they sum up a whole tradition of nineteenth-century science wherein men and women compared human and animal skeletons to try to work out the boundaries between the non-human, the human and different gradations of the latter, as denoted by the concept of 'race'.[2] Anthropology grew out of this tradition of measuring human difference via comparative anatomy and also from a much longer trend of scientific observation and travel writing stretching back to the Renaissance, part of a process of delimiting what Michel-Rolph Trouillot called the 'savage slot'.[3]

A transformation took place in this field of research about the 'savage' in the latter half of the nineteenth century: it was professionalising. Anthropology began to be communicated in scholarly societies, argued about in periodicals and monographs but also, and with the greatest public reach, displayed in museums and shows of living people.[4] Amidst this tradition of observing and displaying human difference, scholars in the medical and natural sciences sought to differentiate their techniques from those of amateurs and the non-expert public. Professionalising experts burnished their scientific credentials to secure their status as authoritative first-hand observers of human nature. By the turn of the century, observation in the field marked out these professionals from a public who could read tales of exotic travel and witness displayed peoples in travelling shows, at worlds' fairs and on cinema screens.[5] Professional anthropologists in new university departments sought to differentiate themselves from mere amateurs. The main aim of this chapter is to outline this shift towards professionalisation in anthropology during the early twentieth century in order to better understand the discipline's subsequent development.

It is important to note at the outset that these changes took place within a wider transformation of expertise and higher education in Britain. In the late Victorian and Edwardian eras, universities were expanding, and a new culture of academic training for leadership of the nation and empire was taking hold.[6] In 1910 there were 626 academic staff in the redbrick universities and 202 in London, rising to 1,349 staff in the rebricks and 1,057 in London by 1938–39.[7] Amidst this numerical expansion, a new emphasis on capacity building in the social sciences gripped a small group of reformers looking to France and Germany for inspiration. As a result, the teaching of history, anthropology, economics, political science, accounting and social administration was transformed in the three decades following the founding of the LSE in 1895.[8] Anthropology was a comparative minnow even in this small world of academic social science. In 1900 there were as few as a dozen researchers whose professional lives were spent studying anthropology, and only one man amongst this dozen, the great Victorian evolutionist E. B. Tylor, was teaching others to become professional anthropologists.[9]

Expansion of the discipline began modestly over the following two decades, with new courses for colonial cadets set up in the 1900s at Oxford and Cambridge. The fact that cadets could seek out training in anthropology reflected a turn to administrative expertise within the British Empire. In Britain's African Empire, for instance, the number of technical officers rose from six hundred in 1919 to approximately two thousand in 1931.[10] Agricultural and medical sciences were their main focus, and funding followed these 'practical' interests.[11] But like their colleagues in these other academic fields, anthropologists increasingly marketed their knowledge to the growing administrative state and were turning their attention to questions of social reform, especially in Britain's expanding empire.[12]

In the 1880s and 1890s the British Empire was swallowing up huge new domains in the 'scramble for Africa', and from the islands of the South and West Pacific, to the vast interiors of Canada and Australia, to the highlands of South and Southeast Asia, administrators and soldiers exerted increasing control over a huge diversity of what they called 'tribal' and 'primitive' peoples.[13] Yet with such a diffuse set of research questions about 'natural history' and 'the races', how could anthropologists hope to persuade administrators that their studies could be useful, especially in comparison to other kinds of more obviously practical knowledge such as engineering, agricultural science or chemistry? What use would an inquiry into 'man's relation to the brutes,' as the *Chambers* dictionary put it, offer a British civil engineer recruiting peasants to build a bridge in Borneo or a soldier trying to quell an anti-colonial rebellion in Nigeria?

On this basis it may come as little surprise that early attempts by anthropologists to lobby the Colonial Office largely ended in failure.[14] India was a separate case, with its own civil service and a tradition of in-house anthropological study undertaken by the Civil Service as part of its mammoth projects of census taking.[15] In the new colonies in Africa and the Pacific, however, imperialists tended to draw on schoolboy memories of Greek and Latin literature to understand other cultures, not anthropology.[16] A lone anthropologist was put on the government payroll in West Africa in 1909, but he worked only on a fixed term contract that was not extended, with one civil servant recalling exasperatedly that he had done very little to help, 'wore sandals[,] ... lived on vegetables and was generally a rum person.'[17] This idea of the anthropologist as a curio-hunting crank was widely held. For the first decades of the twentieth century, academic anthropologists lived largely on the margins of the colonial state, seeking patrons and influence amidst the affectedly amateur, anti-intellectual administrative milieu of the British colonial and civil service.[18]

Where anthropologists did seek to apply their knowledge, their expertise was often seen as competition by the professional 'men on the spot'.[19] These men tended to think that their class, gender, sporting prowess, classical education and muscular Christianity were knowledge enough to run an empire. It was only from the 1940s onwards, as we shall see later in this book, that university posts started to expand, with thirty professionals employed by 1953, and that the colonial services began to patronize the social sciences with central government funding.[20] Until then, anthropology remained a small academic discipline practiced at a handful of universities, with almost no job opportunities for graduates. We should keep this in mind when we come to think about the development of the discipline in the late 1920s, when Malinowski wielded enough Rockefeller funding in the 1930s to support practically the same number of PhD students as there were professional anthropologists appointed at all the other British universities put together. Before we get to that part of the story, we still need to know what the small band of professionals between the 1900s and 1920s meant by 'anthropology' and what possible help they thought they could offer to the British soldiers and district officers, who ruled their violent, rapacious empire from the business end of their maxim guns.[21]

One answer to this question was offered in the *Times* on 17 January 1925. 'Sir, – No reader of the daily papers can fail to be aware of the tremendous importance of racial problems in the sphere of domestic and especially international politics at the moment,' wrote Grafton Elliot Smith, professor of anatomy at University College, London (UCL). Britain's huge empire with its many different cultures made studying 'the biological aspect of race' indispensable, and Elliot Smith decried the fact that there was 'no one who can strictly be called a whole-time specialist' on the subject in Britain. A supportive editorial responded to Elliot Smith's plea: 'The time has certainly come ... to make much better provision in England, the heart of the Empire, for the encouragement and direction of studies that are so obviously important, not merely for the advancement of science, but from a purely administrative point of view. ... No country has such opportunities as our own for wide and fruitful anthropological study. No country has so much to gain from it in every sense.'[22]

Elliot Smith's medical background as professor of anatomy at UCL and his biological view of race certainly fit well with the wider cultural connotations of anthropology found in the *Chambers* dictionary that I cited at the beginning of this chapter, and his letter provoked several replies, including one from the Polish-born anthropologist Bronislaw Malinowski. At the time a just-appointed reader at the LSE, Malinowski agreed that anthropology was necessary and useful for colonial administrators, but as 'relations between the white settler and the aboriginee [sic]' were 'as a rule, of an economic nature,' the most important topics for study would be 'native custom and native belief,' not race science. 'Primitive economics, the psychology of native races and, above all, the theory of savage jurisprudence' would be key, he argued. Taking a dig at Elliot Smith, he wrote that anthropology should be led 'towards concrete realities' not 'sensation-mongering antiquarianism into which it has now and again fallen.' There is, Malinowski concluded, 'a useful as well as a useless Anthropology.' His letter was not published.[23]

These letters reveal the relative importance of these men in British anthropology. Malinowski was very much the junior figure to Elliot Smith in the 1920s. This does not fit well with folk histories of the discipline that speak of Malinowski's transformative and paradigm-shifting 'discovery' of fieldwork and participant observation. This approach has become paradigmatically associated with his 1922 book *Argonauts of the Western Pacific*, which includes the now-famous invocation to his colleagues to adopt the 'native's point of view, his relation to life, to realise *his* vision of *his* world.'[24] He argued that anthropologists should study people in situ, taking part in their rituals in order to reconstruct the way their societies functioned as working wholes. Clearly the force of this argument – taken by later anthropologists to have inaugurated a total transformation in method – had not secured him authority over his peers three years after its publication.

The publication of *Argonauts* alone was not sufficient to secure a letter in the *Times* or to influence the ideas of his colleagues. No matter how influential Malinowski's ideas became, no matter how inevitable the 'revolution' in British anthropology (as one commentator saw it in 1964) might look in retrospect, not all intellectual-historical roads led to Malinowski's methods in the 1920s.[25] Other men, long forgotten now, like Charles Seligman and Arthur Keith, were published in response to Elliot Smith instead of Malinowski.[26] These men's methods tended towards the kind of race science promoted by Elliot Smith, not Malinowski's 'sociological' interests in economics and law. Malinowski's criticism of 'sensation-mongering antiquarianism' may seem to point towards a future in which the 'social' sciences would become professionally and methodologically decoupled from the natural sciences.[27] But at the time it was Grafton Elliot Smith at UCL, not Malinowski at the LSE, who was the leading contemporary theorist in British anthropology. Before explaining Malinowski's rise to prominence we need to explain other contemporary trends in the discipline and then give an account of how he was able to sideline Elliot Smith.

PARROTS OR ELEPHANTS? DIFFUSIONIST THEORY IN INTERWAR BRITISH ANTHROPOLOGY

Elliot Smith's letter represented an important strand of anthropology that was engaged with the science of race and drew on a tradition of studying human society by medics and natural scientists. His main job, after all, was as professor of anatomy at UCL, where he specialised in the evolution of mammalian brains. Elliot Smith had been fascinated by anthropology since the early 1900s when he excavated ancient Egyptian tombs, and he had published his theories for specialist and non-specialist audiences.[28] We can get a sense of the ideas motivating his anthropological research by dwelling briefly on a dispute in 1924 about carved stone animals.

Elliot Smith thought that he had found evidence of an ancient carved elephant in Honduras and saw in these stone pachyderms support for his theory of cultural 'diffusionism'. This theory proposed that a migration of sun-worshipping, metal-working men and women had spread out from Egypt around the world in the first or second millennium BC. If the carvings were elephants, it would support his contention that this great migration had taken an Egyptian culture of astrology, megalith building and mummification to the Americas. A. C. Haddon, another prominent anthropologist, pointed out that this argument rested on an error: what Elliot Smith thought were carved elephants were, in fact, parrots.[29]

This dispute may seem bizarre in retrospect, but it gets to the heart of a key debate in contemporary anthropological theory. The disagreement also demonstrates just how fuzzy anthropology's disciplinary boundaries were. Archaeology was a source base, as was anatomical and biological research into 'race', a topic, recall, that Elliot Smith put front and centre of his letter to the *Times*. Note also that Elliot Smith's findings came from a museum collection and from an object, not from observations of human behaviour in the field. In this fecund era of interdisciplinarity, some academics, especially in Cambridge, saw anthropology and classics as close cousins, with speculations about ritual and ancient Greek drama driving research.[30] Another strand of research married anthropology with linguistics, which could be used to track the diffusion of culture. Elliot Smith and his colleague at UCL, William Perry, for instance, thought that Egyptian migrants went in search of pearls around the world hoping for a key to eternal life, and the two saw in the global value of pearls and pearl shells evidence of the influence of this history. They hypothesised that the Persian word for pearl, *margan*, had an etymology of *mar*, giver, and *gan*, life. However, Haddon stuck his oar in again to point out that *margan* means coral in Persian, not pearl, and, after consulting with the professor of Arabic at Cambridge, Haddon wrote, 'If one wanted to make wild etymological shots . . . one would rather connect it with the root *marg*, "death", *murdan*, "to die", though of course it has nothing to do with either.'[31]

Language, stone carvings, skulls, architecture and material culture all formed a grab bag of evidence to answer a huge variety of research questions that associated anthropology with the study of the past and its persistence in the present. In this sense, the diffusionists agreed with a previous generation of Victorian evolutionary theorists that conjectural histories of the deep past should be used to understand the lives of peoples on the fringes of the British Empire. This previous generation of Victorian anthropologists tended to think that culture evolves in a more or less unidirectional manner in stages out of a more simple past towards the complex, modern present.[32] Elliot Smith may have been an evolutionist when it came to comparative anatomy; he was a world-leading expert on the development of the mammalian brain. But he refused to connect the evolution of the brain with the evolution of culture: 'The explanation of the intellectual and moral outlook of every individual and community,' he wrote, 'is to be sought mainly in his or its history, and not in some blind mechanically working force of evolution.'[33]

Instead of a direct line from past to present, Elliot Smith narrated the history of civilisation as one of great disruption. The really consequential changes in culture and civilisation did not happen as a result of biological or cultural evolution but as a result of cultural 'diffusion'. Like the evolutionists before them, diffusionist anthropologists like Elliot Smith speculated about the conflict between 'races' and thought that this conflict was written into the distribution of human remains around the world. But rather than see this distribution of remains as evidence of progressive evolution, the diffusionists thought they could discern the historical blowback from a migration that had spread from the eastern Mediterranean outwards to overrun the ancient world's existing cultures, bringing irrigation, agriculture and aristocratic warfare to existing Stone Age societies.[34]

Unlike the Victorian evolutionists, Elliot Smith's vision was tragic rather than optimistic: the warlike Egyptian sun worshippers had conquered mostly peaceful Stone Age cultures. It was possible to see the diffusion of this warlike culture in the archaeological and anatomical records: those stone 'elephants', ceremonies associated with worshipping the sun and the building of giant megaliths and practices of mummification in places as far apart as Egypt and the South Pacific. By using a comparative method (another nineteenth-century mainstay), these scraps of information were pieced together into collages of conjectural history.[35] Anthropology, according to Elliot Smith, remained a species of natural history, as explained in the *Chambers* dictionary, although it was not an evolutionary science.

By the 1920s, diffusionism was overturning Victorian evolutionism and having a brief moment in the sun. Perry and Elliot Smith published several monographs and embedded themselves at UCL, where Elliot Smith was director of the Institute of Anatomy and Perry had offices in the same building, decking his rooms with maps of migration and the diffusion of cultures. They were soon able to recruit students and had begun to train colonial cadets. Part of this was due to Elliot Smith's power as an academic patron and discipline builder in anatomy (at the time of his death in 1937, twenty of his former anatomy demonstrators filled professorial chairs in the British Empire and the USA).[36] But he was not popular amongst the anthropologists, described by recent commentators as a 'scientific Pharaoh ... more often feared and resented than well liked.'[37] Diffusionism's authority in anthropological circles would not have been so great without the support of the much-admired W. H. R. Rivers, who had been perhaps Britain's most distinguished anthropologist until his death in 1922 and who, late in life, had become enamoured of Elliot Smith's ideas.

RIVERS, HADDON AND THE TORRES STRAITS

It was, in part, Rivers's legacy that was being fought over by Haddon and Elliot Smith when they publicly argued about elephants and parrots and pearls. Rivers had begun his anthropological career at Cambridge alongside A. C. Haddon. And like both Haddon and Elliot Smith, Rivers had studied natural science before moving to anthropology. He did ground-breaking research in physiology and psychology by cutting open the arm (and electrocuting the penis) of his friend Henry Head in his rooms in St. John's College, Cambridge, to come up with new theories about the functioning of the nervous system.[38] Rivers was also an early reader of Sigmund Freud in Britain and was famously involved during the First World War in the diagnosis of shellshock. It was this inventive and wide-ranging mind that attracted Haddon's attention in the 1890s as he set about planning the first anthropological expedition sent by a British university to do intensive field research abroad.

The plan was to take a team to study the inhabitants of the string of islands between New Guinea and Australia known to the British as the Torres Straits. Like their post-Darwinian contemporaries in the natural sciences, Haddon, Rivers and their colleagues sought to judge the differential effects of the environment on adaptation. They would treat the islands of the Torres Strait like natural laboratories, setting up experiments to judge the way that humans adapted to their environments and to find out how these ecological niches created social structures within which humans were socialised. Rivers, especially, sought to study adaptations with the latest advances in experimental psychology, taking colour perception and acoustic tests out of his lab in Cambridge to the field.[39]

The test results threw out some long-standing assumptions in the social sciences. The Victorian sociologist Herbert Spencer had theorised that the more 'advanced' a culture, the more brain power was taken away from the senses by abstract thought. People living in supposedly more 'primitive' societies with less division of labour, and with little or no written culture, would have more sensitive sense perception, by comparison, he assumed. The findings from the Torres Straits repudiated this view, and once back in Britain, the data was compared with villagers living just outside Cambridge, with people from a community near Aberdeen and with inmates in a convalescent home near Manchester. According to one historian of psychology, 'this process of replication confirmed the lack of meaningful differences in the perception of "primitive" and "civilised" people.'[40]

Of course, many psychologists carried on fusing race science with intelligence testing and justifications for global and imperial inequalities, but a minority report arose alongside this strand of psychology, drawing on these results from the Torres Straits to feed into a new relativist paradigm that suggested broad similarities in the minds of 'primitive' and 'civilised' peoples. This latter argument relied, in large part, on the scientific authority of these mostly Cambridge-based academics. The validity of their arguments also rested on the perceived accuracy of the tools and techniques used and the relatively recent elevation of fieldwork into a source of authority in the natural sciences. 'The field' had become a bounded domain in which authoritative knowledge could be gathered and trusted. Part of the trustworthiness of fieldwork was generated by an association between scientific expeditions and late Victorian ideas of heroic masculinity. Reaching 'the field' was equated with vigour, virtue and stoicism.[41] Stories of great adventures and triumphant observations began to be braided together: the more difficult the terrain overcome to record the object of enquiry, the more putatively authentic the data.[42]

This emphasis on fieldwork and first-hand experience differed from a previous tradition of observation and marks a difference between the research of Haddon and Rivers and Elliot Smith and those who had gone before. In the age of the Victorian evolutionist anthropologists, a division of labour and associated class ascriptions existed between the non-experts who collected specimens and made ethnographic reports (the labourers) and the scholars who catalogued objects and compared and taxonomized them (the gentlemen). Fieldwork tended to be the job of the amateur, a mucky and often dangerous affair that did not befit an upper-class man. The scholar's role was to compare and adjudicate the data the labourers returned and reported.[43]

A turn to anthropological fieldwork thus meant a move away from 'armchair' anthropology and its separation of hands-on labour from scholarly reflection. While recent commentators have questioned the starkness of the purported division in method between the 'armchair' theorist and the fieldworker, nevertheless a transformation was clearly occurring, and the Torres Straits expedition had a marked effect on the subsequent history of anthropology.[44] From then on, fieldwork became a key part of anthropologists' research.

An index of this transformation can be discerned in the Royal Anthropological Institute's 1912 edition of its *Notes and Queries*. This was a book for travellers, administrators and missionaries to elicit them to collect anthropological information. Rivers contributed material that urged readers to spend prolonged time with subject communities and to cross-check facts gained through interviews. Charles Seligman, another Torres Straits veteran and Malinowski's teacher and patron at the LSE, said that fieldwork had become by the First World War 'as the blood of martyrs is to the Roman Catholic Church.'[45] The result was the emergence of a 'new occupational persona' in anthropology: the scholar-fieldworker.[46]

The aim of anthropological fieldwork in the tradition of Rivers, Haddon and Seligman was to generate detailed studies that could then be compared with others along the lines of the survey research in the Torres Straits.[47] To further this aim, Haddon, Rivers and Seligman spread their students out amongst the islands of the Western Pacific in the first decades of the twentieth century to survey and compare the different groups and cultures interacting in this area.[48] Through comparison across populations, they sought to understand migrations and the diversity of human cognition. Open questions remained. Should anthropologists double down on the comparative and historical aspect of Rivers and Haddon's project? Or should anthropologists transform the intensive fieldwork suggested in *Notes and Queries* into the study of one particular society? Should anthropology carry on down the path of Rivers's sense perception tests and dissociate the study of psychology and sociology from anatomical studies of human physiology? Or should anthropologists study the past as archaeologists and historians or look to present systems of marriage and religious beliefs in the here and now?

We can see these different strands of British anthropology converging on Australia for the 1914 British Association for the Advancement of Science (BAAS), where the current and future stars of the discipline gathered at the meeting of BAAS's section H.[49] Malinowski (Seligman's student) was there in 1914 and presented a paper titled 'A Fundamental Problem of Religious Sociology,' which used the recently published work of the French sociologist Émile Durkheim to explore whether there was a meaningful distinction between the 'religious' and the 'profane' amongst 'primitive peoples'. Elliot Smith spoke, too, on 'the Origin and Spread of certain Customs and Inventions,' focusing on the familiar theme of the distribution of mummification and megalithic monuments. Four days later he gave another talk, this time titled 'The Brain of Primitive Man.' The proceedings then moved from Melbourne to Sydney, where the participants gathered to hear Rivers present on marriage in Australia, followed by another Cambridge man, A. R. Brown (a student of Rivers and Haddon who later changed his surname to Radcliffe-Brown), who gave a talk on totemism in Australia.

Of the twenty-seven talks given to 'section H' at the BAAS that year, ten were on skulls or some other kind of human bone, five were on Stone Age technology, stone circles or caves (a man called C. Hedley talked about Polynesian fish hooks, R. Ethridge delivered a paper on dingo teeth found in a cave, and Thomas Ashby spoke on Roman roads). Two papers (by Elliot Smith and Rivers) were on diffusionist theories. Only Radcliffe-Brown and Malinowski gave papers that would be understood three decades later as standing in the recognisable tradition of method and theory that would mark British social anthropology.[50] Clearly we still need to understand how these diffuse approaches to anthropology were transformed into a new paradigm, and here we must turn to Malinowski, who, after presenting at the BAAS meeting in Australia, went on to do the fieldwork that has often been seen as a turning point in the history of the human sciences.

MALINOWSKI IN THE TROBRIAND ISLANDS

With the outbreak of war in Europe shortly after presenting his paper, the Polish-born Malinowski was officially an 'enemy alien' as a subject of Austria-Hungary. To remain free from internment in Australia, he depended on the liberality and hospitality of local administrators and government officials. Through his contacts at the Australian universities he was able to proceed to New Guinea for his anthropological research, taking with him some of Rivers's books, a copy of *Notes & Queries* and a large number of novels. At this stage, his plan was to carry out work in the tradition of Haddon and Rivers's recent advances in the Oceanic and comparative tradition of anthropology.[51]

Malinowski's first extended period of fieldwork was on the small island of Mailu. He followed Rivers's advice by living on the island for an extended period of time. But he was not principally interested in the questions of experimental psychology that had motivated researchers like Rivers and Haddon in the Torres Straits. He took village censuses, trying to work out the patterns of marriage amongst the islanders, and he took note of the role of communal dancing and ritual in the organisation of labour and village gardening. At one point, Haddon arrived by boat on Mailu to research canoe building. Malinowski's biographer writes that this provides for us 'a fortuitous juxtaposition of old [Haddon's] and new [Malinowski's] anthropology,' drawing a contrast between 'Haddon's peripatetic prospecting surveys versus Malinowski's methodological impulse to stay in one place and excavate deeply.'[52] By this time, Malinowski's stubborn investigations of local life led him to uncover new and intriguing information about the mode of life of the people of Mailu. Haddon, meanwhile, was not principally interested in Mailu as a unique place whose social life should be uncovered. Rather, he was interested in contributing to his ongoing comparative research in material culture and migration. He wanted to show how the different forms of canoe technology could be mapped onto the region to reveal the ancient migration of different 'races' of islanders (see figure 1), in particular the impact of Melanesian trading and raiding around the coast and interaction with indigenous Papuans.[53]

But it was not only Malinowski's 'impulse to stay in one place' that mattered; he was asking different research questions to Haddon. Haddon was invested in a historical paradigm and, although he disagreed with the grandiosity of Elliot Smith's theory of ancient, worldwide Egyptian migration, he was similarly interested in writing conjectural histories of culture change. Haddon travelled to Mailu to answer historical questions. The people who lived there were important to the extent that their canoes might tell him about the history of the region. To Malinowski, it was the people's current society that mattered most

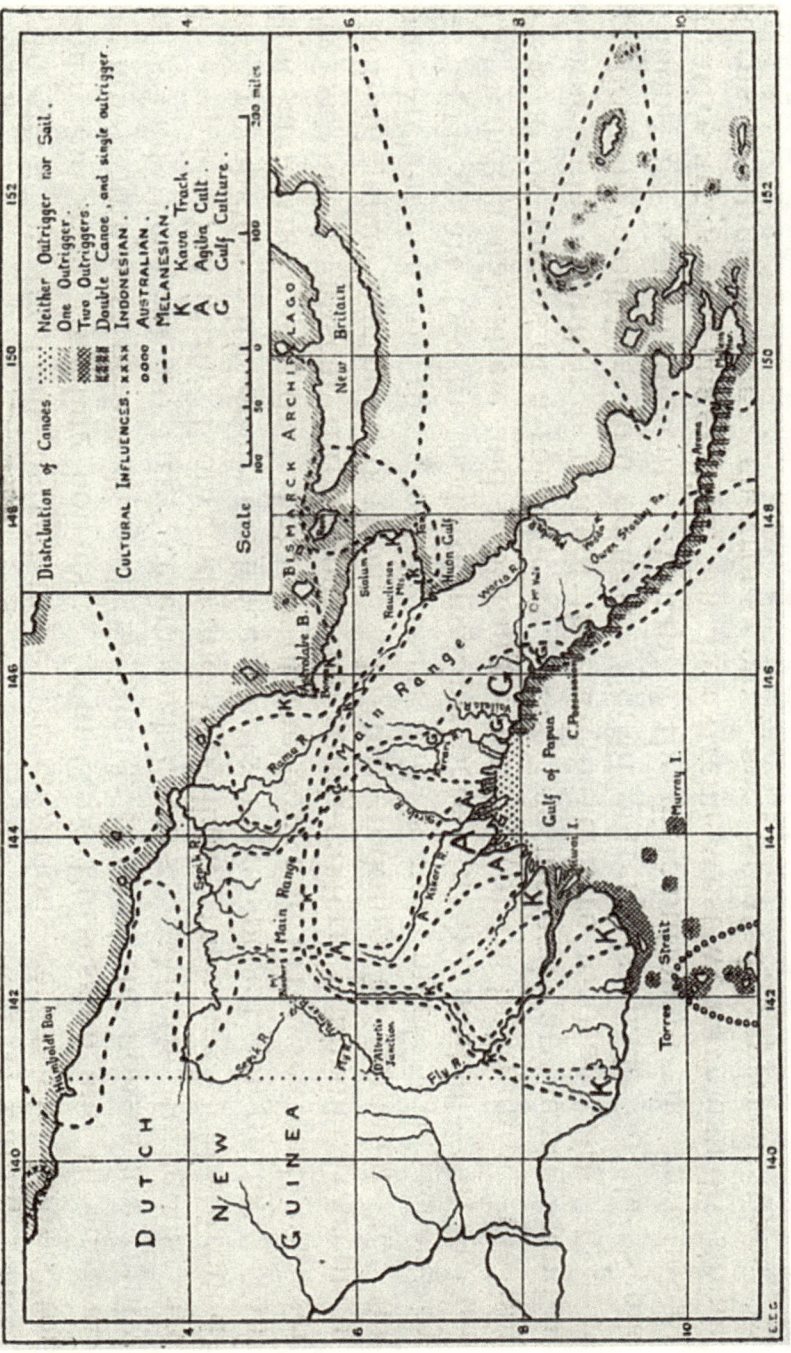

FIGURE 1. Distribution of canoes in eastern New Guinea and surrounding islands. *Source*: A. C. Haddon, 'Racial and Cultural Distributions in New Guinea,' *The Geographical Teacher*, 11.1 (Spring 1921), 15–19. Reproduced with permission from the Geographical Association.

and what their social organisation might tell him about different questions; as evidenced by his paper in Australia earlier in the year, he was interested, for instance, in the same kind of sociological questions about the 'sacred' and the 'profane' as French sociologist Durkheim, who, like Freud, and Radcliffe-Brown and Malinowski, was using new ethnographic data to reconfigure European theories about the 'primitive' and the 'modern'.[54]

Malinowski was also interested in economics and custom, in how a community might function as a collective of interlocking institutions to make meaning for its members and how common rules and norms might work together to allow people to house and clothe themselves. He took these interests further on another island, Kiriwina. As on Mailu, he focused on understanding family life, rituals and economic exchange and left the tools of the physical anthropologist – callipers, skin-colour gauges and measuring sticks that he had bought in Berlin – in storage with a local trader.[55] Instead, he used his diary as his research tool, recording his observations and feelings, cross-checking his notes with later observations and then reflecting on his entries to synthesise and integrate his thoughts. Participation in the life of the people around him over an extended period allowed him to develop his methods and sharpen his insights. This was a kind of 'resident science' that situated scientific observation in the context of a particular locale.[56]

This implied a degree of immersion in the local and imperial politics of the Trobriand Islands. Most immediately, Malinowski was only able to do this research because of his demonstrations of respect to Chief Touluwa, whose village Malinowski camped in.[57] And recall that Malinowski had only remained free from internment as an enemy alien because of his academic connections. After some months under the watchful eyes of Chief Touluwa and the other residents of Kiriwina, Malinowski returned to Australia, where he gave a deposition at an inquiry on trade in Australia's Pacific territories in October 1916. His evidence provides a sense of his contemporary political commitments and suggests how he connected his observations to the imperial context of his work.

The inquiry was prompted by Australia's recent capture of the northeast part of New Guinea from the German Empire.[58] The Australians inherited a system of plantation labour in the region, mostly supplying copra (dried coconut used for palm oil and animal feed) for trade on the world market.[59] Malinowski had just returned from doing fieldwork nearby and told of his worries that the plantation system was significantly disrupting community life. The absence of men for long periods had been leading to demographic problems. The birth rate was falling and, on the workers' return, venereal diseases and alcohol were brought into their villages. On the subject of the 'development of the country' he was sceptical that islanders' self-interest lined up with increasing exports. 'I think that the native Papuan is not very keen on working for the white man,' he explained, before adding, 'it is quite evident he does his own work, and if he is left to his own conditions he has plenty of work on hand, work which is not exactly of a purely economical description, but which for him makes life worth living.' He ended his deposition by comparing this practice with the Nama and Herero genocide in German Southwest Africa, where colonial authorities had 'transplanted numerous tribes from one place to another, and decimated them.' The Germans, he stated, 'did not discuss at all whether that was a fair way to treat the natives.' In light of these dangers, he proposed some measure of administrative amelioration: 'Once the natives come into contact with white civilization it is always better to take some measures to prevent their dying out.'[60]

With this interest in economics, 'which is not exactly of a purely economical description,' and with its connection to colonisation worldwide, Malinowski set off again for another round of fieldwork in October 1917, eventually returning to Kiriwina as a more fluent speaker of the local language and having processed many of his earlier observations. His research covered a range of topics, from law to sex and reproduction to gardening and magic, but it is his insights on the *Kula*, as described in *Argonauts of the Western Pacific*, that are most famous and that would influence generations of commentators on economics and sociology.

After long study and observation, Malinowski reckoned that he could discern a pattern. Around the archipelago of the Trobriand Islands a ceremonial trade of shell armbands (*mwali*) for shell necklaces (*soulava*) called the Kula took place. These shell objects were not money, in the way that money exists in a capitalist economy, but they were traded for each other and had different values. Extensive and sometimes dangerous expeditions set off to carry on the Kula, and Malinowski realised, through noting who exchanged what armband for which necklace, a picture of an economy of prestige and esteem emerging. By, as he put it, taking the 'native's point of view', the Kula could be understood as an integrated system that brought the scattered island populations into a circuit of exchange that cemented social ties. He wrote about the Kula in *The Economic Journal*. About the *soulava* and *mwali* he wrote:

> Their main economic function is to be owned as signs of wealth, and consequently of power, and from time to time to change hands as ceremonial gifts. As such, they are the foundation of certain kinds of native trade, and they constitute an indispensable element of the social organisation of the natives. For, as mentioned above, all their social life is accompanied by gift and counter-gift.[61]

An economy of gift and counter-gift marked almost all the relations in Kiriwina and the other Trobriand Islands: a vision of exchange that would have a profound influence on the social sciences.[62] Malinowski argued that these gift exchanges were not mere utilitarian bartering. Yams, for instance, formed part of a complex economy, given as part of a ceremonial offering to kin and displayed to demonstrate the social power of their owners to the other members of the community. Exchange – gift and counter-gift – underpinned a kind of economic cum social system unlike a 'national economy' with a 'free competitive exchange of goods and services,' Malinowski argued. He found, instead,

> a state of affairs where production, exchange and consumption are socially organised and regulated by custom, and where a special system of traditional economic values governs their activities and spurs them on to efforts. This new state of affairs might be called – as a new conception requires a new term – Tribal Economy.[63]

These arguments would make him justly famous, and his methods would be applied and amended by his many distinguished students. His ideas also had a number of effects outside anthropology, as we will see later in this book, on notions of 'moral economy' and in analyses of early-modern capitalism in England.

But the result of Malinowski's participant observations did not simply persuade everyone who read *Argonauts* in 1922 that this approach represented the future of anthropology. By moving away from conjectural history, physical anthropology and the study of race, Malinowski was drastically narrowing the focus of the received definition of his discipline. Recall that Elliot Smith's theories were, at the time of the publication of *Argonauts*, more popular, although they were also controversial. In comparison, Malinowski's studies of the 'native's point of view' seem far more circumscribed than the natural history of man's 'relation to the brutes, his evolution, the different races' written about in the 1908 *Chambers* dictionary. Malinowski's colleagues would take some persuading that intensive fieldwork in one community could ever substitute for this more expansive definition of anthropology, and some never would be convinced.

STEAMERS, UNIVERSITIES AND CIRCUITS OF ANTHROPOLOGICAL MOBILITY ACROSS THE BRITISH WORLD

'Anthropology' in this period, argue John Forrester and Laura Cameron, 'would not have been possible without steamships and trains that kept tight schedules from the Pacific to Southampton and from London to Cambridge.'[64] W.H. R. Rivers for instance, could be in Cambridge for the start of the year in 1898, travel to the Torres Straits over the Easter break and be back in time for the start of term in October to deliver his lectures. In fact, Rivers had only agreed to travel to the Torres Straits on the basis that he would be able to return to teach at Cambridge that same year. This is what steamships and rail timetables made possible. But Rivers's commitment to university teaching also speaks to the increasing importance of the professionalisation of the discipline and that university teaching was done alongside anthropological fieldwork.

It seems like a simple point to make, but it is nevertheless very important to point out that the different theories of Elliot Smith, Haddon and Malinowski in the 1910s and 1920s were being propounded by university-based academics. This represents a huge change from the largely amateur milieu and the gentlemanly ethos of late nineteenth-century anthropology. It was the union of steamships and universities that underlay the newly professionalising academic anthropology and the emergence of a new kind of anthropologist in the 1910s and 1920s: the university-based fieldworker. But without university posts for the new fieldworkers to fill, any advances in theory would have been moot. All of the men discussed here were trying to professionalise their discipline and to carve out a new scientific basis for it, but there were hardly any jobs. Until 1900, Haddon had to work two jobs to support his gentlemanly lifestyle, one in Dublin as a professor of zoology and another in Cambridge as an anthropologist. He longed to secure a post with a high enough salary in Cambridge and endured a crushing commute to spend part of the year in the two universities. In 1900 he finally gained a fixed term appointment at Cambridge and scraped by on short-term contracts until he was appointed reader in ethnology in 1909 at the age of fifty-four.[65]

A process of professionalisation led to the narrowing of the very broad definition of anthropology then current in British society. As soon as the subject had to be taught to students rather than disseminated to gentlemen amateurs, hard decisions about syllabi, reading lists and institutional affiliation had to be raised. Would anthropology, as a 'natural science of man', be taught in a manner more like classics, or, as in Cambridge, the 'moral sciences', or would it be closer to a natural science or, indeed, engineering or business? Would it be taught in the late Victorian institutions of museums and natural history collections? Or should the discipline be taught in labs and anatomy theatres?

Before the 1920s, these questions did not seem that urgent because professional appointments were so scant and there were so few opportunities to study the subject as a consequence. While a survey in 1900 found that students could take anthropology courses in eight universities in Britain, most of the teaching was piecemeal and taken as part of a natural sciences degree. In 1905 Oxford offered courses to colonial cadets and in 1906 instituted a school of anthropological studies (closely tied to the Pitt-Rivers museum), although the university had no permanent professorship in social anthropology until 1936.[66] In 1907 Liverpool created a professorship in anthropology, although it was unsalaried. Cambridge made anthropology a component of an undergraduate degree in 1913, after significant lobbying from Haddon, but only instituted a professorship in 1932. Students could study anthropology at the LSE with the Torres Straits veteran Charles Seligman, who was on a part-time contract, and with Malinowski after 1924. By then, the number of institutions offering courses in anthropology had grown to eleven. UCL, with William Perry and Elliot Smith in post, led the field in terms of the diversity of courses offered, and UCL awarded the first PhD in anthropology by any British university in 1925.[67]

Universities in the British Empire offered a handful of other jobs. Alfred Radcliffe-Brown, like Malinowski, had been stuck after the outbreak of the First World War after travelling to the BAAS. (Rivers, meanwhile, telegraphed to Cambridge asking if he could postpone his return, on account of the war's inevitable interruption of student life, to do some more fieldwork. The university agreed.) During the war, Radcliffe-Brown found employment at Sydney Grammar School in 1915, then held a job as director of education in the kingdom of Tonga between 1918 and 1919.[68] In 1921 he took up a new professorship in anthropology at the University of Cape Town, after lobbying by Haddon.

At Cape Town he explained to his students and the colonial cadets seconded to him for training that anthropologists should study societies as social wholes rather than as parts of hypothetical diffusionist histories.[69] In his theoretical approach he was strongly influenced by Durkheim, one of the founders of modern sociology and whose work had also influenced Malinowski (although the latter tended to be more sceptical about his ideas than Radcliffe-Brown).[70] Radcliffe-Brown shared an investment in Durkheimian theory with his colleague Winifred Hoernlé (who had studied under the French sociologist at the Sorbonne and also under Haddon and Rivers at Cambridge), and together they founded a tradition of liberal-aligned anthropology in South Africa.[71] Radcliffe-Brown and Hoernlé were, like Malinowski, writing more 'social' and less 'physical' anthropology in comparison to the diffusionists Elliot Smith and Perry. In 1926 Radcliffe-Brown spread these interests further when he moved from Cape Town to take up a professorial chair at the University of Sydney. As in South Africa, he built a department that trained colonial cadets and nurtured graduate students.[72] Hoernlé stayed on in Cape Town and between them they circulated students between their seminars: mostly sending students to London after Malinowski had been promoted to Professor at the LSE in 1927. These connections between South African, Australian and British institutions meant that the university was increasingly becoming the institutional base from which anthropological authority emanated and from which theoretical innovations would emerge in the 1920s and 1930s.[73]

These anthropological connections between Australia, South Africa and Britain nested in a dense intra-imperial academic network that stretched across Britain's settler colonies.[74] A centripetal pull drew academics and students from the settler peripheries to British universities, maintaining and creating links between professors in the colonies and in Britain. Peripheral circuits existed too, linking professors in settler colonies with one another. The fact that the 1914 BAAS meeting was held in Australia reveals how academic connections were being forged between the settler colonies and the metropole. 'British' anthropology grew up within this wider ambit. These British and 'British world' universities certainly helped accelerate the professionalisation of anthropology, and institution building slowly expanded the job market.[75]

But universities were not the only places to get a job as an anthropologist. After much scepticism, colonial administrations began to employ a small number of professional anthropologists in Africa and the

Pacific Islands during the interwar years. R. S. Rattray was appointed in the Gold Coast in 1920, and C. Meek, H. F. Matthews and R. C. Abraham took up posts in Nigeria.[76] In Australia's Mandate of New Guinea and its colony Papua, three government anthropologists were employed: E. P. Chinnery, W. E. Amstrong (both students of Haddon) and F. E. Williams (an Australian who had studied at Oxford). These men published intermittently in scholarly journals. But their main task was to gather political intelligence and strengthen the tax-raising functions of the colonial state.[77] Government anthropologists did not tend to innovate theoretically, but they often acted as gatekeepers for the university-based researchers who did.[78]

The interests of these two groups (university academics and government anthropologists) were largely distinct. For one thing, their institutional bases were different. Academic anthropologists reproduced themselves in university departments. This meant that they had to secure funding if they wanted to attract students. The Torres Strait expedition had been preceded by extensive fund raising, although the funding did not cover all of the costs, and most of the group had to travel at their own expense.[79] Radcliffe-Brown's institution building in South Africa was warily supported by the state, but in Australia he relied on the largesse of the Australian National Research Council (a Rockefeller Foundation–funded body).

In the 1920s, then, British anthropology existed in a state of multipolarity with no single centre of gravity: Haddon in Cambridge, Malinowski and Seligman at the LSE and Perry and Elliot Smith at UCL. Far-flung minor stars were tied to them, principally Radcliffe-Brown in Sydney and Hoernlé at Cape Town. These schools taught different kinds of anthropology. Haddon and Elliot Smith differed over the histories of cultural diffusion but agreed that the proper study of anthropology was the past and its impact on the present. Malinowski, Hoernlé and Radcliffe-Brown, on the other hand, pursued a more 'sociological' agenda and sought to witness the functioning of societies in the present through extended fieldwork. While the approaches of these anthropologists differed, some commonalities persisted. Most important was a general lack of money for research. Two large injections of Rockefeller cash in 1926 and 1931 transformed all this. Rockefeller money, more than any other source of funding, was crucial to the institutionalisation of social anthropology in Britain and its empire. With central government spending on the social sciences so scant in this era, the importance of American philanthropy cannot be overstated.[80] It was American money that decisively transformed British anthropology by concentrating power to reshape the discipline in the hands of one man: Malinowski.

ROCKEFELLER PHILANTHROPY AND BRITISH ANTHROPOLOGY: TOWARDS THE FUNCTIONALIST 'REVOLUTION'

The favour of the Rockefeller philanthropies could, and did, decisively reshape the balance of academic power within academic disciplines in the interwar decades.[81] Between 1919 and 1940 the Rockefeller, Carnegie and Harkness philanthropies together gave approximately £690,000 to fund the British social sciences.[82] The Laura Spelman Rockefeller Memorial (LSRM), a large philanthropy made up of the profits from the Standard Oil petrochemical empire, was the main funder of anthropology in the 1920s.

Why would the Rockefeller philanthropies be interested in British anthropology? Anthropology was conceived by foundation officers as a way to bring race science and administrative expertise together. By the 1920s foundation investments were spread far beyond America to universities and institutes around the world. The ideology of these research officers has been characterised as 'sophisticated conservatism', a mindset focused on 'efficiency', 'planning' and 'control'.[83] While they funded a good deal of social science research, most of their money was directed at the natural sciences, especially disease control and public health. In the view of these officers, academics would act as vectors for reform, such that by building capacity in universities the foundation could change the public sphere. As Selskar Gunn (vice president of the LSRM in Europe) wrote to Raymond Fosdick (John D. Rockefeller Jr's sometime lawyer and eventual president of the foundation): 'That a close contact exist between the experts in the universities and the responsible men in government (central, provisional or district) seems to me a <u>sine qua non</u> for success in the development of social technology.'[84] This emphasis on 'social technology' and the desire to influence government gives a sense of the technocratic worldview of the Rockefeller philanthropies, which tended to favour impact on public administration via practical knowledge.

In the 1920s the Rockefeller officers made increasing investments in British and imperial universities, warping the institutional networks of the 'British world' by offering academics and students fellowships to travel to, train in and teach in the USA.[85] This process was felt in anthropology as well, with British academics increasingly courting the Rockefeller philanthropies. A principal early beneficiary was Elliot Smith at UCL.[86] Since 1921, he had been trying to get the LSRM to fund a significant school of anthropology at UCL. But from 1927 Rockefeller money for anthropological research went to Malinowski's LSE instead. As the next chapter explains in much greater detail, this redirection of funds came about via a new organisation, the International Institute for African Languages and Cultures (IIALC). The Rockefeller-funded fellowships distributed by the IIALC went to Malinowski's LSE, meaning that Elliot Smith was unable to attract the best graduate students to his school or promote his theoretical agenda in the prestigious publications begun under the IIALC's auspices (such as the journal *Africa*). He was furious at this turn of events and in a letter raged at the 'amazing action of the Laura Spelman trust in subsidizing those who are wrecking anthropology in this country' (a pencil note by a funding officer in the margin stated: 'means Malinowski of the London School of Economics').[87]

The marginalisation of Elliot Smith had an important effect on the kind of anthropology that was institutionalised in British universities: the study of human anatomy and human culture was gradually pulled apart in British anthropology, although never completely and never neatly. The triumph of a more sociological anthropology over diffusionism did not, however, as some commentators have suggested, lead to the separation of race science from the study of culture. Race science, of course, carried on in other forms, with a tenacious hold in the academy.[88] The realignment from 'biological' to 'social' anthropology in Britain owed more to professionalisation and philanthropic funding than to ideas and methods alone, and the 'victory' of social over biological anthropology was never total.

As we shall see in future chapters, Malinowski's 'sociological' approach ultimately won out over Elliot Smith's ideas by being allied to prominent patrons and then by being taught as a method to students at the LSE during the 1930s. These men and women would then go on to hold faculty positions in the expanding university system. In short, Malinowski's arguments did not so much overwhelm his colleagues, many of whom carried on studying race, natural history and anatomy, as set his discipline on a path of divergence from these interests; in the process he secured a niche in the academy for the disciplinary reproduction of his 'social' agenda.[89]

Meanwhile, to his Rockefeller funders, culture, race and society were not to be separated. The Rockefeller philanthropies classified anthropology as part of the broader study of 'human biology', and in the Rockefeller accounting books, grants to the IIALC were entered under the heading 'Race Relations'.[90] At the other end of the funding pipeline, anthropology at the LSE was a major beneficiary of school director William Beveridge's attempts to bridge the gap between the natural and social sciences.[91] To British anthropology's principal funders, biology and the study of society should go together, and Malinowski did nothing to disabuse his patrons of this idea.[92]

As we shall see in the following chapter, Malinowski's interests were soon redirected by all this funding from the South Pacific to sub-Saharan Africa, with a particular focus on East Africa. The eminent historian of anthropology George Stocking noted the significance of this shift from the Pacific to Africa in his compendious history of British anthropology but admitted his 'failure to treat (save incidentally) either domestic debate about colonial policy and practice or other domestic concerns that might have been reflected in anthropological discourse.'[93] The IIALC promised to unite anthropology and colonial administration, reflecting, as Stocking put it, imperialist concerns in the discipline. Colonial policy was not merely reflected in, but redirected by, its members. Its main backers in Britain were, in fact, promoting a particular policy agenda in opposition to other alternatives.[94] Social anthropology's patrons, the British representative on the League of Nations Permanent Mandates Commission, Lord Lugard, and Joseph Oldham, secretary of the International Missionary Council, were united in opposing the triumph of white settler interests in East Africa and adamant that colonial administration there should proceed under the rubric of trusteeship. Like Malinowski in Melbourne in 1916, they shared a common concern about depopulation and wanted to make sure that British imperialism would be reformist, paternalist and developmental, rather than genocidal and expropriative. The next chapter explains how this combination of interests ushered Malinowski into the position from which he was able to decisively turn the discipline away from Elliot Smith's diffusionism and towards his own ends.

CHAPTER 2

Philanthropists and Imperialists

Indirect Rule, the Rockefeller Foundation and the Rise of LSE Anthropology

What, if anything, did the founding of the International Institute of African Languages and Cultures (IIALC) have to do with colonial politics? One answer can be found in the figure of the IIALC's chairman, Lord Lugard, former governor general of Nigeria and author of *The Dual Mandate in Tropical Africa* (1922). The *Dual Mandate* has often been taken as a blueprint for the ideological sine qua non of British imperialism: 'indirect rule'. According to this theory, the imperial state should collaborate with local elites and, taking inspiration from the work of the Victorian jurist Henry Maine, vaunt 'customary' authority, often inventing traditions in the service of imperial power.[1] This model was formulated first in India in the 1860s and then spread to West Africa, where Lugard synthesised his experience as an administrator into a kind of doctrine. His *Dual Mandate* should also be understood as a pitch for his future job as Britain's member of the League of Nations Permanent Mandates Commission, which purported to oversee formerly German- and Ottoman-ruled territories after the First World War according to Article 22 of the League charter: 'inhabited by peoples not yet able to stand by themselves under the strenuous conditions of the modern world.'[2]

In the margins of his personal copy of the *Dual Mandate*, Malinowski drew a connection between his own theories and Lugard's ideas, writing that 'Indirect Rule is a Complete Surrender to the Functional Point of View.'[3] Malinowski's note has since been taken as confirmation of social anthropology's ideological alignment with the policy.[4] One recent history of indirect rule has even gone so far as to state that social anthropology bears 'a specific and intimate, as opposed to an incidental, relationship to the dynamics of colonial power and late imperial ideology.'[5] But while Malinowski may have thought that Lugard's ideas must 'surrender' to his own theories, this does not tell us anything about what Lugard himself thought or, indeed, whether indirect rule had anything whatsoever to do with anthropology. In fact, as we shall see in the second half of this chapter, the two men held quite different ideas about what 'indirect rule' meant with regard to laws concerning magic and witchcraft. Malinowski's note says more about his overweening intellectual narcissism than it does about the administration of the British Empire in Africa.

Yet the fact that Malinowski saw a similarity between Lugard's theorising and his own ideas is surely significant. Recall Malinowski's 1916 deposition about Australian trade in the Pacific, discussed in the previous chapter. He thought that capitalist expansion, if left unchecked, would result in the eventual extermination of the island inhabitants of the Pacific, destroying, in the process, the labour supply the colonial plantations relied on. It was by comparison to German rule in South West Africa and the genocide of the Nama and Herero peoples that Malinowski pled for 'protection' in Australia's colonies. Lugard also sought to differentiate indirect rule from contemporary variants of settler colonialism.[6] His idea of the 'dual mandate' sought to secure peasant proprietors' native title to the land while welcoming international firms to buy and trade their crops. Both Malinowski's ideas and Lugard's policies fit under the rubric of an ideology that contemporaries labelled 'trusteeship': a very broad concept of rule that sought to protect 'natives' from slave trading and from the most expropriative kinds of imperialism associated with settler colonialism.[7] This meant that they were also united by a common ideological enemy, what the historian Patrick Wolfe has called the settler-colonial policy of 'elimination'.[8] Both the family resemblance between their ideas and what they opposed are the focus of this chapter.

My aim in this chapter is to explain how competing visions of colonial development intersected with the funding of the IIALC and with the formation of social anthropology in the late 1920s. It is not enough simply to assert that anthropology was a colonial discipline; how could it not be? The apposite issue is to ask how colonial politics (understood as *political* and hence about contest and conflict) influenced the discipline's formation.[9] For with a Conservative, settler-friendly government in power in the late 1920s seeking to boost British migration to its East African colonies, those like Malinowski and Lugard who favoured imperial trusteeship were in a position of relative political and ideological weakness when the IIALC was founded.[10]

The crucial political dilemma, so far as the politics of social anthropology was concerned, was a policy debate carried on by politicians and administrators about whether to push forward with the widespread white settlement of East Africa – an issue I call in this chapter the settler question. Reformism, indirect rule and liberalism were certainly one answer to the settler question. But arguably more influential was a c/Conservative push to sponsor European emigration to East Africa allied with the interests of white farmers to subordinate African peoples under settler minority rule. By recovering this dispute over the settler question, and by explaining Malinowski's stake in the debate, we will be able to understand better how colonial politics affected the consolidation of social anthropology in Britain during the late 1920s and 1930s and the discipline's relationship with indirect rule via the International Institute of African Languages and Cultures (IIALC).

POSING THE SETTLER QUESTION
IN 1920S EAST AFRICA

In a memorandum written for the Laura Spelman Rockefeller Memorial (LSRM) before a 1926 trip to America, Malinowski criticised physical anthropologists for directing themselves at the wrong objects, not for asking the wrong questions. 'Anatomical and craniometric studies have been insufficient even to describe, classify and define human races,' he wrote. Really fruitful research would come from the 'correlating of race with culture.' On this note, he mentioned 'the Negro problem' as 'one of the most important and instructive subjects of sociological study.' The 'question of race, the mixing of races, of human Mendelism, might be studied in the United States,' but it was in the British Empire that some of the most explosive tensions over the racial division of labour were occurring. 'In the Pacific, in West Africa, above all in East Africa (Kenya Colony) recruiting and the mode of employment of labour have been incessant subject of wrangles, disputes and maladjustments ... and in one colony, at least, the disputes have led to threats of civil war (Kenya).'[11] When Malinowski returned from travelling in America in 1926 at the Rockefellers' behest, he wrote to his wife that his main research would henceforth be on the 'Negro question'.[12]

That year the IIALC was founded and a year later Malinowski began a course of lectures at the LSE with the ex-colonial officer Jack Driberg. In the second lecture on 'culture contact' in Africa he told his students that 'the problem of race but be [sic] approached from the cultural point of view.' The apposite question was, accordingly: 'Can we make out of the Negro a white man in a trice or not?' Malinowski immediately linked this question of race and culture to contemporary politics when he mentioned two names: 'Delamere v Norman Leys' and wrote in his lecture notes, 'both are fools!'[13]

Who were Delamere and Leys, and what did their arguments have to do with race? Hugh Cholmondley, Lord Delamere, was an aristocratic farmer in Kenya and leader of the settler caucus there. Norman Leys was a former medical officer who lobbied for equal rights for Europeans and Africans and for widespread land reforms. Throughout the 1920s Leys and Delamere clashed in a charged debate that connected the colony to a metropolitan context of imperial reform.[14] Land tenure was often at the heart of these arguments; so too was welfare spending.[15] Malinowski pointed out that cultural and racial differences sat at the core of both of these men's ideas. To Leys, land reform and increased welfare spending would harmonise the interests of Africans and Europeans. To Delamere, expanded settlement should clear what he saw as racially inferior people off the most fertile land in the colony. The dispute between Leys and Delamere was part of a much wider conversation about the relative merits of either a policy of 'trusteeship', often associated with West Africa, or the promotion of white settler dominion, as in South Africa.[16]

It is worth pausing for a moment over what exactly this dispute meant to contemporaries and why it provoked such explosive debate. As Malinowski put it to the officers of the LSRM in 1926, labour recruitment had 'led to threats of civil war' in Kenya.'[17] The 1920s saw a number of crises in the settler empire, especially, as Malinowski pointed out, in Eastern and Central Africa. For the Conservative colonial secretary between 1925 and 1929, Leo Amery, emigration from Britain was the key to the whole issue of labour in the colonies, and he sought to carry forward Cecil Rhodes's vision of a white man's Dominion running from the Cape to Cairo.[18] But Amery's breezy optimism in Whitehall belied the troubles brewing at the peripheries. South Rhodesian farmers had declared self-rule from Colonial Office oversight in 1923, and agitation was mounting in Kenya, where plans were being hatched to kidnap the British-appointed governor and install Lord Delamere, the settlers' preferred representative, in his place.[19] This was the political context in which Malinowski warned the Rockefeller officers of an impending 'civil war' in the region.

On the other side of the ideological divide to Delamere and Amery were the founders of the IIALC, Lord Lugard and J. H. Oldham, and in a supporting role to these much more influential men, Malinowski. Both Lugard and Oldham had been on manoeuvres against Amery's vision for East Africa since campaigning on the question of forced labour in the early 1920s.[20] As secretary of the International Missionary Council, Oldham was especially sensitive to questions of 'native welfare'. He was eager to promote a form of Protestantism that could accommodate local customs and beliefs.[21] Amery's vision of a white settler 'counter-empire' running from the Cape to Nairobi was, one historian writes, his 'worst nightmare'. It chafed against his humanitarian views and challenged his position as a proselytising missionary whose great fear was that the settlers' victory would make the conversion of Africa impossible.[22]

For Lugard, meanwhile, sitting on the League of Nations Permanent Mandates Commission from 1922, Amery's vision for East Africa was intolerable for different, though related, reasons. Lugard never clarified his views on the ultimate source of sovereignty in Tanganyika, but he sought to maintain the line that the territory was held in trust by Britain under the oversight of the League. Tanganyika, Britain's East Africa Mandate, provided a case of best practice that Lugard could use to justify British imperial administration in international society.[23] Under its governor, Donald Cameron, the British were pursuing a policy of 'peasantification' rather than settler colonialism.[24] Yet despite the fact that Tanganyika was committed to such a policy, Delamere's agitation over the border in Kenya was affecting its Mandate neighbour. In 1926 Tanganyika's governor, Donald Cameron, rushed off a letter to Lugard warning that Kenyan settlers were being urged to cross the border and 'dig in . . . before the Germans got back.'[25]

Amidst these worries of contested sovereignty and competing models of imperial development, the IIALC was founded, uniting Oldham's long-standing anxieties about the direction of missionary activity in Africa with Lugard's Geneva-oriented politics and funnelling Rockefeller funds to Malinowski's students at the LSE. Lugard and Oldham did not question the justice of colonial rule in principle, but they were adamant that it should conform in practice to 'autocratic paternalism'.[26] On this model, Africans should not be cleared off the land and replaced by white farmers, but nor should Britain pursue a colour-blind policy of modernisation, as Norman Leys wanted. Africans should be protected in trust, afforded an education offered by whites, and their societies should be developed as part of a system of 'indirect rule' – with all of the patronizing, racist and paternalist assumptions that this suggests.[27]

In the same year that the IIALC was founded, the Hilton Young commission was formed to report on a possible union of Britain's East African colonies. Its findings, however, satisfied neither the pro-trusteeship camp nor the settlers. The commission proposed a 'dual policy' that favoured a settlement between Africans and Europeans in East Africa, and the report called for the limited coordination of mail and transport infrastructure across the colonies.[28] Malinowski took the opportunity to review the commission's report in the IIALC's house journal *Africa* and spun its findings towards the interests of his patrons. While Hilton Young had supported a 'dual policy', Malinowski clung to the principle that, over and above the interests of settlers, African interests should be 'paramount'. The idea of 'paramountcy' had been touted since the Devonshire Declaration of 1923.[29] Much like the idea of trusteeship, the language of paramountcy belied the violence of colonial rule.[30] But it offered a vital rhetorical opening from which settler interests could be attacked in the metropole. White settlement, Malinowski argued, would only be compatible with this overriding principle of paramountcy 'in so far as' it would 'not conflict with the native races.' The report declared that colonial rule should provide 'the creation of a field for the full development of native life.' In Malinowski's comment on this proposal he urged that only after this 'full development' had been fulfilled 'should surplus resource[s] be utilized for fostering immigrant enterprise.'[31]

The report's notion of 'field' is ambivalent. It could well be read as a justification for the further entrenchment of divisions between white highlands and native reserves in Kenya. But after quoting the report, Malinowski immediately followed up with the claim that paramountcy would only make sense if 'the native tribes have adequate land'. The implication was that they might not have sufficient space to develop at present. Indeed, for anyone of a remotely liberal persuasion in the 1920s, stories of expropriation, confiscations and settler violence caused periodic outrage.[32] Issues of land tenure clearly motivated much of this conflict, and Malinowski put the issue at the heart of his critique of Kenyan policy. When Malinowski cast settler farmers as 'immigrants' and proposed that their numbers be limited until Africans developed their land sufficiently on their own, while ploughing the profits of the colony into education and welfare projects, he was totally inverting settler-colonial visions of white-led economic development supported by the colonial secretary, Amery. Malinowski took a radical reading of the Hilton Young report and planted the flag of functionalist anthropology in its midst.

We can find further evidence of Malinowski's intervention in the settler question in his writings published in *Africa*. In two articles in 1929 and 1930, Malinowski set out a political manifesto for social anthropology.[33] While in principle anthropology could be used to buttress settler-colonial politics, this would mean supporting, he wrote, 'in the last issue forced labour, ruthless taxation, a fixed routine in political matters, the application of a code of laws to an entirely incompatible background.'[34] Having cleared away that particular issue, Malinowski proceeded to trumpet the utility of anthropology for a policy of trusteeship. Social anthropology, he argued, would help to ensure that trusteeship triumphed.

A very different position was put forward in October 1929 when the South African statesman Jan Smuts delivered the first of his Rhodes memorial lectures at Oxford. Like Malinowski, Smuts drew on the Hilton Young report, but he used that ambiguous document in support of a quite different political position: 'From the native point of view ... just as much as from the white point of view, the policy of African settlement is imperatively necessary,' he declared. White settlement was the 'only way to civilize the African native,' providing the 'steel framework of the whole ambitious structure of African civilization.'[35] Amery attended, calling Smuts's lecture 'a very challenging affirmation of the white settlement doctrine' with which, he noted in his diary, 'I agreed'.[36] Oldham, meanwhile, hurried an anti-Smuts broadside into print, declaring that administrators should concentrate their efforts on ameliorating the conditions of the inhabitants of East Africa, rather than merely focussing on the most efficient way to extract the wealth of its minerals and boost the export of crops.[37]

Smuts's idea of the 'native's point of view' was diametrically opposed to Malinowski's methodological argument discussed in the previous chapter. Recall that Malinowski urged anthropologists to enter into the worldview of the 'natives' in order to understand the different values underpinning their social life. In the Trobriand Islands, Malinowski explained, the Kula ring was its own kind of exchange that created meaning and secured the welfare of the islanders by stimulating trade. In comparison to Smuts's ideas, white settlement would be disastrous for the people of the Pacific, and presumably for the people of Africa, too. This might all be left in the realm of textual and contextual reconstruction of Malinowski's political views, apart from the fact that we can see him explicitly making these arguments in an article published in the BBC magazine the *Listener*, where he repeated in public what he had noted during his private studies of Lugard's writings. 'Perhaps the fairest statement of an ideal colonial policy is the doctrine of the *Dual Mandate*,' he wrote. But he qualified his support for Lugard's policy with the suggestion that the two sides of the mandate – to develop the colonies for the world, and rule 'for the benefit of the natives' – were not compatible if what he called 'the "get rich quick" principle ruthlessly followed by settlers or exploiters' was left undisturbed. Rather than going 'full steam ahead' with the Dual Mandate, 'native interests should be regarded as supreme.'[38] And this, in his view, meant that development must be 'slow, gradual, and constantly subordinated to the question of whether it does not deplenish and permanently cripple the native supply of labour.' Too much emphasis on 'development', he thought, would disturb the labour supply and lead to gluts of 'over-production'.[39]

Emphasis on Africans' interests would lead in the long run, he thought, to better prospects for economic gains and would avoid practices that seemed ethically abhorrent, like forced labour, which Malinowski suggested was, in reality, a 'new kind of slavery'.[40] In short, Malinowski may have supported Lugard's Dual Mandate, but his sympathies lay decidedly with one side of its dualism over the other: protectionism for colonised peoples rather than boosting production for export. And Malinowski set these ideas against contemporary Conservative colonial policy, taking a swipe in his article at the arguments of Lord Milner, who had been Amery's patron and inspiration. Malinowski's emphasis on the coherence of so-called primitive peoples' culture went hand in hand with a politics of development that sought to protect that culture and to ensure that land tenure and legal rights were recognised. His pro-trusteeship position was, in essence, an anti-Conservative politics. And it was stated in such bald terms that the *Listener's* editors were forced to plead with him to tone down the incendiary language of the original draft. He refused, and the BBC had to include a note at the top of the article stating that Malinowski's arguments were not the views of the corporation.[41]

A LABOUR GOVERNMENT
AND THE JOINT COMMISSION

Malinowski's understanding of the party-political context of the settler question was understood by Lugard, too, who attributed his continuing involvement in debates about colonial policy to the influence of the

Labour Party.[42] Thus, when a Labour minority government was elected in May 1929, Lugard, Malinowski and Oldham felt they had a stronger hand in their struggle over the future direction of policy in East Africa. Lugard wrote in a letter that at a meeting with Oldham in his offices, Prime Minister Ramsay MacDonald 'said that he thought that his Party entirely shared what he understood to be our views.'[43] The new colonial secretary, Sidney Webb (Lord Passfield) was no friend of the white settler community either, declaring in a speech in Parliament in 1930 'that every Colony, equally with the Government of a Mandated territory, is under an express obligation to promote the welfare and advancement in civilisation of its native population.'[44] Malinowski explained to Rockefeller Foundation officers that he felt confident he could persuade Webb, his LSE comrade, to push the anthropologists' agenda at the Colonial Office.[45]

But despite this cosy alliance at the top, the question of settler sovereignty and whether to unite Britain's East African colonies in one Dominion had to be met head on, and Webb decided to call a Joint Committee drawn from both houses of Parliament to debate the issue.[46] The committee encompassed a wide range of views drawn from both sides of the debate over the settler question. Hopes were high that a clear position on East Africa would emerge, but in that cherished tradition of British high politics, the commission's findings were a fudge. The fact that the commission did not plough on with a political union was a blow for Amery. Proponents of native paramountcy were disappointed, too, and a compromise was struck that left neither side happy: the restatement of the 'dual policy'. This effectively meant that Africans and settlers would be offered 'equality of opportunity'.[47] Opportunity, of course, was almost exclusively in the hands of European mining and farming interests.

While the commission's report made few politicians happy, for Malinowski it was something of a coup. On the basis of evidence given by the former Kenyan commissioner for native affairs, C. M. Dobbs, the report stated that all administrators should be offered training in anthropology. 'Social anthropology' was needed in order to 'lead the native through the necessary stages of development.'[48] The paternalist tone of this idea is typical, but the argumentative thrust should be noted. Anthropology would be used to *understand* and therefore *develop* the societies subject to colonial rule, rather than subjecting them to endless white-settler overrule, as Smuts had suggested.

Just as 'trusteeship' was a peculiarly vague concept, so the 'dual policy' could be bent into any shape in accordance with its promoters' ends.

In the wake of the Joint Commission's reporting, Lugard began promoting a particularly extreme vision of 'dualism'. He suggested that only total segregation of European and African communities could solve the economic and political tensions between them.[49] This pushed the 'dual policy' in the direction of 'paramountcy' – but in a limited fashion. Africans would be 'paramount', but only on their own reserves. Foreshadowing justifications of apartheid in South Africa, segregation would supposedly protect African societies and keep European economic interests from interfering in them. Ever eager to follow Lugard's lead, Malinowski wrote an article for the *Spectator* titled 'A Plea for an Effective Colour Bar' in which he pushed Lugard's argument considerably further. He did not think that Lugard had worked out his own logic, and Malinowski proposed that white settlers should emigrate wholesale back to Europe rather than stick to the white 'highlands'. 'The only just and therefore wise policy,' he wrote, 'would be to leave East Africa for the Africans, even at the expense of a few thousand whites, and of the capital investment which their repatriation would demand.'[50]

This was a radical response to the settler question, to say the least. By 1931 three possible answers had arisen: native paramountcy, white supremacy and the vaguely defined 'dual policy'. Native paramountcy on the model expressed by the League of Nations was the hope of many European radicals and humanitarians, but it was a vague sentiment that could be interpreted in many ways – from Lugard's limited segregationism to Malinowski's invocation of a politics of 'Africa for the Africans' and the repatriation of European settlers.[51] While many scholars have emphasised the braiding of colonial ideology (especially indirect rule) and anthropology together and have seen in this alliance evidence of the discipline's role as a handmaiden of colonialism, others have argued that it was precisely Malinowski's engagement with colonial politics in the 1930s that made his seminar at the LSE a place that drew African intellectuals and politicians living in London.[52]

For Malinowski was pushing a radical reading of the Hilton Young commission's findings and the report of the Joint Commission. Advancing along the path of the 'necessary stages of development' set out in the Joint Commission would mean a politics of 'Africa for the Africans', opening alliances with nascent African nationalism and repudiating Britain's 'civilizing mission'. This was clearly not on the minds of those like Lugard. But within the polysemous meaning of 'trusteeship' this was certainly one lesson that could be drawn, and it was drawn by some of Malinowski's African students, like Z. K. Matthews and the future president of Kenya, Jomo Kenyatta.[53] It was social anthropology's association with a particular form of trusteeship and Malinowski's opposition to settler rule that made his theorising a potent source for the West African historians Nnamdi Azikwe's and Ladipo Solanke's criticisms of the colour bar in Britain's colonies.[54] Without understanding the diversity of different engagements with the settler question, we are left with a false sense of the hegemony of 'indirect rule' that fails to analyse what it seeks to explain: the politics of social anthropology and furthermore why social anthropology was, for a time, an appealing body of knowledge for colonised peoples.

All of the positions on the settler question discussed here sought to apply expert knowledge to the matter of African economic development, but they clearly differed over the politics of how to go about developing eastern Africa.[55] What *sort* of research did they want? And *to what end*? Jan Smuts wanted to increase science funding in order to support South African subimperialism.[56] Malinowski wanted research on farming and education to defend peasant production in East Africa from the menace of settler encroachment.[57] These were deep and consequential fault lines, and these differences are crucial if we are to understand the Rockefeller Foundation's decision to support the IIALC for a second round of funding in 1931.

THE 1931 GRANT AND THE OXFORD SCHOOL

So far we have seen that the alliance in the late 1920s between Lugard, Oldham and Malinowski was not incidental, nor was it merely instrumental. Oldham, Lugard and Malinowski differed on details, but they had at least worked out a common position against the politics of Smuts and Amery. In short, Oldham, Lugard and Malinowski's network strength derived from the consolidating force of a common enemy. But what did this have to do with the Rockefeller Foundation?

We can see the connection between the politics of the Oldham-Lugard-Malinowski axis and the Rockefeller Foundation when the IIALC applied for a second round of funding in 1931. The Rockefeller Foundation almost funded a rival institution at Oxford, only the intervention of the international relations expert Raymond Buell halted the plan.[58] In a confidential letter to foundation officers, Buell made clear the links between the proposed Oxford Institute and the policies of Smuts and Amery. The Oxford Institute's plans were ostensibly similar to Oldham, Lugard and Malinowski's at the IIALC: to apply scientific expertise to questions of colonial administration. 'Of course no one objects to a school for African studies,' Buell wrote. The problem with the Oxford application lay in the fact that 'General Smuts himself would like to become principal of this school for the purpose of expanding his ideas of white settlement throughout the continent of Africa as a whole,' and, Buell warned, 'nothing could be more injurious to that continent than such a development.' Citing Smuts's lectures at Oxford, he concluded: 'It would be nothing more than a calamity to have the South African doctrine expanded, especially through the aid of American money.'[59] Edmund Day, director of the Division of Social Sciences at the Rockefeller Foundation, replied with a tactful note – 'I think I understand your general point of view. The same impression has been brought to our attention from other sources' – and pulled back. The Oxford Institute was not funded.[60]

This episode makes clear the 'gatekeeper' function of philanthropic funding in the interwar social sciences.[61] As Donald Fisher has argued, the Rockefeller Foundation certainly favoured the stabilisation of capitalism in this period, but the relationship of capitalism to colonialism was complex, especially where white settlers mediated between metropolitan finance and the expropriation of a colonised workforce.[62] The settler question makes clear that contemporaries could not agree on imperial policy. It is not enough to state that foundation money was aligned with attempts to make imperialism more efficient.[63] On that basis, Amery and Smuts's side of the debate might seem a better capitalist proposition.[64] More important than economic exploitation alone was the vision of world order espoused on either side of the debate. Buell's letter warned of the impact of settler policies for 'race relations' on a global scale.[65] The Rockefeller Foundation was heavily invested in research into race relations. In fact, as part of their strategy to gain funding, Malinowski and Oldham made comparisons between East Africa and the American Deep South in their letters to foundation officers, presumably to spell out the global stakes of their research and its relevance to an American audience.[66]

The decision not to fund the Oxford Institute also forces us to consider the political context in which calls for colonial expertise were made in the interwar decades. The Oxford Institute promised a scientific approach to questions of colonial administration. But its alignment with Smuts and Amery made it politically unpalatable to the Rockefeller Foundation. Weighing the relative claims for anthropology's collusion in colonial politics, one historian has concluded that 'anthropology needed empires far more than empires needed anthropologists.'[67] But treating 'empire' and imperialism as merely one form of politics occludes the rival policies at play during the decades of social anthropology's institutionalization. So, too, does too great an emphasis on the politics of 'expertise' ignore the stakes of broader political debate. As one colonial officer exasperatedly explained to gathered students at one of Malinowski's LSE seminars in 1933, 'expert opinions are not a final criterion in British Government.'[68] Colonial expertise was always subordinate to colonial politics.

As a consequence, one recent history has come to the conclusion that social-scientific expertise was inherently 'frail' in the British Empire.[69] Clearly in comparison to such giants of international and domestic politics as Lugard, or a leader of an important missionary organisation such as Oldham, Malinowski played only a marginal role in the grand political struggle over the settler question; we should not confuse anthropologists' political interventions with real influence on matters of policy. And Malinowski was not only expressing his opinions, he was also making his voice heard for intradisciplinary, academic reasons. For as we saw in the previous chapter, Malinowski was opposed to Elliot Smith's 'diffusionist' methods and was in the process of building up his own disciplinary power base at the LSE. The way to do this was to court the Rockefeller philanthropies and Lugard and Oldham, via the IIALC, who had significant sway in that regard. Malinowski was a shrewd academic entrepreneur and sought to ally himself to these powerful men. But this does not mean that Malinowski was merely 'cloaking' his academic interests in language designed to assuage his funders and patrons, as one commentator has argued.[70] Nor was he simply a cheerleader for imperialist power with an interest in concocting an ideology for some putatively hegemonic ideal of indirect rule. His writings should be seen in their political context and amidst the unstable and underdetermined politics of the 'settler question'.

LEGAL RATIONALITY AT THE LIMITS OF INDIRECT RULE: WITCHCRAFT, ANTHROPOLOGY AND COLONIAL JUSTICE

A prominent legal case in 1931 further illustrates the tensions between anthropological and administrative expertise, even though the two were supposedly brought together under the umbrella of 'indirect rule'. In that year a murder in Kenya sparked a public debate about witchcraft, the rule of law and the role of anthropology in colonial administration. Mwaiki, a woman from the Kamba tribe in Kenya, had been killed.[71] Two men, Kumwaka and Mnyoki, confronted her after Kumwaka's wife stopped talking. Mwaiki was accused of casting a spell on Kumwaka's wife. She was captured and held prisoner. She attempted to escape that night, but was chased, caught and beaten to death by a large group of men. The case came before the Supreme Court of Kenya in 1932. Sixty men and ten minors stood in a dock set up in a makeshift court inside the train station at Nairobi. Sir Jacob Barth, the presiding judge, passed a death sentence on the sixty defendants over the age of sixteen. But as he did so, he appealed for clemency from the governor-in-council. The sentences were contested, and the case moved to the East African Court of Appeal, where the charges were upheld.[72]

As the Supreme Court passed judgment, a Reuter's telegram was sent from Nairobi and published in the *Manchester Guardian* with the headline 'African Village Tragedy'.[73] The death sentence for such a large number of men and the complications of colonial justice turned the case into a sensation. The *Manchester Guardian* ran the story on 6 February, 30 March, 1 April, and 2 April. The case was reported in the *Times*, the *Washington Post*, the *New York Times* and newspapers in Australia and India.[74] There were two facts that almost all of the journalists noted: the unusually large number of defendants and the way that the case revealed the tension between Western legal practices and African customs; Mwaiki's fate was largely effaced. At the eleventh hour, the governor-in-council intervened and granted clemency to the group. Kumwaka was sent to jail, and the others received sentences of hard labour.

On 13 April, just over ten days after the governor's intervention, a two-thousand-word article by former colonial administrator and amateur anthropologist Frank Melland was published in the *Times*. The article suggested that accusations of witchcraft should be aired in colonial courts and that anthropological expertise should be deployed.[75] This provoked Lord Lugard to write a letter to the *Times* a few days later. Lugard avoided criticising the juridical logjam the case raised – wherein the governor was called on to overturn a judicial sentence in the very act of sentencing – while arguing, like Melland, for the application of expertise to stem the tide of witch murders: 'It is a job (as Mr. Melland says) for the anthropologist and psychologist and it is a job which the International Institute of African Languages and Cultures, with the aid of a psychologist and of anthropologists of international reputation, is now engaged upon.'[76] But in a private letter sent to Melland two days later, Lugard disagreed with him on a matter of substance. Melland had argued that witchcraft accusations should be tried in British colonial courts. Lugard, on the other hand, thought that witchcraft beliefs could not form the basis of colonial justice. He wanted to keep customary and colonial law separate.[77]

For Malinowski, on the other hand, the connection between magical beliefs and the rule of law was central to his theorizing, and he contrasted his ideas with prevailing opinion in Britain's colonies. In a letter sent to an officer at the LSRM, he explained that many colonial administrators seemed to be struck by 'moral indignation, or at least superciliousness with regard to primitive belief.' Functionalists, like him, treated seemingly irrational 'superstition' as part of a cultural whole, a 'working and vital system of forces ... which are all organically connected and mutually adjusted.'[78] In another letter he made the connection between governing and theorizing more explicit still: 'It is impossible to administer law and justice in a society with an entirely false view of its constitution.'[79] Malinowski's belief in the utility of his theories resulted in his expressed amazement in a lecture to his students at the LSE that 'in some colonies native law has been declared non-existent!'[80]

'Primitive jurisprudence,' Malinowski wrote in his extended treatment of law and anthropology, *Crime and Custom in Savage Society* (1926), 'has received in recent times the scantiest and the least satisfactory treatment.'[81] The argument that 'primitive' societies were governed by 'authority, law and order' had been a theme since writing *Argonauts* in 1922.[82] In *Crime and Custom* he explained that the difficulty of understanding the law in non-literate cultures resided in the fact that law is 'only one category within the body of custom.'[83] Law was a part of custom and maintained the social rules that held each culture together. Magic and sorcery were seen as crucial conduits for law making and the organisation of labour.[84] Malinowski thought that magic was a crucial part of the legal process: it mediates relationships, stresses dependencies and is deployed as a mark of status, danger or power. Colonial laws were clearly completely mismatched with primitive laws. They worked on utterly different bases. One kind, the colonial law, was a form of command issued by a sovereign authority, written down and meted out by specialised functionaries in specialised zones of contestation. Primitive law was dispersed, constitutive, social and tacit. As Malinowski put it in a lecture at the LSE: 'To the layman the law means a code, court, cop. To the functionalist it is an aspect of culture.'[85]

He expanded on these ideas in a series of notes he took in the late 1930s while reading C. K. Allen's influential textbook *Law in the Making* (1930). He wrote that 'genuine law is but the charter of institutions, and of tendencies within organized life.'[86] He gave as examples of these 'charters': 'chieftainship versus district autonomy; matriarchy versus patriarchy; sorcery as instrument of law and its criminal agency.'[87] Any attempt to override these customs would be a threat to the true source of law that resided in the maintenance and reproduction of the social order of each particular community.

When *Africa*, the house journal of the IIALC, published a special edition on witchcraft in 1934, all of the contributors noted these tensions between anthropological theory and administrative practice. The former senior magistrate in Uganda and assistant attorney general in Nyasaland, C. Clifton-Roberts, wrote, 'The legislation affecting witchcraft emphasizes the urgent need for a change in native policy, with consideration of what we mean by trusteeship in its practical application. I have no hesitation in saying that the legal system we have imposed is entirely unsuited to African peoples.'[88] Edward Evans-Pritchard's headline article, titled simply 'Witchcraft', suggested that both 'offensive' and 'defensive' witchcraft were crucial to the constitution of the society he discussed, the Azande. Amongst the Azande, almost all deaths were attributed to witchcraft. Witchcraft accusations are an 'essential concomitant to social organization' because the society is based on patrilineal kinship, wherein groups of related men act as both a 'blood-revenge group' and a 'mutual assistance group in paying compensation for homicide.'[89] So when someone died and witchcraft was suspected (it was almost always suspected), the male relatives of the deceased asked an oracle to confirm whether witchcraft was to blame and who the culprit might be. The offending individual, if found, would then be required to pay compensation to the claimants, and often has to raise the funds from amongst their male kin. If witchcraft is so intertwined with such a central fact of social life, and society is mediated through who dies, and their reasons for dying, then making witch-hunting, or witchcraft beliefs illegal *tout court* would mean denying a central plank of customary law.

Clearly the anthropologists were setting themselves up against the fact that indirect rule was hardly very indirect. Under indirect rule, laws were supposed to be based on 'native custom'. But if considered 'repugnant', the law could not recognise their reality without undermining the supposedly 'civilised' basis of colonial power.[90] To cope with practices like witchcraft, magistrates and judges applied a 'repugnancy test'. This acted as a kind of judicial loophole, allowing officials to strike down any aspect of customary law offensive to notions of 'justice, equity and good conscience.'[91] Anthropologists like Malinowski and Evans-Pritchard troubled these distinctions and theorized about a far more expansive application of customary law.

Thus despite the anthropologists' claims to be able to offer advice on the subject of witchcraft and the law, and Lugard's public support for applied anthropology, one of Malinowski's students, Meyer Fortes, wrote in a letter from the field: 'I fear that there may be a diversity of opinion on some matters between the Administration and myself, as to what is or is not "law".'[92] Fortes was right to be concerned. The appeals court judge in the Kamba case, for example, seemed to have a completely different conception of the law to the anthropologists. He reminded the court that the 'Government does not tolerate the killing of witches.' The adoption of a different policy would, he remarked, 'encourage the belief that an aggrieved party may take the law into his own hands, and no belief could well be more mischievous or fraught with greater danger to public peace and tranquility.'[93]

Lugard did not subscribe to anthropologically relativist ideas, either. Despite his support for social anthropology as part of the IIALC, when discussing the appropriate response to witchcraft beliefs in his *Dual Mandate* he wrote: 'Stamping out such practices compels recourse to deterrent penalties, and since fear of death was the motive, no less penalty than death will be deterrent.'[94] Lugard here sounds exactly like the British judge in the Kamba case, his views hardly 'surrendered' to the 'functional point of view', as Malinowski wanted to believe. Likewise, Hubert Murray, governor of Papua (under whose authority Malinowski had done his own fieldwork), held similar views, especially in regards to witchcraft and the rule of law. The anthropologist 'cannot be allowed to encroach upon the province of administration. In administration the stakes for which we play are too high to allow of experiment and chance work.' He went on: 'The principals of the functional school [i.e., Malinowski and his students] if pressed to their logical conclusion must end in a refusal to admit "that the white race can under any circumstances govern the black or the brown."'[95]

Murray intuited that Malinowski and his students clearly thought of sovereignty and the rule of law in a quite different way to administrators like Lugard and himself. Legitimacy did not reside in the commands imposed upon, or in spite of, existing social organization. If magic and sorcery formed part of a society's 'tendencies', then they were valid expressions of customary law. Malinowski increasingly thought in the 1930s that indirect rule, if it was to be properly implemented, must steer a middle line between native and European customs. Indirect rule, as a species of 'collaboration' between coloniser and colonised, had to 'develo[p] by its own laws of growth and ... its own determinism' rather than merely tracking Western positive law and 'civilization'.[96] He blamed the missionaries' teaching, and, he wrote acerbically, their 'enlightened influence,' for increasing the prevalence of witchcraft accusations in Africa.[97] They cleaved too closely to the European side of what he called 'culture contact'. He rejected the idea that colonised societies should be brought up under British power to be 'caricature[s] of the European' and threw this idea out as a form of direct rule.[98] Colonialism was creating new forms of social organisation. In order to make this bargain worth wagering for colonised peoples, some way had to be found toward a middle ground. The implication was that a new source of law was arising out of the interaction of European and colonised societies, and with it, the diminution of any claims by whites to be the sole arbiters of the colonies' political destinies. This made Malinowski's legal theories so radically 'indirect' that, as Hubert Murray recognised, they offered little theoretical space for any form of legitimate colonial law making at all. What anthropologists and colonial officials meant by 'indirect rule' clearly suggested different things.

ECONOMIC DUALISM AT THE LIMITS OF INDIRECT RULE

So far, this half of the chapter has explored interwar social anthropologists' theories about law and magic and indirect rule; attention now briefly turns to economics. Malinowski was centrally concerned with explaining the differences between Trobriand Island life and the kind of extractive colonialism going on in the plantations of the colonial Pacific. In *Argonauts* he did this by couching his critique in an argument about the difference between a 'national economy' marked by the circulation of goods equated with the exchange of money and a 'tribal economy' functioning according to a logic of social reciprocity. The implication was that by drawing labour away from coastal villages to boost profits in the plantations, the tribal economy would be inevitably degraded. Movement between these dual systems meant moving between two worlds structured by different, and opposing, values. As with his ideas about primitive law, Malinowski's economic theories represented non-Western peoples as possessing their own delicately balanced social systems particularly attuned to maintain and reproduce their social life.

The fact that the peoples populating the Trobriand Islands did not possess a 'a system of free competitive exchange of goods and services' did not mean that they existed in a 'pre-economic stage', an argument Malinowski used to score a point against the German sociologist and economist Karl Bücher. Instead, 'production, exchange and consumption are socially organised and regulated by custom.'[99] Kinship ties, customary usages and magical rites all interacted to generate values in the Trobriand Islands, but this did not make the islanders 'irrational' or uneconomically minded. Malinowski trained his early graduate students in these assumptions, and his first PhD student, Raymond Firth, gave a brief history of his supervisor's approach in his doctoral dissertation, published in 1929 as *Primitive Economics of the New Zealand Maori*.

Firth contrasted the 'Functional study of Economic Institutions' (in short, Malinowski's views) with a previously dominant tradition that sought to tell an evolutionary story of societies progressing via distinct stages. In that tradition, each stage was considered as a 'fixed point', a 'pause and then a forward movement,' Firth explained. But there was no way to tell how these stopping-off points were maintained or why some societies decided, or were forced, to decamp and march on to the next staging post.[100] Evolutionists argued amongst themselves about the proper order of stages, positing that many customs currently practiced were survivals of earlier epochs and, Firth pointed out, they were often only interested in 'primitive economics' in order to tell different origin stories for Western economic structures. As a result, they had generated a 'hopeless welter of hypotheses' linked to purely hypothetical historical narratives and untethered from current observations of economic life amongst non-capitalist peoples.[101]

Firth's dismissal of this form of grand synthetic sociology formed part of the death 'slowly and unspectacularly', as John Burrow put it, of evolutionary social theory in the early twentieth-century social sciences.[102] Rather than look at hypothetical 'stages' to explain institutions, Firth and Malinowski proposed a pragmatic methodology that stressed present functioning, rather than historical reconstruction as the key to sociological method. 'The root of the matter,' Firth wrote, 'lies in the fact that it is by consideration of what a thing *does* that one is likely to understand what it *is*.'[103] Malinowski put things similarly in a class at the LSE four years later: 'The theories of the evolutionary and historical schools . . . diverts attention from things which are really there, from realities, from customs now practiced.'[104]

These attacks on both evolutionary social science and the figure of the rational economic man (the infamous 'homo economicus') became particularly sophisticated in Firth and Malinowski's arguments about the inadequacy of Lionel Robbins's recently published theories in the 1930s. Robbins was Firth and Malinowski's colleague at the LSE, and he mounted a challenge to the economics profession in 1932 with his short book *An Essay on the Nature and Significance of Economic Science*. In it Robbins famously argued that economics is 'the science which studies human behaviour as a relationship between ends and scarce means with alternative uses.'[105] Economics, Robbins wrote, 'serves for the inhabitant of the modern world with its endless interconnections and relationships as an extension of his perceptive apparatus. It provides a technique of rational action.'[106] As a result, he argued that

> economic analysis has most utility in the exchange economy. It is unnecessary in the isolated economy. It is debarred from any but the simplest generalisations by the very *raison d'etre* of a communist society. But where independent initiative in social relationships is permitted to the individual, there economic analysis comes into its own.[107]

While the economists' techniques may not be so 'illuminating' in the case of the 'isolated man' or the 'communist society', all action can still be described in economic terms because all actions are basically 'subsidiary to the main fact of scarcity.'[108]

Malinowski, two of his students, Raymond Firth and Margaret Read, and another IIALC-funded anthropologist, Richard Thurnwald, posed three broad problems to Robbins's ideas. First, they pointed out that the communities anthropologists studied were exchange societies but neither free market societies nor communist ones. Second, there was no common market in which goods could be exchanged, and crucially, no medium – that is, money – that could be used to intermediate exchanges or read off prices to seek to find out what people valued. Furthermore, and relatedly, individuals in the societies studied by anthropologists did not act individually, and so many of the resources collected were disposed along customary and communal lines. They did not quibble with Robbins's account of ends and means, then, but with the supposition that economic action could be understood by the play of prices in an open market when no such market existed in non-capitalist societies.

Thurnwald's *Economics in Primitive Societies* (1932) affirmed, as a point of principle, that in 'primitive communities' 'economic values do not stand isolated in their own special field, but are closely interwoven with the whole texture of society.'[109] Despite the variations in complexity of social structure and forms of tribute and redistribution, he argued that there was 'the continuance of direct barter between the people whether privately or in markets.'[110] The nature of these exchanges was highly personal. And the 'rationality' of these exchanges was social. Thurnwald therefore argued that Western economics is best fitted to describe systems of market-based money exchange and unhelpful when describing non-capitalist economic relations.

Malinowski raised similar criticisms in his 1932 lectures on primitive economics at the LSE. He contrasted his approach to Robbins's: 'Problems of production, exchange value etc. are not an autonomous body of customs and institutions in every community. We are not arbitrary in this division, but there is no dictatorial step afterwards. If we are arbitrary in this, we are in good company from Adam Smith to Professor Robbins.'[111] The 'dictatorial step' of making an 'arbitrary ... division' between economic and non-economic institutions was a logical move necessitated by preconceived, and misplaced, ideas, not the result of observing facts. Robbins had written in his *Essay* that 'each individual entering the market may be conceived to have a scale of relative valuations. . . . Any given price, therefore, has significance only in relation to the other prices prevailing at that time.'[112] However, prices and values in non-capitalist societies were different. In the Trobriand Islands, Malinowski had written, 'in almost all forms of exchange ... there is [no] reason for looking at it from the purely utilitarian or economic standpoint, since there is no enhancement of mutual utility through the exchange.' Exchanging goods, he pointed out in the case of the Trobriand Islands, was rarely to the mutual benefit of price-optimizing individuals determined to negotiate the most rational distribution of resources. Giving was often done for its own sake, which is to say, for a social sake. Giving, as one part of an exchange, often implied a burdensome reciprocal obligation to offer a counter-gift. Exchange in this sense is driven by 'the fundamental human impulse to display, to share, to bestow.' Exchange situates the exchanging parties in a social order that their giving serves to reinforce and sustain.[113]

Developing these insights, one of Malinowski's students, Margaret Read, took aim at a theory of economic development that she presented as ubiquitous in British colonies in Africa: the inducement to grow cash crops, the introduction of cash wages and the marketing of consumer items to increase spending. While this logic applied across any number of official policies, Read explained that it played out in two different ways. The first way that the society she studied, the Ngoni, might raise their standard of living was to work for a European for a wage. The second way that they might improve their lot was to raise their own crops, manufacture goods themselves and sell them in local markets. Read strongly suggested promoting the latter.[114] How to achieve this aim was unclear, though: 'We shall not by pressing a button and dangling a bicycle in front of him, at once persuade an African to grow more crops and sell them in the market in order to buy the bicycle.'[115] Amongst the Ngoni a great deal of production was done within the household and was unwaged. Furthermore, many exchanges were done by bartering, and others were owed to kin: 'It is at least a debatable point,' she pointed out, 'whether the market price of grain is a real equivalent for the utility to the consumers of the grain which they themselves have grown.'[116] Amongst the Ngoni a mixed economy reigned, and many villages existed in conditions of semi-subsistence.[117]

In Central Africa, Read argued, neither a 'modern economic system' nor a 'primitive economic system' existed.[118] So Malinowski's idea about 'tribal economics' would not hold. Rather, peoples like the Ngoni were subject to three 'divergent and contrary lines of development': one was the 'traditional economic life' of kinship dues, wherein 'economic life is closely bound up with the social and political organization of the people'; then there were the changes 'come through European contact' that 'pressed most hardly' on traditional, chiefly authorities who had 'command[ed] labour and resources' prior to colonial conquest; and finally there was 'Indirect Rule', which attempted to rule through chiefs but left them 'shorn of economic supremacy' and which was opposed by 'those subjects who possess wealth in the European sense' – that is, settlers and South Asian traders.[119] In this context, 'the problem of raising the standard of living is not a matter of simple arithmetic.'[120]

Clearly, measurement would be difficult when there were no prices set in a free market, and more fundamentally, exactly what should be measured? In order to work out how to raise the Ngoni standard of living 'we must discover the values which govern their present production.'[121] Economists would only be able to do this with the help of anthropologists, Read argued. Intensive observation in the field might allow the social scientist to 'examine those institutions by means of which goods are produced and distributed' and then, crucially, judge the 'extension of production' into other institutions, such as kinship and religion. Once this ethnographic data was collected, the anthropologist and economist could then judge whether 'the tribal resources, consisting of the natural environment, the people, and their knowledge and organization and work can be developed without destroying the entire basis of their former economic life.'[122] To do otherwise would be to totally misunderstand how values were formed amongst the Ngoni. As an example, Read described how attempts by administrators to make the Ngoni raise and exchange their cattle 'economically' had spectacularly backfired. Administrators had no sense that the animals were used in such complex ritual ways and that the exchange of animals enmeshed them in webs of kinship, neighbourly obligation and political display. Cattle, to the Ngoni, were not merely goods to be matched with a cash price. They were crucial vessels for the reproduction of their society.

Amongst the Ngoni, the paramount chief's market attracted Read's approbation. Here was an institution in which 'the old and the new are in unison and not in conflict.'[123] The paramount chief's involvement in the economic life of his people united the economic and political functions that indirect rule sought to sever, and that Read and her anthropological colleagues thought should be reconnected. If 'economic progress must be in line with . . . political development' in order to 'achieve stability and permanence' of the population and, presumably, of British rule, too, then an 'uneconomical' economic system like the market at Lizulu in Nyasaland should be supported.[124]

Firth, writing also in the late 1930s, described the problems faced by economic anthropology in *Primitive Polynesian Economy* (1939) in the following way. It is not so much then, 'by the presence or absence of economic organization or the rational control of the environment that primitive peoples differ from civilized, but the different types of ends towards which this organization and control are aimed, resulting in the creation of a very different scale of values.'[125] Rather than merely read off the relations between means and ends in a value-neutral manner and look to prices as a guide, as Lionel Robbins suggested, the task for the economic anthropologist must be to understand how wants are 'determined' and 'the organization by which . . . means are brought into relation with the ends desired.'[126] The key point to stress is that individuals do not determine these relations between means and ends individually. Social relations of reciprocal obligations and communal dues determine values. And under the conditions of colonial expansion, new ends, which Firth described evocatively as 'bait . . . held out to them by the new economic and social system,' created new incentives.[127] Understanding the workings of the baited traps set by business and missionary interests provided the means by which anthropologists could describe and explain the newly emerging values arising in societies meeting Western economies from a position of social difference and colonial dependence. In order fully to understand the economic action of individuals deploying their scarce means and limited time, this behaviour must be set in its social, which is to say colonial, context.

For Robbins, of course, all of this was part of the 'sociological penumbra' he had hoped to cut through with *Essay*. Human actions could be described in much the same way in all places – as responses to the problems of scarcity. Yet in an article in the magazine *Science and Society* in 1937, Firth argued that this limited idea of rationality was unhelpful. 'Co-operation with sociologists is of prime necessity,' he wrote, 'if the economist wishes to use his generalizations to predict the behaviour of human beings.' Some account must be given of the reasons for choosing amongst means and an explanation offered for the emergence of new ends under the conditions of colonialism.[128] Freedom of choice could not be assumed in this context, and economists' ideas were leading to faulty logic on the part of administrators who insisted on applying policies developed for capitalist, market-based societies to those that possessed very different forms of economic life.

CONCLUSION

An interest in what Firth had called 'functional correlation' in his dissertation suggested a methodological protectionism connected to a politics of trusteeship that saw new anthropological theories about law and economics emerge in the 1920s and 1930s. The interlocking nature of political, economic and familial ties in the societies anthropologists studied suggested that any changes to their workings would disturb the coherence of the culture as a whole.[129] The coherence of a culture was always linked by anthropologists to the society's ability to reproduce itself, not only in terms of ideas or technologies but also in demographic and economic terms. For anthropologists like Firth, Read, Thurnwald and Malinowski, cultural exchange, appropriation and consolidation were set in a critical history of catastrophic sociological destruction. The missionary, trader and soldier, Firth wrote, 'are primarily concerned in dealing with the people of the country.' The settler, on the other hand, 'applies his energies to subduing the country itself.' 'It is the slow almost resistless advance of settlement,' Firth went on, 'that holds the most menace for the freedom and autonomy of the native and the retention of his characteristic economic structure.'[130] In Firth's model of cultural change, the rhythm of colonisation could be described as equilibrium disturbed by new forces and a resettling after a dynamic period of interaction into a new pattern, if, after the preceding process, he wrote chillingly, 'enough of them' are left 'to undergo the change.'[131]

Bringing together the two halves of this chapter – the first on the 'settler question' in East Africa and the second on law and economics – we get a different sense of Malinowski's notes on how Lugard's ideas must 'surrender' to his own. The eminent historian of anthropology George Stocking quoted this remark to argue that this was proof that Malinowski's theorizing was stuck 'in the historical present, [thus] maintain[ing] a certain distance between anthropology and the actual process of colonial policy and practice, both on the ground and in the metropole.'[132] This cannot be right. Malinowski's desire was to ally his methodology to Lugard's politics and so change the discipline away from the diffusionism of Elliot Smith discussed in the previous chapter. But he simultaneously hoped to transform indirect rule into a more truly indirect policy, devolving law making as well as economic power down to the level of the societies currently subject to imperial control.

Malinowski's work seems less distant from metropolitan and peripheral colonial policy if we pay attention to another piece of his pencilled marginalia, this one on cultural change in Africa: 'The goal or end result. African nationalism, not exactly on Europe's pattern but same type.'[133] Demanding that law and economic power in Britain's colonial possessions should be determined by colonized peoples placed significant strain on the legitimacy of a form of imperial rule based on exclusionary ideas of race and on ideologies of civilizational hierarchy. However, as we have seen, this did not mean that Malinowski discounted ideas of race.[134] Rather than situate race in physiology, he thought that cultural factors were more important and did little to challenge the paternalism of the British ideology of trusteeship.[135] In terms of his professional politics he was willing to promote his African students, but only so far. The personal prejudices of individual anthropologists, including Malinowski, and the structural racism of the British academy endlessly frustrated black intellectuals' ambitions. Professional appointments and publishing contracts were subject to an effective colour bar.[136]

Malinowski's ideas about jurisprudence and economics did challenge a significant component of British colonial ideology that proposed that

Western norms exist at the developmental apex of social evolution, as the alibi of indirect rule seemed to suggest.[137] Malinowski and his students offered accounts of a vast plurality of civilizations existing within the bounds of the European empires, to be protected and recognized. According to the functionalists, all civilizations had value; none could claim to be the *fons et origo* of political order. This raised the question of how one could go about finding out how these communities functioned. As we will see in the next chapter, social anthropologists faced significant issues in the field when they investigated politically sensitive topics, and by the 1930s they were increasingly divided over questions of methodology.

CHAPTER 3

Pencils, Schemes and Letters

*Fieldwork and Pedagogy in 1930s
Social Anthropology*

When Audrey Richards embarked for her first bout of fieldwork in 1930, she recalled Malinowski seeing her off at Victoria Station with a fistful of coloured pencils, 'saying "remember what I told you: brown for economics, red for politics, blue for ritual".' Then he gave her 'a great many cards and he said, "now this is the linguistic stuff, yellow for adjectives, blue for 'so-and-so' and red for proverbs or sayings".' Bemused, Richards 'bundled into the carriage with the elastic bands breaking in their unwonted burden that they had to carry.'[1]

After a long journey from Victoria Station to what its British colonisers called Northern Rhodesia, Richards received two packages from Malinowski.[2] One contained even more writing material: 'Such a grandeur of pencils I never looked for,' she wrote in reply. In the other parcel was a copy of her mentor's monograph *The Sexual Life of Savages in Northwestern Melanesia*. 'I clasp them lovingly,' she wrote about the pencils, 'fired to initiate new schemes of notes.' The book provided 'a lovely fresh feeling of field brotherhood so to speak.' That lovely feeling was mixed, though, with a sense of bewilderment. As she thumbed through Malinowski's book, Richards found herself 'longing to stop and ask "How ever did you manage to get that[?]".' 'I mean', she went on, 'that you don't see the difficulties at home however much they are fitted into the theoretical pattern. I would give a lot for a seminar, even over the fuggy radiators of the L.S.E. now.'[3] Later in life, Richards explained that all this stationery was connected to Malinowski's functionalist 'theory, of course'. But, she asked sceptically, 'how do you study a whole society, how do you do it?'[4]

Richards's attempt to 'study a whole society' was carried out as part of a community encompassing face-to-face encounters and also other forms of sociability that stretched over great distances (as in the case of writing letters) and extended over time via training (as in the case of Malinowski's coloured pencils and cards). This chapter explains how the anthropological field was intimately connected to other spaces: to other field sites, as well as the university seminar back at the LSE, where field notes were discussed and theories refined and reiterated, and where norms and behaviours were passed down through the generations. In this sense, the chapter's task is to move from the focus on the ideas found solely in texts in the last chapter to how those ideas were transmitted via pedagogy and how they worked in practice. Jack Goody grasped the essential sociability of anthropologists' pedagogy by calling Malinowski's seminar a kind of 'collective apprenticeship' and by noting that the seminar often spilled into the pubs surrounding the LSE.[5] Goody's insight can be stretched a step further, though. According to Richards's testimony, the LSE's collective apprenticeship spread far beyond the bars of Aldwych and the Kingsway, out beyond Victoria Station to the peripheries of the British Empire, entrained in a particular way of seeing, enveloped in the correspondence between Malinowski's acolytes (and detractors), connecting a web of researchers attacking common problems with similar methods.

My aim in this chapter is to turn away from the emphasis on 'high politics', ideology and the intellectual history of law and economics in the previous chapter to tell of the 'collective apprenticeship' formed by fieldwork in the 1930s. My argument is that anthropological knowledge was constructed in dialogue with research assistants, through pedagogy and via the sociality of Malinowski's seminar. I also argue that the turn to fieldwork in the 1930s created the conditions for intradisciplinary feuding that turned some of Malinowski's students away from his functionalist ideas in the late 1930s and 1940s, a story taken up in chapter 6. From the previous two chapters we now have a good sense of Malinowski's ambivalent relationship with the ideology of indirect rule and how his connections to the Rockefeller Foundation helped fund many of his students' fieldwork. We have also been introduced to many of the functionalist ideas that made his work so powerfully inspiring for his readers. The task of this chapter is to see how, with their funding in hand, social anthropologists connected their training at the LSE with the contingencies of life in the field. After all, social anthropology was not only a collection of texts making arguments about law and economics in political contexts; it was a subculture of real living, breathing humans working stuff out in conversation and on paper.

Audrey Richards gave a sense of how this subculture functioned in terms of pedagogy, affect and material culture. She also suggested that anthropologists were not tied down to studying one particular thing. Rather, they sought to study a 'whole society' via extensive research in a wide variety of domains, from law to economics, from religion to nutrition. This vision of holism and functionalism and the catholicity of research topics pursued by social anthropologists made their texts and their methods hugely influential. We can witness in the 1930s the 'collective apprenticeship' of social-scientific field research being formed by looking 'under the hood', as it were, and then we will see in the following chapters how their functionalist ideas ramified and reached out to transform ideas of 'the social' more widely.[6]

CHARTS, SCHEMES AND OBSERVATION IN THE FIELD

Like Richards, Lucy Mair longed for life back in London. Her research left her experiencing a sense of alienation. Mair was one of the first of Malinowski's students to profit from the infusion of funding offered by the Rockefeller Foundation via the International Institute of African Languages and Cultures (IIALC) in 1931. She was a specialist on League of Nations policy towards minorities in Europe and had been a lecturer in international relations at the LSE before travelling to Uganda.[7] She wrote to Richards for advice as she began her field research. She was shy and worried about how to interact with European settlers and with Africans, relating, with a racist turn of phrase typical of paternalist liberals of the time, 'I wonder sometimes just how one applies the Functional Method to the modernised savage. I suppose the thing will work itself out.'[8]

Her sense that things would fall naturally into place soon subsided into resignation, however. Turning her paper over to continue writing, she speculated that 'it may be tropical lethargy undermining my character, but I have decided that it is lifeless to aim at covering the ground someone like Bronio would, or even to fill out every section of a previously worked out plan.' She committed herself, however, to 'carry on with what comes to hand and be content to get one's own problem and as much as can be managed.' She hoped that this pragmatic approach was in accordance with Richards's advice before setting off for the field and conformed to what 'Bronio means by the line of least resistance.'[9] Mair's and Richards's identification with each other and with 'Bronio' (the name used by Malinowski's close associates) sustained an epistolary community of anthropologists attacking similar problems with the same techniques in the 1930s. Mair's racist allusion to the 'modernised savage' gestures to a new emphasis in the 1930s on what social anthropologists were then euphemistically calling 'culture contact' as they sought to judge the impact of European colonialism on mostly African societies.[10] Richards's mention of a 'theoretical pattern' and Mair's referral to a 'previously worked out plan' suggest that neither of them were doing research with a naively positivist disposition. They had prepared themselves to look at the world around them with a particular kind of attention.

Malinowski's students' emphasis on observation, standardization and training owed a great deal to his teaching. And his ideas drew, in turn, on contemporary developments in European science and culture.[11] In one class Malinowski inveighed: 'In order to speculate or "explain" a phenomenon' it is 'necessary to understand it – incidentally in order to find – know [sic] what to look for.'[12] He stressed that this seemingly tautologous position was part of a broader appeal to sharpen his students' awareness. His intention, he told them, was to reconstitute their 'capacity to see'.[13] Such an epistemological recalibration would allow his students to reveal what he called 'the invisible facts of Anthropology.'

Malinowski knew well enough that seeing facts and looking for them were part of the same process. 'Facts', he told his gathered students, 'do not walk on the surface of tribal life. You have to construct them.'[14] This constructivist approach posed the danger that the student's gaze would be utterly theory laden. If anthropologists merely saw what they expected to see in the field, then they risked producing a purely hypothetical series of deductions about culture and society unmoored from reality. 'Diffusionists' [Malinowski explained with reference to the theories of Grafton Elliot Smith we encountered in chapter 1] go about 'finding that everything diffuses; and people who believe in Functional Theory that everything functions!'[15] Despite these problems, however, there was no virtue in imagining that one could adopt a neutral stance of untrammelled objectivity. 'If you go out [to the field] with a blank mind you will find nothing.... [T]he blank mind does not exist,' he explained. While 'theories will stupefy, the absence of theories makes field-work impossible.'[16] Some protocol had to be found to connect observation, theory and practice. He thought that a solution lay in the deduction that cultures reproduced and maintained themselves through a collective of interlocking institutions. This insight formed the starting point from which researchers could work out the ways in which institutions in particular locations locked together.

In his most famous work, *Argonauts of the Western Pacific*, Malinowski pursued a narrative form to help his readers 'see' the *kula* as a functioning social whole. As his interests shifted to Africa in the late 1920s, to comparative ethnography, and as he began to teach students, he had to find ways to operationalize his methods.[17] At some point during the early 1930s he began representing key social institutions that he thought underlay all communities in schemes made up of rows with titles like 'Economics', 'Magic' and 'Education'. These charts were to be filled in by fieldworkers to reveal the different ways in which each culture maintained itself. 'What is the function of our diagram?' Malinowski asked his students. 'It leads us to new lines of inquiry and to correlating details of concrete observation. If you investigated certain of these details we would miss the correlations, and these relationships themselves yield further facts.'[18] There is evidence from Mair's correspondence that Malinowski's techniques changed at some point between 1931 and 1932: 'I understand that the Scientific Method of Approach has undergone a number of fundamental changes since I was last in contact with the Master's mind,' she wrote from Uganda.[19] It is possible that less emphasis was being put on the use of different-coloured writing to bring out the different functions of institutions, as Richards recalled. It was perhaps at this moment that Malinowski was introducing his students to his ever-more-complex charts (see table 1).

Mair does seem to have been working in light of some kind of scheme during her research in 1932. She had, she wrote to Malinowski, finished researching land tenure and was now 'attacking' government.[20] On the subject of economics she regretted that she did not have the chance to test 'either my favourite theories or yours.' From her field experience in the Ngogwe district of Uganda, Mair could not see evidence of the distinction Malinowski had drawn in the early 1920s between a 'tribal economy' and a capitalist economy.[21] The use of cowry shells had died out, and money was so much taken for granted by the subjects of her research that 'it is far too late to analyse what specific results' its introduction had 'produced'.[22] Christianity had been taken up enthusiastically too, and she could only find evidence of people seeing magical practices

TABLE 1. AUTHOR'S REPRODUCTION OF A CULTURE CHART MADE BY BRONISLAW MALINOWSKI

CHART I. Copyright of B. Malinowski

SCHEME OF CULTURE

A — External Factors determining Culture	B — Descriptive Approaches	C — Functional Aspects	D — The Fundamental Factors of Culture
1. BODILY NEEDS OF MAN Nutrition Procreation Shelter and Temperature Safety Movement Recreation & Rest Growth. 2. ENVIRONMENT Habitat Climate Natural Routes (Land & Water) Bacteriological Endemic Diseases Flora Mineral Resources Meteorological & Astronomical periodicities Season, Morns, Day & Night (i.e. everything we cannot otherwise explain) 3. RACE 4. HISTORY Recorded Reconstructed (Archeological evidence; Speculation) (Evolutionary Level) – Relegate to another pair 5. CULTURE CONTACTS: Pre-European With Western Culture Modern Race and Culture Mixture	1. LIFE HISTORY: Birth Childhood Puberty Adolescence Manhood (Maturity) Courtship Marriage Parenthood Full citizenship Old age Death 2. COMMUNAL LIFE ON TRIBAL SCALE: Cultural Map of the Tribal territory Seasonal Calendar Profane – Ceremonial Phases Peace and War Private & Public Phase 3. GROUP LIFE ON DOMESTIC AND LOCAL SCALE: The Schedule of Daily Life The Meals Cooking and Domestic Work Daily Division of Labour Amusements and Recreations 4. DEMOGRAPHIC SURVEY Type of Settlement House to House Census Vital Statistics (Samples)	1. ECONOMICS: Resources, ownership, production; exchange; consumption. 2. EDUCATION: Specialized agencies Domestic Training Apprenticeship 3. POLITICAL CONSTITUTION Authority at home, in village, district, tribe Chieftainship and Military Organization. Change in custom Political Unit and Intertribal (International relations) 4. LAW AND ORDER Survey of norms and rules Types of Sanction Morals, manners, custom, law, etiquette Machinery of Law (Codes; court; policing) 5. MAGIC – RELIGION: Dogma: Ritual: Ethics Myth 6. ART Folk-Tales, Music, Drama, Dancing, Decorative Art 7. KNOWLEDGE: Analysis of technical Tradition Historical and Legal Tradition Assessment of Empirical and Logical Power. 8. RECREATION	1. MATERIAL SUBSTRATUM (Tools & Commodities) Engineering Works: (terraces, roads, waterways irrigation) Buildings Implements Clothes Goods for Consumption 2. SOCIAL ORGANIZATION Family and Kinship (Clan system) Territorial Grouping (Local Units, Political Divisions) Associations by age, initiation, occupation Cultural & Racial grouping Spiritual Symbolism of language, gesture, artifact. 3. LANGUAGE Descriptive (Phonology (Grammar (Vocab. Texts Social Differentiation Contextual types Language of each aspect Scientific ideas Mythological ideas Economic Values Moral " Spiritual factor of Cullane

Reproduced by permission of the Malinowski family.

in a negative light (Mair's early observations on this point would soon be radically revised).

Margaret Read seems to have used one of Malinowski's newer schemes when she set off for the field a few years later. In a letter containing instructions to write to him regularly, Malinowski urged Read to let him know 'whether you find our schemes of real use, and how you have to modify them in order to adapt to local conditions.'[23] The schemes, Read reassured him, were helping to keep her on the right track, and the accordion file that Malinowski had recommended to her was proving to be of great use when organising her notes. Without a conceptual scheme and an organised filing system, she could well understand how 'the non-functionalist anthropologist of old gathered scraps of unrelated information,' thought that they had gathered all there was to know 'in a week and could move on to the next tribe.'[24] Using a scheme was slowing her down and forcing her to collect information under all of its headings. The accordion file, we can presume, was split into different sections, perhaps one for each of the topics listed in the scheme. In its very materiality, the file reflected the additive and interlinked functionalist theory that Malinowski taught in his class and promoted in his monographs and articles. Like the coloured cards and pencils employed by Richards, the very stuff of note-taking and note-organising reinforced the theoretical underpinning of his pedagogy and practice.[25]

Employing a scheme to prompt the collection of ethnographic data was not an idea that was original to Malinowski. His interest in such a technique might have developed as a student of physics and psychology in Poland and Germany.[26] But there was a more immediate precursor to his charts. His schemes were in competition with others within his own discipline. The Royal Anthropological Institute (RAI) published a guide for fieldworkers called *Notes & Queries* that had gone through four editions between 1870 and 1920. These were books filled with questions and designed to direct merchants, missionaries and administrators to provide ethnographic material for anthropologists studying back in Britain. The type of data being gathered was, however, 'fragmented', James Urry argues, into discrete realms of facts, reflecting the approach of the RAI, which sought to maintain studies of physiology, material culture, sociology and arts and crafts under one roof.[27] This reflected an older model of expertise, wherein professional scientists acted as interpreters of diverse data, comparing and sifting the observations of others and forming a new synthesis out of the result. Malinowski's charts can be seen as an attempt to supersede the RAI's methods. They were to be used by trained graduates of his seminar, not by amateurs, thus closing the epistemological loop between theorising and observation. His students would embody simultaneously the ethnographer, the theorist and the data gatherer, bridging the divide between the 'armchair' and the 'field'.[28]

Malinowski's charts emerged, then, as a rival to an already-existing knowledge infrastructure. And his anxiety about maintaining his intellectual property can be ascertained by the words 'Copyright of B. Malinowski' at the top of the chart's first page.[29] Unlike *Notes & Queries*, these charts were only available to students trained by him. They can be seen as a material means to form a new, professional cadre of experts within a wider disciplinary formation. Their use meant that discussion would be centred at his seminar rather than at the RAI – shifting, as a result, the locus of disciplinary authority away from this older learned society towards the academic milieu of the LSE. Malinowski's correspondence with Read reveals, however, that he maintained some doubt about whether his schemes were actually useful to the field researcher. After all, Malinowski's own field research was carried out on the *Notes & Queries* model, nuanced somewhat by pushing further down a reflexive approach to intensive questioning than had been proposed by W. H. R. Rivers.[30]

Indeed, his charts never approached the kind of universality afforded to other instruments used by field scientists in different disciplines, even amongst his most loyal students. 'In order to function as a scientific instrument,' Ursula Klein explains, 'a material device cannot itself be considered as an object of research.'[31] As we will see, Malinowski's charts were never so transparent to their users. They remained rather opaque and became sites of significant theoretical struggle. They were more like 'paper technology', in Boris Jardine's terminology: 'a material grid laid over the world, visible in itself: classificatory, controlling, empowering - and susceptible to a more socially oriented analysis.'[32] Applying this approach to the history of anthropology calls into question Kohler's notion that social anthropology can be understood as just another instance of 'resident science'. Ornithologists and botanists developed complex taxonomies that allowed them to speculate about plant and animal evolution alongside their extended bouts of fieldwork.[33] And other field scientists, such as meteorologists and astronomers, devised precise instruments to make measurements across different sites. Their findings could then be shared and compared according to the supposed virtues of aperspectival objectivity.[34]

Malinowski's paper technologies built up neither the kind of instrumental charisma that the telescope possessed nor that physiographic analysis offered ecologists.[35] What did have an impact, though, was a new way of orienting field research and anthropological theorising via the research seminar. Unlike the *Notes & Queries* model, theorising and observation were carried out by the same person at the LSE, although at different stages of their career: entering the field and exiting it, joining and leaving the seminar, developing their epistemic authority and contributing to a wider series of debates at a more abstract level of comparison. For despite their limitations as scientific instruments, Malinowski's charts were prompting social anthropologists to keep collecting more and more material and to sort this material in such a way that the stylised facts of their ethnography could be rearranged at a later date, either to pursue more investigations in the field or when writing up their notes. Furthermore, once sent back to Malinowski, they could be used to train the next wave of social anthropologists before they went on to do their own research. Malinowski explained the importance of sticking to a common set of protocols in part because of this pedagogical function: 'Any uniformity in schemes which I have been urging on the class is justified mainly by the fact that we want to have the results from the various fields presented in similar form,' he wrote to Read.[36] This would allow students back at the LSE to compare the conditions in each field site and create theoretical connections between them.

Malinowski demanded that his students write to him regularly about informants, important episodes and any difficulties they faced. After a number of highly detailed letters from Read, Malinowski sent a grateful reply:

> I am very glad to have such full reports and they will allow me, not only to give you occasional advice, but also to visualise your work and to follow it, and to be better prepared, when you come back, to discuss with you detailed problems of organising your material. . . . I can visualise from it your mode of living, of feeding, and to a certain extent, your mode of work.[37]

The notes Mair, Read, Richards and other students sent to Malinowski meant that those back in London could feel, at least in part, like the fieldworkers really were there amongst them by visualising the particularities of their fieldwork experiences and discussing their methods.

This back and forth between the field and the seminar became a great deal easier and less expensive at exactly the time that Read and Malinowski were corresponding. The Empire Air Mail was introduced in

1934, a few years after Richards and Mair did their fieldwork and a year before Read did hers. It greatly reduced the cost of sending letters and increased the speed of their distribution, with large and rather ungainly flying boats plying the route between London and South Africa, depositing mail and passengers along the way.[38] In January 1935 Malinowski explained to Read that this new service, and the use of thin airmail paper and cheaper first-class rates, made sending him regular reports easy and economical.[39] Piggybacking on this service offered Malinowski ever-greater opportunities to survey the work of his students and presumably provided far fewer excuses for lax communication on their part.

All of this correspondence kept fieldworkers in touch practically and emotionally with life back home, and their letters reveal evidence of the disciplining effect Malinowski had, even at a great distance. During the first few weeks of her fieldwork, Mair admitted: 'I suppose I spend a lot of time "muckin abaht", and then your voice rings in my ears telling me to work hard.'[40] Read, too, wrote of how Malinowski's 'words come back at every turn.' The new airmail scheme was all very well, but she imagined a more immediate and hi-tech telecommunications solution to the dilemmas of fieldwork, wishing that she was 'able to radio questions to you often.'[41]

Internalising the seminar's ethos could be a stumbling block, however. For instance, Read wrote, 'Memories will rise up of devastating criticisms round your seminar table ... you see yourself joining that distinguished company who have "omitted all the real essentials".'[42] Without the radio technology she desired at hand, and with still only patchy correspondence available via airmail, the LSE had to be kept in mind through largely imaginative endeavours. These were certainly acts of the 'self upon the self', as previous historians of anthropological fieldwork have explained, but the form of subjectivity that emerged was highly sociable rather than individualistic.[43] They invariably sought ways to increase their sociability with each other via available technology, through hopes for new technologies and in their imaginations.

LOCATIONS AND RELATIONS IN THE FIELD

Malinowski's hold over his students' emotional and social lives obviously had its limits. Relations between Malinowski and his students were crucial to the consolidation of the discipline in the 1930s, but perhaps just as, if not more, important were the local relationships developed between anthropologists, administrators and the subjects of their research. As in the other field sciences, location matters in anthropology. But perhaps more than in any other discipline, interpersonal relationships matter most for the social anthropologist because sociality is the very stuff they study.[44] Social anthropologists famously study social life through participant observation. Malinowski had arguably pioneered this method in the Trobriand Islands in the 1910s, as we saw in chapter 1. But it only became a key aspect of the persona of the social anthropologist in the 1930s.

Like Mair and Richards, Read was one of the method's early pioneers in Eastern Africa and wrote to Malinowski from what its British colonisers called Northern Rhodesia (present-day Zambia) that she was feeling like a 'stage anthropologist ... typing in a grass shelter, complete with sun helmet and moisture pouring off back and front.'[45] Like Read, a new generation of social anthropologists drew on practices of fieldwork and associated symbols of authority that Malinowski had imbued with charisma and that they attempted to reproduce in their own research.[46] Malinowski's example helped them to project a common disciplinary identity, creating a mystique about their method that was often, another anthropologist admitted, based more on myth than reality.[47] For despite their self-presentation as fieldworkers deeply immersed in life in the field, few anthropologists of the 1930s could speak fluently the language of the society they studied, and most relied for a great deal of their information on privileged informants who mediated and controlled their understanding.

Yet even though anthropologists may not have been as deeply submerged in their cultures of study as the myths of fieldwork that they projected, correspondence between Malinowski and his students is full of evidence of involvement in local life. Writing from Uganda in the early stages of her fieldwork, Mair admitted that she had done few formal interviews. Instead, she found herself helping to type villagers' love letters, picking cotton with local farmers, caring for babies and acquiring 'a native godchild'.[48] As such, she soon found herself inducted into community life. And after contributing her customary share of beer to a local funeral party, she was invited to the proceedings and then adopted by both the dead woman's clan and that of her husband.[49] Read remarked on the gendered experiences of life in the field and, like Mair, was included in women's work. She took part in hoeing the fields with the women of Mchakhatha village and was regularly invited to 'any special ceremony, as for example the puberty ceremony of a girl.'[50]

She was relieved to note early on in her research that she had so far avoided questions about whether or not she had a husband. When older women greeted her, 'after the conventional "We see You" [they] always add "And you are a woman like ourselves", and that in spite of my living in breeches, which are the only possible garments for a wet spell in camp.'[51]

Clearly differences of clothing were not the only thing stopping anthropologists like Read and Mair from seamlessly fitting into village life. Britain's African empire was divided along the so-called colour bar, which racialised its subjects through violently policed pass laws. Some minimal recognition, for instance in terms of gender, did not mean acceptance from the local population. The fact that anthropologists often asked the same sorts of questions as administrators; were often seeking to advise the administration along paternalist, reformist lines; and were often, although not always, white, means that the people they studied often understood the anthropologists and the administrators as part of the same class of colonial oppressors.[52] We can see these relationships playing out in the fieldnotes and letters of Malinowski's students and can also witness their strategies to try to deal with the epistemological repercussions of the unequal power relationships that upheld the field.

For instance, Read's research on economic organisation meant asking questions about taxation, which made her a figure of considerable suspicion to her informants. To mitigate the worst of these problems of difference and resistance, she suggested that choosing to live in a hut rather than a tent significantly improved the 'psychological attitude of one's stay.'[53] Her cook, interpreter and assistant, Jonathan, Mumambwe and James, stayed in an adjoining hut that also served as a kitchen. Their small compound was set in between the chief's old hut and the new one he was having built. This meant that Read could see, either from her porch or from the shade of a large nearby tree, 'all that is happening of import in the village, without appearing to be watching all the time.' Her assistants aided her, too. Jonathan was a trusted advisor, and Read reported to Malinowski that he was 'anthropologically-minded, though not in the functionalist tradition' and proved to be a great help by knowing 'who to fetch from the village to ask about things.'[54]

Mair also stressed the importance of location to knowledge production. She found that she was able to gather more material after moving to a new field site. She had previously been staying in what she described as a 'dilapidated house once inhabited by missionaries.' This was more comfortable than a traditional dwelling but, in her opinion, made people less likely to talk to her. The sense one gets is that the early months of her fieldwork were not a particularly productive period.[55] However, after moving to a new site at some point in late March or early April 1932, she made a real breakthrough. She had noticed a large house with a clock in a glass case above the door soon after she first moved. She supposed that it must belong to some local dignitary. On enquiring further she was told that it was inhabited by a man who had made a fortune growing cotton. A child gave her more information. The house, it turned out, belonged to a 'native doctor' whose magical cures and medicines were sold as far afield as Kampala and whose clients included the royal family there.[56] After a great deal of negotiating she secured an interview.

She opened the meeting with a greeting, saluting her subject as a great doctor 'and also a prophet'. Immediately the man, called Andeyera in the published report, became hostile and explained that 'he knew nothing about it. . . . [T]here had been prophets in the days before the people knew religion but they were a very bad thing and now there were none left.'[57] Mair felt a great deal of frustration at her lack of tact. By trying to flatter Andeyera, who was, as she well knew, acting as a prophet, she had been insensitive to the politics of religion and magic in the colony.[58] After her blunder, one of her African assistants managed to get him to perform a divination, but Mair was repeatedly refused. Mair's tactlessness and her uncertain status as a member of the oppressive British occupying forces, if not actually an administrator, made it impossible to have a frank and open conversation about possibly subversive, and certainly illegal, activity. Her efforts to get at what Malinowski had called in class 'the invisible facts of anthropology' were not in vain, however. Within a month of moving to the new village she found someone else willing to perform a prophecy. The fee was twenty shillings.

In a dark tent, with a burnt down fire of hot embers in its middle, Mair sat and took notes. After a while the lamp she was writing by was put out by order of the prophet. After she protested that she could no longer see, three canes were lit, and their intermittent flickering allowed her to keep writing from time to time. The prophet was agitated by Mair's note-taking and asked her repeatedly what she was doing. When it came to her turn to ask for a prophecy, she 'forgot that [she] was the principal enquirer.' Assa, her research assistant, was quicker thinking and made up a story about Mair's relatives being sick back in England, and the ceremony went on. After the fact, Mair had serious doubts about the authenticity of the ritual performer, or indeed, whether the other participants who huddled in the tent really believed in the powers of the divination at all (there was much laughing at the antics of the prophet, apparently). But she was nonetheless pleased that she had gathered evidence that prophecy still played a role in the life of the people, even if Christianity was so prevalent and government sanctions so stern. The report from this letter found its way into her book *An African People in the Twentieth Century* (1934), written up almost verbatim from her correspondence with Malinowski.[59]

Malinowski's injunctions to write regularly thus functioned as a way to anchor his students' experience amidst the complexities of life in the field and as aids to writing up. But they could also lead to difficulties. Reflecting on her notes gathered six months after enthusing about the utility of her accordion file, Read admitted that the result of all of her endeavours had been merely to bring together 'a great deal of ill-assorted material, in spite of working on systematic schemes.' This groundwork, however, apparently stood her in good stead when she moved to a different area and reassessed her findings.[60] More troublesome than the large amount of material they prompted her to collect, the schemes and the questions they provoked were provoking hostility from the subjects of Read's research.

When she looked at Malinowski's scheme for economic study, for instance, she thought to herself 'you cannot get this particular point until you have got the language,' and 'you must establish full confidence with a people frightened by the Boma before they will tell you this.' 'Boma' was the general word for a stockade enclosure, but often referred to British administrators' compounds spread across Northern Rhodesia.[61] Read found that it was economic life 'above all (and their religion and magic too) that the people want to hide from the Boma – the result I think of harassing for taxes.' 'For some reason or another,' she wrote naively, 'certain essentials in that scheme are connected in the people's minds with the Boma hunting for tax defaulters.' Her frustration was considerable. 'Many times a day I say "Blast the tax" and still more times a day I say "blast the methods of catching defaulters".' Quite apart from the difficulties that administrators' investigations caused for her own enquiries, Read expressed sympathy for her informants, writing that it seemed 'damnable, that a man should feel he has to hide any efforts he is making to make a little extra income.'[62]

Just as in economic life, so Read reflected that 'only by very slow degrees can you penetrate the almost blank wall on any subject connected with magic and religion.' In matters of ritual and belief, it was not only the authority of the colonial state that mattered: 'What the Boma has failed to quash, the Dutch Mission with its hell fire has stepped upon.'[63] Read found herself increasingly sympathetic to the people she lived amongst, and she acted, she explained, 'as an intermediary between them and the Boma on more than one occasion.' 'They wanted to make use of me,' she wrote to Malinowski, but 'the path of the anthropologist then is a slippery one.'[64] The kind of information anthropologists collected made their enquiries suspect, and their sympathy with their subjects made their political position precarious. Clearly good relations had to be maintained with local district commissioners, but the sympathy that grew amidst the socialization of the field (becoming godparents and adoption into clans, for instance) reinforced a political identity formed, in part, in opposition to the colonial authorities. Indeed, the colonial authorities increasingly became part of the anthropologist's own subject of study as responses to questions about seemingly unrelated issues circled back to questions of power, politics and taxation.[65]

When she wrote up this research (discussed in part in the previous chapter on Ngoni economics), Read drew on her observations to develop an original anthropological account of economic and social change. New goods, technologies and processes do not appear in a society as if in a *'tablua rasa'*, she wrote. 'On the contrary', she went on, 'they disturb profoundly the traditional balance of labour and natural resources,' sweeping away 'the former rhythm of work and recreation, and effort and reward.'[66] When we draw out the conclusions of anthropologists' often guarded contemporary writings, we are left with a critical view of colonial policy and repeated demands to devolve the sovereign functions of the state onto local African elites. These elites, however, as African intellectuals like Archie Mafeje would later lament, were hardly harbingers of a progressive future.[67]

Negotiating between elites, research assistants and the colonial authorities in the field was a vital skill. Mair's encounter with Andeyera showed how bad manners and ignorance could backfire spectacularly on the anthropologist. Balancing these allegiances in the field with Malinowski's demands back home and with one's fellow students required highly complex performances of sociability and unsettled the neutral, and supposedly apolitical, persona that social anthropologists were constructing in this period.[68] This persona was ambiguously gendered. While the bulk of the primary sources used to reconstruct fieldwork in this chapter are from letters by women, this selective source base might give a misleading impression that Malinowski 'loyalists' were women and the 'rebels' (encountered later in this chapter) were men. This gender breakdown did not reflect the reality, with Raymond Firth, Edmund Leach and Godfrey Wilson all in the 'loyalist' camp. Certainly, however, fieldwork was gendered, and when it came to the students who sought to critique Malinowski's authority, it is pertinent to think about their turn to 'abstract' 'theory' also as a gendered response to a personally and professionally acrimonious relationship.

MEYER FORTES, EVANS-PRITCHARD AND THE LIMITS OF FUNCTIONALIST COMMUNITY

In the 1930s Malinowski was attempting to make social anthropology into something like a paradigmatic 'ordinary science', subjecting his students to 'a dogmatic and authoritarian process by which they are drilled through exercises to master the craft of the professional practitioner.'[69] From the evidence of Mair's, Richards's and Read's letters, his endeavours were proving to be successful; the competitive, disciplining and clubby ethos of Malinowski's seminar had been internalised and was having a salutary effect. But as we will see, the authority of his methods relied to a large extent on his hold over his students.

As part of this disciplinarising process, Malinowski made a point early in his students' fieldwork to request regular updates on their progress. In a letter sent in November 1934 to Godfrey Wilson he warned that only those who wrote often would 'have full access to the Seminar on their return to England and will have those benefits which an active membership of the functional group might bestow.' 'Those, on the other hand, who remain silent or aloof,' he went on, 'cannot expect me naturally either to take an active interest in the progress of their field work, nor of course to help with any criticism or suggestions, nor yet to welcome them here on their return.'[70] Malinowski used his control of the seminar and the 'benefits' it might 'bestow' as a way to keep his charges in line. These benefits were presumably obvious: reference letters, patronage and access to funding for fieldwork. Despite the success of his bids to the Rockefeller Foundation throughout the 1930s, Malinowski clearly thought that his position was precarious. Keeping close tabs on his students meant that methods taught at his seminar, rather than any possible rivals to his disciplinary supremacy, would become the norm for anthropological training in the British Empire.

Malinowski may have had a particular student in mind when he wrote those threats to Wilson. Meyer Fortes had left for the field toward the end of 1933; he was a lousy correspondent. 'I must frankly say that I am very disappointed not to have heard from you since your departure about six months ago,' Malinowski wrote to him in May 1934.[71] And almost a year later Malinowski wrote again, caustically comparing Fortes's relative lack of contact with 'the Fellows working in East Africa [who] I have been exchanging letters [with] about once a month,' which, he asserted, 'has been very profitable to both sides.'[72] As he had done with Wilson, he had threatened Fortes in his earlier letter that he would cease to accept 'for further cooperation at my department' those Fellows funded by the Rockefeller grants handed out via the IIALC if they failed to send reports 'at intervals not longer than, say, three months.'[73] But while his worries about Wilson's loyalty seem to have been misplaced, the anxious, sometimes fierce, sometimes fragile letters to Fortes were being sent to someone who had long held oppositional views to Malinowski's ideas and his overbearing seminar style.

Unlike Read and Richards, Fortes had extensive graduate training in another discipline, having completed a PhD in psychology at UCL, and he was, on the whole, unimpressed with Malinowski's functionalism. His scepticism about Malinowski's theories led him to try to get funding to train with Alfred Radcliffe-Brown at Chicago.[74] Radcliffe-Brown would soon become the pretender to Malinowski's crown in the eyes of a subset of the younger social anthropologists that included Fortes. Those who were personally or professionally opposed to Malinowski's authoritarianism, or who prickled at his demands for methodological conformity, invested their energies in organising themselves around Radcliffe-Brown's theories and looked to him, rather than Malinowski, for their inspiration.

So while Malinowski may have desired to position himself affectively at the centre of his students' affections, his control was, of course, never total. Not only did students send letters medially, between the seminar and the field; their letters circulated laterally amongst students, too. These lateral connections could undermine his students' faith in their skills. 'I find my fellow Fellows' reports the most depressing reading because they have done everything already in an astoundingly short time,' Read wrote despairingly after a few months of research.[75] The difference between the difficulties the students expressed in personal correspondence and the constructive reflections on progress they typed up for wider consumption amongst their peers clearly caused anxiety. Student-to-student correspondence could form doubts, but at least in Read's case, it did not lead to a break with her mentor's methods. However, lateral communication between students could, and indeed did, generate networks of resistance to Malinowski's authority. Antagonistic sentiments about the seminar could be aired, and new alliances and theories could be formed away from Malinowski's prying eyes. Despite this, his students all agreed that fieldwork was central to their practice. The emergent persona of the anthropologist researching in the field, immersed in the life of their subject communities, was capacious enough to contain contending theoretical agendas. This explains how social anthropology could form into a common discipline despite significant internal disagreements about theory.

In chapter 1 we saw how Malinowski and Radcliffe-Brown had bonded over a common interest in attacking evolutionism and diffusionism in anthropology during the 1910s and 1920s.[76] Relations began to sour in the 1930s, however, as the differences between their theoretical agendas became clearer and as they began to compete for the loyalty of students.[77] The turning point came in 1931, when Radcliffe-Brown involved himself in the IIALC pitch to the Rockefeller Foundation and gained the confidence of one of its most important patrons, Joseph Oldham. On the way from Sydney to take up an appointment at Chicago, Radcliffe-Brown stopped in London and caused a stir in anthropological circles. Malinowski was a jealous man. The idea of losing influence over his students, or patronage via the IIALC, was too much to bear. He blocked Fortes's plans to travel to Chicago after reports from Richards suggested that Radcliffe-Brown's popularity was increasing amongst the younger anthropologists at the LSE.[78] Malinowski wrote spitefully to Oldham that if Radcliffe-Brown ever got an appointment in England, 'it would be a damn bad job for our Institute as well as for everybody else.'[79] Malinowski made sure that Fortes was trained solely at the LSE. He could not risk losing the allegiance of one of his most talented young charges and one of the IIALC's most promising new fellows.

One of the anthropologists who was most enthusiastic about Radcliffe-Brown on his London visit in 1931 was Edward Evans-Pritchard, who had briefly attended Malinowski's seminar in the 1920s.[80] Evans-Pritchard was friends with Fortes, and from their correspondence in the field it is clear that Fortes was similarly impressed with Radcliffe-Brown's theories.[81] Evans-Pritchard had been personally and professionally hostile to Malinowski since at least 1928, when the two men had spectacularly fallen out after a seminar at the LSE. Malinowski had accused his former student of massaging his findings to score methodological points, and in response, Evans-Pritchard flew into a rage.[82]

They soon patched up their relationship for professional reasons. But in a letter from 1931 Malinowski mentioned the continuing feuding between the two, referring to 'the bitter hostility he has shown to me and is showing to me, openly and above all underground.'[83]

A few months after they arrived in the field, Evans-Pritchard wrote of his relief that Fortes and his wife Sonia had finally broken free of Malinowski's clutches after years 'wasting ... time in London like hostages kept at a foreign court.' Evans-Pritchard sent the Forteses rugs from Egypt and along with these gifts, sent news and personal greetings.[84] Evans-Pritchard also sent working papers to the Forteses in the field, and they discussed methodological issues that gestured towards both men's later break with Malinowski's functionalist program. In short, Fortes was treating Evans-Pritchard in exactly the way Malinowski wanted to be treated himself, as an interlocutor and a research partner.

In a letter sent to Evans-Pritchard in September 1934, Fortes expressed the differences between 'ethnology' and 'sociology' that had occurred to him recently. He cast Malinowski's functionalism in the former category and Radcliffe-Brown's idea of 'structure' in the latter. He praised Evans-Pritchard's scholarly productivity as a good thing for his career, especially, he wrote, 'if the Bronosaurus is ever likely to be bumped off.'[85] Radcliffe-Brown's notion of 'structure' directed anthropologists towards explaining social cohesion. Kinship was centrally important. The interrelation of social groups, and the obligations they demanded, held a society together in a tight mesh of reciprocal dues. Social anthropologists should go about comparing these structures in order to explain the society being studied. After his move to Chicago in 1931, Radcliffe-Brown would describe this analysis as a 'natural science of society'.[86] This research, the historian George Stocking writes, 'moved always away from observation toward the formulation of general social laws.'[87]

Radcliffe-Brown's was a different vision of the discipline to Malinowski's, who used charts to explain the institutions that functioned to meet the needs of individuals. What's more, Malinowski's analysis was not aimed at an abstract social science but at an applied policy agenda united with nascent projects of colonial development.[88] Fortes and Evans-Pritchard rejected this approach and broadly subscribed to Radcliffe-Brown's comparative project of abstracted analysis. We should also see this shift in terms of the phenomenon explained by historians of science, who have now detailed a number of cases in which a turn to abstract theory meant a gendered repudiation of more 'applied' work that was deemed 'feminine'.[89] This certainly seems to have been the case in the history of social anthropology more broadly and specifically with the 'rebels' in Malinowski's seminar.[90] Richards, Mair and Read all did more 'applied' research and generally sought to follow Malinowski's theoretical lead (although, as I explain later, the existing source base of surviving letters considerably skews the gender balance away from a more mixed male-female group of applied researchers). Despite their criticisms, Evans-Pritchard's and Fortes's masculinised turn to 'theory' did not, however, solve the problems Malinowski set his students and that he tried to square with his schemes. As Fortes wrote to Evans-Pritchard, the more he developed the new theories they were discussing, the more he saw 'a conflict of the two roles in the field': ethnographic observation and anthropological analysis. This was a view, he wrote, that 'I am going to defend in the strong holds of London's anthropological sophists' (i.e., on his return to Malinowski's seminar). The problem, though, is that Fortes does not seem to have developed an alternative form of competing paper technology with which to reconcile the 'conflict of the two roles in the field.' 'If one did not have to write notes, anthropology would be ideal fun,' he wrote laconically.[91]

Like Fortes, Evans-Pritchard united a personal animus with methodological critique, and he took special aim at Malinowski's charts and schemes, writing that

> B.M. and his friend do their sociological analysis in the notebooks when they get home & not among the natives whose culture they have studied. The best sociological weapon in their hands is a pair of scissors to cut out sections of their notebooks & the glue pot to stick them together in a 'functional' order. It is all done by verbal juxtaposition & not by noting real behaviour links & sociological associations.[92]

In this telling, Malinowski's functionalism was a kind of post hoc rationalisation, breaking the totality of the social situation found in the field into neat boxes in a scheme without a convincing account of how the system hung together. We can see from these letters a kind of running critique of Malinowski's 'cut and paste' schemes, before Evans-Pritchard wrote in November 1934 that he was 'coming more & more to the conclusion that the real sociological problems are political – that is, the way in which local groups live together & the manner in which this inter-behaviour is organized.'[93] This 'political' view gave primacy to only one aspect of Malinowski's extensive schemes and marked a new 'structural-functional' approach to social anthropology.

Some time later, probably in 1935, Evans-Pritchard wrote to Fortes that he had recruited the young South African anthropologist Max Gluckman to their fold: 'I have thoroughly conscripted him,' he wrote, 'but leave the final stages of dissolution to you.'[94] Such an overlap between the personal and the academic-political makes it clear how, after Malinowski left for a job at Yale in 1938, the theoretical bent of British social anthropology shifted so quickly away from Malinowski's functionalist schemes towards 'structural-functionalism'. This new research agenda was driven by Gluckman, Fortes and Evans-Pritchard, who drew on Radcliffe-Brown's writings to foreground social structure and the political function of kinship, alliance and descent.[95] This was different to Malinowski's approach, which stressed the functional interrelation of institutions to meet the biological needs of individuals. Evans-Pritchard suggested that anthropologists look, by contrast, from the top down at social structure rather than the bottom up from biological needs. This analysis foreshadowed the argument he and Fortes would make in their 1940 collection *African Political Systems* and in Evans-Pritchard's *Nuer* (1940).

Towards the end of his life Evans-Pritchard seems to have had some kind of psychic rapprochement with Malinowski, but in the 1930s he was perhaps at the peak of his opposition to Malinowski's theoretical and social power.[96] Despite Evans-Pritchard's criticisms, later commentators have argued that he owed a great deal to Malinowski, taking up the technique of gathering vernacular texts to understand Zande society, for instance.[97] Sadly he left tantalisingly little material from which to reconstruct his field practices. Recent scholarship has analysed his large cache of fieldwork photographs, suggesting that he put photography to different use than Malinowski's staged tableaux of Trobriand life, using photographs alongside written notes and histories derived from Zande oral culture to analyse, interpret and record the events he witnessed.[98] While we await further research on Evans-Pritchard's field techniques, we can find the early shape of his subsequent theorising in the letters sent between him and Fortes in the field.

Paying attention to materiality and practice recasts the standard narrative given by disciplinary historians of the supersession of Malinowski's functionalism by Radcliffe-Brown's structural-functionalism.[99] Looking at the correspondence between Fortes and Evans-Pritchard shows the underside of the debate between Radcliffe-Brown and Malinowski. Rather than tell this story as merely a theoretical change, I have argued in this chapter that it is better to see changes in the discipline in terms of frustration with Malinowski's increasing centralisation of training at the LSE and with the methodological limits of his 'paper technology' of note-taking and schemes. The difficulties of fieldwork and the inadequacies of Malinowski's methods offered openings for students who opposed him to develop alternative approaches. Correspondence about new ideas, a sense of being slighted and intergenerational hostility against a more established figure all led to the 'acrimoniousness', as Randall Collins put it, of their intellectual dispute.[100]

It is worth returning to the gendered nature of these conflicts. The surviving documents quoted here threaten to present the women discussed in this chapter as 'loyal' and the men as 'rebellious'. In fact, Malinowski's closest 'loyalist' was a man, Raymond Firth, and he fulsomely supported the career of Wilson, along with many other men not discussed here. Mair's and Read's gendered experiences of fieldwork certainly suggest that women and men experienced the 'collective apprenticeship' of Malinowski's seminar very differently. And these differences persisted via the sexist strictures of the academy after Malinowski's death in 1942, when Richards, Read and Mair tended to be passed over for the most senior positions and often worked in 'applied' anthropology or in regional research centres, never leading their own seminars in the UK. When it came to the post-war professoriate, all of the major positions in the 1950s and 1960s were held by Malinowski's male students: at the LSE (under Firth), at Cambridge (under Fortes and Leach), at Oxford (under Evans-Pritchard), and across the British Isles (Siegfried Nadel at Durham) and out into the Empire and Commonwealth (Gluckman in Northern Rhodesia and then at Manchester; Nadel at Canberra after Durham).[101] The women discussed in this chapter did end up in prominent positions, but never at the very peaks of the discipline: Read ended up as a professor, but at the Institute of Education, not as a professor of social anthropology; Richards became head of the Centre of African Studies at Cambridge, but never led the anthropology department there. Mair did eventually gain a professorial position at the LSE in 1963, but in applied anthropology, not in control of the main seminar, which was run by Firth. This outline of the post-war academic scene is filled in in chapter 6, but before that our attention will turn to England and to the development of another trend in British social anthropology, which turned the techniques of fieldwork onto Britain itself and sought to compare 'primitive' societies with metropolitan cultures.

CHAPTER 4

Popularising the Field

Interwar Anthropologists on the Radio and in Literary Culture

While his students were studying in his seminar and then doing their fieldwork, Malinowski was becoming an increasingly influential author. In a letter sent to his wife, he recounted that his new book, *The Sexual Life of Savages in Northwestern Melanesia* (1929), was being sold 'on the boulevards alongside *The Well of Loneliness*, *Lady Chatterley's Lover* (a porno-gramme by D.H. Lawrence), and Frank Harris's *My Life and Loves*.' Such scurrilous company, Malinowski thought, would doubtless improve its sales.¹ But he soon recanted his happy association with Lawrence, Harris and Radclyffe Hall, worrying in the third edition of his book that 'merely sensational details were picked out, and wondered or laughed at while the synthesis, the integration of details, the correlation of aspects, the whole functional mechanism was missed.'² Only a few readers had properly engaged with the monograph's main argument: that 'kinship presents an organic unity that cannot be disrupted.'³ Those who took the theory seriously included Bertrand Russell in *Marriage and Morals* (1929) and Floyd Dell in *Love in the Machine Age* (1930). Malinowski recommended these books, while generally expressing disappointment at the public's response to his findings, which tended towards the sensational and was less engaged with his anthropological theories.

The extent of Malinowski's popular reach in the late 1920s and 1930s might come as a surprise. According to one prominent historian, the discipline's increasing professionalization in the 1920s swiftly led to its 'decline . . . in popular relevance.'[4] According to this view, British anthropology diverged from debates going on in the wider culture around it, supporting Perry Anderson's argument that British anthropology only survived by being 'exported' and 'displaced' outside the positivist and intellectually desiccated metropole.[5] It was supposedly in other national cultures, especially across the Atlantic, that anthropology had the greatest cultural and intellectual impact. In America, Franz Boas, Margaret Mead, and Ruth Benedict loom large in political and intellectual debates about race, class and gender.[6] In Britain, by contrast, social anthropology was supposed to have separated itself from the wider culture and begun a slow, steady decline into self-referential navel-gazing.[7]

In this chapter I take a different view and explain that Malinowski's writing on the family had some appeal amongst writers and intellectuals. He even presented his ideas to a broader public via radio broadcasts. However, as he explained in his preface to the third edition, readers did not always follow his arguments or understand the novelty of his approach. As we shall see, Malinowski's greatest effect was on a group of novelists and social critics thinking about love and marriage and social change, who all found different ways to rework and rethink these topics via his ethnographic research.

The appeal of Malinowski's ideas needs to be understood in light of the political and intellectual context of metropolitan Britain. The interwar years saw a recognition that a demographic transformation was sweeping through many Western societies, and that sex, marriage and the family were undergoing great changes. At the same time, the way that sex, marriage and the family were being understood was also changing. Since the late nineteenth century, sexologists like Marie Stopes, Havelock Ellis, Theodoor van de Velde and Magnus Hirschfeld had reframed discussions about same-sex desire and premarital sex and were concerned with examining sexual pleasure and behaviour in a self-consciously 'modern' and secular, rather than religious, fashion.[8] Meanwhile, some communists were calling for the complete dissolution of bourgeois marriage, arguing that the institution was a capitalist sham that was destined to disappear.[9] Freudians focused on the disorder of the bourgeois family as well, but with a different aim: they did not seek to explode the family's strictures but to reform them. Children were endowed with sexual desires, neuroses proliferated and complexes were fixed.

There was, in sum, an 'explosion of discussion' about marriage, contraception and sexuality during the first decades of the twentieth century.[10] This discussion centred on politics and economics, too, as discussion of family allowances became a crucial part of the incipient welfare state.[11] Coupled with spasms of anxiety amongst demographers and eugenicists about the birth rate, the family was the site of great interest and worry in what one historian has called Britain's 'morbid age'.[12] It was in this context that Malinowski offered a view of kinship and intra-family dynamics that allowed his readers to compare British society to others. Rather than take a Marxist path down a route of economic determinism or drill a Freudian tunnel into the formation of the psyche in childhood, Malinowski offered a mutable middle road that focused on parenthood to explain social reproduction. As all human groups are enmeshed in webs of kinship, he argued, variation between forms of family relationships could help uncover similarities and differences between societies. Specialising in kinship studies hooked Malinowski, and anthropology more broadly, into contemporary debates about sexuality, patriarchy and marriage.

These debates formed one of the 'great dramas of the early twentieth century,' according to the historian Dagmar Herzog.[13] This drama implied, for some, a backlash, but it also led to meaningful advance for others. Its cast of actors was extremely diverse: radicals, socialists, liberals, conservatives, Christians and eugenicists were all involved, pulling in different directions, but often with their focus on motherhood and on marriage.[14] The huge diversity of interwar writings on marriage and sexuality formed an amalgam of conservative and progressive forces.[15] Most authors promoted the ideal of the procreative couple, which later feminists and some contemporaries critiqued as socially regressive.[16] Malinowski's work, and the legacy of social anthropology more generally, was constituted amidst these impulses of progress, reaction and social reform and went on to push the discussion of the family into cross-cultural contexts. The chapter begins with some background on the intellectual history of kinship, then explains Malinowski's uptake amongst novelists and critics, before exploring his part in a BBC debate on marriage that reveals the outer limits of the diffusion of ideas in the 1930s.

ANTHROPOLOGY AND THE HISTORY OF KINSHIP

European readers had long sought out anthropological texts for frank discussions of human sexuality in a sociological idiom before the 1920s.[17] But amidst this history of cross-cultural comparison, the anthropologists of the 1920s and 1930s offered something new. Ethnographic evidence was used to construct a mutable account of the psychological dynamics of the family, shifting away from orthodox Freudian approaches and from the kind of grand evolutionary stories of social evolution of Victorian social science towards less rigid, less deterministic theories.[18]

To get a grip on Malinowski's contribution to the reimagining of kinship, it is first necessary to briefly outline the longer trend of writing in the West about the 'primitive', the 'barbarian' and the 'savage'.[19] Artists, scientists and philosophers had speculated for centuries on the origins of society and how customs surrounding sex and marriage had influenced human history. Something important happened to this tradition in the 1860s. It was related to anthropology, to Christianity and to new scientific theories of evolution. When the naturalist Charles Darwin reached for evidence to explain the early development of the human animal, he found it in the works of Edward Tylor and John McLennan.[20] As we saw in chapter 1 of this book, anthropology at the time was forming itself into a respectable science of the 'primitive'. Amongst these anthropologists, one of the most important differences between 'civilisation' and 'barbarism' was thought to lie in the structure of the family. The American jurist and polymath Lewis Henry Morgan had amalgamated a huge tranche of questionnaires on the families of non-Western peoples in his book *Systems of Consanguinity and Affinity of the Human Family* (1871). The results led him to argue that human societies progressed through a number of stages towards the eventual adoption of the form of patriarchal family prevalent amongst the light-skinned denizens of European descent living on the East Coast of the United States of America. The most primitive societies consisted of groups of men marrying groups of women, with society slowly evolving towards a Western, Protestant ideal.[21]

Many others followed in Morgan's wake, with a number of important texts published by the turn of the twentieth century, including Lorimer Fison and Alfred William Howitt's *Kamilorai and Kurnai* (1880) and Baldwin Spencer and Frank Gillen's *The Native Tribes of Central Australia* (1899). Speculations about the family relations of aboriginal peoples in Australia would soon inspire Émile Durkheim and Sigmund Freud to write on the division of labour in society and the origins of the Oedipus complex.[22] Friedrich Engels contributed an intervention too and titled it *The Origin of the Family, Private Property, and the State* (first published in 1884 and in English translation in 1902). Engels drew on Morgan's arguments about the promiscuity of supposedly 'primitive' peoples but proposed that, far from being the high point of social evolution, the monogamous modern family was merely another exploitative economic institution, which communism would sweep away. With the publication of J. G. Frazer's *Golden Bough* and the increasing interest in comparing cultures amongst novelists, poets and painters, and political thinkers, it is little surprise that one prominent anthropologist should have written that by 1910 his discipline had become 'the latest form of evening entertainment.'[23]

In this context Malinowski was at pains to point out how much of this literature rested on faulty misconceptions about the family's origins and how these false pictures led to political arguments that were based on unsound premises. To Malinowski, the Freudians, Marxists and traditionalist conservatives on the Edwardian right all naturalised faulty ideas about 'primitive' families. His ideas were self-consciously different to existing strains of anthropological theories germinating in Britain's intellectual culture. Malinowski did not tell grand evolutionary narratives of the sort that Morgan, Engels and McLennan had proffered.[24] He told of the way that particular societies were held together by the mutual support of institutions, the family being an undergirding structure in all societies. This research led him into an interdisciplinary debates with Freud's British followers and to write in the highbrow press, and resulted in his entry into the upper spheres of British intellectual life, where he danced the Charleston with Dora Russell, spoke on the radio and published books, hoping to make large sales. He was, in short, becoming a public intellectual, and his writings on the family from the mid-1920s to early 1930s were often crafted in a literary style in order to make public interventions.

FUNCTIONALISM AND THE FAMILY

The American anthropologist Margaret Mead pioneered a similar approach to Malinowski's in America. When she sent Malinowski a copy of her book *Coming of Age in Samoa*, she hailed him as the figure who had 'originated, ploughed, sowed and made fruitful' the new type of 'psychological field work' she practiced.[25] Malinowski replied with a statement on what he considered to be their shared critique of contemporary culture. On the topic of 'New Guinea Puritanism' he wrote:

> A distinct predilection for copulatory pastimes seems to me to be the natural thing, and if our maiden aunts, who worshipped Queen Victoria, the White Lily, and the unwashed ... affected a considerable detachment, we, usually, had the price of their bad temper, and pre-Freudian complexes, that is unless there was something wrong with their ovaries.[26]

Here we can find many of the tropes of the interwar progressive: the sense of a new era having opened up, an emphasis on sexuality, a contrast with Victorian attitudes and a misogynist, sexologically inspired denigration of the spinster. Like Mead, Malinowski was not merely describing a novel form of social organisation amongst 'primitive' peoples; he was publishing books that presented these practices as a critique of European culture and sexuality, comparing the 'maiden aunts' with people from New Guinea to criticise the former.

The prominent sexologist Havelock Ellis framed Malinowski's *Sexual Life of Savages* in just these terms when he contrasted three eras that corresponded with three different understandings of 'savage' peoples: a fantastical world of primitive promiscuity found in eighteenth-century travel writing, a more 'sombre' mood in nineteenth-century accounts and a final turn to science, meaning that 'only to-day' had proper investigation into sex 'become possible'.[27] Recent commentators concur and argue that Malinowski contributed to a shift in Edwardian anthropology whereby an earlier ideal of the 'over-sexed savage' was transformed into the 'under-sexed savage'. The new picture Mead and Malinowski offered of Pacific islanders presented a vision of men and women 'having passionless and boring but stable and sexually well-adjusted marriages.'[28]

These depictions of primitive marriage were not merely neutral representations. Anthropologists like Mead and Malinowski thought of themselves as progressives aiding an ultimately successful agenda of social reform. Explanations for the shift towards smaller family sizes and more companionate forms of marriage in Britain and America in the first half of the twentieth century have generally moved away from an emphasis on the heroic actions of a small cadre of 'sexual modernists' like Mead and Malinowski.[29] Yet even if anthropologists were intervening at the margins of this broader historical process, they were unarguably at the forefront of a major cultural and social change. Anthropology, especially Malinowski's, influenced elite opinion formers clamouring for marriage reform, and, through them, a wider readership associated with 1930s 'middle opinion'.[30] The key texts were *Sexual Lives of Savages*, *Sex and Repression in Savage Society* (1927) and the short book *The Father in Primitive Society*, published in the Psyche Miniatures series in 1927, with radio broadcasts and publications in the press helping to spread his ideas further still.

Malinowski often couched his interventions as part of a critical commentary on the work of Freud.[31] The 'first problem' of Freud's theorising, he wrote in *Sex and Repression in Savage Society*, is that 'the *family* is not the same in all human societies.'[32] Anthropologists must take it upon themselves to discuss the 'outstanding types of family constitution . . . and state the corresponding forms of the nuclear complex.'[33] Melanesian families exhibit a particularly coherent 'nuclear complex' because 'the social forces of custom, morals and manners' all conspire to unite in 'the passionate intimacy of motherhood.'[34] The first months of childrearing are supposed to be a 'state of bliss' broken decisively by the '"trauma" of weaning'. In a critical aside, he noted that exceptional aberrations from this state of affairs are to be found only among the 'higher strata of civilized communities'[35] (here he was presumably criticizing practices of wet nursing and the role of the nanny and governess from infancy). Relativism may stretch to different family structures, but the nucleus – apart from aberrant cases amongst the European upper classes – would be formed by the mother and child. The major differences lay in the relationship of the father to the 'nucleus': whether he would be authoritative and emotionally distant or accommodating and supportive of the mother and child.

These culturally specific differences between paternal roles lay at the heart of Malinowski's famous criticism of the universality of the Oedipus complex.[36] In the Trobriand Islands the father's sexual activities are not considered to be connected to procreation, and the mother's brother maintains a paramount role with respect to social discipline and the inheritance of property rights. As such, the Freudian emphasis on the father as both the head of the household and the figure of ultimate political and social authority over his children – the ideal of the *patria potestas* – looked only relevant to Western, bourgeois families. Other family nuclei might, and do, exist. In this shift away from large-scale evolutionary accounts of kinship, the relations between individual and society were reformulated as a matrix of possible sentiments within the family, an institution taken to be universal.[37] Always at the centre of any particular matrix, according to Malinowski, are a mother and child forming a bond that should be unbreakable.

Recall that to late Victorian writers, such as Engels and Morgan, the early history of marriage was an era when the individual bond of mother and child did not hold. Their writings included the idea that social relations amongst early humans consisted of a horde dominated by group marriages with no sense, or a shared sense, of parenthood. Freud had read this literature and baked it into his theories. But this makes his work look distinctly Victorian. By the Edwardian era, anthropologists were replacing these ideas with fieldwork-informed studies that posited marriage as a universal institution in all human societies and with motherhood as the static centre amongst all variations in family life and marital practices. Following the anthropologist-cum-sociologist Edward Westermarck, Malinowski toed this line. Speculating about the prehistory of societies when the family did not exist was done away with.

Some laudatory recent commentary has suggested that this shift away from orthodox Freudianism in Malinowski's work represents a move from a 'pathologizing psychoanalytic view' to 'an alternative nonbiological discourse.'[38] Anthropologists like Malinowski, and those belonging to the 'culture and personality' school in America, like Mead, are often discussed as part of a change that saw the increasing dissociation of sociological methods from the biological sciences – a move often simultaneously celebrated for driving a stake into the heart of scientific racism.[39] However, it was precisely Freud's lack of interest in biology that drew Malinowski's ire. In the preface to the third edition of his *Three Essays on Sexuality*, Freud had stated that his research was done 'deliberately independently of biology'.[40] In the margins of his own copy of the book, Malinowski wrote: 'This is absurd.' Rather than follow in the wake of this nonbiological understanding of human sexuality, Malinowski added, contra Freud, in a penned scrawl in the flyleaves, 'Biological laws must supremely control all that happens in [human?] organisms.'[41] In short, Freud's theories were not *too* biological; they were not biological enough.

Parsing contemporary distinctions between 'biology' and 'sociology' is difficult, and sometimes simply the wrong way to think about what these concepts meant.[42] For instance, after travelling to America in 1927, Beardsley Ruml, an officer at the Rockefeller Foundation, praised Malinowski's work because it so clearly put 'social science interests in cultural matters on a more fundamentally biological basis.'[43] This view was hardly idiosyncratic, and Malinowski's own institution, the London School of Economics, was at this time building a case for a department of social biology that would support the school director, William Beveridge's, long-standing desire to unite the natural and social sciences.[44] It was in these terms of cross-disciplinary research that Malinowski understood his own work. He argued that motherhood and childrearing were the locus of a sociobiological unity ('an organic unity that cannot be disrupted,' as he put it in the preface to the third edition of *Sexual Lives*).[45] But this fact did not mean that Malinowski thought that biology was *determinative* of social relations. Instead, the particular forms of the family – the variability of the kinship nucleus and its orbiting electrons – became the subject of study. This nucleus could form the basis of a comparison across cultures: each culture might have its own nuclear form.

MALINOWSKI AND INTERWAR LITERARY CULTURE

Malinowski tried his hand at diffusing these thoughts on kinship to a broader audience of educated lay readers in an essay published in 1930. He chose a venue that reflected his outlook: *The New Generation: The Intimate Problems of Modern Parents and Children*, edited by Victor Calverton and Samuel Schmalhausen, known to contemporaries in America as the 'sex boys'.[46] The book included essays by Bertrand Russell and Margaret Mead. The editors hailed Freud as an important pioneer. But his ideas were recontextualised as an analysis of a particular form of family life at a particular time and in a particular place: late nineteenth-century bourgeois Vienna. Relativising Freud led the 'sex boys' and their fellow-travellers, like Malinowski, to reach for other accounts of the psyche's formation. Their gaze fell on parenting and the particular, plural, culturally distinct forms of childcare that were exhibited amongst the world's different peoples. Malinowski's 'initial situation' of kinship seemed like a perfect place to start.

In *The New Generation*, Malinowski argued that the family, as the institution through which society and its members were reproduced, should be taken as the primitive baseline for all comparison between cultures. The 'relationship between parents and children remain[s] stable and universal' whether in the South Pacific, in Eastern Europe or modern Britain, Malinowski argued. Delineating the forms of attachment between parents and between parents and their children 'is the real task of scientific anthropology.'[47] Malinowski proposed that this emphasis on the importance of the family meant that 'functional anthropology' was an 'essentially conservative science.' Because 'the institutions of marriage and the family are indispensable, they should be saved at all costs in the present wrecking of so many things old and valuable.'[48]

Here he was critiquing contemporary Bolshevism and Marxist and feminist ideas of abolishing the family. But his ideas also stood against traditional, conservative mores that placed fatherly authority at the heart of family life. A tension exists between Malinowski's avowed 'conservatism', which did not seem very conservative at all by contemporary standards, the social circles he moved in, and the influence his ideas had. Amongst the wider world of humanist and liberal society, he was delighted to be made an honorary associate of the Rationalist Press

Association in 1930. This put him in the hallowed company of fellow LSE academics and leftists Harold Laski and Graham Wallas and with the scientists Julian Huxley and J. B. S. Haldane.[49] He was no radical, and certainly he was not a Marxist, but neither was he politically or intellectually a conservative: he was a liberal with a scepticism about religious teaching and a faith that science could improve humankind's lot. His emphasis on the mutability of the family made him popular with other contemporary marriage reformers in the broadly progressive wing of British politics.

On this count, Malinowski would surely have agreed with birth control advocate and novelist Naomi Mitchison's sexologically informed feminism that 'intelligent and truly feminist women' want 'to have masses of children by the men they love and leisure to be tender and aware of both lovers and children: and they want to do their own work, whatever it may be.'[50] Mitchison drew on Malinowki's research in the Trobriand Islands; she thought that Malinowski's books would usher in a 'revolution in consciousness'. '[M]utual physical passion' might become the basis of heterosexual union, displacing the prevailing archetype of the pre-married woman as a 'coldly chaste and flower-like maiden.' Malinowski described Trobriand women as having premarital sex, yet there seemed to be little evidence of children born out of wedlock, or divorce, or affairs. Mitchison put this down to the fact that individual Trobrianders must be somehow 'in communion with one another, so that impulses and ideas of a kind travel through them as through a single body.' Women realise 'the good' with their bodies, not with their minds, enforcing the injunction to avoid pregnancy in some kind of mystical union of social and individual consciousness. (This idea was very anti-Malinowskian! He had repeatedly spent his professional career arguing against the idea of the 'collective consciousness' favoured by Durkheim and his descendants.)[51]

Mitchison's collectivist reading of the ethnographic evidence led her to hope that, with enough scientific reform of society, a similar ethic might one day prevail amongst Britain's atomised and individuated moderns. While she characterised the current scene as a 'prison' of social dislocation for women, some hope lay in the fact that more positive ideas about female sexuality had begun to be published in the preceding decades and had been 'slowly ... filtered down' to the masses. With enough filtering down of elite ideas, she implied, a new society might come into being; with the most modern scientific techniques a revolution might occur, and women could experience the 'same kind of happiness as the Trobrianders.'[52] Mitchison and Malinowski's relationship was also personal. She entertained Malinowski at her family home at least once in 1926.[53]

Malinowski maintained personal relationships with other progressives seeking to usher in a revolution in consciousness. He was on friendly terms with Marie Stopes and visited her house with his children.[54] He frequently went out dancing with Dora Russell, buying a gramophone to practise the Charleston in his spare time.[55] Bertrand Russell was another avid reader. It was the fact that in the Trobriand Islands the paternal role was delinked from 'power and inheritance' that particularly impressed him. In his book *Marriage and Morals* (1929), Russell wrote that Malinowski's theories had thrown a 'flood of light on the psychology of paternity.'[56] Contrasting the traditional authoritative ideal of the father, the *patria potestas*, with the Trobriand father-helpmeet suggested that there were many ways in which the father could function in the family. This insight made Malinowski's work 'quite indispensible'. Yet Russell saw in it a worrying aspect to the flexibility of a child's attachment to their father. For there was nothing, in that case, to stop the state becoming the primary object of filial affection. Thus while Russell generally favoured the diminishing power of the authoritarian father, with 'the family decaying fast, and internationalism . . . growing slowly,' the threat of militarist states demanding obedience from their children-subjects 'justifies grave apprehensions'.[57] For Russell, then, anthropological studies of small-scale communities offered up a vision of social plasticity that had worrisome implications in a political world of states geared for war.

Aldous Huxley read Malinowski in the same spirit of hope and despair about modern Britain. Writing to his friend Norman Douglas, he noted that *The Sexual Lives of Savages* was 'an interesting and instructive book,' but, nevertheless, 'very depressing in as much as it demonstrates the incomparable superiority, intelligence and decency, of the neolithic inhabitants of the Trobriand Islands to the English.' 'A *Sexual Life of Ladies and Gentlemen*,' he quipped, 'ought to be written as a pendant volume.'[58] To Kethevan Evans he recommended reading Malinowski and Mead alongside Virginia Woolf's *To the Lighthouse* and E. M. Forster's *A Passage to India*, suggesting that it was particularly among modernist writers that sexological, and – we should add – anthropological works were interpreted and disseminated.[59]

Evidence of Huxley's anthropological reading can be found throughout his own book *Brave New World* (1931).[60] In 1929, Huxley wrote to Mary Hutchison that these Melanesians... can afford to spend their childhood and adolescence in idyllic flirtations under the hibiscus bushes. We can't. But, *per contra*, can we afford to spend our childhood and adolescence learning to be, not merely intellectually efficient, but also unhappy, nervously unstable, perverted, mad? It's a nice question.[61]

The children's sexual play under the bushes outside the Central London Hatchery and Conditioning Centre towards the beginning of the novel clearly refers to his reading of Mead and Malinowski, as do Mustapha Mond's (the World Controller) references to Pacific Islanders and to the institution of marriage.[62] But Huxley's comparison of 'the savage' John with the sterile, bottle-born moderns shows that he had a very different idea to Mitchison about the kind of world that modern science might bring about and the comparative insights anthropology might offer for social reform.[63] In his letter to Mary Hutchison, Huxley clearly felt that there were significant differences between what the Melanesians and 'we' (meaning the modern British) could 'afford' to spend their childhood doing. Huxley was sceptical that the way of life of a people so distant in culture and climate could be compared with the British.

This scepticism was married to a more general criticism of his contemporaries seeking political ideas in the Trobriand Islands or in Britain's medieval past for their 'snug little Utopia[s]'.[64] Huxley worried that this tendency was spreading. 'With every advance in industrial civilization,' he wrote critically in *Music at Night* (1931), 'the savage past will be more and more appreciated.'[65] *Brave New World* was not simply an attack on the modernist utopianism of H. G. Wells, as he wrote in a preface to the novel, but of the primitivist utopianism represented by his recently deceased friend D. H. Lawrence and, we might add, Naomi Mitchison. In this light, one commentator has characterised Huxley's critique of anthropologically informed social engineering as 'satiric primitivism'.[66] This is because the world of A.F. 632, with its gyrocopters and Malthusian contraceptive belts, is not, another critic argues, 'in relation to us... moving... into the future,' but 'into the past, into the savage past.'[67]

John, the Shakespeare-quoting 'savage', cannot fit into either the native reserve of Malpais (in Spanish, literally 'bad country') or the 'ultramodern primitivism' of England.[68] By the novel's end he is driven to suicide in despair. Huxley's lesson is an ultimately aristocratic one. He did not trust that the spreading of leisure and technology would create more happiness or a more elevated culture, nor that social engineering would lead to a more equal society, as even in future England a strict hierarchy is maintained through social conditioning.[69] He represented his contemporaries' enthusiastic reading of anthropology as an exercise in self-congratulation by the denizens of a small scientific circle, finding in supposedly savage mores justification for their own sexual practices.

The reception of social anthropology amongst highbrow writers was marked by ambivalence, then. Mitchison found, as Malinowski intended, inspiration for sexual reform in his Trobriand ethnographies, but she applied a collectivist reading to the evidence that he would have found objectionable. Huxley, while fascinated, took a more tragic view, seeing little possibility of recreating the culture of the Pacific islands in England and satirizing the ideals of those who thought such a project was realizable. Russell was both excited and troubled by the mutability of the paternal role in childrearing. So far we have seen the reception of functionalist ideas of the family amongst an elite audience. A series of radio addresses by Malinowski and a representative of an older current of thinking, Robert Briffault, offers a tantalizing glimpse into social anthropology's wider cultural reach. But the broadcasts also point to the limits of its uptake in a society marked by class and generational divisions and highlight the limits of radio as a medium for conveying complex ideas to non-elite audiences.

POPULARISING THE FUNCTIONALIST FAMILY OVER THE AIRWAVES

Talks on the interwar BBC were at the forefront of attempts at informing public opinion with elite ideas. They engaged with more outré subject matter, such as sexuality, after a change of policy in 1928. Under the direction of Hilda Matheson, the corporation broadcast debates on contemporary politics and controversial social questions.[70] Matheson was head of talks at the time of the radio debate between Malinowski and Briffault, and she has been characterised as a 'typical post-war liberal'.[71] A feminist, sympathetic to socialism and interested in modernism, she persuaded a cast of the broadly liberal great and the good to talk at the BBC. For Matheson, radio possessed great potential to mediate expert opinion and popular attitudes, allowing, in this elitist model of cultural diffusionism, progressive sensibilities to percolate outwards from the centre. Yet her aim to engage audiences with programmes of social reform was beginning to founder by the beginning of the 1930s. One of the problems was a question of genre, the other was a matter of the medium of radio itself.

Getting listeners to engage with complex subject matter was difficult. Radio rewarded a conversational style and lightness of tone. By the late 1920s listeners were beginning to move away from crystal sets and headphones towards mains-powered multiple valve radios with loudspeakers.[72] This seemed to favour Matheson's ideals because programmes had more didactic potential when families and groups of friends could listen together at the same time. But these technical improvements did not solve the problem of squaring an ephemeral sonic medium with the desire to make radio broadcasts carry an educational or political message. Matheson responded to these challenges by broadcasting some talks programmes in the style of a debate between figures on opposing sides of a controversial question. Malinowski's series on marriage and kinship mixed some of these debate-style broadcasts with more straightforward addresses. The differences between these two types of talks were mostly superficial, however. Neither was spontaneous, and both were heavily scripted.

Malinowski opened the series of debates with a broadcast called 'The Present Crisis in Marriage,' in which he immediately dismissed most talk of 'crisis' in Britain. He took an extreme version of its tendencies as his theoretical and rhetorical foil: the marriage reforms of the USSR. According to Malinowski, new laws allowing group marriages would ultimately lead to the 'disassociation of kinship and marriage.'[73] Having no concept of adultery or of illegitimacy and no punishment for incest in Russia would lead to a situation wherein 'several men and several women may run a communal household, and indiscriminately share as much of their lives as they like.'[74] Despite this legal background and its apparent boosters amongst Western psychologists like the behaviourist J. B. Watson, Malinowski dismissed the possibility that such a 'degenerate' social arrangement could, in fact, exist. Far from posing some novel social arrangement, Soviet-style group marriage reflected 'a very old' and 'familiar concept' to any anthropologist who had read Morgan and Engels. These theories, and their present incarnations in Soviet policy, contradicted what Malinowski thought was the true social and biological link between kinship and marriage: parenthood.

As we have seen, Malinowski's 'initial situation' of kinship united the personal, the biological, the psychological and the social in the act of childrearing. Parenting, according to Malinowski, could only ever be a bond between a mother and a father and a child. Marriage was concerned with parenthood, not with sex or property. The anthropologist Robert Briffault saw things differently. Briffault was an exemplar of the older style of non-academic anthropology that told evolutionary tales of human institutions. And his ideas were recognisably more feminist than Malinowski's. In the second BBC broadcast in the series, titled 'The Origins of Patriarchal Marriage,' he proposed that economic forces had always underwritten the ever-evolving forms of marriage. 'Matrimonial unrest' did not come from the Soviet Union or from American psychologists but from 'the women of England' who were made to adopt a 'subordinate position' under contemporary legal and economic strictures.[75] The subordination of women constitutes the 'patriarchal conception of the marriage relation.' Found in Greece and Rome, sanctified by the Church and ossified by the Victorian jurist Henry Maine, patriarchal ideals of marriage are supposed to be how things have always been and how they should be.[76] Patriarchy was not, in short, originary. 'Adam-and-Eve anthropology', as Briffault called it (a view that bases ideas of the family on biblical authority and the social customs of pastoral peoples in the ancient Middle East) cannot provide an explanation of the foundations, or a model for the future reform of, the family.[77] Unlike Malinowski, who wanted to find a comparable sociological basis of human relations in forms of parenting, for Briffault 'to know the truth about social relations and institutions means to know their origins and history.'[78] Briffault wanted to tell an evolutionary story of increasing control over women's lives through the civilising process. This had the revolutionary implication that only overturning the whole system would liberate women from their subordination.

In the third broadcast 'What Is a Family?,' the two men engaged in a dialogue. In reality a scripted and intensively edited production, it gave the impression of a discussion in which the previous two programmes' ideas could be developed further. Briffault's definition of 'family' took account of its 'variety of meanings' in the historical record. The concept of the family meant different things at different times in the evolution of culture. In Latin, *familia* meant a man's goods, chattels, animals and wife. Amongst cats, meanwhile, 'Papa, as a matter of fact is not there. The animal family consists essentially of mother and young.' Briffault drew from this the conclusion that 'the primitive human family resembled the animal family more closely than does the civilised family.'[79] The implication was that groups of mothers reared groups of children with men circulating between them. This picture was very different from modern marriage. But the foundations for Briffault's argument look rather shaky: it is certainly a strong kind of evolutionism that would use the behaviour of cats to criticise human institutions.

The nub of the debate rested on the plausibility of the idea of group motherhood. For Malinowski it simply did not seem psychologically possible that parenting could be a communal activity and he turned Briffault's arguments towards contemporary politics. Briffault's idea that marriage was a 'capitalistic institution' led Malinowski to propose that the alternative to individual parenting would be that the 'State, the Community, the Workers' Union ought to educate the future citizen from his early childhood.'[80] There could be no 'group-marriage without group parenthood.'[81] He was more than sceptical that this would be an option that women would choose. 'Parenthood, and above all maternity, is the pivotal point in the anatomy of marriage and family,' he declared.[82] Women were gaining increasing autonomy in modern Britain, and he agreed with Briffault that they 'will have the last word in deciding what the future of marriage will be.' But the idea that women would choose group marriage and group parenting led him to the following conclusion: 'Will a woman, however intelligent, feminist, or progressive, consent to undergo the hardships and dangers of childbirth in order to give over her child to a glorified foundlings' hospital or State incubator?'[83] The answer to Malinowski clearly seemed to be: no.

Briffault was allowed a final stab at making his argument, and then Malinowski concluded with two broadcasts in which the illusion of debate was jettisoned. Having started out on good terms, the experience of working together led the two men to become increasingly hostile. Malinowski's summing up reiterated his claim that marriage was an individual contract everywhere. The whole experience had been gruelling and unproductive. In a letter sent to John Reith, the BBC's director general, after the final broadcast, Malinowski admitted that the series had been something of a disaster.[84] The obvious hostility between Briffault and Malinowski, and both men's tendency to turn the debate towards contemporary politics so readily, meant that they hardly conformed to the smooth style favoured by the Talks department.

The talks provide a sense of the shifting terrain of debate about marriage and motherhood in interwar Britain. Malinowski's views represented the ideals of a new generation of marriage reformers engaged in the drama of eroticizing marriage. Briffault, on the other hand, represented an older, Victorian tradition that sought to historicize forms of kinship in the vein of McLennan, Morgan and Engels. Despite the lofty ideals of Matheson and the BBC, if these talks were meant to change people's minds from the former idea of the family to the latter, there is little evidence that they did. Malinowski hoped 'the general effect of the Talks will, in spite of all, be on the whole constructive.'[85] Charles Siepmann, a senior Talks producer, let him in on the bad news. 'Looking back upon the series it does seem to me now that it was side-tracked too early on to academic issues that cannot grip the interest of ordinary listeners,' and, Siepmann concluded, 'although it is a hard saying, I think the best that can be said of these talks is that they are over.'[86]

Siepmann's intuition is supported by evidence from a group of between twenty-three and fifty men and women who sat down at a public library in Lancashire to follow the debate over a number of weeks. Sophie Munn-Rankin, convener of the Carnegie-sponsored listening group, sent a report to Malinowski a day after the final broadcast. 'Discussion has been enthusiastic,' she wrote. She was glad to report that both men and women had been active participants, although, 'as might be expected in this town, the Communist attitude was very strong.' She accounted for the 'Communist attitude' by explaining that 'class feeling ... is very bitter.' Amongst the listeners in Munn-Rankin's radio group was a man who claimed to have memorized large sections of books by Lewis Henry Morgan. Morgan, like Briffault, proposed an evolutionary account of kinship relations beginning with a stage of 'primitive promiscuity'. The man had quoted large sections of Morgan's work to refute Malinowski's theories. It is safe to presume that he was part of the 'Communist element'. Morgan's work was, after all, central to the argument made by Engels in *Origins of the Family, Private Property and the State*.[87]

In Munn-Rankin's view, class feeling meant that the discussion kept getting sidetracked. The audience apparently had a tendency to mistake their own views for those expressed by the anthropologists. When listeners attributed arguments to Malinowski that Munn-Rankin thought were incorrect, she reached for the transcript to rebut their claims: 'The chief difficulty has been for an audience like this, uneducated, to grasp fully the matter broadcast.'[88] She thought that distributing transcripts in printed form in advance of the broadcasts might help to guide discussion more effectively.

While communist and non-communist politics split the group, gender did not seem to have much of a marked influence; men and women participated equally willingly, according to Munn-Rankin. Generational differences, however, did make a big impact. Young people did not seem to want to discuss the broadcasts. This might have been due to the subject matter. For the older members of the listening group there was a lot to complain about and, for Munn-Rankin, a lot to be scandalised by. (A Poor Law doctor informed her that on one street in the town twenty-four of twenty-six couples lived in 'Tully' – informal relationships – and that divorce was not seen as an issue amongst many of the listeners, who simply broke off partnerships if the couple wished.) For the silent, embarrassed youths things seemed to look different. They apparently asked Munn-Rankin for a separate session just for them. They chose as their representative a young woman, who approached Munn-Rankin on their behalf. She explained the need for youth group in the following way: 'We cannot . . . discuss in front of them what we regard as sacred. They have forgotten their youth – what love is – we want some Ideals, real Ideals.'[89] Munn-Rankin seemed to be discouraged by the woman's unwillingness to state her case in the listening group, but she approved of her sentiments. Malinowski did too, writing in reply that he was 'very glad' that the young people seemed to have 'a more decent outlook' than their elders.[90] Despite this, Munn-Rankin's experience supports Siepmann's criticisms. Even though there were some young people who seemed to agree with Malinowski's arguments, the subject matter proved difficult to engage with as a topic for radio broadcast.

Interwar talks radio was expected to be a reciprocal medium, and radio broadcasts were surrounded by associated print media and institutionalised forms of group listening like this one in Lancashire. Listeners were encouraged to correspond with speakers, and groups like Munn-Rankin's were set up to carry on the conversation by groups of interested participants.[91] Feedback between listeners and speakers formed part of an approach to radio that sought to distinguish the BBC from communist and fascist propaganda, which adopted more obviously didactic forms.[92] The style of address at the BBC was mirrored in Malinowski's own ideological positioning between Soviet reforms and Italian fascist approaches to marriage.

In theory, the audience was left to make up their own minds. But when promotional material was sent out in advance of the broadcasts, almost all of the preparatory reading material had a distinctly Malinowskian slant. On the list were Malinowski's articles on anthropology in *Encyclopaedia Britannica*; books by his LSE colleague Edward Westermarck, whose views about the individual, contractual nature of marriage Malinowski followed almost verbatim; and literature from the Social Hygiene Council, a group Malinowski supported. None promoted Briffault's views.[93] Future listeners, the pamphlet suggested, could read these books and articles and, duly prepared, might send the speakers some questions before the broadcasts began. There is no evidence in Malinowski's papers that any questions were sent.

Malinowski did receive other forms of feedback on his broadcasts, though. For instance, a letter from a man born in the Gold Coast living in London wrote to Malinowski to express his anger at Briffault's patronising statement that 'primitives' did not marry for romantic reasons. A note from someone called Ronald Rushworth expressed the opinion that marriage was an individual contract and should be kept apart from intermediary institutions such as the state or the church. Malinowski wrote back a frustrated reply.[94] A letter from a Gillingham Workers' Educational Association group, meanwhile, suggested that Briffault's argument was more sensible than Malinowski had made out. Briffault was concerned with the communal raising of children by multiple women rather than their 'impossible conjoint production'. 'Economic conditions' in modern Britain meant that families were often limited to one or two children and so 'deni[ed] ... companionship of children of their own age.' The letter writer concluded that the 'present development toward nursery schools, and other additions to home rearing are beneficial for the children and desirable from the racial standpoint.'[95]

Dismissing his correspondent's claims that groups of children should be socialised together by multiple women, Malinowski sent a reply asking whether 'any experiments in "communal" motherhood had been tried? Will you be able at Gillingham to stage such an experiment? If you cannot even think of instituting an experiment in "communal" motherhood is it not futile to think whether it is "better" or "worse"'.[96] Despite Malinowski's focus on the psychological and sociological, rather than the economic, aspects of marriage in his radio responses to Briffault, he stressed that economic considerations must, in the end, pose a limit to marriage reforms in his correspondence with the Gillingham WEA. Group motherhood – 'gigantic nursing homes for children' – would, he wrote, 'probably increase our taxation to treble the amount it is now – we might perhaps be able to retain 1/- in the £1 for our private incomes.' Trebling the tax burden seemed intolerable to him. Furthermore, the state might have to run services like the post and telegraphs, but, he wrote, 'it is hopeless when it comes to finer re-adjustments. Would the State as the "communal" mother be any good?' He signed off by writing sarcastically 'If you discuss these matters and reach any results I should be glad to hear about it.'[97]

Malinowski's resolute focus on the virtues of heterosexual union; his liberal attitude to political economy; and his emphasis on the singular, universal and fundamental importance of motherhood makes him an awkward ally in feminist, anti-Freudian histories of the family.

He is a difficult figure to rope into a liberatory narrative about the 'non-biological' and 'non-essentialising' approach to social relations in opposition to orthodox Freudianism.[98] Malinowski's writings from the late 1920s and 1930s reveal his position arrayed in a resolutely anti-communist position that, while aligned with maternalist feminists such as Naomi Mitchison, looks distinctly conservative in relation to later feminist writings on marriage and childhood or in comparison to contemporary Marxist theory.[99] Rosalind Coward, writing in 1983, wondered whether anthropologists in this era were really interested in gender at all, or if their discussions about women and childrearing derived from attempts to describe social relations in general, in which sex between men and women was incidental to broader discussions about economics, populations and the origins of political order.[100] Malinowski, after all, had written that social anthropology was an 'essentially conservative science'.

CONCLUSION

The equation of motherhood and domesticity with the formation of the personality is often associated with psychoanalysis rather than anthropology in Britain, and especially with the work of Melanie Klein, John Bowlby and Donald Winnicott in the post-war decades rather than Malinowski in the 1920s and 1930s.[101] In the existing literature, the Second World War and particularly the experience of the blitz and evacuation play a large role in explaining how motherhood came to be endowed with such value and why such a maternalist conception of personality formation became embedded in the British social sciences.[102] In this chapter we have seen how strains of maternalist thinking were present in social anthropology from the late 1920s and that a number of prominent writers amplified Malinowski's ideas in their writings. The presence of this public debate about kinship in a post-Freudian key suggests that we need to revise the chronology of the centrality of the mother and child in the history of the social sciences in Britain back into the interwar years.[103]

The broadcasts also revise the argument that academic professionalization necessarily meant a move away from public engagement. Malinowski's interventions were wide-ranging and frequent. Focusing on the works of interwar intellectuals, broadcasts and listeners' reports, rather than reading texts designed for academic audiences alone, allows us to see the history of anthropology from an often unstudied perspective: in its popular reach and interaction with public life. Furthermore, we do not only need to look to non-academic writers to uncover this popular reception.[104] Thus while debates about kinship and social structure have become associated with the dry, scholastic stereotype of 'British social anthropology', for listeners in Lancashire, or novelists and intellectuals like Russell, Mitchison and Huxley, questions of sex, marriage and reproduction were far from exotic or academic questions. As a result, Malinowski has been revealed as an arch populariser alongside the arch professionaliser discussed in the previous chapters.

The second way that these sources contribute to the history of anthropology in Britain stems from the exasperation of the young woman in Lancashire at the lack of 'high Ideals' on the part of older listeners. Her comment might suggest a set of pervasive tropes with a long history that set the youthful romantic versus the old and jaded. But it also points to a shift in attitude that historians have come to recognise as a patriarchal, Christian view of marriage began to change towards a more companionate, romantic model.[105] Ideals of romance, freedom and a concomitant commitment to family planning and female sexual autonomy marked out a growing cultural movement that united a diffuse generational transformation with an academic sea change in anthropology.

In this case, though, the lack of reciprocal dialogue between Malinowski and his correspondents, and the large diversity of their views, suggests that 'companionate marriage' failed to gain a foothold in the majority of people's lives, a fact borne out by social histories of the period.[106] While Malinowski's listeners generally did not share his views, none of his correspondents complained about the overwhelmingly non-religious manner in which he debated. Malinowski praised the 1930 Lambeth Council of Bishops' decision that contraceptive methods could be used within marriage, but the movements he pinned his hopes on were not spiritual associations. Instead he looked to the Council on Social Hygiene and the eugenics movement, groups the likes of which had an undeniably increasing influence on policy making over the twentieth century.[107] As secular languages of human sociality proliferated throughout the universities, over the airwaves and in print in the first half of the twentieth century, so did progressive arguments against the *patria potestas* take hold, however unevenly and incompletely.[108]

By the mid-1930s, then, social anthropology of the Malinowskian kind formed part of a wider uptake of anthropological ideas amongst the intellectual and upper classes in Britain. The plurality and diversity of these ideas should be noted. As the likely communist in Lancashire quoting Morgan demonstrates, functionalist accounts of the family co-existed alongside older, evolutionist theories. So, while academic anthropology was increasingly influenced by Malinowski's ideas, outside the academy newer ideas competed with older ones: currents of comparative anthropology continued to influence public discussions of British society.[109] And when it came to understanding British society in the late 1930s, it was not, at least initially, the ideas and techniques of social anthropology that had the most immediate impact. What was missing was the kind of study that Huxley longed for: a *Sexual Life of Ladies and Gentlemen*.

In Malinowski's public broadcasts, the comparisons he made between Trobriand marriage and British marriage were anecdotal and exemplary. They were not based on anything like Huxley's dream of an anthropological investigation into British society. The group that did end up studying Britain anthropologically during the 1930s was called Mass Observation (MO), which Malinowski certainly influenced, but whose methods met with his scepticism. The next chapter explains how MO ran out of steam by the early 1940s and how Raymond Firth's students carried Malinowski's hopes forward to apply anthropological field methods to British society, informing the social sciences with new concepts, from the 'traditional working-class neighbourhood' to 'race relations sociology' and the 'social network'.

CHAPTER 5

From Kinship Studies to Community Studies

'Race Relations', the 'Traditional Working-Class Neighbourhood' and the 'Social Network' in Post-war British Sociology

The Second World War precipitated huge social change in Britain, and the victory of a Labour government in 1945 led to the foundation of the modern welfare state. Soon 'affluence' became a description of increasing wealth and also a marker of anxiety about changes to supposedly 'traditional' working-class identities.[1] At the same time, migration to Britain from the Commonwealth recast notions of national and imperial citizenship and led to a new discourse of 'race relations'.[2] Gender roles were challenged, too, as new norms arose around working motherhood and women made demands for better living standards for themselves and their families.[3] Amidst this new world lay older patterns of social relations. By describing the transformations occurring around them, a genre of anthropologically inflected community studies formed part of a new discourse of social change in post-war Britain.[4]

With their selective foci and fields of vision, these community studies prompted readers to experience and interpret Britain's urban milieus in new ways. Of course, investigators had travelled through urban neighbourhoods commenting on the poor, on migrants and on mores for well over a century.[5] But to link the study of a locale to the culture of a community within it via fieldwork was a novelty drawn from social anthropology. In much the same way that we saw Audrey Richards, Lucy Mair and Margaret Read doing their fieldwork in central and eastern Africa in chapter 3, so the community studies researchers did their fieldwork in the UK during the 1940s and 1950s. The books they subsequently wrote influenced the way that race, community and culture were imagined in the British social sciences well into the 1960s and have shaped the way historians have subsequently reconstructed these decades ever since.[6]

My aim in this chapter is to reconstruct this brief moment when a common tradition of 'community studies' united anthropology and sociology. These field studies took a number of different forms, but they generally married ethnographic fieldwork with some pressing contemporary issue. My second aim is to build on recent research that has stressed the centrality of anthropological methods to these community studies.[7] For, as Malinowski told his students at the LSE in 1933, 'Modern Sociology is Anthropology applied to a modern district or town.'[8] Perhaps this statement reveals little more than Malinowski's overweening self-importance, but the two disciplines clearly did share some commonalities at mid-century.

For instance, when a letter was sent to the *Times* in 1951 announcing the founding of the British Sociological Association, two of the thirteen signatories were anthropologists: Raymond Firth and Meyer Fortes.[9] And in that decade the most cited authors in the *British Journal of Sociology* were the usual suspects – Marx, Weber and Durkheim – who received twenty-one, sixteen and fourteen references, respectively. But following close behind was the doyen of structural-functionalist anthropology, Alfred Radcliffe-Brown, with eleven citations, bettering Freud's ten; then there were Malinowski with eight and Edward Evans-Pritchard with seven.[10] When John Rex published his influential overview of the discipline, *Key Problems in Sociological Theory*, in 1961, the two most prominent academic sociologists in Britain of the preceding decades, Morris Ginsberg and Leonard Hobhouse, did not rate mentioning, while Malinowski and Radcliffe-Brown both came in for extended commentary and analysis.[11]

Yet Michael Young, one of the pioneers of the community studies tradition, would disown his extensive debts to anthropology, recounting much later in life how Raymond Firth had raged at him, '"You don't understand the academic world, or decency, or procedure or anything – you've written as though *you've* discovered the bloody extended family; well I did!"'[12] Whether or not this blow-up happened (Young's biographer Lise Butler suspects that it did not), this statement signals how acrimonious relations between sociology and anthropology became as the two disciplines competed for students, funding and prestige after the 1960s.[13] In 1986 the anthropologist Anthony Cohen wrote that ethnographies of Britain were seen as 'poor man's anthropology' and not sufficiently exotic or 'other' to count.[14] But this was not always the case. By pursuing what Stefan Collini calls 'lateral' 'intellectual' rather than 'vertical' 'discipline' history, which presupposes that anthropology and sociology always existed as totally distinct enterprises, we can see how ethnographies of urban community in Britain sprang up across what would later become increasingly siloed disciplines.[15]

Beyond this act of historical recovery, I also want to point to these studies' limitations. These problems arose when researchers applied the methods discussed in chapter 3 to understanding urban life in Britain. By doing so they confronted some serious misgivings. How should they delimit and define their 'field' when cities were so huge? And could they generalise about individual and collective behaviour in the same way that anthropologists thought could be done in 'primitive' societies? In the case of 'race relations' sociology, these questions stored up a powder keg of resentment that ultimately exploded in an insurgent critique of the discipline in the 1970s. As radical researchers at the Institute of Race Relations argued, racism, capitalism and imperialism had put men and women into marginalised groups in Britain in the first place, and sociology, law and science had colluded in this process.[16] Perhaps race relations sociology itself was complicit in the maintenance of defined, and fictive, group identity?

While race relations sociology was subject to especially withering critique, the problem of naturalising community in terms of a locale-bounded, face-to-face web of thick interactivity plagued the whole community studies tradition. This ultimately unrealistic vision of 'the social' was one reason community studies did not take stronger hold either in anthropology or in sociology. These community studies failed on their own terms to describe discrete groups acting together in bounded locales. The rapid changes suggested at the outset of this chapter concerning gender roles and relations, ethnicity and migration, work, leisure and consumption, to name only a few, burst out of the often static accounts of 'community' that researchers employed to understand their contemporary milieus.[17] Other analytical problems came from the emphasis placed on intra-family dynamics and childrearing, carrying over the Malinowskian emphasis on the role of motherhood as the basis of social life discussed in the previous chapter: feminists have been rightly suspicious of the validity of these arguments.[18]

But despite these limitations, or perhaps precisely because community studies trucked in already available stereotypes, many community studies monographs were incredibly influential, reaching out into a wider public conversation about British society and post-war social change. Michael Young and Peter Willmott's *Family and Kinship* became a classic of the genre and was read widely in universities and by a wider public. Exploring Young and Willmott's work alongside some other, less well-known, community studies gives a sense of the importance of social anthropology in the intellectual culture of 1950s Britain. We will see how a number of landmarks in the social sciences of that era – the 'traditional working-class neighbourhood', the 'race relations' paradigm and the 'social network' – all drew on anthropological theory for conceptual and methodological inspiration.

The chapter begins with a brief analysis of Mass Observation (MO), the first, stuttering and incomplete crossover between LSE anthropology and the British social survey tradition, before moving on to discuss the work of Raymond Firth in Bermondsey. Then Young and Willmott's study of Bethnal Green is introduced. The third section discusses Kenneth Little's 'race relations' sociology. Finally, Elizabeth Bott's social network theory is analysed. My argument is that all of these pioneering and famous works of social science owed far more than is currently understood to the methods and theories of social anthropology. Anthropological methods and arguments prompted sociologists to reinvent their theories of British society. By telling this history we can better understand the strengths and weaknesses of these books, as well as provide a richer account of social anthropology's place in Britain's mid-century intellectual culture.

MASS OBSERVATION AND THE ANTHROPOLOGY OF ENGLAND

A precursor to the community studies tradition can be found in the work of Mass Observation (MO), formed in 1937 by Charles Madge and Tom Harrisson. Harrisson had done fieldwork in the New Hebrides (now Vanuatu). Madge was a poet. Madge and Harrisson attempted to survey, explain and describe everyday life in Britain, with a special focus on the working class.[19] But the group's activities were always plagued with problems, an overabundance of field notes and internal squabbles over method.[20] Harrisson tended to favour intensive observation of overt behaviour. Madge urged volunteers to write in with reflections, answers to questions and diaries to collate a patchwork of responses to contemporary life in Britain.

Harrisson and Madge were generally dismissive of contemporary academic social science. They poured particular scorn on the value of 'opinion' drawn from survey research. In general, they favoured a more 'subjective' type of data, drawn from multiple observers' experience and valued for its particularity.[21] This did not mean that they thought of themselves as amateurs. Quite the opposite. As Madge explained, MO would 'produce . . . a scientific theory as useful to mankind as the atomic theory or the theory of natural selection.'[22] The general theory they landed on was less grand and much more schematic than this, however. The theory consisted of the idea that people related to the wider society in three broad areas. Area one included regular face-to-face contacts, from family members to friends and fellow members of civic associations. Area two encompassed those people whom an individual might encounter going about their everyday life, such as shop customers or police officers. Area three was rather more abstract: it was made up of all those people, or ideas or associations that had 'peculiar power in influencing' people's 'life', from journalists and radio hosts to ideas of national belonging and advertising jingles.[23]

The Mass Observers' intention to capture the totality of social life in Britain possessed a family resemblance to the work done by the LSE social anthropologists in the British Empire, although the idea of 'areas' was different to the schemes and charts we encountered in chapter 3. The methods were similar enough, though, to warrant Harrisson an invite to give a talk at the LSE departmental seminar in December 1937, where he was met with an appreciative audience. Malinowski agreed to join the group's advisory committee and was, according to Harrisson, 'interested and vigorously sympathetic to our work,' and Raymond Firth arranged for Harrisson to give a talk at the Royal Anthropological Institute.[24]

But after his initial enthusiasm Malinowski wrote an equivocal essay in Madge and Harrisson's publication *First Year's Work 1937–38 by Mass-Observation*. He wrote that ever since landing in the Trobriand Islands to carry out his fieldwork, it had been his 'deepest and strongest conviction that we must finish by studying ourselves through the same methods and with the same mental attitude with which we approach exotic tribes.'[25] As a 'nationwide intelligence service' MO might offer something like Malinowski's longed-for application of anthropology to the 'modern district or town', but on an even larger scale. The reality, though, was a disappointment. The ever-caustic Edward Evans-Pritchard, meanwhile, called MO's findings 'bilge' in a letter to Meyer Fortes.[26]

Firth followed up with a critical, although sympathetic, review of MO in the *Sociological Review* in 1939. He concluded that MO offered a 'recreative outlet for its thousand or so Observers and enabling them to learn something about the behaviour of others than themselves.'[27] Hardly the foundation of a new science of society, then. To achieve something more than a merely recreational activity, Firth suggested that the Mass Observers would have done better to 'concentrat[e] [their] attention on the analysis of a single institution.' If they had done this, 'it is likely that [their] results would have been of more value to sociology.'[28] And sociology was in dire need of this kind of analysis, Firth argued. 'Anthropologists have long been aware of this lack of a body of material comparable in empirical depth to their own, and Malinowski, in particular, has insisted on the need for a study which might be called the anthropology of civilization,' he wrote.[29] Mass Observation, with its eclectic methods and diffuse, non-academic ethos, did not provide the kind of insights Firth and Malinowski longed for.

After Malinowski's death in 1942, Firth himself would end up pioneering this kind of research. The Second World War delayed his research (he ended up working in the Admiralty, producing handbooks on the South Pacific). But once the war was over, he sent his students into a block of flats in Bermondsey to try to do exactly the kind of 'anthropology of civilization' in a single institution he had called for in *The Sociological Review*. This work and Firth's support and mentorship would have a profound effect on the community studies tradition, influencing a host of pioneering studies of British society in the 1950s. Under the new regime of Britain's welfare state, sociologists applied the field methods developed by social anthropologists and wondered whether the family and its intimate connections to place and space might mark the limit of social engineering in the 'new Jerusalem'. In this respect they took up the hopes and dreams of Malinowski to study Britain anthropologically. And, as MO veered into market research, they carried forward the group's original intentions to cast an anthropological gaze on British society.

FROM TIKOPIA TO BERMONDSEY

After returning from his wartime service and after Malinowski's death in 1942, Firth took over Malinowski's vacated professorial chair at the LSE in 1944. During one of his seminars, students were comparing 'primitive' kinship systems with 'modern' ones. They realised that they knew very little about the structure of the British family and its relation to broader social structures beyond anecdote and personal experience. Reference was made to recently published works by Talcott Parsons and Margaret Mead. But Parsons and Mead put their emphasis on the 'nuclear' family, assuming that this was typical of modern kinship. Firth thought that this was probably wrong. He suggested that the students find out whether the distinction between 'primitive' and 'modern' families lay in the difference between an extended and a nuclear kinship structure. The result would be the beginning of a two-year research project, a monograph published twelve years later in 1956 as *Two Studies of Kinship in London* and inspiration for all other community studies to come.[30]

Firth had already done a research project on families and social structures, publishing his findings ten years before. This study was not of London, though, but of the island of Tikopia in the Pacific. In his monograph *We, The Tikopia* he concluded that 'the relation between kinship system . . . and . . . local organization' constitutes a 'fundamental problem of analysis.'[31] He 'attacked' this problem from 'two sides'. First, he gave 'an indication . . . of the kinship affiliations of the people as they are distributed in residential groups' and then followed this up with 'the spatial distribution of the members of the various kinship groups.' The result would 'represent a superimposition of the members of the genealogical record upon a residential plan of it, and if carried out in its entirety would fix as by a system of co-ordinates the position of every individual from the point of view of kinship and locality.'[32] Plotting each person on his hypothetical map would have been far beyond the scope of one researcher's capacity. So he proposed to study two villages and compare them. After more than five hundred pages of detail he concluded that he had achieved 'a kind of dissection of the anatomy of the society, viewing the kinship links as part of the skeletal structure giving the society its form.'[33]

Firth and his students decided to study a block of flats near the LSE in Bermondsey in the same spirit, but without having to pay heed to the colonial authorities, a significant relief for Firth.[34] Their goal was to uncover the kinship relations of those living in the block, treating the building in much the same way that Firth had investigating social relations in the two Tikopian villages. They hoped to plot a map of its residents and of their relations with each other. After some initial planning, a general approach had been formulated by December 1947. Index cards would be filled in with information on individuals, a daybook would be used to keep a note of progress and genealogies were to be drawn up of all the families. The group of fourteen students was split into three groups. Each team would have a leader who would make sure to keep in touch with the others in the hope of avoiding too much overlap and to ensure that the groups could share information and tips on best practice.[35]

Unlike MO's three area theory, Firth's team focused almost exclusively on kinship. Like their decision to study one building, this had the advantage of narrowing the study down to a seemingly manageable scope. It was decided to measure the 'range' of kinship relations in three ways: total, nominal and effective. The total range would be reconstructed using census data and interviews to create genealogies for all the families in the building. The nominal range was understood on a shifting scale that included the kin that any member of the family could name in an interview setting. The effective range included those relatives who could be relied on in times of hardship, who exhibited some aspect of more mundane solidarity or who came together on important occasions such as christenings and funerals. At first the researchers spent their time in the local social club and talking to people in pubs. After two months of drinking together and observing darts matches, a new approach was taken. This 'pub-and-club' stage was followed by more intensive interviews in residents' flats.[36] Tables were drawn up describing who received Christmas cards from whom, how many family photographs lined the walls of the residents' rooms and which family members talked to each other on a regular basis.

All of this investigation created a great profusion of material. And like their predecessors in MO, the researchers soon found that things were running out of control as the system of index cards and notebooks strained under the weight of so much information. Having too much data was one problem, but this was compounded by the partiality of the research that the LSE students were able to undertake. The anthropologists soon realised that information could only be gathered from a limited number of residents. Beside the practical issue of gaining access to families regularly, the band of international students decamping regularly at the flats caused some residents considerable anxiety. One man, described as an 'informal chief', likened the anthropologists to the Gestapo – which, in a particularly tasteless moment of ethnographic self-reflection, one researcher wrote in their notes might fit if it meant the acronym: 'Gregarious Expert Subversifying Through a Political Organisation.'[37]

The 'Gregarious Experts' ceased their research in 1949. There is no explanation in the project files about why the project ended when it did. But it is clear that the undertaking had already consumed a vast amount

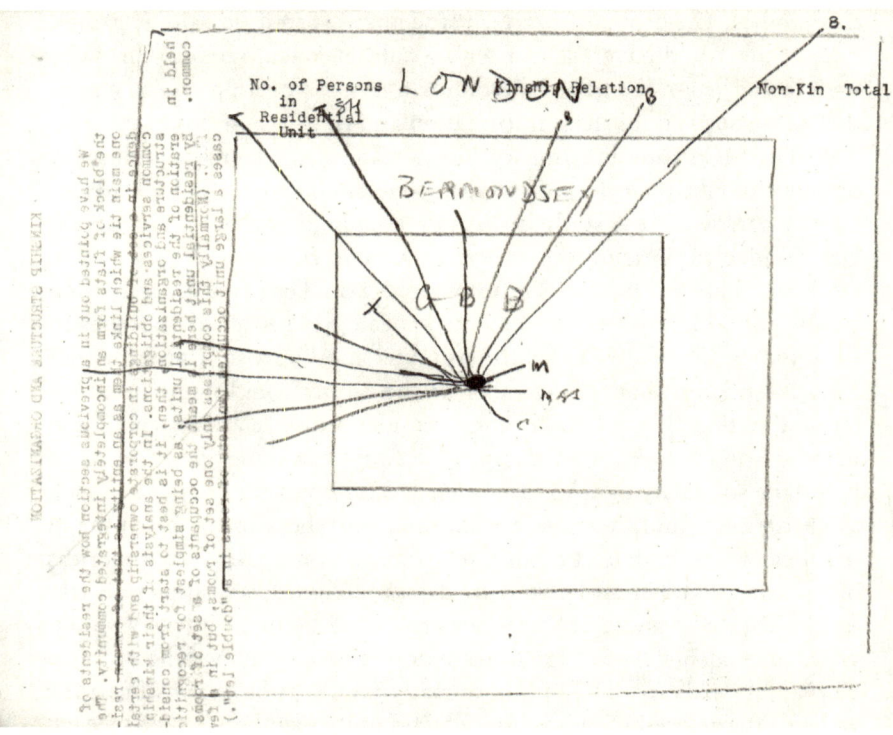

FIGURE 2. Hand-drawn diagram from Raymond Firth's kinship research in Bermondsey. Reproduced with permission from Firth family.

of intellectual effort for relatively little pay-off. Where did one end one's investigation? How was one to know what to observe and write down when anything might be significant? What's more, kinship types were proving hard to pin down. The anthropologists' original assumption that residents would experience their social relations with reference to the building itself proved to be untrue. The attempt to bound these relations within its walls and study them as a coherent set of institutions had failed, and Firth, or one of his researchers, sketched the diagram shown in figure 2 to represent these problems. (GBB is the Guinness Trust building at the centre, with lines radiating out showing the dispersion of kin relations beyond the building.)

The diagram revealed the limits of their approach, and when the report was finally written up a number of differences between the types of societies the anthropologists usually studied and the families in

Bermondsey were noted and proved to be a crucial part of the group's findings when they finally appeared in print in 1956.

Firth's introduction to *Two Studies of Kinship* made it clear that Margaret Mead and Talcott Parson's idea of the 'nuclear', or 'elementary' family as a 'self-sufficient social unit' was inadequate.[38] Yet while the nuclear family was a myth, this did not mean that modern families conformed to the model that anthropologists were used to studying. 'Whereas in a primitive society,' Firth wrote, 'one normally expects to have patterns which can be described as universal for that society, in modern Western conditions there may be a high degree of variation.'[39] He put this variation down to what he called 'permissiveness'. The permissiveness of modern Western societies resulted in a high degree of choice on matters of marriage and the extra-familial kin whom individuals chose to spend their time with.

While in 'primitive' societies kinship relations determined a large part of a person's social life, in Bermondsey relations with kin were only part of a broader range of social interactions. In South London, economic, legal and religious norms did not overlap with kin relations to anywhere near the same extent that they did on Tikopia or in Malinowski's Trobriand Island studies. Regularities could be discerned, but these could not be described as 'systematic': 'For general categorisation, terms such as aggregate, set, configuration, constellation, web, network, grouping, and group are suggested to describe the entity empirically composed by and represented by the people who communicate or come together on certain social occasions because of their kin relations.'[40] The anthropologists employed the same 'intensive techniques of first-hand research' in their research in Bermondsey, but the 'complex conditions of Western society' meant that they 'ha[ve] of necessity to break up the field.'[41] Firth concluded that anthropologists 'cannot make the holistic type of appreciation which he is accustomed in the primitive society.'[42] Instead, 'the pattern' of kinship relations 'may be said to be statistical rather than normative in character.'[43]

There was simply too much variation in the lives of metropolitan British subjects to draw a total picture of their culture and society. Statistical variations, a vast crunching of data, may throw up some interesting results, but field study could not hope to capture the complexity of a permissive society. Parts could not be taken for wholes. Things were too complicated for that. However, one of the few concrete findings that Firth did feel was enough of a commonality proved to be hugely important: the realisation that despite the family name passing down the male line, the families studied in South London maintained 'a strong matrilineal bias with particular emotional significance.'[44] And his suggestion that the metaphor of the 'web' or 'network' would more accurately capture the nature of kinship relations would prove to be consequential.

FAMILY AND KINSHIP IN BETHNAL GREEN

Young and Willmott's *Family and Kinship in East London* (1957) was published a year after Firth's *Two Studies of Kinship*. The book took up many of Firth's findings and made the role of mothers in working-class families even more central. Furthermore, Young and Willmott related kinship more clearly than Firth had done to the politics of the welfare state and to debates within the post-war Labour Party.[45] The result was a resounding success by any standard, let alone for an academic monograph. The discovery of an urban 'village' of face-to-face community existing in the heart of London has delighted hundreds of thousands of readers since the book's first publication.

Part of *Family and Kinship*'s immediate impact resulted from Young and Willmott's strident challenge to a tradition of urban social investigation that tended to portray working-class Londoners as slum-dwelling masses huddled in poor conditions in need of philanthropic uplift. In their hands, the terraces, streets and 'turnings' of Bethnal Green were fixed in a new paradigm: the 'traditional working class neighbourhood', a shorthand that spread throughout British and American sociology in the 1960s to become a widespread social scientific, and even popular, idea during that decade.[46] Scholars have recently outlined the debt both men owed to social anthropology. It is the task of this section to further explicate the connections between their ideal of the 'traditional working class neighbourhood' and their anthropological methods.

Family and Kinship was one of the most cited works of British sociology published in the 1950s, beaten into second place only by Bott's *Family and Social Network*, published in the same year. (I discuss Bott's work later.)[47] *Family and Kinship* had an undoubtedly larger impact beyond the academy, though, where it was waved around in Parliament by MPs on both sides of the House, and in its 1962 reprint, it formed a key part of the culture associated with the new Pelican-reading public.[48] Its main political lesson was, to put it baldly, that the family should form the outer (or inner) limit of state planning. Social engineering, Willmott and Young inveighed, must follow the contours of family life or risk generating anomie rather than utopia. These ideas echoed Malinowski's theories about the mother and child discussed in the previous chapter. In fact, Malinowski's influence was more direct than that, providing an exemplar for Young of how to apply social science to contemporary concerns. In a funding application written by Young in 1954, he asked: 'Will Malinowski sit down with Rowntree? Will the interest of anthropologists in the advance of fundamental social theory mix with the interests of sociologists in policy and practice?'[49] The Ford Foundation officers were intrigued and offered £70,000 to find out, and the Institute of Community Studies was born.

Analysing what Young meant by 'fundamental social theory' makes the connections between the community studies tradition and social anthropology clearer still. These connections can be readily seen in the 1957 first edition of *Family & Kinship*. But the book's anthropological inheritances have to be dug out from the mass-market edition on closer reading. One reason the 1962 edition's anthropological references are harder to spot is the chopped down scholarly apparatus. Excised from the second edition are references to a 1955 article by Bott, 'Urban Families, Conjugal Roles and Social Networks' (this was the first footnote in the first chapter and included the statement that Bott's interviews had been 'far more searching than the ones we were able to do').[50] Also cut were references to Edward Evans-Pritchard's *Kinship and Marriage among the Nuer* (1951), Firth's *We, the Tikopia* (1936), Meyer Fortes's *The Dynamics of Clanship among the Tallensi* (1945) and his *The Web of Kinship among the Tallensi* (1949), Malinowski's *The Sexual Life of Savages* (1929), Mead's *Male and Female* (1949), George Murdock's *Social Structure* (1949), and Audrey Richards's essay 'Some Types of Family Structure Amongst the Central Bantu' (1950).

Surprisingly, this general shortening of scholarly apparatus has led (if we exclude Young's own publications and government reports) to the cited anthropological works going *up* as a percentage of the total when compared to the 1957 bibliography: from 29 to 35 percent. But in absolute terms, the number of references to anthropological works (those canonical monographs and essays listed previously) drops by nine. As a result, the formation of the traditional working-class neighbourhood via the techniques of social anthropology is harder to recognise.

The Pelican edition was, for whatever reason (perhaps to keep costs down), lopped at both ends. The bibliography was shortened, and Richard Titmuss's low-temperature introduction did not make it out of the first edition. Titmuss had critically remarked on the book's 'impressionistic flavour' and called into question its scholarly rigour, stating that conceptual difficulties in presenting the material were 'resolved, to put it simply, to favour readability.'[51] To put it less simply, and perhaps more clearly, the conceptual slippages that resulted from Young and Willmott's use of anthropological concepts are still there in the 1962 book but are left for the clued-up reader to sleuth for themselves.

Family and Kinship overlaid geometric space, kinship relations and economic activity in ways that Firth thought was appropriate for Tikopia but had found impossible to square in Bermondsey. Part of this might be to do with locale. The studies were of different neighbourhoods, after all. Perhaps Bethnal Green possessed more Tikopia-like characteristics than Bermondsey? There is also a difference in scale between Firth's work and the work of Young and Willmott at the Institute for Community Studies. The LSE group studied a block of flats. Their methods broke down under the mass of material. Young and Willmott did their fieldwork in a much larger urban area but were nevertheless able to come up with generalizable conclusions. This should make us suspicious. As we will see, questions of scale, space and normative versus statistical reasoning plague the book's findings and skew the way its readers are encouraged to envision the community being described.

The density of connections in Bethnal Green was the primary object of study. Young and Willmott asked their subjects about the frequency of family visits and the distance between the houses of married couples and their parents. The result was that two out of three of those interviewed had parents who lived within two or three miles of their own homes.[52] We are not told where the other one-third lived. Two to three miles is a long way, especially through busy London streets. It might take up to an hour to walk that far with small children in tow. Young and Willmott seem to have found something similar to Firth's sketched diagram: a large box with smaller boxes inside. The data is represented, however, in a table listing only those whose parents live in Bethnal Green. *Family and Kinship* focuses on the innermost group of close family connections, gradually normalizing this rescaling of the sample so that by the end of the first section – with its discussion of urban 'villages' of '100 or 200 people' – we have in mind these particular relations as if they were normative, rather than statistical. We do not think of the one-third with kin outside the two to three miles or, indeed, of those whose kin lived within that radius but outside the small cluster of nearby streets (as the crow flies, a three-mile radius from Bethnal Green tube station encompasses areas as far afield as Lower Holloway, Clerkenwell and the Elephant and Castle: hardly a village!).

So too did Willmott and Young use temporal compressions to construct the bounds of their community. Like Firth, they were interested in the connections between fathers' and sons' occupations. This is discussed in the book as part of the phenomenon of 'speaking for'. Practical mutual aid was achieved by parents 'speaking for' their children, or for their 'kindred' more generally, in the hope of securing social services. Thus the 'large round mother' with 'slim and anxious daughter behind her' had more power with informal rent collectors than with the government functionaries at the Housing Office.[53] State authorities, with their bureaucratic procedures, took little account of kinship ties. The same seemed to go for jobs, or at least, the authors suggest, it used to. During the Great Depression, they write, families were able to secure work for their relatives, meaning that 'the kindred constituted an informal union within the formal trade union structure.'[54] While the connections between fathers and sons had frayed considerably since the 1930s, 'the mothers represent tradition', and this had apparently prevailed.[55]

Through these slippages of time and telescopings of scale, Young and Willmott constructed in their reader's mind the 'village' of Bethnal Green, filled with rich connections between residents, especially women. The book contains no maps or diagrams, but the front cover of the Pelican edition gave a sense of the argument: a man looking at a group of women, two holding babies. The women and children form the centre of the drama, separated, in this case, from an older man who is making a face at the children, or perhaps leering at the women, perhaps both, while the latter get on with talking and caretaking.

In comments later in life, Young admitted that he may have drawn from rather untypical cases a picture of a false social totality (in a 1994 interview he said that he had 'generally lied in a small way' about being surprised at finding extended networks of kin in Bethnal Green).[56] This admission demands that we put his idea of 'community' in question, and recent studies have argued that it is almost impossible to separate Young's sociological research from his political beliefs.[57] Young had been a part of the wartime think tank Political and Economic Planning and had written Labour's 1945 election manifesto. During Labour's time in office, however, he had become increasingly frustrated with top-down approaches to governing. He worried about the dangers of the 'bigness' associated with large-scale social engineering. He worried about 'bigness' because he saw a fundamental tension between the intimate communal needs of individual human beings and the economies of scale and centralized organisation demanded by the modern state.[58] In contrast to the potentially dehumanizing actions of the welfare state, his construction of community was a paean to 'smallness'. And what would have seemed a more attractive alternative to 'bigness' than social anthropologists' accounts of a plurality of small, self-organising societies, each existing without a state?

Young was part of a growing chorus of anti-statist voices on the left that was swiftly joined by Conservative MPs like Keith Joseph touting the findings of *Family and Kinship* as a critique of 'bigness' too.[59] Under the hawkish eyes of Joseph, the 'tenement buildings standing guard, like dark fortresses, over the little houses' that Young had employed to stand in for social-reform-done-badly must have seemed like a synecdoche for the menaces of state-sponsored planning in general, and Joseph quoted *Family and Kinship* in speeches at the House of Commons to make his case.[60] The political upshot of the book's argument was that the 'improvement' of peoples' lives by 'slum' clearance was bound to destroy the community ties of the residents. On the book's last page Young and Willmott made a plea to protect the 'spirit' of community found in places like Bethnal Green and urged planners to 'build the new houses around the social groups where they already belong.'[61]

Family and Kinship did not invent this 'spirit'. Young and Willmott clearly found evidence of the families they wanted to find; the tables and relatively large sample size support their case. But the slippages between norms and numbers mean that we should read the book with some circumspection. After all, Firth had concluded that he and his students 'had of necessity to break up the field' in order to study it – and could not find the kind of regularity presumed to exist in societies like that on Tikopia.[62] By reinserting this regularity, the 'traditional working class neighbourhood' as a sociological shorthand was born; Young and Willmott created it.[63] While the political context of mid-1950s Britain is crucial to understand the particular argumentative thrust of *Family and Kinship*, its main contention – that community was located in space and connected by kinship ties – was only available *as an argument* because of social anthropology.

Young and Willmott not only drew on anthropological theory but also presented early drafts of their work at Firth's seminar at the LSE, where their time with the anthropologists changed the terms in which they analysed their material.[64] The relationship between Young and Firth was strained, however. As we have seen, in the book's second edition an acknowledgment of Firth's help and advice was cut. This scholarly slight led to decades of resentment on Firth's part. Perhaps the appearance of

Two Studies so soon before Young and Willmott's book was the result of Firth's rush to get his findings out before the Young Turks stole the limelight. As it turned out, his efforts were in vain. Young and Willmott's bravura display of politicised social science emerged to great fanfare at a particularly propitious time. And the cutting down of the scholarly apparatus excised many of the clear references to social anthropology from their intervention. Young's subsequent disavowal of Firth's influence and Firth's apparent rage at this sleight further elided the extent of the overlap in *Family and Kinship* with contemporary LSE anthropology, an elision that has also marked our understanding of the subject of the next section of this chapter, race relations sociology.

KENNETH LITTLE AND 'RACE RELATIONS' SOCIOLOGY

While Firth and Young and Willmott were doing their research in London, a new generation of anthropologists-cum-sociologists were carrying out pioneering community studies of a different kind in Edinburgh. These researchers of 'race relations' wrote a cluster of important monographs in the 1950s and 1960s, including Michael Banton's *The Coloured Quarter* (1955) and *White and Coloured* (1959), Sydney Collins's *Coloured Minorities in Britain* (1957) and Sheila Patterson's *Dark Strangers* (1963), while in London, Ruth Glass's *Newcomers* (1960) and Pearl Jephcott's *A Troubled Area* (1964) were part of a different but cognate trend.[65]

The study of 'race relations' in British towns and cities was strongly associated with the University of Edinburgh, where a student of Firth's, Kenneth Little, took over the anthropology department in 1950. Little's own study of Tiger Bay in Cardiff had begun as a PhD project at the LSE under Firth's supervision. It was published in 1947 as *Negroes in Britain: A Study of Racial Relations in English Society*. This book has been read as a British offshoot of the Chicago School of urban sociology because he drew on Chicago sociology's tradition of understanding cities in terms of habitats and ecology.[66] American sociology offered a way of thinking about racial difference as a matter of culture and of homogenous 'in' and 'out' groups.[67] Social investigation of city populations and a sense of shock at urban living conditions had longer antecedents, however: a recognisable trope of writing on social reform stretching at least as far back as the Victorian era. The urban poor and destitute were often described in terms of civilisation, of savagery and barbarism, either as analogues or as part of a theory of racial degeneracy or, indeed, immutable difference.[68]

A more proximate, and likely decisive, influence on Little's work was the anthropological training he had done at the LSE.[69] His research there took social anthropology in a new direction by linking urbanization in Africa with race relations in Britain.[70] Little had also been amongst the field researchers on Firth's project in Bermondsey.[71] But unlike Firth in Bermondsey or Young and Willmott in Bethnal Green, he thought that studying history was crucial to explain the community he was observing. The prejudice faced by Black men and women in Cardiff, he argued, could not be understood without taking account of Britain's long history of imperialism. Britain's history of slaving, conquest and jingoism had created a widely dispersed visual and literary culture of stereotyped inferiority that was applied to people of African descent.[72]

Studying history did not mean that Little had become less of an anthropologist. Nor did the fact that he studied British society rather than a culture overseas mean that he had left behind his disciplinary training. He incorporated these approaches in his new anthropology curriculum when he arrived at Edinburgh from the LSE. In 1951–52 the 'ordinary course' on social anthropology at Edinburgh contained a 'part I' that included many familiar names from previous chapters of this book, from Firth and Malinowski to Mair and Fortes and Evans-Pritchard. He changed 'part II', however, from a course on 'culture contact' that had been taught by his predecessor, another student of Firth's, Ralph Piddington, to a course on 'anthropology and modern life', in which Little set Conrad Arensberg's *The Irish Countryman* (1937), Robert Lowie's *Are We Civilized?* (1929) and Helen and Robert Lynds' *Middletown* (1929) as part of his students' reading.[73]

Outside the classroom, Little extended his interests in 'anthropology and modern life' by applying for grants from the Nuffield Foundation and the Buxton Trust. He and his students and colleagues sought to study the experience of students from British colonies in metropolitan universities. Eyo Bassey N'Dem and Violaine Junod did fieldwork of this kind. Michael Banton was granted money to do research on the 'coloured quarter' in Stepney, and Sydney Collins won a Carnegie Trust grant to study in Tyneside.[74] Little's own contribution to applied research focused on the working of the colour bar in Britain via the prevalence of racism amongst landlords and landladies and the importance of challenging stereotypes in the press and in educational institutions.[75]

His research on race and racism had begun in a very different manner, however. Ten years before his appointment at Edinburgh, Little had worked as a physical anthropologist and an anatomy demonstrator at

Cambridge. In 1941 he published an article in the *Eugenics Review* with the title 'The Study of Racial Mixture in the British Commonwealth'. Little took the opportunity to dispel some myths about the biological basis of race and urged that there 'can in no sense be any idea of racial "purity" attaching itself to the individual' and that 'differences in mentality' were not 'scientifically demonstrable' between groups, drawing on the research of Franz Boas.[76] He wrote as an anthropologist about questions of human difference and similarity, but rather than apply the methods of social anthropology, his techniques at Cambridge were statistical and his vision was global and departicularising rather than local and ethnographic.

This was very different to the work he promoted as department chair in Edinburgh. Part of the explanation must lie in the experience of studying for his PhD with Firth at the LSE. When he wrote up this PhD dissertation as a book in 1947 he had moved away from statistics and population studies and was applying himself to a recognisable form of social anthropological research based on intensive observation of a community in a limited locale. He finished his PhD in 1944, at the same time that Firth returned to the LSE and when he would subsequently send his students out to Bermondsey. These studies should be seen as part of the same research program.

In the same spirit as Firth's review of MO from 1939, Little wrote in *Negroes in Britain* that his intention was to 'draw the attention of anthropologists in this country in concrete terms to the possibilities of applying their discipline more positively to the study of urban society.'[77] But unlike Firth or Young or Willmott, Little made a 'plea, also for scientific attention to be given to the study of racial relations (or group relations, if the generic term be preferred) in its own right.'[78] And unlike in his *Eugenics Review* article of 1941, Little applied himself to studying 'race relations' or 'group relations' via ethnographic fieldwork, rather than genes and heredity, focusing on intergroup *behaviour* rather than intergroup difference, on race *relations* rather than race per se.

In a methodological introduction he explained that in many cities there were quarters and sections that were inhabited as 'racial colonies', small subgroups often limited to households or interhousehold association with a more limited relation with neighbouring districts.[79] This small space and its inhabitants might be conducive to field research. But attempting to narrow a large, modern city into a limited field for intensive study was difficult. Even in the case of the 'racial colony', 'such communities, it might be argued, are fundamentally different from those conventionally dealt with by the anthropologist in a pre-literate society' or those studying a 'peasant group'. This is because in cities 'individual aims tend to be thought of vocationally rather than socially; experience is the product of diverse and often conflicting opportunities, and, above all, personal values and incentives are often based on sanctions unacceptable to the consanguineous or immediate social group.'[80]

Kenneth Little packed a lot into that terse sentence. Several things should be noted. First, he was interested in values and aims, much in the same way as Malinowski and Firth. Second, unlike their studies of island communities in the Pacific, he felt that he could not extrapolate from a social role what expectations any individual might have. Third, in fact, an individual's values and incentives and aims may be unacceptable and inimical to close kin to an extent that would have been destabilising in a smaller scale society. Nevertheless, the family, he thought, should be considered the basic structure of society; it was the institution that most 'produc[ed] and exercise[ed] social cohesion.'[81] This repeated emphasis on the centrality of the family is a now familiar refrain of post-Malinowskian community study in Britain and of a piece with Firth's research in Bermondsey. Studying these families would mean reversing the procedure promoted by A. F. Wells in his *The Local Social Survey in Great Britain* (1935), Little argued. The subjects of anthropological study should be known to the anthropologist, and the social researcher should even take part in their everyday lives, in direct contrast to the more distant social survey tradition.[82] This is a familiar technique from the discussion of Richards, Mair and Read in chapter 3, and he approvingly cited Richards's essay on field research in F. C. Bartlett's *Study of Society* as an example of his own method.

The application of social anthropology to the study of 'race relations' in Britain has been the subject of some strong criticism. Little has, however, sometimes been read more sympathetically than his student Michael Banton. When Little wrote about Cardiff he noted the importance of class analysis when discussing the interrelation of Black and white Britons and for setting his analysis of race relations in terms of the history of racist attitudes.[83] Banton, on the other hand, has been accused of naturalising a supposed propensity for certain groups (themselves supposed to be homogenous) to treat so-called outsiders as strangers and react to other groups in a hostile manner. In the hands of his most stringent critics, this tendency has been equated with the thought of the post-war New Right, who posited a quasi-functionalist model of national identity that migrants were imagined to interrupt and threaten.[84]

Little's research was certainly not motivated by this sort of concern. As he wrote, 'My attitude is affected by sympathy for the victims of this prejudice and by a considerable amount of irritation with the ideas and factors which underlie it.'[85] Despite some criticism of race relations sociology, this was an attitude that was widespread amongst this diverse group of researchers, whose political biases were, on the whole, resolutely anti-racist and some of whom, like Sydney Collins and Eyo Bassey N'dem, were Black and presumably faced the humiliations and exclusions of the British colour bar.[86] Nevertheless, a tendency to naturalise the functioning of 'in-groups' and 'out-groups' was prevalent in contemporary anthropological writings on race. This was a view shared by many social anthropologists in the post-war decades, such as Max Gluckman, who took to the airwaves via the BBC to discuss racism as a purportedly natural expression of hostility to supposed outsiders.[87]

Little did not subscribe to these ideas that naturalised 'in-group' and 'out-group' identification, and later commentators have lamented the fact that British social scientists tended to ignore his fusion of history and sociology and his emphasis on class and prejudice and racism.[88] Little's influence was diminished by the fact that he never produced the kind of seminar culture that Malinowski had created or that post-war anthropology's charismatic patriarchs like Gluckman, Evans-Pritchard and Leach reproduced in Manchester, Oxford and Cambridge. And after a few publications on race relations in Britain, Little's research interests moved to the study of urbanization in West Africa. In time Banton, rather than Little, became the doyen of British race relations sociology, and Little's work had a relatively small impact on social anthropology from the 1960s onwards.[89] Outside the academy, meanwhile, the Institute of Race Relations sprang up, with a decidedly patrician approach to what it saw as the problems of 'integration'. Both Little and Firth cast a suspicious eye on its workings.[90] Social anthropologists in the 1950s and 1960s did not generally work on racism or its sociological causes. And those who did, like Gluckman and some of his Manchester School colleagues, seem to have had little, if any, conversations with Little at Edinburgh about how to theorise racism or the impact of imperialism and colonialism on Britain's social structures.[91]

So while Little did have some small impact at Edinburgh, his influence on the tradition of community studies was less marked than Young and Willmott's and less decisive than Banton's influence on race relations sociology. He did, however, recognisably take forward the Malinowskian intention to apply anthropological techniques to a modern district or town. And like Young and Willmott and Firth, Little grappled with a series of fundamental issues in the process: How do you go about applying ethnographic methods that presume social homogeneity onto a diverse urban population subject to a high degree of division of labour? How do you, as Firth put it, 'break up' the field?

ELIZABETH BOTT AND THE BIRTH OF SOCIAL NETWORK ANALYSIS

The thinker who, perhaps more than any other, thought through these issues, and perhaps even transcended them was Elizabeth Bott. Her notion of the 'social network' allowed her to abstract from geographical space to social space and to explain the connections amongst people spread over a dispersed and variegated urban landscape. Once again a key contribution of 1950s social science, often subsumed wholly into the history of sociology, like the community studies of Michael Young or race relations research, emerged out of the productive application of anthropological methods in urban Britain.[92]

Bott's work was one of the references that had been cut from the 1962 Pelican edition of Young and Willmott's *Family and Kinship*, and Young and Willmott described her interviews as 'far more searching than the ones we were able to do.'[93] Bott's influence did, however, stretch to the book's terminology. Young and Willmott borrowed the idea of the 'network' from her. It was a new concept with a particular meaning, but in *Family and Kinship* it was misapplied, taken to mean 'all the kin recognised as such by any given person.'[94] In short, it meant merely, in Firth's terms, the 'nominal relations' of an individual dressed up in new packaging. Bott meant something different.

The concept of the 'network' in the hands of Bott allowed her to blast through the difficulties Firth, Little and Young and Willmott had all run into as they attempted to map social space onto geometric space. The network was a metaphor that connected space in an unbounded way. Solidarity might exist at long distances; strong networks might not map onto neighbourly proximity. Furthermore, the tightness or looseness of a network – rather than the connections within a particular locale – might be analysed to see if network density could be correlated with other aspects of a person's social life.

Bott had come to London in 1949 to work at the LSE as an anthropologist. She was a lecturer there for two years. She then moved to the Tavistock Institute to do further research. While working at the

Tavistock, Bott began researching the lives of twenty 'ordinary families'. She had come to many of the same conclusions about the importance of mothers as had Firth, Young and Willmott. But she reckoned with the difficulty of applying functionalist methods to British subjects in ways that they didn't.

In November 1954 she presented her initial findings at Firth's anthropology seminar at the LSE. The discussion notes do not make for very positive reading. Her study was criticised for its lack of emphasis on 'community'. Her twenty families were spread all over London, and as a result she was criticised for failing to adequately delimit her 'field'. By contrast, the sociologist Peter Townsend's paper, presented at the same seminar, was lauded for its focus on a particular location and the relations within it.[95] Bott had been butting up against the problem of representativeness and the difficulty of getting sufficient participants since beginning her study. In her PhD prospectus, which she sent to Firth for comment, she listed under the 'disadvantages' of her study: 'no study of the real environment; environment seen from the perspective of the families, except for material provided by contact agencies and their relations with families'; 'a great deal of interviewing but relatively little observation'; and 'difficulties of access, hence of studying a large number of families by this method.'[96]

She was confronted with a relatively few, highly detailed interview transcripts and a brief to combine the interests of her colleagues at the Tavistock Institute with her own anthropological methods. At Firth's seminar there is no evidence that she had achieved the methodological breakthrough that would appear in print almost exactly a year later. How were the families she studied related to the wider social structure? How could one avoid, or better, how *could*, one generalize from particular cases to broader trends? And how did the data she had collected fit with the ideas of class, culture and motherhood Young had presented in Firth's seminar a year before?

Bott's breakthrough came sometime between her dispiriting appearance at the LSE in 1954 and the publication of her article 'Urban Families: Conjugal Role and Social Networks' (1955). The argument represents a considerable advance on the handling of the questions Firth, Little, Young and Wilmott all shared. Bott's key insight lay in placing the family in a larger set of relations, but to divorce these relations from a necessary connection to locale. She put this like this: 'The immediate social environment of urban families is best considered not as a local area in which they live, but rather as the network of actual social relationships they maintain, regardless of whether these are confined to the local area or run beyond its boundaries.'[97] It is worth remembering that *Two Studies* and *Family and Kinship* presented the family in some connection with a broader social structure that was presumed to be anchored in a bounded space. This social structure was a system of social reciprocity. It was influenced by the functionalist idea of culture that had been first advanced by Malinowski and designed to study island communities and supposedly 'primitive' tribes. Young and Willmott presented their Bethnal Green families in much the same manner. By contrast to his writing on Tikopia, Firth saw that this clearly would not do. *Family and Kinship*, however, conveniently underplayed these problems. Bott's contribution to this theoretical logjam was to reject its terms and move beyond them.

The idea, which came to her, she said, as if it had 'floated into my head from nowhere,' was to abstract away from the tie between space and community.[98] Bott's move was to introduce the idea of the 'network' into her analysis. She landed on this insight at the same time as another anthropologist, John Barnes, who was similarly trying to make the tools of social anthropology work in a locale with a high degree of variation and division of labour. Barnes's 1954 article 'Class and Committees in a Norwegian Parish' is an ethnography of the parish of Bremnes on Norway's west coast. It details the existence of two fields, the 'fluid' and the 'stationary'. The fluid field exists when men step on board the fishing boats in the harbour, entering an industry that stretches from their villages around the world. The stationary social field refers to the relatively immobile fixtures of houses and interpersonal relations on land, which contain, of course, a gendered assumption about the fixity of women's domestic labour in the household. As in Bott's study, the concept of the network allowed Barnes to explicate a multidimensional field that could capture the complexity of the villagers' social relations. The network was not a 'totality', as it had no clear external boundaries and its densities and dimensions looked different from each person's position within it. The 'network' also allowed him to recast the distinction between the 'primitive' and the 'modern'. So-called primitive societies tended to have networks with tighter 'mesh'.[99] This meant that the relationship of any individual A with B, and B with C (moving outwards) would likely result in C knowing A too. The key was to pay attention to the density of connections. In a looser mesh, odds are that if A knew B who knew C, C would not know A.

What all of this meant for Bott's data can most easily be grasped by the diagram she provided in her 1955 article (see figure 3). Bott had

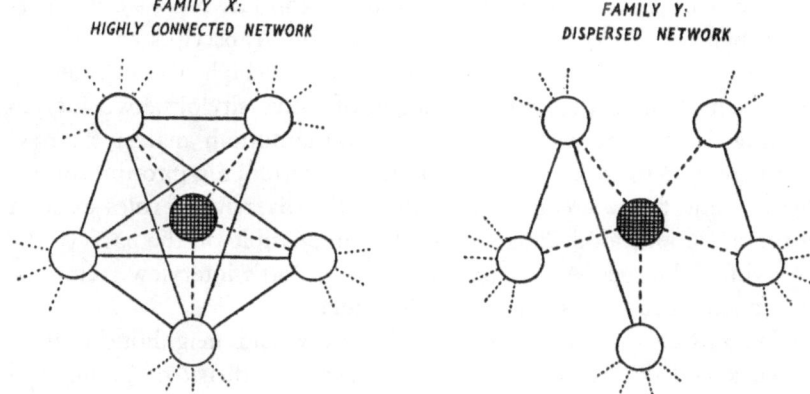

FIGURE 3. Diagram of a social network. *Source:* Elizabeth Bott, 'Urban Families: Conjugal Roles and Social Networks', *Human Relations*, 8.4 (1955), 345–84. Reproduced with permission from SAGE Publishing (and the journal *Human Relations*).

been criticized for her inability to grasp the *total* relations of marriage partners in a particular neighbourhood in 1954. This failure proved to be the spur to her greatest success. In a similar way to Barnes, she disaggregated the relationship between locale and community and began to pay attention to the density of connections between men, women and other groups regardless of their spatial location. What she found on closer inspection made her reputation.

Bott discovered that families with greater 'network connectedness' tended to go along with a greater segregation of 'conjugal roles' in the household.[100] The denser the mesh, the more likely the husband's and wife's division of labour would be distinct. In families with loose networks, men and women were more likely to have joint conjugal roles, spending leisure time together, sharing more domestic labour and seeing their marriage as a common project. The looseness and tightness of networks was correlated with class, but it was not *determined* by it. The reasons for network density were infinitely various, related, but not limited to, mobility, occupation, religion, and, perhaps most importantly, personality and psychological disposition.

The failure to explain this diversity was what made Firth's and Young and Willmott's studies unsatisfying. They were unable to account for variation and so had provided incomplete, or oversimplified, analyses of their data, taking statistical findings for norms. In Bott's terms, some of the families in *Family and Kinship* display the classic hallmarks of high network density. Similarly, the crux of Jon Lawrence's critical reassessment of Young and Willmott's interview transcripts can be said to contrast the purported homogeneity of these high network-density families in Bethnal Green with evidence of a diversity of network types existing side by side with each other.[101] To the Bottian analyst, the next step would be to seek to understand this variation, dig into the contradictions and try to create an account of the diversity of roles existing in the neighbourhood. This may well be impossible on the basis of the surviving fieldnotes. As Young pointed out, Bott's interview technique was much more sophisticated than his own.

The upshot of moving from community and neighbourhood to network and density was to reset the narrative thrust of Young and Willmott's findings. A denser network provided a huge help to many residents of Bethnal Green, especially to young mothers who could rely on mutual aid with childcare. The flipside of high density was a concomitant increase in 'social control', however. Mothers may have appreciated the help of family members and neighbours, but they were subject to levels of gossip and surveillance that could be stifling; amidst these networks 'one has to put up with being included in the gossip . . . no gossip, no companionship,' Bott concluded.[102] So too did women face the possibilities of disastrous dependence on men. One of Bott's informants, Mrs N., is the ideal-type high network-density wife. Her appreciation of her husband's generosity with her weekly allowance is marked, as is her happiness that her mother and husband have a good relationship. Both of these crucial aspects of Mrs N's life are described in terms that foreground the ultimately underdetermined good luck of things having worked out this way.

Much of the criticism of *Family and Kinship* has justifiably been aimed at the rose-tinted portrayal it gives of grandmothers, mothers and daughters. An emphasis on luck would make a sharper intervention. Dense networks might provide satisfying conditions for those psychologically amenable to high density and lucky enough to have a kind husband and a good relationship with their mother and mother-in-law. For those women who did not thrive in such compact social groups and were not so lucky with parents and/or mate, the experience of places like Bethnal Green would be very different. The advantages of a loose network consisted in relative freedom from the social control that generally goes along with a tighter network mesh. Sex would likely be different too.

Between partners like Mr and Mrs N it was difficult to ascertain but, Bott hypothesized, 'it seems likely that she [Mrs N.] felt that physical sexuality was an intrusion on a peaceful domestic relationship rather than an expression of such a relationship; it was as if sexuality were felt to be basically violent and disruptive.'[103] Sex between couples with more joint roles, we can surmise, might have been more equal, or at least have had the potential to be. However, Bott also worried about something lurking under the surface of her loose-network interviewees' responses: 'In some cases one almost got the feeling that these husbands and wives felt a moral obligation to enjoy sexual relations, a feeling not expressed or suggested by the Ns.'[104] Regardless, the possibility of more equal sex and less social control was experienced as a boon. On the other hand, the extra workload faced by young mothers with dispersed networks was marked. Amongst the type at the opposite end of the density gradient to Mrs N, all the women expressed the fact that the amount of work devoted to childcare thwarted opportunities to advance careers and the pursuit of personal interests. The advantages and disadvantages of varying network density were clearly explicated. Bott's findings do not lend themselves to reversing the negative view of *Family and Kinship*. Rather, she offered a nuanced analysis of mobility, class and family that presented pay-offs as well as benefits to moving between denser and looser networks, especially for women stuck at home looking after children.

Bott had managed to cut through a knot of methodological complexity with her analyses of role and network. This new approach allowed her to escape the vexed relations between conceptions of geometric, social and familial space that dogged her contemporaries. A recent commentator has written that 'to understand [Bott's] work we should not see her as a nascent sociologist or anthropologist so much as a core Tavistock researcher and loyalist.'[105] Which is all very well, but Bott described herself throughout the 1950s as an anthropologist, not as a 'Tavistock loyalist', and in the two years between 'arriving in London' and beginning work at the Tavistock, she taught social anthropology at the LSE in Firth's department as a lecturer.

However, there were clear signs that professional, if not methodological, divisions were hardening at this time. In 1952 Bott sent a letter to Gluckman resigning from the Association of Social Anthropologists. It was not due to any difference in approach that she was resigning. Indeed, she wrote that she adhered to 'a body of theory and research techniques characteristic of anthropologists,' meaning that her 'basic sociological theory is the same and much of the research is similar.' It was her lack of research in a 'primitive society' and her decision not to pursue a career as an anthropologist that led her to resign her membership.[106] Again, in a letter sent to Firth she wrote, 'I find I have to talk to anthropologists occasionally; they are really the only social scientists in England, in that they test a sociological theory by studying social groups as wholes.' Her Tavistock colleagues, she avers, 'do that too, but the sociological theory is a bit different.'[107] When Gluckman wrote the preface to the second edition of *Family and Social Network*, on Bott's invitation, he cast the book as a classic of social anthropology, not sociology.[108]

In his book *Identities and Social Change*, Mike Savage argued that post-war sociology had only become 'modern' by escaping the 'gentlemanly' methods of social anthropology. Regardless of the misapprehension that Mair, Richards, Read and other women did 'gentlemanly' social science, the centrality of Bott to Savage's history of sociology, and the fact that Bott was a social anthropologist, mean that we must recast his narrative. The shift he discerns can now be understood as the waning of a broadly functionalist ethnography to one based on social networks. This was an intradisciplinary transformation brought about by social anthropologists like Gluckman and Bott and Barnes. If we wish to tell a convincing history of post-war sociology, therefore, we must reinsert the social anthropologists into the narrative and see that the pertinent differences between the disciplines were not so much methodological but, as Bott wrote to Gluckman, increasingly a matter of where one happened to do one's research: sociology in Britain, social anthropology elsewhere.

CONCLUSION

All of the writers discussed in this chapter tried to coax their readers to *see* the 'society' they were studying. That 'society' existed in some relationship with 'culture' was a relatively novel idea, drawn from the works that Young and Willmott cited in the 1957 version of *Family and Kinship*: Malinowski, Evans-Pritchard, Fortes and Richards. This chapter has reconstructed a moment when anthropologists applied these concepts to British society.

Ever since, the anthropological invocation to think of culture as a 'whole way of life' and as 'ordinary', to quote a Raymond Williams essay from 1958, has inspired generations of post-war British social scientists and humanists.[109] The contrast between the anthropologists' 'ordinary' concept and earlier ideas that 'culture' was a matter of refined taste and a hierarchy of value goes some way to explaining the anthropologists' popularity in an era of growing egalitarianism and diminishing deference.[110] If the culture of the middle and upper classes were deemed to be 'reasonable' and 'rational', so too could the lives of the working classes be understood to be their own sphere of dignified social action. If working-class Londoners and Black men and women in Cardiff had culture, so too might Britons of the past have had it. How did cultures change, and how might that process be linked to the modernizing trends of the contemporary world? These questions were posed most extensively by anthropologists in the British Empire. The next two chapters take up the story begun earlier in this book about anthropology and colonialism and carry forward an emphasis on shifting patterns of patronage associated with institution building and funding for the social sciences.

CHAPTER 6

The Development Decades

The African Survey, *the CSSRC and
Three Approaches to Social Anthropology
in the British Empire, 1935–1955*

This chapter explains how the growing demand for 'development' in the British Empire affected social anthropology between the mid-1930s and the mid-1950s. My aim is to show how imperial histories intersected with anthropology's institutional development and how wider developments in the discipline framed anthropologists' willingness to advise and influence policy. As told in chapters 1, 2 and 3, during the 1920s and early 1930s social anthropologists did not have much power individually to shape or direct colonial policy. Any influence they did have came from their alliances with imperial grandees and from their ability to create and sustain institutions within which their expertise could be reproduced. During the decades under discussion here, anthropologists certainly saw their influence grow. This took place in the context of a wider transformation of the Colonial Service, which began large research programs in agriculture, geology and soil science during the 1930s, a turn to expertise that was capped by the *African Survey* (1938), written by Lord Hailey.[1] In the social sciences, psychologists became increasingly interested in questions of colonial administration and debated the validity of cross-cultural intelligence tests and the social bases of cognition.[2] Economists, for their part, largely steered clear of questions of colonial development.[3] So it was left principally to the anthropologists, especially those at Malinowski's seminar at the London School of Economics (LSE), to study the impact of British administration on colonised peoples.[4]

While a technocratic push for development began in the 1930s, the Second World War dramatically raised the stakes of these studies. A wartime crisis gave new force to the emergent politics of 'development' in the wake of crushing debts, interrupted trade, destroyed capital stock and the deaths of millions of men and women. Anti-colonial rebellions were growing, and in 1947 India, hitherto the garrison of British imperial power east of Suez, declared independence. In this atmosphere, and with US loans to repay, the rest of the empire, especially in Africa and Southeast Asia, was seen by successive British governments after 1945 as a source of raw materials with which to pay down post-war debts.[5] Even though this exploitative context was obvious to many, British politicians, experts and administrators sought to persuade international public opinion that the British Empire and Commonwealth was a 'multiracial partnership' led by Britain for the mutual benefit of all its subjects. This coincided with an almost total repudiation in Whitehall of the revanchist white settler supremacy discussed in chapter 2 that had been associated in the interwar decades with Jan Smuts and Leo Amery.[6] Rather, administrators tended to favour development that focused on peasant-led farming under the aegis of agricultural planning and technical assistance. 'Development' in the 1940s and 1950s went along with an attempt to represent Britain's imperial project as a rational, planned exercise in spreading the 'Westminster' model of representative government overseas and the purported uplift of the peoples of the empire.[7] With enough 'development', officials patronisingly proposed, Britain's colonies might be able to 'achieve' independence.

This led to a fundamental realignment in thinking about the colonies and their terms of trade, which in turn had a knock-on effect on the academic social sciences. This chapter and the subsequent one explain how anthropological expertise became valuable in this era, how it was eclipsed by economics and how anthropologists differed over how and whether to advise the colonial state. The ubiquitous Lord Lugard (introduced in chapter 2) remains in the picture at the outset, but he is joined by new protagonists. Margery Perham, a historian, was an expert on African affairs and a member of Malinowski's seminar at the LSE. Malcolm Hailey, a civil servant and governor in India, is another crucial figure. Malcolm Macdonald, secretary of state for the colonies between 1938 and 1940 and architect of the 1940 Commonwealth Development and Welfare Act (CDWA), makes a brief cameo. These three people would have a large impact on the fortunes of social anthropology in the run-up to the founding of the Colonial Social Science Research Council

(CSSRC) in 1946, which funded many anthropological projects until it was wound up in 1955 and a further set of intellectual and geopolitical changes challenged anthropologists' expertise (as recounted in the next chapter).

The CSSRC funding ended up in the hands of some of Malinowski's most famous students, paying for more fieldwork and helping to set up regional research centres that hosted anthropologists studying government development programs. The cumulative effect was to give social anthropologists in Britain a higher level of prestige and greater self-confidence than they had ever had before and, arguably, ever would have again. This chapter explains how anthropologists allied with Lord Hailey's *African Survey* project and then how three different approaches to colonial development emerged after Malinowski's death in 1942 as his former students quarrelled over the future direction of social anthropology and the inheritance he had bestowed.

HAILEY AND THE *AFRICAN SURVEY*

Students attending Malinowski's seminar on 2 May 1933 heard a paper presented by historian and expert on colonial administration Margery Perham. In her presentation she fantasised about a future in which the LSE would 'multiply Malinowski indefinitely to staff our districts.'[8] A discussion was held a week later, and students at that event sat alongside the former governor of Nigeria and Britain's permanent member of the League of Nations Mandates Commission, Lord Lugard. A transcript of the ensuing discussion exists in the archives of the LSE. In it, Malinowski declared that 'the most interesting point for us anthropologists here is to realise the difficulties of the political officer.' 'The anthropologist,' he went on, 'must often lower the prestige of white people, he must say and do things at the cost of being discreet. And this would not be approved of by government officials.'[9] Such a willingness to court controversy impressed Perham. Hilda Beemer, a twenty-two-year-old South African student and later a prominent anthropologist, disagreed with Malinowski's views, however. She thought that the anthropologist should play a more detached role, stating that 'a government anthropologist is an anomaly.' But Beemer only got this single sentence out before Malinowski cut her off. 'It is futile and a sign of mental laziness,' he snapped, 'if the man of science pretends he can keep away from ethical questions or that he should not state it when his scientific outlook contributes to real welfare of humanity.' After some time speaking, he concluded: 'It is our duty to present these facts. Are we then political or scientific?'[10] Malinowski's question and the context in which it was uttered strikes to the heart of this chapter's discussions of differences over development, expertise and policy advice.

By the late 1930s, Malinowski's seminar at the LSE was attracting students from across the world and across the British Empire, keen to make sense of, and sometimes to challenge, British colonial policy. It was a hub of research and activism, with colonial civil servants (like Lugard) contributing to classroom discussion alongside an increasingly cosmopolitan, multiracial student body. Malinowski's African students included Jomo Kenyatta and Z. K. Matthews. Other attendees were critical of British imperialism, like the African American political scientist and critic of imperialism Ralph Bunche and the anti-colonial activist, actor and academic Eslanda Robeson, as well as many other critics of the British Empire.[11] With an emphasis on applied research and with extensive discussions of colonial policy, Malinowski's seminar has been described as the first school of colonial studies in Britain. Although as one administrator remarked drily after a long discussion of how useful anthropology might be to men like him: 'Expert opinions are not a final criterion in British Government.'[12]

Nevertheless, when the former Indian administrator and civil servant Malcolm Hailey began research for his compendious and influential book *An African Survey: A Study of Problems Arising in Africa South of the Sahara*, it must have seemed natural to rely on the anthropologists at the LSE for a great deal of relevant information and advice. The reams of information quickly became too much for Hailey to handle alone, however. Perham acted as an advisor, and her friend Hilda Matheson became Hailey's secretary, although Matheson's role is better described as the *Survey*'s executive manager.[13] This meant that Malinowski and Malinowski-aligned intermediaries, like Perham, became ever more important to Hailey. The result was the addition of Hailey to the Lugard-Oldham pro-trusteeship network described in chapter 2 and, as a result, a ramification of that network's power and influence.

Part of Hailey's impact came about simply because his *African Survey* ended up being so long. Hailey had planned to write a short book, but in its final form the *Survey* ran to over sixteen hundred pages, ranging over a vast number of topics that administrators could dip in to, from educational provision to soil erosion. In this sense, it mirrored, as well as concentrated, the contemporary turn to scientific expertise in Britain's Empire, with Malinowski's students acting as key intermediaries in this process. For instance, Lucy Mair did most of the writing of the chapter on land tenure. Mair began by arguing that no matter 'is so conspicuously' affected by colonial policy as who owns the land.[14] In her potted history, she wrote that early colonisation was based on 'expropriation . . . designed to place Europeans in a position to exploit their [Africans'] production.' Taking an optimistic view in more recent times, however, Mair stated that 'native rights in land' were increasingly being 'considered on a purely legal,' rather than an economic, basis.[15] Mair's gloss of colonial history occluded contemporary forms of exploitation executed on a vast scale, especially in the settler colonies. Yet the effect of narrating recent history as a transition from expropriation to recognition of rights had clear rhetorical force. By making expropriation merely a stage in the history of colonialism she suggested that the future belonged to a world of secure legal title to land. The economic imperatives of efficiency and production – wherein rights to land depend on the uses towards which it is put – might give way, Mair suggested, to a juridical discourse of universal rights. This would be a legal framework of land and its uses that would escape an instrumentally economising logic: in short, a significant blow for settler-colonial justifications for land use by white farmers and of a piece with notions of trusteeship associated with the Mandates commission of the League of Nations.

Mair's connections to the League of Nations and its ideal of colonial 'trusteeship' proved to be an important point of contact between her and Hailey, who had recently taken over Lugard's role as Britain's representative on the Mandate's commission. And her internationalist ideals explain the pro-trusteeship tenor of her chapter in the *African Survey*. Audrey Richards was also a Hailey informant, and Perham was also sympathetic to the League. Richards was described during her fieldwork in Uganda as being '"closer to Geneva than to Whitehall," an epithet from the white settler community by no means intended as flattery.'[16] Malinowski supported the League, too. When deciding whether to travel to Ohio for a lecture tour in 1930 or travel to Geneva to deliver a series of lectures to be titled 'The Anthropological Approach to International Relations,' Malinowski chose Geneva; this was, as he repeated a number of times to his friend, the classicist and international relations scholar Alfred Zimmern, despite the fact the Americans were offering him $1,500 to speak and the League of Nations was paying him nothing.[17]

These threads of internationalism connecting social anthropologists and their allies are not incidental. Throughout the interwar era, the

League pushed a technical approach to political and economic problems, and the American foundations, like the Rockefellers and the Carnegie Corporation, provided considerable financial resources towards nudging the way these problems would be framed away from settler supremacy (as we saw in chapter 2's discussion of the non-funding of the Oxford Institute in 1931). While the context of metropolitan British policy remains the primary cause for social anthropology's rise to prominence at the LSE, a growing body of internationalist opinion was forming around the idea that colonial rule should cleave to policies of human development rather than settler colonialism and that independence, however far down the road, should be the final end of British rule.[18] Mair's ideas of land tenure accorded with the spirit of trusteeship promoted by the League and by ameliorist imperialists like Oldham, Lugard and Malinowski.[19] Hailey's *Survey* was conceived in a spirit of internationalism, too, funded by the Carnegie Corporation and pitched as a comparative study encompassing all the European powers' policies and territories. The *Survey* promised a new, scientific approach to administration that rejected settler colonialism and discounted racist assumptions about African backwardness and difference.[20]

Hailey's international framing of policy influenced the way many readers thought about their empire after its publication. The shape that debates over trusteeship and native paramountcy had taken over the previous fifteen years deeply affected it, and the *Survey* became a touchstone for administrators in its wake. As Hailey's influence rose, so did the prominence of Malinowski and his students. When Perham organized a summer school at Oxford for colonial administrators in 1938, she invited four anthropologists - Malinowski, Alfred Radcliffe-Browne, Edward Evans-Pritchard and Meyer Fortes – to address them. By then Perham, Lugard and Hailey had made significant investments in 'Soc. Anth. Ltd.', to borrow Stefan Collini's evocative term, and its stock price was reaching an all-time high.[21]

THE 1938 SUMMER SCHOOL AT OXFORD

The proceedings at Oxford opened with an address by Secretary of State for the Colonies Malcolm Macdonald. He began by declaiming that 'we in this country have a passion for liberty.' The empire spread this 'freedom amongst all His Majesty's subjects, in whatever part of the earth they live.' Progress was often 'a slow – sometimes a painful – evolutionary process' and 'pace varies from place to place,' but in the Dominions, liberty had been achieved, apparently (although this was liberty for white settlers, with no mention of the violence meted out to First Nations and Aboriginal peoples). In the dependent colonial empire, however, 'it will be generations, perhaps even centuries, before that aim is accomplished in some cases.' But the experience of coming together to discuss matters of colonial policy was salutary, and Macdonald hoped that the summer school would result in 'the setting alight of many torches destined to be carried away to many lands,' with each light 'always throw[ing] back at least one beam of gratitude to the original source of illumination at Oxford.'[22]

Lugard and Donald Cameron (former governor of Tanganyika and then of Nigeria) then proceeded to address the gathered administrators. Lugard used the opportunity to score some points against his old enemy, Leo Amery, criticising Amery's support for tariffs and imperial preference and blaming these policies for Nazi Germany's demands for colonial possessions. Typically bombastic, Lugard reiterated the argument of the Dual Mandate, despite its seeming supersession by increasing emphasis on development in the policy sphere. The British Empire was not ruled for 'national advantage', he claimed. The assembled administrators were really 'trustees alike for natives and for the economic requirements of the world.'[23] He celebrated the drift towards trusteeship in the British Empire – a phenomenon that would have been 'inconceivable a decade or two ago.' A new anthropological spirit apparently gripped the colonial services, reflecting a desire to 'understand the cultures of the indigenous races and to help them to attain a higher standard of life.'[24]

While Lugard seemed to claim that this change had occurred in the ethos of the administration itself, Perham was more circumspect. She claimed that colonial officers could only 'carry' this new spirit 'a certain distance'. Anthropologists, with the 'necessary concentration and detachment' and the 'training' to undertake field research, were necessary to push through the new reforms. 'This is why anthropologists have been invited to play such a large part in our lectures and discussions during the next few days.'[25] The terse foreword to the printed proceedings states merely that the anthropologists' addresses 'led to a lively debate.'[26]

Despite Perham's boosterism, social anthropology had not gained the wholehearted support of the colonial services by the late 1930s and, indeed, it never would. Hailey was clearly pro, but even Lugard maintained a studied scepticism about the discipline, writing mockingly of Perham's support for anthropology as 'bowing the knee to Baal,' a reference to the purportedly false gods worshipped by Canaanites in the Old

Testament.²⁷ Meanwhile, Radcliffe-Brown's address at Oxford certainly suggested that, amongst the anthropologists at least, a heady sense of self-importance had set in. Radcliffe-Brown, by now professor of social anthropology at Oxford, claimed that his discipline was a 'pure theoretical science, like physiology or biology,' and cast the colonial administrator as a mere 'practitioner'. The scientist should not get their hands dirty worrying about the administrator's needs. Anthropological science was 'theory pursued for its own sake,' and he compared the discipline's potential impact to Robert Boyle's researches in chemistry.²⁸

Malinowski, on the other hand, proposed a more 'applied' vision that served what he called the 'administrative charter' of imperial rule. The role of anthropology was in line with Perham's hopes – to extend the interests of the administrative officer – only with a more specialised research apparatus. These divisions between 'applied' and 'pure' research would wrack the discipline for the following decades. For Perham, as for Malinowski, Mair, Richards and Raymond Firth, anthropology was a reformer's science intended to redirect the administration of Britain's colonies. The interests of anthropologists should be driven by political needs. For Radcliffe-Brown and, as we will see, his successor to the chair at Oxford, Evans-Pritchard, research in social anthropology had to be kept separate from political concerns, or the discipline risked becoming merely a routine part of the imperial state's bureaucratic machinery. If this came about, anthropologists would be unable to ask the grander questions about human nature and the fundamentals of society that they had traditionally made their concern. When Macdonald announced that the wartime administration would make significant investments in colonial research in 1940, these differences between the value of 'pure' and 'applied' anthropology structured the ensuing disputes about the future direction of the discipline.

THE COLONIAL DEVELOPMENT AND WELFARE ACT, THE ASA AND THE CSSRC

When the CDWA was passed into law in 1940, £500,000 of the £5 million a year was set aside for research. A number of prominent social anthropologists held the purse strings.²⁹ After 1945, the act was folded into the post-war Labour administration's welfarist agenda.³⁰ However, in an empire of over five hundred million people, the amount of money spent per capita in the dependent colonies was clearly risible.³¹ A minimal commitment to welfare spending certainly mirrored, if only in a much diminished manner, some aspects of the domestic welfare state. More crucial was the CDWA's emphasis on planning. The trend towards increased expert involvement in economic policy had been gestured at in the 1938 Oxford summer school, where the economist and technocrat Arthur Salter told the gathered colonial administrators at Oxford that behind its largely unmodified 'visible structure . . . the whole pattern of the state is changing.' 'The outstanding characteristic of our age,' he went on, 'is that the state has become an active and important participant in economic enterprise.' In Britain at least, Salter told his audience, 'enterprise is largely replaced, and largely controlled' by government, though private enterprise 'remains the main foundation of the national economy.'[32] The empire must follow suit. Research was needed to plan effectively.

In this spirit of planning for development, two important social scientific bodies were set up: the CSSRC and the Colonial Economic and Development Council (CDC). David Rees-Williams, a minister in the Colonial Office, explained that the CDC would be the 'focal point in the Colonial Office for all development projects.' Its aim was to link the Colonial Office with the Treasury and the Central Economic Planning Staff of the Cabinet Office.[33] Social scientists were represented on the CDC: W. Arthur Lewis, Keith Murray and Sydney Caine. But these were economists; there were no anthropologists in this crucial body. The anthropologists sat on the CSSRC, whose remit was less clearly aligned with the growing economic power of the active, developmental state. As O. G. R. Williams, assistant secretary at the Colonial Office, wrote sceptically in 1940 upon receipt of a research plan sent in by Evans-Pritchard and Fortes, 'I see that Dr E-P hopes that the Kenya Govt. will allow him access to its files etc. This strikes me as rather naive, but perhaps he does not really expect permission to browse into Secretariat files at will.'[34]

Clearly the anthropologists were not trusted with sensitive information and were not allowed into the information order of the colonial state. The CSSRC gained its prestige from the success of Hailey's *Survey*, which had explained that anthropologists could help research how government policy could be delivered more effectively.[35] As we have seen, social anthropologists had been key intermediaries in Hailey's project, and in June 1944 they reaped their reward when the CSSRC met informally for the first time. The group concluded that large-scale surveys would be needed to implement the government's new economic policies, and 'the council was of the opinion that the programme of

ANTHROPOLOGICAL work was important, as it formed the basis for so many of the other social sciences with which it was necessary that it should be closely associated in fieldwork.'[36] In 1949 the CSSRC's standing committee on anthropology and sociology included Evans-Pritchard, Firth, Margaret Read, Daryll Forde, professor of anthropology at UCL, and David Glass (four anthropologists and one sociologist).[37] Firth was the CSSRC's secretary, with considerable power over procedure. In short, Malinowski's vision of an applied social science directed at problems of policy appeared in full bloom shortly after his death in 1942. And with his sometime students well placed to carry on his legacy, his idea of anthropology as a science of social development seemed destined to grow over the following decades.

While the CSSRC acted as a means to dispense funds, the founding of another organisation, the Association of Social Anthropologists (ASA), meant that only a chosen few would be able to gain access to the money and do the anthropological fieldwork. At an initial meeting of the ASA held on 15 July 1946, Radcliffe-Brown, Evans-Pritchard, Richards, Siegfried Nadel, Daryll Forde, Max Gluckman, Anthony Arkell (an archaeologist and the only non-anthropologist), Edmund Leach, Brenda Seligman and Firth discussed Evans-Pritchard's proposition that 'Social Anthropology is not sufficiently distinct a study to have its own Association and Journal and that a co-operative undertaking of this kind is desirable in the interests of science.'[38] They agreed that something should be done and clubbed together to more clearly define their field, excluding anyone who threatened to don the mantle of 'anthropologist' without the necessary accreditation and socialization.[39] The ASA restricted its membership to those who held – or had held in the past – as an early committee minute put it, 'a teaching or research appointment in Social Anthropology.'[40] One black ball was enough to exclude an applicant. The ASA's initial members were almost exclusively drawn from former members of Malinowski's seminar at the LSE, with a few close associates who had not studied with him but who had influenced those who did, such as Seligman and Radcliffe-Brown.

Early on, the CSSRC had decided to reinforce the provision of anthropology in existing university departments – UCL, LSE, Oxford and Cambridge – rather than create new departments. This neatly consolidated power in the hands of the ASA's principal grandees. By 1950, Evans-Pritchard had succeeded Radcliffe-Brown at Oxford; Gluckman led a new department at Manchester; Fortes was William Wyse Professor at Cambridge; Leach and Firth were at the LSE, the latter in Malinowski's chair (Leach would soon join Fortes at Cambridge); Richards was director of the East African Institute of Social Research; Mair taught colonial administration at the LSE; Read was a Professor at the Institute of Education, and a number of junior appointments and research posts were held by other members in Britain and in the empire. (Nadel moved from a professorial position at Durham to Australian National University in 1950, while Isaac Schapera moved from the University of Cape Town to join Leach and Firth at the LSE.) In turn, these men and women were bringing on a new generation of students who would, in time, gain fieldwork funding from the CSSRC and subsequent faculty appointments. In 1947 the first twelve CSSRC postgraduate studentships were awarded. Over its lifetime, twenty-one studentships were handed out.

Such a combination of exclusive in-group membership overlapping with access to funding from the CSSRC put social anthropologists in a powerful position to form a group identity. The social anthropologists associated with the ASA were beginning to hold all of the principal positions of power in the discipline (in 1963 all fifty-five professional anthropologists employed in UK universities were ASA members).[41] Yet despite the strong centripetal forces holding the CSSRC and the ASA together in a close embrace, these institutions contained divergent visions about anthropology's future. At Oxford in particular there was disagreement, both about the suitability of applied research and the place where students should do their training, whether in Britain or in the colonies. This Oxford approach has been contrasted with the LSE approach to applied anthropology in regional research centres.[42] Somewhere between these two visions was a third approach associated with the Rhodes-Livingstone Institute, in which students would train at Oxford and then go on to do applied social research in Central Africa. The following sections describe each of these different visions of post-war social anthropology in turn.

THE LSE TRADITION OF APPLIED RESEARCH

The LSE tradition drew on the spirit of technocratic planning founded in the wake of Hailey's *Survey*. At the initial meeting of the CSSRC in 1944 the group decided to fund anthropological fieldwork alongside government development programs. By 1950 the CSSRC had its own budget of £325,000 a year for the next five years. The main targets of this funding were four regional research institutes: the Rhodes-Livingstone Institute in North Rhodesia (RLI), the East African Institute for Social Research (EAISR) at Makerere College in Uganda, the West African Institute of

Social Research in Nigeria and the Institute for Social Research in Jamaica. Over fifteen years these centres consumed £1 million of funding, twice as much as the money directed at individual research via graduate bursaries.[43]

Richards (whose fieldwork experiences were discussed in chapter 3) fought a long battle to have the EAISR be funded and run as a hub for applied research in East Africa. She had to struggle with sexism, scepticism and hostility from local administrators and the governor in Kenya, as well as opposition to the very idea of the institute from Evans-Pritchard and Radcliffe-Brown. William Stanner was chosen as the founding director of the EAISR over Richards, in part, it seems, because he was a man.[44] Stanner resigned within a year. (Gluckman was secretly pleased by this development, writing to his one-time student and colleague Clyde Mitchell that the EAISR's difficulties left the RLI at an advantage as a 'unique' institution.)[45] But Richards picked up successfully where Stanner left off, overseeing the construction of buildings and bringing an exploratory survey of Uganda to completion in 1954, published as *Economic Development and Tribal Change*.

That book was based on team research focused on labour migration from the Belgian colonies of Rwanda and Burundi into Britain's colony of Uganda. The study aimed to address 'one of the main problems confronting Buganda, that is to say the extent to which its whole economy depends on foreign labour.'[46] This posed problems, according to Richards, of an 'inva[sion] of strangers', making clear, as we saw in the previous chapter, how anthropology and migration studies were united in this era, both in Britain and in the empire.[47] The administration of Uganda supported new capitalist enterprises and also the 'rapid democratisation of local African councils' in order to make local government 'resemble more closely' institutions in the UK.[48] However, Richards's team pointed out that policies that encouraged and relied upon significant immigration posed significant possibilities of political instability when 'tribal' identities were in flux.

Richards set out to woo local officials and persuade them that anthropology could play a useful role in development planning and in coping with the influx of Belgian colonial subjects into British territory. She met with support from Uganda's new governor, Andrew Cohen, but had less luck with the Kenyan authorities; one official snidely, and perhaps accurately, remarked that anthropologists' appeals to administrative utility were due more to '"pressure from job-seekers" rather than "the value of the services".'[49] Richards's tenure at the EAISR fits an established pattern familiar from Malinowski's overtures about applied anthropology in the 1930s. Claims to utility were tempered by administrative scepticism, and works that ostensibly aimed at practical ends were often scholarly publications lacking clear policy prescriptions.[50] The rhetoric, though, was one of applied social science, familiar by now as based on an LSE attitude to advising government. Richards sought to offer the services of anthropology to the territories the EAISR was meant to serve. The regional research centres would, she hoped, form the basis for new universities that would go on to train anthropologists of their own, multiplying the LSE in the colonies.

In short, Richards saw the role of her discipline in a similar way as Perham and Hailey: as a great reforming science. This vision was only partially fulfilled. The EAISR would remain an important hub of social research in East Africa, but when the CSSRC's funds ran dry in 1955, the rapid expansion of the research centres slowed, and anthropologists' position became increasingly shaky in the face of economists' new ideas and increasingly influential American development expertise, a story told in the next chapter.[51] Perhaps Richards felt the way the winds were blowing, for in 1956 she returned to England to take up a fellowship at Newnham College, Cambridge and a job as the first director of the Centre of African Studies there.

THE OXFORD APPROACH

The LSE approach of applied social research was a far cry from the postwar tradition of social anthropology being carried out at Oxford, where 'pure' anthropology was highly valued. This vision of the discipline was associated with Evans-Pritchard, who was appointed a lecturer in African sociology at Oxford in 1935 and where Radcliffe-Brown was made the inaugural professor of social anthropology in 1936, after spending the first half of the decade at the University of Chicago. When Radcliffe-Brown arrived he found Oxford's institutional structures stifling and struggled to push through reforms to the curriculum. In Oxford, anthropology had traditionally been aligned with the Pitt-Rivers Museum, and students were taught material culture and anatomy, alongside linguistics and sociology. The kind of field-based, intensive study pioneered by Malinowski and Radcliffe-Brown in the 1910s and 1920s barely registered. Radcliffe-Brown wanted to institute a new diploma in 'social anthropology' to nudge things in the direction of his own interests, but he was resisted vociferously by the old guard of Oxford anthropology – John

Myers, Ranulph Marett, Henry Balfour and Leonard Buxton – who wanted to maintain the traditional links between museology, anatomy and sociology.⁵²

Perhaps to escape such a conservative intellectual climate, Radcliffe-Brown held informal seminars in pubs in North Oxford with Evans-Pritchard, Fortes, Brenda Seligman and Gluckman. These discussions consolidated the 'structural-functional' anthropology that Radcliffe-Brown had theorised in a few scattered papers and that we saw Fortes and Evans-Pritchard working out together in the field. Radcliffe-Brown's 1940 presidential address at the Royal Anthropological Institute, 'On Social Structure,' clarified his ideas and was a call to arms. His main argument was that 'every human being living in a society is two things: he is an individual and also a person.' 'As a person', he went on, 'the human being is the object of study for the social anthropologist. We cannot study persons except in terms of social structure nor can we study social structure except in terms of the persons who are the units of which it is composed.'⁵³ By pursuing a 'comparative morphology of societies', anthropologists could build 'some sort of classification of types of structural systems.'⁵⁴ Fortes's and Evans-Pritchard's monographs from that decade, on the Tallensi and the Nuer respectively, as well as their jointly edited *African Political Systems* (1940), would extend the reach of Radcliffe-Brown's views.⁵⁵ A focus on kinship, ritual and belief, and the political systems of stateless societies marked the new agenda. By the mid-1950s, most social anthropologists in Britain had left behind Malinowski's psycho-biological functionalism in favour of Radcliffe-Brown's 'sociological' emphasis on social structure; the contributors to Malinowski's posthumous festschrift *Man and Culture* (1957) generally agreed that he would be remembered as a pioneering field worker rather than as a groundbreaking theorist.⁵⁶

These theoretical differences partly mapped onto different approaches to colonial development. The LSE-associated researchers and the Oxford group confronted one another along two axes: first, on the matter of 'pure' and 'applied' studies, and second, over the primacy of regional research centres. Radcliffe-Brown and Evans-Pritchard wanted their students to take graduate classes in Britain, specifically at Oxford, before leaving for their fieldwork. And they sought to keep social anthropology and the Colonial Office at arm's length, using CSSRC funds for student funding, but not to let their research agendas, or those of their students, be driven by the exigencies of late imperial politics. The LSE approach, taken by anthropologists like Richards, wanted to recreate the ethos of the LSE in regional research centres that would form hubs of training and research.

While this latter approach gained the lion's share of funds, Radcliffe-Brown and Evans-Pritchard fought a rearguard action, using the CSSRC and the ASA to lobby the Colonial Office in support of their own view that students should be trained at Oxford rather than at the new regional research centres. They also wanted to defend a firm distinction between 'pure' and 'applied' anthropology.[57] In Evans-Pritchard's view, anthropologists should be driven by a general interest in the 'science of man'. Spending too much time on 'settlement schemes, land tenure difficulties, labour migration, and such-like problems,' he declared at the Oxford University Anthropological Society in 1946, would mean diverting attention from the foundational issues of the discipline, such as 'ritual' and 'mythology'. 'We are not social cobblers and plumbers,' he concluded, 'but men of science.'[58] The disparagement of Richards and the LSE approach to applied research was presumably obvious to those who listened.

Evans-Pritchard made a forceful intervention on similar lines in his Marett lecture, given at Exeter College, Oxford in 1950. He had recently replaced Radcliffe-Brown as professor of social anthropology at Oxford University and held the presidency of the Royal Anthropological Institute at the time of his address. By 1950 he had dropped the idea that anthropologists were 'men of science', and he used the occasion to lambast his colleagues who still thought in those terms. In direct contrast to his statement in 1946 and in stark opposition to the views held by the previous holder of his chair, Radcliffe-Brown, Evans-Pritchard now argued that anthropology was not, after all, a natural science of society. In fact, it was futile and misguided to try to seek the laws guiding social relations. Anthropologists may speak of discovering laws, testing hypotheses and forming typologies, but rather than applying the methods of the natural sciences, they were merely making false analogies. Anthropologists had, in fact, been writing what he called 'cross-sections of history' all along. Talking about these cross-sections as if they offered timeless truths was misleading.[59] It would be far better, he told his audience, if they wrote books like the historians Numa Fustel de Coulanges, Paul Vinogradoff, Henri Pirenne, Frederic William Maitland, and, in an obsequious nod to the then current Regius Professor of Modern History at Oxford, Frederick Powicke. 'When we read the words of these historians,' Evans-Pritchard declared, 'we feel that we and they are studying the same things in the same way.' All 'good modern historians', he went on, seek to describe the institutional connections making up past societies. The fact that these historians wrote 'diachronic' rather than 'generally synchronic' accounts of social institutions, as anthropologists did, merely marked a 'difference of emphasis . . . and not a real divergence of interest.' It was a cause for regret that anthropologists had not realised that they were really quasi-historians and that some historians were, in fact, quasi-anthropologists. The anthropologists' method of freezing social relations at one moment offered a false sense of objectivity and meant that they had paid too little attention to studying change over time. Taking a swipe at Malinowski in particular, Evans-Pritchard called functionalist theory 'little more than a literary device' despite 'the wide claims he [i.e., Malinowski] made for it.'[60]

Evans-Pritchard argued that the endeavour to uncover the scientific laws of social life was associated with 'predicting and planning' and an approach to studying social forms that 'constantly stressed the applications of its findings to affairs, the emphasis in England being on colonial problems and in America on political and industrial problems.' Those anthropologists most enamoured of 'discovering the sociological laws in terms of which . . . actions, ideas and beliefs can be explained' are those most keen to see them 'in the light of which they can be planned and controlled.'[61] The sense that Evans-Pritchard might be opposed to planning is confirmed in his book *Social Anthropology* (1951). There he repeated the now familiar line that historical study was important for methodological reasons and, furthermore, that the subjects of anthropological study 'are rapidly being transformed and must be studied soon or never.'[62] Unlike many of his colleagues, such as Richards, Evans-Pritchard did not then go on to argue that social change should be studied to guide the resulting transformation. Instead, he argued that anthropology had value because its descriptions of non-capitalist, pre-industrial peoples 'are interesting in themselves'. This interest lay, for Evans-Pritchard, in total opposition to the developmentalist urge. Non-industrial societies should be studied because they offered moral lessons about 'the values, and the beliefs of peoples living without what we have come to regard as the minimum requirements of comfort and civilization.'[63] These societies should be studied because they proved that increasing material abundance did not necessarily lead to the spread of more civilized values. This was a view wholly at odds with the leftist political agenda of many of his colleagues.

Evans-Pritchard made the same case in a lecture given at Victoria University in Manchester eleven years later. The lecture was printed as a pamphlet and then found its way into wider circulation as part of the collection *Essays in Social Anthropology* (1962). Evans-Pritchard's argument seemed perfectly designed to create a controversy, and it did. Almost immediately the pages of the Royal Anthropological Institute's monthly journal *Man* began to fill with defences and rebuttals.[64] In his presidential address to the Royal Anthropological Institute that same year, Isaac Schapera argued that Richards, Godfrey Wilson, Monica Wilson, Hilda Kuper, Ian Hogbin and Firth (all Malinowski's students) described change over time in their work. Where government documents, published books and archival sources existed they were consulted by all of these anthropologists, who gathered as much evidence as possible. Furthermore, the fact that they often studied societies undergoing rapid change meant that a historical frame of reference 'was virtually forced upon them by the conditions prevailing in societies with which they had to deal.'[65] In short, Evans-Pritchard's stark distinction between 'anthropology' and 'history' was little more than a 'red herring' according to Leach.[66] What Evans-Pritchard really seemed opposed to was planning. This meant that he ultimately had little to offer to the burgeoning apparatus of economic development, severing the ties between anthropology and the other social sciences and pushing the discipline towards the humanities instead.

THE RHODES-LIVINGSTONE INSTITUTE

The RLI formed a third type of post-war social anthropology that ultimately became known as the Manchester School after Gluckman moved there in the late 1940s. The RLI had served as a model for the other centres funded by the British government after 1940. It proved that a local research station could function as a base for fieldwork.[67] But unlike the regional centres discussed previously, the RLI was founded in 1937 without central government spending from Britain. Nor was it imagined as a foundation for an independent university. Money had come from a combination of business interests (mostly mining companies) and from the governor of Northern Rhodesia, Hubert Young. Its first director was Wilson, one of Malinowski's favourite students. Along with Richards, Firth and Mair, Wilson tended to stress the importance of applied research, although he had a testy relationship with the authorities in Northern Rhodesia and never saw his vocation in such an administrative-directed ethos as, for instance, Richards at the EAISR.[68] Wilson's assistant, Gluckman, was appointed in 1939 and took over the directorship of the RLI after Wilson's resignation in 1941.

Gluckman had studied under Winnifred Hoernlé in Cape Town. He had also been a weekly attendee of Malinowski's seminar at the LSE in 1935 and was a product of the late 1930s Evans-Pritchard/Radcliffe-Brown milieu at Oxford. His job at the RLI might suggest that he would have supported the development of regional research centres. But under Gluckman's directorship, the RLI fell somewhere between the two stools of 'Oxford' and 'LSE' anthropology He carried out fieldwork in South Africa and in Northern Rhodesia with his students and research assistants – John Barnes, Elizabeth Colson and Clyde Mitchell – and then sent them to Oxford to write up the results as part of their training.[69] The RLI was, in short, not conceived as a new university like the East African Institute of Social Research, but as a research outpost for trainee social scientists who would be schooled at Oxford in the structural-functionalist mode. Gluckman, though, was a political radical, unlike Evans-Pritchard, and the research he sponsored at the RLI had a Marxist edge that owed something to his leftism and anti-racism (he and Wilson read Marx together sympathetically in the 1940s).[70] The young RLI researchers who had carried out initial fieldwork in South Africa under Gluckman's guidance discussed at great length his now famous paper 'Analysis of a Social Situation in Modern Zululand' (1940),[71] popularly known to Gluckman's students as the 'The Bridge'.[72] The text was published in two parts in *Bantu Studies* in 1940 and 1942, before being published together as *Analysis of a Social Situation in Modern Zululand* as a Rhodes-Livingstone Paper in 1958.

Analysis has since been taken to constitute a new direction in social anthropology and as a foundational text of the Manchester School.[73] In it, Gluckman proposed that the opening of a bridge could be submitted to a 'situational analysis' wherein differences of dress, behaviour and race were linked to the dynamics of power that contained the whole structure in one frame. The bridge opening in a native reserve was linked to the broader structure of South African society, and widening the frame further, to the global economy. This was a far cry from Malinowski's mode of ethnographic writing about the Trobriand Islands. Early in his career Malinowski presented colonised societies as if they were self-contained social wholes. Later he recanted, admitting, in an appendix to his 1935 work *Coral Gardens and Their Magic* that he had insufficiently accounted for the social changes wrought by colonialism on the society he studied.[74]

While Malinowski's monographs tended to present pictures of societies untouched by colonial domination, in his teaching and articles from the 1930s he promoted a theory of 'culture contact'. This theory proposed that a hybrid third culture was emerging out of the interactions of colonised and coloniser. In *Methods of Study of Culture Contact in Africa* (1938) he argued that the anthropologist must keep the three cultures in frame at one time rather than trying to treat Africans and Europeans as part of a common culture, as he criticised two of his students, Schapera and Fortes, for doing.[75] In *Analysis*, Gluckman took a self-consciously anti-Malinowskian line and treated South Africa as one culture.[76]

This was, in part, due to Gluckman's views on segregation.[77] Gluckman had been raised a liberal and was committed to a multiracial future for South Africa. In response to the settler question in the late 1920s, on the other hand, Malinowski had proposed a segregationist answer in East Africa. Malinowski thought that the only way to mitigate the destructive, predatory land alienation of European settlers was for the British government to buy them out and exclude them from East and Central Africa. However, it seems that by the mid-1930s Malinowski's ideas had shifted in the face of the clear impracticality of this suggestion. In a collection of essays on culture contact edited by Mair, he attested to the inevitability of cultural loss and dislocation occurring in Africa and around the world. His functionalist response, and that of his students, such as Mair, Richards, Read and Wilson, was to slow the pace of such change and seek to protect those parts of the society that still existed. This put his ideas in line with what Saul Dubow has called 'adaptationist' policy in South Africa.[78]

Gluckman, on the other hand, rejected this approach. In *Social Situation*, Zulus, white South Africans, the anthropologist, labourers, administrators' wives, dancers, magistrates and a whole cast of characters all performed a complex ceremony together. This was not an homage to either the sanctity of 'native' culture or the overwhelming force of white South African power (although Gluckman was clear that the threat of force and of economic exploitation structured the whole event). *Analysis* was a study of how anthropologists could describe the workings of racism and colonialism and show that the differences generated upheld a broader social and economic order.[79]

While Gluckman's political beliefs were certainly enough to challenge the implications of Malinowski's theories, the analytical tools to do so came from his willingness to range in scale from the local to the global. And this surely must have resulted from the discussions he had with Godfrey and Monica Wilson as they completed their monograph *The*

Analysis of Social Change (1945), and as Godfrey wrote *An Essay on the Economics of Detribalization in Northern Rhodesia* (1941, 1942).[80] The Wilsons proposed that conflicts between large-scale and small-scale sociological phenomena were causing disequilibriums in Central Africa. The colonies contained local economies that were part of global supply chains, and individual Christians, while members of local congregations, were part of a world religion. Zooming out from the experience of particular field sites to the realm of international finance, war and religion allowed the Wilsons to explain the phenomena they observed in Central Africa. And their findings from that region captured some universal themes of sociological adaptation and maladjustment in turn. In *An Essay on the Economics of Detribalization*, Godfrey Wilson used the Trotskyist notion of uneven and combined development to capture this process. Gluckman shared a comparative spirit with the Wilsons and was similarly committed to a broadly Marxist understanding of conflict and crisis in the global economy. This theoretical bent went along with a commitment to anti-racism that resulted in a tendency to treat African informants and colleagues in a familiar way that many settlers and administrators found disturbing.[81]

Gluckman left Northern Rhodesia for Oxford in 1947 and moved to Manchester in 1949 to take up a position in social anthropology created especially for him. He left behind a radical research agenda focused on pressing political issues in Central Africa. These were very different topics to those being promoted by Evans-Pritchard at Oxford and tended to have a more critical edge than the kind of government-aligned development work sponsored by the regional research centres or done out of the LSE. Under the directorships of Colson and Mitchell in the 1950s, researchers at the RLI increasingly focused on urbanization, labour migration and the role of trade unions in African politics. The result was a post-war tradition known colloquially as the Manchester School.[82] This 'Manchester' approach tended to focus on the constitutive role of conflict in politics.[83] It influenced a generation of researchers in Central Africa and also in British sociology.[84]

CONCLUSION

We can see, then, three distinct traditions emerging in social anthropology by 1955. The first was the Oxford anthropology of Evans-Pritchard. This upheld a supposedly 'traditional' ideal of the discipline that kept itself apart from what Evans-Pritchard haughtily called the work of social cobbling and plumbing. Then there was the LSE approach of applied anthropology carried out in a broadly Malinowskian vein. This aligned itself with the desire to create regional research centres that would become their own hubs for training social scientists in the colonies. Finally there was the RLI and the incipient Manchester School, which sat somewhere between these positions. Gluckman was initially keen to maintain a link with Oxford. But after moving to Manchester in 1949 he increasingly quarrelled with Evans-Pritchard, seeing the Oxford view (to disavow applied work and focus all efforts on securing funding for home institutions) as a threat to the future of the RLI.[85]

These divisions over the future direction of the discipline also reflected differing approaches to the question of development and planning. Richards at the East African Institute of Social Research was keen to do large-scale survey work. Gluckman, too, employed statistical methods, took censuses and drew up tables for researchers to note the political offices held in a particular locale. Under the directorship of Mitchell, large urban surveys were undertaken, and a Powers-Samas machine was used to sort and count the data on a vast number of punchcards that he and his research assistants created.[86] These methods were alien to Evans-Pritchard's interests, whose opposition to applied anthropology hardened throughout the 1940s. By 1950 Evans-Pritchard's emphasis on kinship, magic and religion and his conversion to Catholicism went along with a distrust of state planning and resulted in a decidedly anti-rationalist politics.

Meanwhile, Gluckman's radicalism had been noticed by the British security services, and two of his most promising students at Manchester, Ronald Frankenberg and Peter Worsley, had their requests for visas blocked on the grounds of their leftist politics.[87] A leftist tradition of social anthropology was increasingly choked off at the RLI. Coupled with Evans-Pritchard's conservatism, the discipline increasingly diverged from the more policy-facing disciplines of economics, sociology and political science. And with CSSRC funding drying up in 1955, the regional research centres were facing tightened budgets and less capacity to engage with development projects. All of this led to what one commentator has called the 'enforced primitivism' of Oxford-dominated British social anthropology of the 1950s and 1960s.[88] Adam Kuper has similarly argued that the 'purism' of Oxford anthropology led to an 'ostentatious refusal to analyse the colonial context,' which in turn 'became the hallmark of theoretical contributions in social anthropology.' This happened, Kuper argues, 'because any acknowledgment of colonial realties would mean engaging directly, rather than implicitly, in debates on colonial policy.'[89]

An attitude of eirenic detachment at Oxford and squabbles between the RLI and LSE approaches seem likely to have blocked avenues for further influence in the burgeoning field of development studies. After all, such considerable differences between the Oxford, RLI and LSE traditions certainly made the field look less 'scientific' when government funders sought theories to apply to practical problems.[90] As we will see in the next chapter, economists would soon be proposing methods and policies that better suited the ethos of late colonial and post-colonial states. In this way, the drying up of CSSRC funding in the mid-1950s took place against the background of increasing intellectual and political critique.

CHAPTER 7

From Development Economics to the 'Moral Economy'

At the Margins of Anthropology, Economics and Social History in the 1950s and 1960s

In 1961, Audrey Richards worried that social anthropology was destined for the 'Scrap-Heap'.[1] The discipline, she wrote, looked 'likely to be blown off the field, like so much else, by the famous winds of change.'[2] Referring to Harold Macmillan's recent speech about decolonisation, Richards argued that anti-colonial politicians like Kwame Nkrumah and Julius Nyerere sought to develop political power at the level of the nation-state, rather than via the subnational organisations traditionally studied by anthropologists.[3] Because of this, they would have little use for anthropological expertise. Economists, on the other hand, promised to help anti-colonial nationalists with state building, planning and development. For these reasons, Richards thought that decolonisation and the rise of development economics threatened the future of social anthropology.

Why was Richards so worried, and what had changed from the story told in the previous chapter? After all, only a decade earlier, social anthropology seemed set on sure foundations, with steady funding and colonial governments seeking anthropologists' advice on their development projects. But by the early 1960s, things were in flux. As recounted in the previous chapter, anthropologists had maintained a close, if contested, relationship with development projects from the late 1930s to the early 1950s. But a set of geopolitical and intellectual changes then began to pull anthropology and development apart. On the political side, both colonial and anti-colonial politicians began making demands for economic and political development.[4] On the intellectual side, new concepts like 'modernization' and 'economic growth' emerged as political scientists and economists turned their attention to those parts of the world that anthropologists traditionally studied.[5]

This alliance of development ideology and post-colonial state building took place amidst the growing tensions of the Cold War.[6] On the 'Western' side of the conflict, a logic of economic growth and raising per capita income was baked into the decisions of states and non-governmental organisations, fomenting an ideal that the historian Alden Young calls 'calculable development'.[7] The Rockefeller and Ford Foundations and new international organisations (like the International Monetary Fund and International Bank for Reconstruction and Development) gave fulsome support to this new approach to development. They funded American and European economists who invented new metrics such as gross domestic product (GDP), new concepts such as 'economic growth', and new methods such as national income accounting, to help jump-start industrialisation at the peripheries of the capitalist world system.[8] Doyens of development economics, like Arthur Lewis, Paul Rosenstein-Rodan and Walt Rostow, called for the 'big push' and 'take off' that would lead 'underdeveloped' societies into modernity.[9]

Richards's essay was written in response to this recent transformation of the social sciences. Surprising as it may seem, before the 1940s few economists in Britain or the USA spared much thought for questions of economic development outside Europe or America.[10] The giants of British economics of the previous decades – Marshall, Pigou, Keynes, Cannan, Benham – may have written on some aspects of colonial economics, but they had little to say about economic development in general. One scholar has argued that before the 1930s economists did not possess a concept of an 'economy' that could be subject to development at all.[11] There is some debate about the exact timing of the concept's creation, but suffice it to say that the widespread idea that an 'economy' could be the target of growth via government planning and state-led development outside Europe and America rose to widespread academic prominence sometime at mid-century.

This new idea of the 'economy' posed a challenge, as Richards well understood, to anthropology's traditional focus on 'the social'. Studying 'the economy' meant abstracting up to the quantitative and statistical rather than following the anthropologists' preferred method of drilling down into the qualitative and specific. Studying 'the economy' also had a political salience for national planners and state builders, whereas anthropologists' emphases on the 'tribe' and tradition did not. As Talal Asad has argued, 'statistics is much more than a matter of representation; it is a tool of political intervention. And as a political tool it is infinitely more powerful than ethnographic representation – for good or for ill.'[12] In short, anthropology seemed out of touch with the modernizing spirit of the age.[13]

My first aim in this chapter is to outline the political and methodological challenges posed by economics in the 1950s. In the first section we meet Arthur Lewis, one of the most prominent contemporary development economists. Here we see how he challenged anthropology's political quietism on questions of welfare and industrialisation. We then move on to a more sympathetic engagement between anthropology and economics in the work of Phyllis Deane, although her ideas were ultimately sidelined when the United Nations (UN) drew up its *System of National Accounts and Supporting Tables* in 1953. The chapter then moves on to outline my second contribution to the literature of the post-war social sciences as I explain how anthropologists responded to this moment of critique and crisis. In the late 1950s anthropologists began to debate the nature of 'market exchange', especially via the ideas of Karl Polanyi, and they offered other disciplines the tools to piece together new histories of capitalism and industrialism. In this way, social anthropology continued to inform debate and scholarship, but increasingly about the past rather than the present. When we shift our focus from the periphery to the metropole of the British Empire, Richards's vision of displacement and intellectual crisis seems overblown. Just as anthropological ideas were squeezed out of development planning, they were being picked up elsewhere. Rather than being thrown on the scrapheap, a number of important historians began to follow Polanyi in seeking to emulate what Raymond Williams called anthropologists' sensitivity to a 'whole way of life'.[14]

We have already seen in chapter 5 how this interdisciplinary borrowing played out in community studies of urban Britain. Social anthropology also inspired research on capitalist development and industrialisation in the past. Economics may have threatened social anthropology with the scrapheap in the post-colonial peripheries, but in Britain, at least, anthropologists' ideas formed a minority report on the process of capitalist development itself. Like a rock stratum from an earlier geological era, anthropologists' ideas persisted throughout the era of 'high modernist' development ideology by informing new histories of modernity 'from below' and new concepts such as the 'moral economy'.[15]

ARTHUR LEWIS AND THE DEVELOPMENT OF THE 'DUAL SECTOR' MODEL

We can discern the outlines of these coming transformations when the economist Arthur Lewis, based at the London School of Economics (LSE), reviewed two key anthropological texts of the 1930s: Raymond Firth's *Primitive Polynesian Economy* (1939) and Richards's *Land, Labour and Diet in Northern Rhodesia* (1939). Lewis wrote appreciatively about both books. The literature on Western economics, Lewis pointed out, was 'large', but the number of studies like this, on societies with no, or limited, price systems, was still 'scanty', and he welcomed Firth's and Richards's contributions.[16] Yet while he applauded their respective strengths, he found their lack of policy prescriptions vexing. What did Firth and Richards think about 'maximizing the satisfactions' of the Bemba and the people of Tikopia that they studied? Their refusal to engage on these questions frustrated him; he concluded, 'perhaps in later writings they may be tempted to forsake the classrooms of descriptive economics for the platforms of political economy?'[17] Lewis's own views on this matter were clear. Maximizing satisfactions would mean increasing per capita income, as he explained in *Theory of Economic Growth* (1955).[18] This would come from industrialising non-industrial societies.[19] In the 1940s, when he reviewed Richards's and Firth's work, Lewis was engaging with leftist critiques of empire via the Fabian movement; by the 1950s he was supporting decolonisation as the best way to ensure increased welfare for colonised peoples.[20]

The mid-1950s saw a number of different theories of industrialisation and development emerge. Lewis's article 'Economic Development with Unlimited Supplies of Labour' (1954) was arguably the most influential.[21] Lewis offered readers a vision of a world thronged with underemployed labourers in places where 'social prestige requires people to have servants, and the grand seigneur may have to keep a whole army of retainers who are really little more than a burden upon his purse.'[22] Alongside this bevy of underemployed and ornamental men were three other pools of untapped potential: women, a generation of young people expanding as a result of growing prosperity and the farmers and labourers who were tied to the land in inefficiently exploited acreages using old fashioned farming techniques. 'The real bottlenecks' in these societies, Lewis argued, 'are therefore capital and natural resources,' not labour, which exists in abundance, ready to enter industry.[23]

To capture the scene, Lewis offered his readers a vision of 'tiny islands' of highly developed 'capitalist sectors', surrounded by large swathes of space constituting a 'subsistence sector'.[24] Lewis's ideas on this count can be contrasted with those of Max Gluckman's predecessor as director of the Rhodes-Livingstone Institute (RLI), Godfrey Wilson, who warned that migration to mines was leading to what he termed 'uneven change' and was thus pushing society in Central Africa towards breaking point.[25] Recall, too, from the previous chapter, that Richards had made a similar argument about the dislocating effects of labour migration in her book *Economic Development and Tribal Change* (1954). Lewis, on the other hand, saw the migration of labour from subsistence farming into the industrial sector as a boon and a political necessity if economic independence and parity between the colonised and colonisers was to be achieved.

Lewis had a different spatial imagination of economics and society to anthropologists like Wilson and Richards. Lewis imagined the capitalist and non-capitalist systems as sectors nested under one overarching conception of an economic space made legible by statistical methods and plannable through targeted investment. In this way Lewis scaled up and away from the subsistence sector to capture the whole of the colonial economy. Anthropologists tended to think of things differently. In chapter 2 we saw how Malinowski had stressed that a dual economy existed on the fringes of the capitalist world system: a 'primitive' sphere of non-money exchange associated with kinship and custom abutted a 'modern' cash economy. These two spheres were not merely two sectors in a larger economic space, as Lewis thought, but distinct zones of social interaction kept in delicate equilibrium to meet the needs of their members. As a result, Malinowski tended to advocate a policy of protectionism of the 'primitive' sphere under conditions of indirect rule and trusteeship in order to secure the welfare of its inhabitants.

Lewis also thought that colonised peoples' welfare should be paramount, but he took exactly the opposite view to Malinowski about how to maximize it. 'Ignorance, disease, superstition, savage customs, a low cultural level,' are all 'hall-marks of most colonial areas,' he argued.[26] Welfare could not be increased by protecting the cultures of the people in these areas. Increased welfare would only come from increasing the wealth of the colonies' inhabitants in order to, as he put it, 'liquidate poverty'. After all, he argued, these problems 'are found wherever poverty is to be found, in the slums of Chicago, no less than under the tropical sun.'[27] Liquidating poverty meant growing a territory's economy. To grow an economy, the industrial sector needed to expand, and savings needed to be piled up. With investment, wages would continue to suck surplus labour out of the agricultural sector until a new equilibrium was reached. These ideas, the Cold War context and the reimagining of the spatiality of development made Lewis and his fellow development economists hugely influential in the 1950s.[28]

Models of economic development, like Lewis's, had a polemical as well as an intellectual appeal. They were designed to hold out the possibility of industrialisation to all the world's peoples and to outline a way to demand it. But Lewis's model only gripped as a piece of political economy if it was combined with his anti-colonial politics. Lewis hoped that political change would come from centralised expert planning, first as a member of the Fabian Colonial Bureau and then as a supporter of post-colonial nationalism.[29] If political independence relied on economic modernisation, how could economists help politicians plan? What data could they rely on? These questions would motivate another economist who also engaged with social anthropology. But unlike Lewis, who criticised anthropologists for failing to write works of 'political economy', Phyllis Deane found value in the granularity of their ethnographic methods. She thought that scaling up from the qualitative and ethnographic to the quantitative and economic could only be placed on a sound empirical foundation by doing village and household surveys, a method pioneered and perfected over the previous decades by social anthropologists.

ECONOMISTS AND ANTHROPOLOGISTS IN THE FIELD

A contemporary of Lewis and a pioneer of the new economics of growth, Deane began her professional career working at the National Institute of Economic and Social Research (NIESR) in London. Deane joined the NIESR after university and developed methods of national income accounting there with James Meade, Richard Stone and Austin Robinson. She initially did her work on colonial accounting from London, synthesizing government statistics published in 1938 from Northern Rhodesia, Jamaica and Nyasaland. These studies were limited by the use of often patchy and incomplete official sources, however. After the Second World War, Deane travelled to Northern Rhodesia (modern-day Zambia) in the hope of gaining more accurate data and to build a better national account of its economy.[30] Deane's subsequent research offers something of a middle road between Lewis's abstract model building and the specificity of the social anthropologists' qualitative field methods.

On arriving in Northern Rhodesia, Deane began to work closely with anthropologists at the RLI. She hoped that fieldwork would plug the gaps in the government sources she had used in London. Deane was interested in economic development. But her experience of using official statistics in London suggested that economists had to enter the field and produce their own data. The nature of Deane's enquiries meant that Gluckman, the RLI's director, and his students had to standardize their field reports for her to study, while Deane relied on their African research assistants for help in translating questions and analysing the information she collected. Gluckman thought of Deane's national accounting project as an 'arid topic', but he nevertheless offered to help. On the other hand, John Barnes, one of the junior researchers at the RLI, was relieved by Deane's presence, noting that it meant he could avoid doing economic research of his own.[31]

Deane soon found that the problem of partial evidence she faced in London was unavoidable, even with concentrated periods of field research and a whole team of anthropological assistants. The data she gathered was more accurate than the statistics she had been reading in London, but the method of national income accounting being pursued at the NIESR simply broke down in Northern Rhodesia. The method used three different metrics to bring the national economy into view: income, output and expenditure. These could be represented as columns in a table. This approach was designed as a repeatable method that could be applied in different territories and to gather data at different intervals of time. The problem in Northern Rhodesia, however, was that what the economists counted as 'economic activity' did not describe very much of the work that Northern Rhodesians did to feed, clothe and house themselves.

For instance, crops farmed for sale could be computed in a national income account, but firewood collected for cooking and heating within the household was often not. As she put it in a 1947 article, 'If a woman spends 6 hours in the day cultivating and collecting food and 2 hours in preparing, cooking and serving it, is she economically occupied for 6 hours only?'[32] And as Firth, Malinowski and Read had argued in the 1920s and 1930s (see chapter 2 in this book), in societies with extensive non-money exchanges, prices were unfit guides to choices about the allocation of time and scarce resources. 'National income includes those goods and services which are normally, if not always, exchangeable for money,' she wrote. 'In an economy where money plays a subordinate role we must seek other criteria. What these other criteria should be is a problem not only for the administrator and economist but also for the sociologist or the social anthropologist.'[33] As so much of the subsistence of the households in Northern Rhodesia was supported by gifts in kind, rather than by cash, it was very hard, and perhaps impossible, to fully quantify income, output and expenditure. Cash transactions only played a small part in most people's lives, to the extent that when Deane crunched her data at John Barnes's field site she found that Barnes's own consumption, and the wages paid to his research assistants, was by far the largest source of money in the local economy, skewing her calculations of the prices of commodities.[34]

Northern Rhodesia did not have a developed market system. Prices could not clearly reflect choices in consumption (as so much was consumed outside the cash nexus). Neither was the household a stable unit of analysis for economic analysis, as the national income accounting pioneers hoped it would be. As Deane found, the sleeping household, the eating household, the income household and the spending household were all different combinations of a larger family unit whose permutations shifted considerably at different times and under different conditions.[35] Should men or women be taken as the 'symbol' of the household? Usually the woman could be taken as the prime mover in the domestic sphere, but in a polygamous society, men may have multiple wives in different villages, spreading the household (as a unit of consumption and expenditure) over a wide expanse.[36] What's more, Deane could not treat the interior of the household as the extra-economic baseline for her accounts, as the NIESR method dictated. One of the largest expenses incurred in any man's life was paying bride price on marriage: Should this be accounted for as domestic or productive activity?[37] In the Meade-Stone method of national accounting, the goods produced within the household and for domestic consumption were not counted as 'economic activity'.

Deane had noted the ridiculousness of maintaining this 'production boundary' in her early desk research in London, and a large part of the reason for travelling to do her fieldwork was to more accurately describe intra-household production and consumption.[38] By shifting the 'production boundary' in ways that made sense of the specificities of economic life in Northern Rhodesia, she thought that she had performed a more accurate reconstruction of economic activity there. Her account was framed by a high level of uncertainty. Nevertheless, she estimated that non-cash transactions of gifts or domestic production stood at roughly 25 percent of household income in the villages of Northern Rhodesia (although there was considerable variation between social groups).[39] She had not succeeded in completing the kind of comprehensive audit that would have been possible in an industrialised market economy, but happy to point to the limits of her studies, she declared that she had nevertheless discovered 'a few large shapes in a thick fog.'[40] More surveys would be needed to get a clearer view. Northern Rhodesia had, she estimated, four hundred thousand households. To do a survey of 10 percent of those households would need three to four economists and twelve assistants working full time for a year.[41] Surveying at this scale would allow for better estimates.

In this sense, Deane was proposing something like the work that the anthropologists at the RLI were already carrying out. Her idea of team-based development research was also similar to the calls by Richards for regional research centres, as discussed in the previous chapter. The need for economic research and anthropological research done together was not lost on Deane. She thanked her anthropologist colleagues in the book-length report on her research, noting that their partnership had been 'such a happy one' that she felt compelled to acknowledge them in full. They had provided the 'advice and practical assistance [that] made the village surveys possible,' and the help of another anthropologist, Isaac Schapera, 'was particularly constructive and [he] suggested many improvements.'[42] If only more money could be raised for surveys, a productive relationship between economists and anthropologists based on the RLI model might dispel some of the fog surrounding development planning.

Deane's research provides a model of careful, contextualised social-scientific thinking about development that took into account differences between social groups, their kinship structures and their differing approaches to domestic production. But in 1953, when Richard Stone universalized the approach to national income accounting in the UN publication *System of National Accounts and Supporting Tables*, his instructions to researchers drew a different production boundary to Deane. He reiterated the assumption that 'the economy' happened largely outside the household, and development economists increasingly did desk research rather than fieldwork. This meant relying on statistics collected by others (mostly governments), rather than gathering the data themselves. The kind of intra-household, 'non-productive' labour that Deane and the anthropologists had quantified was excluded. As a result, much of women's work in the global South disappeared back into uncountability. It was not until the 1970s, when feminist economists challenged the national income accounting models produced by Stone and his colleagues, that these issues were raised again prominently.[43]

This issue of drawing production boundaries in non-industrial economies was a new problem posed by a new conceptual toolkit in the social sciences, in this case national income accounting and growth economics.[44] Social science research in non- or partially capitalist societies was scaling up from the local to the national and from ethnographic methods to desk-bound quantitative studies. But how do you count input, output and expenditure when so much economic activity was carried on without money and within the household? Deane proposed one solution; Stone proposed another. The key, as Deane well understood, was that virtually nothing was known about the 'economies' of the 'underdeveloped' world.[45] This was not only an issue of incorporating data into existing models, such as Lewis's dual sector theory of development. The data did not exist in the first place. And with 25 percent, and more in some social groups, of exchange carried out without money, the construction and interpretation of this data would need to be carried out as a form of field research. Deane's dream team of economists and anthropologists taking regular samples of household budgets never transpired, and she returned to the UK, to Cambridge, in 1950 to become one of the preeminent historians of the Industrial Revolution in England.

Her 1957 article 'The Industrial Revolution and Economic Growth: The Evidence of Early British National Income Estimates' was published in a journal for research on economic development and was one of the earliest studies of the Industrial Revolution to refer to Lewis's theories.[46] Her book *British Economic Growth, 1688–1959* (1962), co-written with W. A. Cole, stands as a landmark of economic history and applied a national income accounting model to the past.[47] Deane's turn to the past and to economic history should be seen as part of an extension of her national accounting project in Northern Rhodesia.[48] The birth of the new economic history of growth and national accounting and the birth of modern development economics were methodologically homologous; they shared a common origin and a common interest in explaining the wealth of nations.[49] We will see how social historians also brought the developing post-colonial peripheries and the English past into dialogue with a similar set of concerns, but at least in the hands of E. P. Thompson, from a much more critical angle.

To return to the 1950s and to anthropology, for now, Deane's experience of economic fieldwork was not unique. On the other side of the continent, in West Africa, Polly Hill was coming to many of the same conclusions as Deane. Her field research on Asante cocoa farmers led her to criticise the policies pursued by Kwame Nkrumah and his advisor on taxation, the Cambridge economist Nicholas Kaldor.[50] Hill was highly sceptical of the new models of development that emerged in the 1950s and 1960s and the paucity of data they were based on, although she recognised that this made her seem intellectually, and perhaps even politically, conservative.[51] Unlike Deane, though, Hill remained marginalised in the academy, picking up temporary posts here and there and pursuing her fieldwork when she could.

Hill's pioneering field research in Ghana and Deane's work with the RLI present a moment of productive interdisciplinarity at a time when most economists ignored anthropology and when anthropologists like Richards worried that their discipline was being eclipsed. Deane's and Hill's experiences were thus unusual. The fact that these pioneering researchers were women may have led to their marginalisation in the highest level debates about the economics of development.[52] And because Deane switched subfields to economic history and Hill never held a permanent academic position, they did not have the opportunity to create schools of anthropologically minded economics within which they could pass on their ideas to students and fellow researchers. Increasingly, anthropologists and economists squared off on opposite sides of a seemingly unbridgeable methodological and ideological divide.[53]

From either side, anthropologists and economists tended to stress their incommensurability rather than their basic similarities, although it might be more accurate to say that economists stressed their uniqueness and had little interest in anthropology. This process was reflected in hostility from the anthropologists, too. Recall that Gluckman thought of Deane's research as 'arid' and, as we saw in the previous chapter, Edward Evans-Pritchard and his colleagues at Oxford left the field of applied policy work altogether, leading one commentator to argue that post-war anthropology had succumbed to an 'enforced primitivism'.[54] Even when anthropologists did engage with economists on matters of development, they did so as junior partners, as in the case of Deane's research, or as marginal actors, like Hill.

The interdisciplinary dialogue between anthropology and economics was also nixed by the post-colonial politicians who demanded development. Anthropologists were not able to offer them theories and policies that promoted the industrialisation many thought was necessary for parity with 'the West'. This meant that in terms of citations, let alone in terms of government advice, economists were an order of magnitude more influential than anthropologists when writing about development.[55] A funding crisis compounded the anthropologists' sense of intellectual and political dislocation. As we saw in chapter 6, Colonial Social Science Research Council (CSSRC) funding had been crucial to the institutionalisation and multiplication of anthropological expertise in the 1940s and early 1950s. But in 1955 CSSRC funding dried up, and anthropologists became increasingly worried about where their money would come from. A year later, in 1956, one of the discipline's major patrons, Malcolm Hailey, expressed his reservations about anthropology in the new edition of his *African Survey*.[56] To many African politicians and intellectuals, sociology, political science and economics, with their focus on modernity rather than tribe and tradition, seemed more appealing and better suited to their politics.[57]

No more striking illustration can be given than the fact that in 1957, Arthur Lewis was invited by Kwame Nkrumah to act as an economic advisor in newly independent Ghana. Nkrumah hung a painting in the anteroom of his offices. The picture depicted three white men fleeing the scene of an African colossus breaking the last chains of colonialism: a businessman holding a briefcase, a missionary clutching the bible and an anthropologist with a copy of Edward Evans-Pritchard and Meyer Fortes's *African Political Systems*.[58] Nkrumah's painting represented a vision of things to come: as the anthropologists left the scene the economists entered the building.[59] Over subsequent decades the prestige of economics would grow as economic discourse became central to international politics, questions of sovereignty, dependence, debt and welfare in the global South.[60]

SUBSTANTIVISM AND FORMALISM

Anthropology did not merely collapse in response to the geopolitical and intellectual challenges of the 1950s. As is so often the case, these external shocks provoked a search for new ideas, renewed relevance and the staking out of differences within and between the disciplines.[61] Nor did every anthropologist feel the reverberations to the same extent, and some seem not to have felt them at all. In Oxford, as we saw in the previous chapter, Evans-Pritchard argued throughout the 1950s that anthropologists had little to offer as advisors on development projects;

which pictures Nkrumah chose to hang in his offices did not much matter to him. At Cambridge, too, a rather abstract comparison of kinship structures reigned, and research carried on in the grooves set down in the 1930s and 1940s.[62] The changes I have been discussing in this chapter did not, therefore, much affect Oxbridge anthropology, which carried on the trajectory outlined in the earlier chapter.[63]

However, to those like Richards who dreamt of a continuing alliance between anthropology and development, one hope was that anthropologists could fill in the blank spaces in economists' models and explain how different social structures created different conditions for development. To other anthropologists, it was precisely *because* their discipline differed so radically from the new breed of economics that it had salience. This group of anthropologists drew from the work of the Austrian-born historian and economist Karl Polanyi to grapple with, and refute, the challenge laid down by the economists to explain how non- and pre-capitalist economic life was 'embedded' in social relations.[64] Because anthropologists tended to think in terms of 'the social', discussions of 'the economy', its development and its growth, seemed abstract, overly general and unempirical.

Polanyi bolstered the anthropologists' critiques by providing a political, social and intellectual history of the economists' ideas. He argued in *The Great Transformation* (1944) that economic theories about market exchange had grown up amidst nineteenth-century fantasies of laissez faire liberalism (the idea that economic agents should be left to trade and invest free from government interference).[65] Market exchange was not merely the interaction of free agents maximising their profits, Polanyi argued, but was a historically specific set of institutional arrangements that liberal political economists had abstracted from the messy reality of their own milieus. Anthropologists learned from these critiques that they should reject the conceptual 'scaling up' to quantitative methods and national income accounting pushed by economists at the UN and World Bank by demanding that these concepts be 'embedded' in accounts of the particular societies economists wanted to develop. Anthropology should thus double down on the qualitative and the ethnographic to reveal how production and exchange took different shapes in different societies. In this sense, anthropology was not facing the scrapheap, as Richards worried, but had renewed relevance as an empirical, observational science of non-capitalist societies. And unlike Richards, who had tentatively proposed that anthropologists could ally with economists to improve their data and do collective research, the followers of Polanyi proposed the radical critique that economics was a busted discipline answerable for many of the wrongs in the world. This view resulted in the well-worn divide in economic anthropology between 'formalists', who thought that economic models could be applied to non-industrial societies, and a group calling themselves 'substantivists', who did not.[66]

We can see the emergence of the 'substantivist' versus 'formalist' debate when, in September 1959, Firth travelled to Chicago to attend a conference organized by the young economist Bert Hoselitz and funded by the Committee on Economic Growth of the Social Science Research Council, a Rockefeller Foundation subsidiary.[67] The participants were invited to discuss the methodological interconnections between anthropology and economics and especially 'the study of socio-economic organization in general and economic development and cultural change in particular.' Hoselitz opened the proceedings by stating that he 'would welcome any conclusions arrived at which would illuminate the problems of economic growth in underdeveloped countries.'[68]

Hoselitz explained that one of the persistent problems economists faced was general bafflement at which 'segments of the society are likely to engage voluntarily in new occupations, and what kinds of social disruptions such moves to new occupations will bring'; that is, Lewis's model of dual sector development looked good on paper when it was published in 1954, but it was still unclear to Hoselitz and the others at Chicago five years later whether surplus workers would in fact leave the 'subsistence' sector, and what inducements might encourage their migration to the 'capitalist' one. Another problem, Hoselitz explained, was the difficulty of 'quantitative analys[i]s of productivity' in non-, or partially, monetized societies: the problems faced ten years earlier by Phyllis Deane in Northern Rhodesia.[69] Unlike Deane, though, who thought that many of these issues could be solved by team-based fieldwork, discussion at Chicago began to revolve around a more foundational issue: the participants diverged on what they meant by the term 'market'.

Arguments about the meaning of 'the market' proved to be extremely divisive. To some of the conference attendees, all kinds of logics may predominate in a market, although assumptions about self-interest and certain economic formulas might be expected to hold, such as laws of supply and demand. But in many of the places anthropologists, and more recently economists, were interested in (the 'underdeveloped' countries), markets only existed as one amongst a number of different spheres of exchange, for example customary dues, such as dowries, blood money and gifts offered to family members and neighbours. These forms of non-market exchange may, in fact, constitute the majority or a large minority of transactions in these areas. Thus, on the fringes of what Lewis called sectors, money may circulate in unexpected ways, and people may not follow higher wages from the subsistence sector into the capitalist sector. Goods may flow through reciprocal exchanges untethered from what economists understood as the rational decision-making of profit-maximising individual initiative.

The American anthropologist Edward Le Clair, however, thought that anthropologists should discuss markets in the same way economists did, as 'any exchange situation between A and B which took place because A and B found the other's good more valuable than his own.' Another participant, Kathleen Gough, thought this idea was ridiculous and proposed that the speakers draw a strict distinction between market and non-market systems. She suggested using historian and economist Polanyi's definitions of 'the isolated market, the market-system, and ... such non-market processes as reciprocity, redistribution, politically administered trade, etc.' The arguments that followed must have been interminable, because the typist, who wrote up the conference proceedings, noted that 'the response to this suggestion seemed chaotic indeed with almost every member having a different conception of "market" and a different notion of how Polanyi had laid out his categories.' The typist concluded laconically: 'There were many other ramifications of this discussion, which probably satisfied no-one.'[70] The debates spilled out beyond Chicago and went on for decades.[71] Economists, for the most part, ignored them.[72]

Firth sought to steer a middle course between Le Clair's and Gough's positions. Neither anthropology nor economics needed to be thrown on the scrapheap. Firth thought that Le Clair's argument meant 'that anthropologists (especially of the British kind) might have to isolate their discussion of values in a way unfamiliar way to them,' because, as a rule, they understood values in the context of 'the total social structure'.[73] Neither did Firth agree with Gough that, as a rule, economics should be rejected as a useful body of ideas. Like Richards, Firth wanted to add nuance to economists' theories, especially with the insight that social structures conferred the values that were deemed to be worthy of maximisation in any given society. In many societies, this might involve acting in ways that would be considered by economists to be distinctly irrational, such as the destruction of large quantities of commodities, choosing to work for kin for lower pay than for a non-kin capitalist or the ceremonial display of ritual objects. In short, economic exchanges were shot through with, and constitutive of, *social* relations.[74]

Polanyi thought along similar lines. In his essay published shortly before the Chicago conference, and which so much conversation swirled around there – 'The Economy as Instituted Process' (1957) – Polanyi argued that 'the economic' had two 'meanings that have independent roots.' The 'substantive' meaning meant 'man's dependence for his living upon nature and his fellows,' while the formal meaning meant simply the 'logical character of the means-ends relationship.' It was 'only the substantive meaning of "economic",' Polanyi argued, '[that] is capable of yielding the concepts that are required by the social sciences for an investigation of all the empirical economies of the past and present.'[75] These ideas seem remarkably similar to those of Malinowski, Thurnwald, Read and Firth discussed in chapter 2, to the extent that for those working in this post-Malinowskian tradition, Firth explained, Polanyi's ideas 'came as no great surprise.'[76]

Polanyi's ideas came as no surprise to Firth because Polanyi had drawn wholesale on Firth's work from the 1920s and 1930s. Out of the thirty-six references in the key chapter 'Societies and Economic Systems' in *The Great Transformation* (1944), twenty-nine, over 80 percent, went to social anthropologists.[77] Polanyi made his debts to social anthropology even clearer in the essay 'Aristotle Discovers the Economy' in his 1957 collection *Trade and Market*. In a genealogy traced from 'Hegel in the 1820's and developed by Karl Marx in the 1840's,' the terms of an 'embedded' and 'disembedded' economy were 'finally, in the more comprehensive terms of economic anthropology, . . . restated by Bronislaw Malinowski in the 1920's.'[78]

In this sense the 'substantivists' at Chicago drew on Polanyi's reading of interwar British social anthropology at second hand. But since the 1950s, social anthropologists like Firth and Richards had begun to see ways for anthropology and economics to work together, and Firth had published a critique of Malinowski's economic ideas in the 1957 posthumous festschrift to his PhD supervisor, in which he wrote that Malinowski's economic ideas were 'unsophisticated', a view at odds with Polanyi, who put Malinowski at the pinnacle of economic analysis.[79] Economists, Firth argued, needed help from anthropologists rather than wholesale critique. Anthropologists could 'help with local institutional data and assumptions, so that input of factors can be more rationally calculated to yield greater output, and this output more equally distributed.' Firth also thought anthropologists could help by pointing out that economic growth would not necessarily lead to increased welfare, as economists like Lewis had claimed in the mid-1950s. 'It is assumed by anthropologists that development should not mean simply increase of *per capita* income or investment per head,' Firth argued. It 'should relate to increase of economic opportunity and raising of levels of living in a broad sense.' This 'broad sense' might be in tension with growth, which was linked by Firth to rapid social change, which might 'not only give distress but lead to dislocation of [the] social structure.'[80]

Thus, Firth sought to unite economics and anthropology by pointing out that both disciplines had much to learn from each other. At least to those like Firth, Deane and Richards, detailed empirical research offered a possible future of economics and anthropology in partnership. For, as Richards explained in her 'scrapheap' article of 1961, economists often end up, after initial 'impatience' with anthropology, nevertheless having to 'turn amateur anthropologist' themselves.[81] The issues the anthropologists raised: of differential responses to development and the importance of social values in social change would not simply disappear even if they were increasingly thrown out or left aside by desk-bound economists citing official statistics. Whether they were thrown on the scrapheap or not, it seemed obvious to Firth and Richards that social anthropology still had a lot to offer the other social sciences. If economists would not listen, would other social sciences take an anthropological turn? And could the past perhaps offer up opportunities for the anthropological study of social change that the present could not?

ANTHROPOLOGY, ECONOMICS AND THE ENGLISH PAST

Amidst all of the debates and different political positions of the 1950s, Karl Polanyi's crossing from history to social anthropology and back again made him pioneering in two senses. We have already seen how his synthesis of anthropological writings from the 1920 and 1930s prompted a spate of writing amongst 'substantivist' anthropologists in the 1960s. Polanyi's turn to history also marked an important turning point. Anthropologists like Richards may have worried that economics would eclipse their authority, but historians of modernization and industrialisation stood poised to recycle and refashion the discipline's core arguments into a central pillar of post-war intellectual culture: social history. Turning from the post-colonial peripheries to the metropole of the British Empire offers a different vision of anthropology's place in Britain's intellectual culture and its ability to generate new research and new ideas.

As the historian Keith Thomas wrote in the *Oxford Magazine* in 1961, a marriage between history and anthropology might create epistemological, ethical and political debate by raising the 'self-consciousness' of historians and their readers, especially concerning economic development and the global comparison of different cultures, 'mak[ing] it possible to see ourselves in perspective.'[82] Much like the post-war community studies researchers encountered in chapter 5, British historians found in social anthropology a method that they sought to emulate. Perhaps most crucially, anthropology 'could provide valuable reinforcement for historians confronted by a paucity of evidence of the mental life of the lower reaches of the distant society they are studying,' Thomas wrote.[83] This commitment to understanding the lives of the 'lower reaches' led him on to a claim about the pedagogical potential of the new history. Rather than forcing undergraduates to remember the 'endless ... gymnastics of minor politicians,' he argued, 'the historical study of more immediate aspects of human experience' would surely 'capture' students' 'imagination[s]' more successfully.[84] Thomas's review piqued the interest of his colleague Lawrence Stone, who invited him to submit a version of the article to the journal *Past & Present*, where it was published in 1963.[85]

In that essay, Thomas wrote that anthropology held out the possibility of uniting religious, ecclesiastical and economic history, which had too often been treated separately, 'like patients in a hospital.' In the past, historians wanting to break the inmates out of the ward had to rely on what Thomas called 'vulgar Marxism'. Social anthropology now provided an alternative that could help 'explain things in terms of each other' without reducing them to an economic bottom line; as anthropologists argued, economic actions 'are themselves culturally determined.'[86] Anthropological texts were thus a vital body of work to understand the social origins of and limits to economic development in a non-Marxist framework: 'The problems of persuading Africans to adopt the rhythms of an industrial life,' Thomas wrote, 'are almost exactly those which confronted Josiah Wedgwood when he endeavoured to convert the feckless, easygoing populace of Staffordshire into "such machines ... as cannot err".'[87] Bringing these anthropological insights to bear on history would create 'a whole new world of historical investigation which might illuminate so much of what is most baffling and most crucial to human existence.'[88] As he put it in a review article of the new social history in *The Times Literary Supplement* in 1966: 'Englishmen are now disposed to see analogies between their history and that of "underdeveloped"

African countries. The gain in understanding and comparative sense is incalculable.'[89]

Thomas's views were controversial, and Stone later characterised the conflict between historians like him, who thought of history as a comparative social science, and those who did not, perhaps most prominently the Regius Professor at Cambridge during the 1980s, Geoffrey Elton, as a 'war'.[90] Over the following decades this war was fought amazingly successfully by the social science–oriented historians, to the lasting diminishment of their enemies.[91] Pioneering monographs by Thomas and Alan Macfarlane, amongst others, brought anthropological theory into the heart of social history.[92] The change in the kind of academic history writing produced in Britain between the 1950s and 1970s, Stone wrote retrospectively, was 'startling'.[93]

Stone characterised the topics motivating much of this new kind of history as 'middle-range problems', typical examples being the emergence of capitalism and the causes of the Industrial Revolution.[94] Thus historians were studying in the past the same kind of middle-range problems economists like Lewis were facing in the present. Anthropology stood at the fringes of both disciplines and provided a way to describe the lifestyles and customs of those societies being transformed by capitalism and industrialism. This is what made their works attractive to historians. Economists, as Lewis had pointed out in his review of Firth and Richards, however, found too little statistical data and too much worrying about industrialisation's dissociating effects to find much use in works of anthropology.

Thomas tackled his own 'middle-range problem' in his classic book *Religion and the Decline of Magic* (1971). This landmark bears the hallmarks of the 'new history', opening with an analogy between early modern England and 'the "under-developed areas" of today.'[95] Thomas recalled in an interview later in life that his 'guiding assumption' in that book was taken from social anthropology, namely that 'we should begin by thinking that we know nothing about people in the past.' The job of the historian, like the anthropologist, was to avoid falsely attributing to the subjects of their research 'beliefs and emotions which are ours, just because they seem natural human and normal.'[96] Earlier in this chapter I suggested that economics and anthropology were in competition in the 1950s. But here, in the English past, social anthropology found new readers eager to draw on its insights.

Summing up the result of almost two decades of this type of history, another scholar of early modern England, E. P. Thompson, concluded that 'just as economic history presupposes the discipline of economics, so social history (in its systematic examination of norms, expectations, values) must presuppose the discipline of social anthropology.'[97] Thompson was a heterodox Marxist and author of *The Making of the English Working Class* (1963). He read works of social anthropology to find examples of pre-industrial and non-capitalist forms of community. As he explained in an essay published in 1965, sociologists and anthropologists 'have sufficiently demonstrated the inextricable interlacing of economic and non-economic relations in most societies, and the intersection of economic and cultural satisfactions.' Like Thomas, he drew on this insight to make a historical argument about the past. '[U]ntil the late eighteenth century,' he wrote, 'the common people of France and England adhered to a deeply felt "moral economy" in which the very notion of "economic price" for corn ... was an outrage to their culture; and something of the same moral economy endures in parts of Asia and Africa today.'[98] Drawing on research from contemporary Asia and Africa might, then, help the historian understand the transition from a moral to an amoral economy. Folding the far away, as it were, back into the long ago, would make the near-contemporary insights of social anthropologists relevant for historians' understanding of past economic development and allow them to pursue what he called a year later 'history from below'.[99]

In 1971 Thompson made good on these arguments in 'The Moral Economy of the English Crowd in the Eighteenth Century.' In this article he put eighteenth-century England in a global frame. He wrote that 'the confrontations of the market in a "pre-industrial" society are of course more universal than any national experience.'[100] He maintained this comparative analysis with a nod to Malinowski and suggested that his works were well known to historians: 'We all know the delicate tissue of social norms and reciprocities which regulates the life of Trobriand Islanders.' But regardless of this knowledge, economists had been guilty of making 'this infinitely-complex social creature, Melanesian man' into 'the eighteenth-century collier who claps his hands spasmodically upon his stomach and responds to elementary economic stimuli.'[101]

Thompson's enemies were what he called the 'growth historians'. Although he did not cite Lewis as one of his targets, Thompson took issue with thinkers who equated industrialisation with increased welfare and who saw in statistics and prices evidence of a better world emerging as a result of the Industrial Revolution, both in the past and in its present incarnation in the post-colonial nations.[102] This led him to quarrel, as he put it in another article, with those who saw the historical record as 'a simple one of neutral and inevitable change.' Thompson saw conflict and exploitation and resistance, where 'values stand to be lost as well as gained.' 'For', he argued, 'there is no such thing as economic growth which is not, at the same time, growth or change of a culture.'[103] The sources for reconstructing what had been lost from this 'culture' came largely from anthropology, which Thompson fused with romantic critiques of political economy. On time discipline he drew on Evans-Pritchard.[104] And for his ideal of the 'moral economy' he used Malinowski (without citing him) to explicate non-market exchange and protest as 'not an involuntary spasm, but a pattern of behaviour of which a Trobriand islander need not have been ashamed.'[105] Thompson thus retooled social anthropology into a weapon to fight about the past and the present; his notion of the 'moral economy' has continued to provoke debate ever since, although with little sense that anthropology played much part in setting the terms of his argument.[106]

Of course, other factors beyond social anthropology shaped the new social history, too. According to one account, it was Lewis Namier's 'painstaking reconstruction of patronage and kinship' and the influence of the French historians writing in the journal *Annales: Economies, sociétiés, civilisations* that best explains the emergence of post-war social history in Britain.[107] Another scholar urges caution when searching for origins, however; 'social history' was never 'monolithic'.[108] It is more prudent, then, to say that within this broad catholicity, social anthropology had the greatest impact on one strand within the emerging field. Thomas and Thompson are, to say the least, names to conjure with if we want to understand the most important, wide-ranging and lasting innovations in post-war historiography. We can find evidence of anthropology's impact on other important studies too, from Peter Laslett's *World We Have Lost* (in which he wrote of the importance of 'contrast[ing] over space, or rather cross-cultural comparison as the anthropologist might put it') to Eric Hobsbawm's *Primitive Rebels* (originally presented to Gluckman's anthropology seminar at Manchester).[109] These texts do not capture the totality of 'social history', but they do encompass a significant amount of what was taken to be most original at the time and what has often been understood as most innovative since.

CONCLUSION

By putting history, anthropology and economics together we have seen how in the era of decolonisation and development economics, social anthropology continued to influence Britain's intellectual culture even as it faced a political crisis in the post-colonial nations. In the field of economics, anthropologists offered aid, inspiration and critical methods for academics grappling with questions of how to measure growth and how to apply national accounting to partially monetized societies. However, it was almost always the case that economists ignored anthropologists, and researchers like Phyllis Deane, who did fieldwork, were in the minority. A different story happened in historiography, where concepts like the 'moral economy' and 'history from below' saw social anthropology take on new salience in debates about the genesis of capitalism and industrialism in Britain's past.

It was in the interstices of these disputes over development, culture and economic life in the 1950s and 1960s that the seedlings of many later debates about 'the market', 'the economy' and 'the social' in the human sciences bedded in and began to germinate.[110] Social anthropology prompted historians to rethink modernization in the past, just as it began to be displaced as a way to think about development in the present. Capturing the shifting terrain of development ideology and decolonisation in the 1950s and 1960s provides a new way to think about the post-war history of the social sciences, when economics emerged triumphant from the detritus of empire and anthropologists inspired critiques of their concepts that would grow and evolve over subsequent decades.

It would not be too dramatic to say that this moment marked the emergence of a new social-scientific *episteme*. Decolonisation reshaped the world, and social science followed in train. How does this interdisciplinary story of anthropology, history and economics change how we see the history of the British social sciences? In the introduction to this book, I quoted Perry Anderson, who argued that British intellectual culture was a desiccated, empiricist husk, meaning that social anthropology could only survive outside the metropole.[111] Clearly this view needs to be revised. In chapter 5 we saw how social anthropology influenced contemporary community studies. Here we have witnessed the discipline's impact in historiography. Anthropology provided a handy cache of functionalist ideas and ethnographic methods to understand society beyond the narrow stratum that Thomas memorably populated with the 'endless ... gymnastics of minor politicians.'[112]

Looking beyond the political elites, anthropology offered researchers ways to make the argument that working-class Britons had their own culture in the 1950s and in the past. 'Early modern' villagers, bread rioters and witchcraft-believing Stuarts all had cultures, too.[113] How did those cultures change, and how might that process be linked to the modernising trends of the contemporary world? Social anthropology provided the functionalist theory that allowed historians to connect changes in one domain of social life to another. Thus, a riot about grain prices in the work of Thompson or the sudden appearance of accusations of witchcraft in the writings of Thomas might be read as a signal of systemic change, and even breakdown, in the wider society. This was an idea borrowed and analogised from anthropologists like Firth, who wrote about contemporary non-capitalist societies being broken apart by settler colonialism and extractive capitalist imperialism. The struggles and tragedies of those facing expropriation on the fringes of 1920s to 1950s global capitalism were folded back into the past to account for the emergence of capital-intensive industrialism and enclosure in the English past.

When we adopt what Stefan Collini called a 'lateral view' and bring the imperial and metropolitan history of social anthropology together, we see how anthropology fertilised so much debate at the margins of the disciplines.[114] And when we look at the shifting terrain of the disciplines we also see how, in many ways, Richards's warnings about the scrapheap were prophetic. For a moment in the late 1930s and 1940s, anthropology looked destined to grow and thrive in the British Empire. Decolonization and development economics changed all that. Social anthropology would, from then on, possess a mostly British rather than post-colonial history as it was shaped increasingly by student demand and government funding in the expanding UK higher education sector. The 1960s were a jarring time for the anthropologists who had trained with Malinowski at the LSE. Anthropology was no longer at the heart of the debate about other cultures and how to develop them. Rather, it formed a kind of minority report on capitalist development itself, with critics drawing on its arguments to challenge top-down programs of 'high modernist' planning.

Epilogue

This book has explained how social anthropology rose and fell as a prop to colonial development and what part it played in Britain's intellectual culture from 1920 to 1960. Tacking from empire to metropole and back again has reset some mainstays of modern British studies in an anthropological key: from 'indirect rule' to 'companionate marriage', from 'race relations' to 'community studies' to 'development'. While Perry Anderson argued in 1968 that social anthropology had been 'useful to colonial administration and dangerous to no domestic prejudice,' this book has suggested that we turn Anderson's thesis on its head: social anthropology was mostly useless to colonial administrators; instead, its lasting legacy lay in shaping debates about social change in Britain.[1] The main part of this book ends in the 1960s for three reasons: first, the intellectual and political critiques discussed in the final chapter intensified; second, social anthropology struggled to adapt to the expanding university sector; and third, new ideas of 'culture' emerged, fraying the coherence of the anthropological enterprise recounted so far.

THE 1960S AND AFTER: INTELLECTUAL AND POLITICAL CRISIS

As we have seen, by 1960 development economics and post-colonial politics both posed fundamental challenges to social anthropology, such that Audrey Richards worried the discipline was due to be thrown on the 'scrapheap'. This crisis was compounded by a generational changing of the guard: over the following decade most of the men and women I have discussed in this book died or retired. Edward Evans-Pritchard retired in 1970 and died in 1973, the same year that Meyer Fortes retired from the William Wyse Professorship at Cambridge. Audrey Richards retired in 1966. Margaret Read retired from the Institute of Education in the mid-1960s, and Max Gluckman retired in 1965 and died in 1973. Lucy Mair retired in 1968 and died in 1986. Raymond Firth retired in 1968 also, and with his death in 2002, Marilyn Strathern wrote that the world lost the 'last of the great founders of modern social anthropology.'[2]

Talal Asad commented on the intellectual drift that resulted. Anthropology in the 1960s and 1970s could no longer claim to study 'the primitive', which left anthropologists with little else but 'a multitude of fragmentary problems ... at a "small-scale"' to offer up to 'cognate disciplines', like political science and economics.[3] The result, Asad declared, was little less than the 'disintegration' of a previously coherent intellectual project. Total collapse was averted by the guild-like power of the Association of Social Anthropologists that kept the discipline together: 'There are today no clear-cut standards in anthropology, there is only a flourishing professional organization,' he remarked.[4]

In retrospect, Asad's sense of intellectual stagnation might seem overblown. The 1960s saw some important research that has stood the test of time. Mary Douglas's *Purity and Danger* (1966) remains a classic. Edmund Leach, whom I have not discussed much in this book, saw his *Political Systems of Highland Burma* (1954) reprinted throughout the 1960s and 1970s.[5] Both Douglas and Leach grappled with the work of the French anthropologist Claude Lévi-Strauss and a younger generation of British anthropologists found in the writings of other French anthropologists, such as Maurice Godelier and Emmanuel Terray, ways to connect anthropology and Marxism.[6] The Manchester School also flourished, with the publication of F. G. Bailey's *Tribe, Caste, and Nation* (1960); Fredrick Barth's *Political Leadership Among Swat Pathans* (1965); Elizabeth Colson's *Social Organization of the Gwembe Tonga* (1960); A. L. Epstein's *Politics in an Urban African Community* (1958); J. Clyde Mitchell's *The Kalela Dance* (1956); and Victor Turner's *Schism and Continuity in African Society* (1957). These writers developed a new approach in anthropology: the 'extended case method'.[7]

Gluckman seems to have guided the anthropology department at Manchester much as Malinowski led his seminar at the LSE in the 1930s: as an overbearing, prickly patriarch overseeing a fractious group of brilliant researchers applying and critiquing their mentor's theories and methods.[8] Yet while Malinowski's seminar decisively transformed British anthropology, Gluckman's did not. The Manchester department in the late 1950s and 1960s was at the fringes of a discipline dominated by Oxford, Cambridge and the LSE and was being pushed to the margins in the field by anti-colonial politics. On the one hand, some of Gluckman's students were barred from travelling to Britain's last remaining colonies because of their political radicalism.[9] On the other hand, Archie Mafeje, who studied and taught in Cambridge in the 1960s, explained the very different context of anthropological research in post-colonial nations.

In the period leading up to independence, Mafeje explained that while Manchester School anthropologists may not have been 'empire builders', their class status and ethnicity meant they still 'enjoyed some prestige and respectability.' In newly independent countries, however, social anthropologists 'were under pressure to account for themselves' in a 'political and intellectual environment' that was 'hostile' to their research.[10] This was a radical change from the situation described in chapters 2, 3 and 6, where some colonial administrators may have been bemused by or uninterested in anthropological research, but anthropologists' status as authoritative and trustworthy observers of 'the social' was largely accepted and they could expect to compel their subjects to respond to their questioning, even if they were often resisted, given selective answers or co-opted into local political disputes. By the end of the 1960s, anthropologists' epistemological authority could no longer be taken for granted because of the very different politics of post-colonial knowledge production.

Turning from the post-colonial nations in the 1960s to the intellectual scene in Britain and America, we can also see critiques emerging that undercut the methodological and epistemological bases of the discipline. Exactly those factors that contributed to social anthropology's prominence in the 1930s and 1940s fuelled the fire of its critics: its functionalism, the centrality of fieldwork to its method, the patronage that resulted from alliances with the colonial state. The 'basic unity of the critique', Peter Forster summarised, 'revolves around discussion of the colonial situation and the place of anthropology within it.'[11] Some writers put their emphasis on British imperialism and others on American 'neo-imperialism', but all of anthropology's critics made the link between 'empiricism', 'functionalism' and the politics of empire.[12] The 'origins' of the critique were 'fairly easy to discern', according to Forster. Nationalist liberation struggles in the 1950s and 1960s and then opposition to the Vietnam War had done much to radicalise anthropology's critics on the left, especially in the wake of the revelations in 1966 that the CIA had funded some American anthropologists' research in South America and Southeast Asia.[13]

Anthropology's critics tended to connect the increasingly maligned functionalism of the mid-century social sciences to a bourgeois, imperialist *Weltanschauung* that, in the words of Mafeje, structured the anthropologist's whole 'ontology of thought categories'.[14] Treating social science as an ideology tended to cast differences over method as 'reflections of deep-lying metaphysical positions' amidst the 'intellectual culture of modernity.'[15] In the case of anthropology's critics, these concerns were foundationally connected to imperialism and neo-imperialism. The braiding of an epistemological critique of anthropology with a political critique of colonialism became a reflex during the 1970s and 'axiomatic', one commentator argues, after the publication of Edward Said's *Orientalism* in 1978.[16]

The 1950s marked the beginning of a break in the imperial and international political contexts that nurtured social anthropology and that I have discussed throughout this book. This trend then accelerated in the 1960s when an increasing number of social scientists, politicians and activists critiqued theories of 'the social' that stressed self-equilibrating and self-stabilising interactions and looked increasingly to dynamics of change, protest and power instead. James Clifford recalls a conversation in the early 1970s with Raymond Firth in which the then retired heir to Malinowski's professorial chair at the LSE 'shook his head in a mixture of pretended and real confusion. . . . "Not so long ago we were radicals. We thought of ourselves as gadflies and reformers, advocates for the value of indigenous cultures, defenders of our people. Now, all of a sudden, we're handmaidens of empire!"'[17]

THE CHANGING LANDSCAPE OF HIGHER EDUCATION IN BRITAIN

Alongside these political and intellectual changes, the discipline also stood in a very different landscape of higher education in the 1960s. Universities were rapidly expanding in Britain, and because of this, Jonathan Spencer suggests, 'the story of British social anthropology in the[se] years . . . is heavily shaped by the story of British universities and their relationship with the British state.'[18] In this context, the professional solidarity of the Association of Social Anthropologists (ASA), which Talal Asad saw as the discipline's last remaining strength, put anthropology at a competitive disadvantage.

The ASA's closed-shop, elitist culture meant that there were barely enough social anthropologists to staff the new departments opening in Belfast, Hull and Swansea and in the joint departments with sociology at Sussex, Kent and East Anglia; in 1963 there were around 50 professional anthropologists in Britain, rising to 90 in 1972 and 120 by 1983.[19] By comparison, there were as many as 1,000 sociologists in post by 1981, more than enough to staff the new universities and polytechnics.[20] The geographical spread of anthropology was smaller, too, with most researchers concentrated in the same universities that had emerged in the 1940s as centres of teaching and research: Oxford, Cambridge and the LSE, with Manchester and UCL at the peripheries.[21]

Part of the reason for anthropology's comparatively slow growth lay with the ASA's strict hold over who could claim to be a 'social anthropologist'. The ASA's elitist attitude and exclusive membership meant that social anthropology was not taught at polytechnics or at the Open University. Social anthropology kept itself aloof from transformations of secondary and post-secondary education that brought social science (as part of a broad-based 'social studies') to a truly mass audience in the 1960s and 1970s.[22] For instance, while 100,000 eighteen-year-olds had studied A-level sociology by the mid-1970s, schoolchildren could only take an A level in anthropology from 2011.[23] Student numbers lagged well behind psychology and sociology throughout the second half of the twentieth century.[24]

The discipline's slow growth was also due to the reproduction of professional anthropologists through fieldwork and via the kind of intensive postgraduate, seminar-based training pioneered by Malinowski and described in chapter 3 of this book. This took time, resources and hands-on experience. In Cambridge, Audrey Richards inducted some undergraduates into field research near her home in the Essex village of Elmdon, but for the most part, anthropology remained a graduate-focused discipline that demanded an intensive period of extended time in the field. This model of socialisation and training could not easily be extended to a growing undergraduate audience. As a result, the anthropological grandees of the 1970s thought it would probably be a waste of time trying to reach out to anyone else beyond their traditional graduate cohorts.[25]

FROM SOCIETY TO CULTURE IN ANGLO-AMERICAN ANTHROPOLOGY

This lofty attitude towards the popularisation of social science research coincided with an intensification of the intellectual crisis diagnosed by Mafeje and Asad. The resulting diminishment of anthropology's standing in Britain and in America has been a cause of lamentation for some.[26] But anthropology did not simply disappear. A new emphasis on culture emerged on both sides of the Atlantic, and some anthropologists took a hermeneutic turn, while others took on Marxist, feminist and postcolonial theories.[27] In this sense, far from diminishing anthropology's standing, the crisis of the 1960s had the effect of extending the discipline's reach by pluralising the range of theories for other disciplines to borrow. Anthropology remained, and remains, a theoretical and methodological storehouse for other academics to explore for inspiration and exemplars.[28]

One of the most successful post-war anthropologists in this regard has been the American Clifford Geertz, who took a turn towards 'interpretive' anthropology but not towards radical politics. While British anthropologists saw this Geertzian focus on 'culture' and 'symbols' as a departure from their emphasis on 'the social', it is questionable whether historians thought about these differences much, or even understood them.[29] Geertz, Lévi-Strauss, Douglas, Turner and a whole host of other anthropologists from Britain, America and France, often with very different theoretical agendas, helped historians redefine the 'early modern' and then the whole discipline, from Natalie Zemon Davis's writings on religious violence, to Robert Darnton's 'great cat massacre', to Carlo Ginzburg's *The Cheese and the Worms*.[30] Meanwhile amongst social scientists who took linguistic, post-colonial and postmodern turns, much of the debate about the 'intellectual culture of modernity' has been, after all, a debate about modernity, as well as culture. As such, it has largely been carried on in anthropology's traditional wheelhouse.[31] Historians and other social scientists continue to draw on Polanyi's and Thompson's ideas of 'moral economy', and some recent theorists of 'the social' like Pierre Bourdieu and Bruno Latour can also be productively read within the traditions of social anthropology discussed throughout this book.[32]

So while British anthropologists might have worried in the 1960s and 1970s that 'culture' would pose as fundamental a threat to social anthropology as 'the economy' had done in the 1950s, their worries were misplaced. At least to outsiders looking in, 'culture' and 'the social' were both holistic concepts that could help reconstruct the 'mental life of the lower reaches' of past societies, as Keith Thomas had put it in 1961, and both concepts would be put to use in criticising reductionist economic ideas about self-interest and individualism.[33] In this sense, social anthropologists' ideas about 'the social' still live on as one particular kind of holism. Like seed pods scattered wide over a changing landscape, many of the anthropological ideas contained in these pages survived the intellectual 'crises' of the 1960s, whether via the idea of the 'moral economy' or in social history; some others did not bed in but may seem fresh or urgent even now, like Phyllis Deane's empirical economic fieldwork.

When Raymond Firth came to write up his dissertation as his first book, *Primitive Economics of the New Zealand Maori* (1929), he ended the manuscript with the following Māori proverb: 'Takoto Kau ana Te Whanau a Tane' (The children of Tane, the trees of the forest, have fallen).[34] Anna Tsing's recent book on life in the ruins of a devastated environment ends with a line from Ursula Le Guin, although it is not this one: '"The world is always new . . . however old its roots."'[35] I hope that this book will carry forward some of these ways of thinking about society, perhaps even to be revivified and debated once again, although with a better sense, perhaps, of the way they reach back into the past. Happily, the history of anthropology is a growing field, with histories of anthropologists and their ideas and anthropological archives being plumbed to write about the people anthropologists themselves wrote about. This latter endeavour is a particularly exciting development.[36] My hope is that this book will inspire further research on the history of social anthropology. There is so much more to say.

Notes

INTRODUCTION

1. Pym drew on her job as an assistant editor at the International African Institute's journal *Africa* to describe the world of social anthropology. Joe B. Fulton, 'The "Enviable Detachment" of the Anthropologist: Barbara Pym's Anthropological Aesthetic', *Papers on Language & Literature*, 39.1 (2003), 91–108. I am indebted to Max Long and Taylor Moore for suggesting I read Barbara Pym's novel and for Taylor's advice to start my book with a discussion of it.

2. Raymond Williams, *Culture and Society* (London: Vintage Digital, 1958; repr. 2015), 157.

3. As opposed to 'the biological'. For the origins of this distinction see Maurizio Meloni, 'The Transcendence of the Social: Durkheim, Weismann, and the Purification of Sociology', *Frontiers in Sociology*, 1 (2016), <http://dx.doi.org/10.3389/fsoc.2016.00011>

4. The literature is large. For some recent books, see Richard Handler, *Critics Against Culture: Anthropological Observers of Mass Society* (Madison: University of Wisconsin Press, 2005); Peter Mandler, *Return from the Natives: How Margaret Mead Won the Second World War and Lost the Cold War* (New Haven, CT: Yale University Press, 2013); and Charles King, *The Reinvention of Humanity: A Story of Race, Sex, Gender and the Discovery of Culture* (London: Penguin, 2019).

5. A good introduction to the diversity and development of American anthropology can be found in Regna Darnell, 'North American Traditions in Anthropology: The Historiographic Baseline', in *A New History of Anthropology*, ed. by Henrika Kuklick (Oxford: Blackwell, 2008).

6. Henrika Kuklick, *The Savage Within: The Social History of British Anthropology, 1885–1945* (Cambridge: Cambridge University Press, 1991), 12; George W. Stocking Jr, 'Radcliffe-Brown and British Social Anthropology', in *Functionalism Historicized: Essays on British Social Anthropology*, ed. by George W. Stocking Jr (Madison: University of Wisconsin Press, 1984), 181.

7. For an important study that bucks this trend, see Grahame Foreman, 'Horizons of Modernity: British Anthropology and the End of Empire' (unpublished PhD thesis, University of California, Berkeley, 2013). Literary scholars have also been interested in social anthropology. See, for example, Jed Esty, *A Shrinking Island: Modernism and National Culture in England* (Princeton, NJ: Princeton University Press, 2004); and Marc Manganaro, *Culture, 1922: The Emergence of a Concept* (Princeton, NJ: Princeton University Press, 2002). For anthropology's influence on literary culture, see Jeremy MacClancy, *Anthropology in the Public Arena : Historical and Contemporary Contexts* (Chichester: Wiley-Blackwell, 2013). For books that mention anthropology in relation to colonial studies and students from Britain's empire, see Barbara Bush, *Imperialism, Race and Resistance: Africa and Britain, 1919–1945* (London: Routledge, 1999); and Marc Matera, *Black London: The Imperial Metropolis and Decolonization in the Twentieth Century* (Oakland: University of California Press, 2015).

8. Wolf Lepenies, *Between Literature and Science: The Rise of Sociology* (Cambridge: Cambridge University Press, 1988), ch. 6. See, for instance, Christopher Hilliard, *English as a Vocation: The Scrutiny Movement* (Oxford: Oxford University Press, 2012); and Guy Ortolano, *The Two Cultures Controversy: Science, Literature and Cultural Politics in Postwar Britain* (Cambridge: Cambridge University Press, 2009).

9. For 'gentlemanly' social science, see Mike Savage, *Identities and Social Change in Britain since 1940: The Politics of Method* (Oxford: Oxford University Press, 2010), ch. 4. On absences in the history of sociology, see Martin Bulmer, ed., *Essays on the History of British Sociological Research* (Cambridge: Cambridge University Press, 1985); A. H. Halsey, *A History of Sociology in Britain: Science, Literature, and Society* (Oxford : Oxford University Press, 2004); and Jennifer Platt, *The British Sociological Association: A Sociological History* (Durham, UK: Sociologypress, 2003); although J. D. Y. Peel has offered some minimal revision of this trend in 'Not Really a View from Without: The Relations of Social Anthropology and Sociology', in *British Sociology Seen from Without and Within*, ed. by A. H. Halsey and W. G. Runciman (Oxford: Oxford University Press, 2005). Martin Bulmer discusses social anthropology only to then dismiss it in 'Introduction', in *Essays on the History of British Sociological Research*, 20.

10. The history of anthropology is one of the paradigmatic examples of the post-war pursuit of disciplinary history, according to Suzanne Marchand in 'Has the History of the Disciplines Had Its Day?', in *Rethinking Modern European Intellectual History*, ed. by Samuel Moyn and Darrin M. McMahon (Oxford: Oxford University Press, 2014).

11. Stefan Collini, '"Discipline History" and "Intellectual History": Reflections on the Historiography of the Social Sciences in Britain and France', *Revue de Synthèse*, 109.3-4 (1988), 387–99 (quotes at 388, 391). For disciplinary

histories outlining the shifting ideas of anthropology in Britain, see Kuklick, *Savage Within*; Adam Kuper, *Anthropology and Anthropologists: The British School in the Twentieth Century*, 4th edn (London: Routledge, 2015); and George W. Stocking Jr, *After Tylor: British Social Anthropology, 1888–1951* (Madison: University of Wisconsin Press, 1995).

12. I. C. Jarvie, *The Revolution in Anthropology* (London: Routledge & Kegan Paul, 1964). For a brief survey of the literature on founders, 'discovery' and disciplinary histories/genealogies, see Simon Schaffer, *From Physics to Anthropology and Back Again* (Chicago: Prickly Pear, 1994), 6–7.

13. Bronislaw Malinowski, *Argonauts of the Western Pacific: An Account of Native Enterprise and Adventure in the Archipelagoes of Melanesian New Guinea* (London: Routledge & Kegan Paul, 1922; repr. 1978), 19.

14. Edward Evans-Pritchard, *Witchcraft, Oracles and Magic among the Azande* (Oxford: Clarendon Press, 1937). The best overviews of these various kinds of 'functionalism' and the theories and debates of the era are Kuper, *Anthropology and Anthropologists*; and Stocking, *After Tylor*.

15. For an overarching outline of a cognate approach, see Daniel T. Rodgers, 'Paths in the Social History of Ideas', in *The Worlds of American Intellectual History*, ed. by Joel Isaac et al. (Oxford: Oxford University Press, 2016), 313–14. I have also been influenced by the ideas of Randall Collins; see Randall Collins, 'On the Acrimoniousness of Intellectual Disputes', *Common Knowledge*, 8.1 (2002), 47–70; and Randall Collins, 'Toward a Theory of Intellectual Change: The Social Causes of Philosophies', *Science, Technology & Human Values*, 14.2 (1989), 107–40.

16. The literature is vast. For a wide-ranging historical essay that reaches back to the Renaissance, see Michel-Rolph Trouillot, 'Anthropology and the Savage Slot: The Poetics and Politics of Otherness', in *Recapturing Anthropology: Working in the Present*, ed. by Richard G. Fox (Santa Fe, NM: School of American Research Press, 1991). For the Enlightenment, see J. G. A. Pocock, *Barbarism and Religion, Volume 4, Barbarians, Savages and Empires* (Cambridge: Cambridge University Press, 2005); and Silvia Sebastiani, *The Scottish Enlightenment: Race, Gender, and the Limits of Progress* (London: Palgrave Macmillan, 2013).

17. Timothy Larsen, *The Slain God: Anthropologists and the Christian Faith* (Oxford: Oxford University Press, 2014).

18. On that count see David Mills, *Difficult Folk? A Political History of Social Anthropology* (New York: Berghahn Books, 2008).

19. For some works in this burgeoning field of the history of social research in Britain, see Lise Butler, *Michael Young, Social Science and the British Left, 1945–70* (Oxford: Oxford University Press, 2020); and Jon Lawrence, 'Inventing the "Traditional Working Class": A Re-Analysis of Interview Notes from Young and Willmott's Family and Kinship in East London', *The Historical Journal*, 59.2 (2016), 567–93. For the wider literature, see Peter Mandler, 'The Language of Social Science in Everyday Life', *History of the Human Sciences*, 32.1 (2019), 66–82; Peter Mandler, 'Good Reading for the Million: The "Paperback Revolution" and the Co-Production of Academic Knowledge in Mid Twentieth-Century Britain and America', *Past & Present*, 244.1 (2019), 235–69; Helen McCarthy,

'Social Science and Married Women's Employment in Post-War Britain', *Past & Present*, 233.1 (2016), 269–305; and Savage, *Identities and Social Change*.

20. In this sense I have been inspired by the methods and approaches of the 'new imperial history': see, for one important collection staking out the methodological terrain, Catherine Hall and Sonya O. Rose, *At Home with the Empire: Metropolitan Culture and the Imperial World* (Cambridge: Cambridge University Press, 2006).

21. Andrew Bank, *Pioneers of the Field: South Africa's Women Anthropologists* (Cambridge: Cambridge University Press, 2016); and Robert J. Gordon, *The Enigma of Max Gluckman: The Ethnographic Life of a 'Luckyman' in Africa* (Lincoln: University of Nebraska Press, 2018).

22. For a statement of this concept, see Michel Callon, 'Some Elements of a Sociology of Translation: Domestication of the Scallops and the Fishermen of St Brieuc Bay', *The Sociological Review*, 32.S1 (1984), 196–233.

23. For an attempt to make a comparative study of national traditions in anthropology, see: Fredrik Barth et al., *One Discipline, Four Ways: British, German, French, and American Anthropology* (Chicago: University of Chicago Press, 2005).

24. For South Africa see note 21 above, and for Australia see Geoffrey Gray, *A Cautious Silence: The Politics of Australian Anthropology* (Canberra: Aboriginal Studies Press, 2007); and Patrick Wolfe, *Settler Colonialism and the Transformation of Anthropology: The Politics and Poetics of an Ethnographic Event* (London: Cassell, 1999).

25. Alfred Gell, 'Introduction: Notes on Seminar Culture and Some Other Influences', in Alfred Gell and Eric Hirsch, *The Art of Anthropology: Essays and Diagrams* (London: Athlone Press, 1999).

26. For a compelling account of how communities of inquiry form and are critiqued, see Isaac Ariail Reed and Mayer N. Zald 'The Unsettlement of Communities of Inquiry', in *Theorizing in Social Science: The Context of Discovery*, ed. by Richard Swedberg (Stanford, CA: Stanford University Press, 2014).

27. George Peter Murdock, 'British Social Anthropology', *American Anthropologist*, 53.4 (1951), 465–73; and Kuper, *Anthropology and Anthropologists*, 102–3.

28. On Stocking as a product of the 1960s and a post-positivist moment, see Marchand, 'Has the History of the Disciplines Had Its Day?', 136–37.

29. Perry Anderson, 'Components of the National Culture', *New Left Review*, series I, 50 (1968), 3–57, at 48.

30. George Steinmetz, 'Defensive Anthropology', *Postcolonial Studies*, 17.4 (2014), 436–50, 443. A debate carries on, meanwhile, about the discipline's role in the undermining of ideas of racial and cultural hierarchy amidst these networks of patronage. For one of the latest interventions in this ongoing dispute, see Herbert S. Lewis, *In Defense of Anthropology: An Investigation of the Critique of Anthropology* (London: Transaction Publishers, 2014).

For a trenchant argument about the field's relationship to colonialism, see Edward W. Said, 'Representing the Colonized: Anthropology's Interlocutors', *Critical Inquiry*, 15.2 (1989), 205–25. For classic statements, see Talal Asad, 'Introduction', in *Anthropology & the Colonial Encounter*, ed. by Talal Asad

(Amherst, NY: Humanity Books, 1973; repr. 1998); Archie Mafeje, 'The Problem of Anthropology in Historical Perspective: An Inquiry into the Growth of the Social Sciences', *Canadian Journal of African Studies/Revue Canadienne des Études Africaines*, 10.2 (1976), 307–33; and Linda Tuhiwai Smith, *Decolonizing Methodologies: Research and Indigenous Peoples* (London: Zed Books, 2012). An important recent intervention that situates the development of social anthropology in the context of the late British Empire and governmentality is Nile A. Davis, 'Empire of Abstraction: British Social Anthropology in the "Dependencies"' <https://jhiblog.org/2020/06/29/empire-of-abstraction-british-social-anthropology-in-the-dependencies> . For one overview of the turn to empire in the history of the social sciences, see *Empire and the Social Sciences: Global Histories of Knowledge*, ed. by Jeremy Adelman (London: Bloomsbury Publishing, 2019). And for some literature in a growing field that links imperial histories and the history of social science disciplines, see Frederick Cooper, 'Development, Modernization, and the Social Sciences in the Era of Decolonization: The Examples of British and French Africa', *Revue d'Histoire des Sciences Humaines*, 10.1 (2004), 9–38; George Steinmetz, 'Sociology and Colonialism in the British and French Empires, 1945–1965', *Journal of Modern History*, 89.3 (2017), 601–48; George Steinmetz, 'A Child of the Empire: British Sociology and Colonialism, 1940s–1960s', *Journal of the History of the Behavioral Sciences*, 49.4 (2013), 353–78; and Robert Vitalis, *White World Order, Black Power Politics: The Birth of American International Relations* (Ithaca, NY: Cornell University Press, 2015).

31. Asad, 'Introduction', 18.
32. Mafeje, 'Problem of Anthropology in Historical Perspective', 319.
33. Helen Tilley 'Introduction: Africa, Imperialism, and Anthropology', in *Ordering Africa: Anthropology, European Imperialism and the Politics of Knowledge*, ed. by Helen Tilley and Robert Gordon (Manchester: Manchester University Press, 2010), 6.

CHAPTER 1. ISLANDS AND INSTITUTIONS

1. *Chambers's Twentieth Century Dictionary of the English Language*, ed. by Rev Thomas Davidson, Project Gutenberg (Edinburgh: W. & R. Chambers, 1908) <https://www.gutenberg.org/files/37683/37683-h/37683-h.htm>.
2. Sujit Sivasundaram, 'The Animal and Human in the Idea of Race', *Comparative Studies of South Asia, Africa and the Middle East*, 35.1 (2015), 156–72.
3. Trouillot, 'Anthropology and the Savage Slot'.
4. Samuel J. M. M. Alberti, 'Museum Nature', in *Worlds of Natural History*, ed. by Helen Anne Curry et al. (Cambridge: Cambridge University Press, 2018); and Sadiah Qureshi, 'Peopling Natural History' in *Worlds of Natural History*, ed. by Helen Anne Curry et al.; and Sadiah Qureshi, *Peoples on Parade: Exhibitions, Empire and Anthropology in Nineteenth-Century Britain* (Chicago: University of Chicago Press, 2011).
5. Qureshi, 'Peopling Natural History', 366–67.
6. Reba N. Soffer, 'The Modern University and National Values, 1850–1930', *Historical Research*, 60.142 (1987), 166–87.

7. A. H. Halsey and M. A. Trow, *The British Academics* (London: Faber & Faber, 1971), 145.

8. Doris S. Goldstein, 'The Organizational Development of the British Historical Profession,1884-1921', *Historical Research*, 55.132 (1982), 180–93; Reba N. Soffer, 'The Development of Disciplines in the Modern English University', *The Historical Journal*, 31.4 (1988), 933–46; and Jill Pellew, 'A Metropolitan University Fit for Empire: The Role of Private Benefaction in the Early History of the London School of Economics and Political Science and Imperial College of Science and Technology, 1895–1930', *History of Universities* 46 (2012), 202–45. An exhaustive overview of LSE's history is given in Donald Fisher, 'The Impact of American Foundations on the Development of British University Education, 1900–1939' (unpublished PhD thesis, University of California, Berkeley, 1977), ch. 3.

9. George W. Stocking Jr, *Victorian Anthropology* (New York: Free Press, 1987), 269.

10. Helen Tilley, *Africa as a Living Laboratory: Empire, Development, and the Problem of Scientific Knowledge, 1870–1950* (Chicago: University of Chicago Press, 2011), 9 and *passim*; Wendy James, 'The Anthropologist as Reluctant Imperialist', in *Anthropology & the Colonial Encounter*, ed. by Talal Asad, 52–60; and 'Anth and Arch Research in East Africa—1930-32', in Colonial Office Files (henceforth CO), The National Archives, Kew, (henceforth TNA), 822/27/17.

11. On histories of expertise, science and colonialism in the British Empire, see Joseph Morgan Hodge, *Triumph of the Expert: Agrarian Doctrines of Development and the Legacies of British Colonialism* (Athens: Ohio University Press, 2007); Brett M. Bennett and Joseph Morgan Hodge, eds., *Science and Empire: Knowledge and Networks of Science across the British Empire, 1800–1970* (Basingstoke: Palgrave Macmillan, 2011).

12. Mafeje, 'Problem of Anthropology in Historical Perspective'.

13. For an overview see C. A. Bayly, *The Birth of the Modern World, 1780–1914: Global Connections and Comparisons* (Malden, MA: Blackwell, 2004), ch 12.

14. Kuper, *Anthropology and Anthropologists*, 66–70.

15. On anthropology in India, see Bernard S. Cohn, *Colonialism and Its Forms of Knowledge: The British in India* (Princeton, NJ: Princeton University Press, 1996); Nicholas B. Dirks, *Castes of Mind: Colonialism and the Making of Modern India* (Princeton, NJ: Princeton University Press, 2001); C. J. Fuller, 'History, Anthropology, Colonialism, and the Study of India', *History and Theory*, 55.3 (2016), 452–64; and C. J. Fuller, 'Ethnographic Inquiry in Colonial India: Herbert Risley, William Crooke, and the Study of Tribes and Castes', *Journal of the Royal Anthropological Institute*, 23.3 (2017), 603–21.

16. T. O. Ranger, 'From Humanism to the Science of Man: Colonialism in Africa and the Understanding of Alien Societies', *Transactions of the Royal Historical Society*, 5th ser., 26 (1976), 115–41.

17. Quoted in Paul Basu, "N. W. Thomas and Colonial Anthropology in British West Africa: Reappraising a Cautionary Tale," *Journal of the Royal Anthropological Institute*, 22.1 (2016), 84–107, 89.

18. For an account of British interwar amateurism with reference to economic expertise, see Marion Fourcade, *Economists and Societies: Discipline and Profession in the United States, Britain, and France, 1890s to 1990s* (Princeton, NJ: Princeton University Press, 2009), 42–49. Imperial bureaucrats in Africa remained sceptical of social science well into the post-war era: Peter Pels, 'Global "Experts" and "African" Minds: Tanganyika Anthropology as Public and Secret Service, 1925–61', *Journal of the Royal Anthropological Institute* 17.4 (2011): 788–810, 795–96; and Erik Linstrum, *Ruling Minds: Psychology in the British Empire* (Cambridge, MA: Harvard University Press, 2016), 158.

19. On struggles over expertise, see Benoît de L'Estoile, 'The "Natural Preserve of Anthropologists": Social Anthropology, Scientific Planning and Development', *Social Science Information*, 36.2 (1997), 343–76.

20. Jonathan Spencer, 'British Social Anthropology: A Retrospective', *Annual Review of Anthropology*, 29 (2000), 1–24, at 3.

21. For an argument about the centrality of violence and resistance in this era of expansive British imperialism, see Antoinette M. Burton, *The Trouble with Empire: Challenges to Modern British Imperialism* (Oxford: Oxford University Press, 2015). And on the necessity of centring violence in imperial history in general, see Richard Drayton, 'Where Does the World Historian Write From? Objectivity, Moral Conscience and the Past and Present of Imperialism', *Journal of Contemporary History*, 46.3 (2011), 671–85.

22. G. Elliott Smith, 'Races of the Empire', *The Times*, 17 January 1925, p. 6; and 'Anthropology and the Empire', *The Times*, 17 January 1925, p. 11.

23. 'Races of the Empire: Useful an Useless Anthropology', LSE Malinowski Papers, 9/3.

24. Malinowski, *Argonauts of the Western Pacific*, 19.

25. I. C. Jarvie, *The Revolution in Anthropology* (London: Routledge & Kegan Paul, 1964).

26. For the context of the letter-writing campaign, see Ian Langham, *The Building of British Social Anthropology: W.H.R. Rivers and His Cambridge Disciples in the Development of Kinship Studies, 1898–1931* (Dordrecht, Holland: D. Reidel, 1981), 188–93.

27. Maurizio Meloni, 'The Transcendence of the Social: Durkheim, Weismann, and the Purification of Sociology', *Frontiers in Sociology*, 1 (2016), <http://dx.doi.org/10.3389/fsoc.2016.00011>.

28. Stocking, *After Tylor*, ch. 5.

29. Langham, *Building of British Social Anthropology*, 162–63.

30. Simon Cook, 'The Tragedy of Cambridge Anthropology: Edwardian Historical Thought and the Contact of Peoples', *History of European Ideas*, 42.4 (2016), 541–53.

31. Langham, *Building of British Social Anthropology*, 163.

32. Stocking, *Victorian Anthropology*; and Stocking, *After Tylor*, chs 1 & 2.

33. G. Elliot Smith, *The Evolution of Man* (Oxford: Oxford University Press, 1924), 133.

34. Ibid., 131–32.

35. On the comparative method, see Stefan Collini, John A. Burrow, and Donald Winch, *That Noble Science of Politics: A Study in Nineteenth-Century Intellectual History* (Cambridge: Cambridge University Press, 1983), ch. 7.

36. Ross L. Jones and Warwick Anderson, 'Wandering Anatomists and Itinerant Anthropologists: The Antipodean Sciences of Race in Britain between the Wars', *The British Journal for the History of Science*, 48.01 (2015), 1–16, at 7n26.

37. Ibid., 8.

38. Schaffer, *From Physics to Anthropology and Back Again*. On the electrocution of Head's penis, see John Forrester and Laura Cameron, 'Discipline Formation—Psychology, English, Philosophy', in *Freud in Cambridge* (Cambridge: Cambridge University Press, 2017), 236–37.

39. Henrika Kuklick, 'Islands in the Pacific: Darwinian Biogeography and British Anthropology', *American Ethnologist*, 23.3 (1996), 611–38.

40. Linstrum, *Ruling Minds*, 26.

41. Henrika Kuklick, 'Personal Equations: Reflections on the History of Fieldwork, with Special Reference to Sociocultural Anthropology', *Isis*, 102.1 (2011), 1–33, at 16.

42. Bruce Hevly, 'The Heroic Science of Glacier Motion', *Osiris*, 11 (1996), 66–86; and Naomi Oreskes, 'Objectivity or Heroism? On the Invisibility of Women in Science', *Osiris*, 11 (1996), 87–113.

43. Henrika Kuklick, 'After Ishmael: The Fieldwork Tradition and Its Future', in *Anthropological Locations, Boundaries and Grounds of a Field Science*, ed. by Akhil Gupta and James Ferguson (Berkeley: University of California Press, 1997), 49, 53.

44. Efram Sera-Shriar, 'What Is Armchair Anthropology? Observational Practices in 19th-Century British Human Sciences', *History of the Human Sciences*, 27.2 (2014), 26–40.

45. Stocking, *Ethnographer's Magic*, 30.

46. Henrika Kuklick, 'Islands in the Pacific', 611.

47. James Urry, *Before Social Anthropology: Essays on the History of British Anthropology* (Philadelphia: Harwood Academic Publishers, 1993), ch. 1.

48. James Urry, 'Making Sense of Diversity and Complexity: The Ethnological Context and Consequences of the Torres Strait Expedition and the Oceanic phase in British anthropology, 1890–1935', in *Cambridge and the Torres Strait: Centenary Essays on the 1898 Anthropological Expedition*, ed. by Anita Herle and Sandra Rouse (Cambridge: Cambridge University Press, 1998), 201–233.

49. Paul Sillitoe, 'The Role of Section H at the British Association for the Advancement of Science in the History of Anthropology', *Durham Anthropology Journal*, 13.2 (2005), <https://citeseerx.ist.psu.edu/viewdoc/summary?doi=10.1.1.123.9527>.

50. Titles and some summaries of the papers can be found in *Report of the Eighty-Fourth Meeting of the British Association for the Advancement of Science* (London: John Murray, 1915), 515–36.

51. Michael W. Young, *Malinowski: Odyssey of an Anthropologist, 1884–1920* (New Haven, CT: Yale University Press, 2004).

52. Ibid., 338.

53. Urry, 'Making Sense of Diversity'.

54. The best overview of these new ideas is Adam Kuper, *The Reinvention of Primitive Society: Transformations of a Myth*, 2nd edn (London: Routledge, 2005). For the place of 'primitivism' in modern art and culture, see Elazar Barkan and Ronald Bush, *Prehistories of the Future: The Primitivist Project and the Culture of Modernism*, (Stanford, CA: Stanford University Press, 1995).

55. Young, *Odyssey*, 402.

56. Robert E. Kohler, *Inside Science: Stories from the Field in Human and Animal Science* (Chicago: University of Chicago Press, 2019), ch. 2.

57. Young's biography provides an exhaustive overview of his methods and the social situation of his fieldwork in Kiriwina and elsewhere; see *Odyssey*, esp. chs. 20 and 24.

58. Cait Storr, '"Imperium in Imperio": Sub-Imperialism and the Formation of Australia as a Subject of International Law', *Melbourne Journal of International Law*, 19.1 (2018), 335–68.

59. George W. Stocking Jr, 'Maclay, Kubary, Malinowski – Archetypes from the Dreamtime of Anthropology' in George W. Stocking Jr, *The Ethnographer's Magic and Other Essays in the History of Anthropology* (Madison: University of Wisconsin Press, 1992), 253–55; Eugene Ogan, 'Copra Came Before Copper: The Nasioi of Bougainville and Plantation Colonialism, 1902–1964', *Pacific Studies*, 19.1 (1996), 31–51; and Patricia O'Brien, 'Remaking Australia's Colonial Culture? White Australia and Its Papuan Frontier 1901–1940', *Australian Historical Studies*, 40.1 (2009), 96–112.

60. Quotations in this paragraph are from *British and Australian Trade in the South Pacific* (Melbourne: A. J. Mullett, 1918), 107–8.

61. B. Malinowski, 'The Primitive Economics of the Trobriand Islanders', *The Economic Journal*, 31.121 (1921), 1–16, at 9.

62. For histories of Malinowski's contribution to theories of the gift and economic thought, see C. M. Hann and Keith Hart, *Economic Anthropology: History, Ethnography, Critique* (Cambridge: Polity, 2011); and Harry Liebersohn, *The Return of the Gift: European History of a Global Idea* (Cambridge: Cambridge University Press, 2011).

63. Malinowski, 'Primitive Economics', 15.

64. John Forrester and Laura Cameron, *Freud in Cambridge* (Cambridge: Cambridge University Press, 2017), 235.

65. Sandra Rouse, 'Expedition and Institution: A .C. Haddon and Anthropology at Cambridge', in *Cambridge and the Torres Strait*, ed. by Herle and Rouse, 69.

66. For a history of Oxford anthropology in this period via the stories of five women, see Frances Larson, *Undreamed Shores: The Hidden Heroines of British Anthropology* (London: Granta, 2021).

67. Henrika Kuklick, 'The British Tradition', in *A New History of Anthropology*, ed. by Henrika Kuklick (Oxford: Blackwell, 2008), 60.

68. Kenneth Maddock, 'Brown, Alfred Reginald Radcliffe (1881–1955)', in *Oxford Dictionary of National Biography* <https://doi.org/10.1093/ref:odnb/37877>. For Rivers's telegram to Cambridge, see Forrester and Cameron, *Freud in Cambridge*, 251.

69. Maddock, 'Brown, Alfred Reginald Radcliffe (1881–1955)'.

70. Robert A. Segal, 'Durkheim in Britain: The Work of Radcliffe-Brown', *Journal of the Anthropological Society of Oxford*, 30.2 (1999), 131–62; and Kuper, *Anthropology and Anthropologists*, 30–31. For a comparative view see Kuper, *Reinvention of Primitive Society*, esp. 88–90.

71. Bank, *Pioneers of the Field*, 34–35; and Isak Niehaus, 'Anthropology at the Dawn of Apartheid: Radcliffe-Brown and Malinowski's South African Engagements, 1918-1934', *Focaal European Journal of Anthropology*, 76.3 (2017), 103–17, at 106.

72. D. Wetherell and C. Carr-Gregg, *Camilla: C. H. Wedgwood 1901–1955, a Life* (Sydney: New South Wales University Press, 1990), 24–28; and Stocking, *After Tylor*, 340.

73. Kuklick, *Savage Within*, 50–51.

74. Tamson Pietsch, *Empire of Scholars: Universities, Networks and the British Academic World, 1850–1939* (Manchester: Manchester University Press, 2013).

75. Ibid., 183.

76. Kuklick, *Savage Within*, 203.

77. Talal Asad, 'Ethnographic Representation, Statistics, and Modern Power', in *From the Margins: Historical Anthropology and Its Futures*, ed. by Brian Keith Axel (Durham, NC: Duke University Press, 2002), 82; and Stocking, *After Tylor*, 382–91.

78. Stocking, *After Tylor*, 340.

79. Rouse, 'Expedition and Institution: A.C. Haddon and Anthropology at Cambridge'.

80. The literature of American foundations and the funding of social science in the UK is large. See, for instance, Donald Fisher, 'The Role of Philanthropic Foundations in the Reproduction and Production of Hegemony: Rockefeller Foundations and the Social Sciences', *Sociology*, 17.2 (1983), 206–33; and Salma Ahmad, 'American Foundations and the Development of the Social Sciences between the Wars: Comment on the Debate between Martin Bulmer and Donald Fisher', *Sociology*, 25.3 (1991), 511–20.

81. David L. Seim, *Rockefeller Philanthropy and Modern Social Science* (London: Pickering & Chatto, 2013).

82. Donald Fisher, 'American Philanthropy and the Social Sciences in Britain, 1919–1939: The Reproduction of a Conservative Ideology', *The Sociological Review*, 28.2 (1980), 277–315, at 284.

83. Ibid., 303.

84. Selskar M. Gunn to Raymond Fosdick, 20 December 1927, Rockefeller Archive Center (RAC), Sleepy Hollow, NY, Rockefeller Foundation (RF), Committee in Review of Soc Sci, FA061 LSRM Series 3.06, box 50, fol. 329.

85. Pietsch, *Empire of Scholars*, 177; and Inderjeet Parmar, 'American Foundations and the Development of International Knowledge Networks', *Global Networks*, 2.1 (2002), 13–30.

86. Kuklick, *The Savage Within*, 186.

87. Grafton Elliot Smith to Edwin Embree, 14 March 1927, RAC, RF, Series 401.AD, box 33.

88. Elazar Barkan makes the argument that social anthropology played an important part in the shift away from race science in *The Retreat of Scientific Racism: Changing Concepts of Race in Britain and the United States between the World Wars* (Cambridge: Cambridge University Press, 1992), 126, 134. As I see it, what happened was a shift of emphasis from biology to culture in one particular field rather than a broader transformation in general.

89. On the continuity of race science in physical anthropology in this period, see Paul Rich, 'The Long Victorian Sunset: Anthropology, Eugenics and Race in Britain, c. 1900–48', *Patterns of Prejudice*, 18.3 (1984), 3–17; and Tony Kushner, 'H. J. Fleure: A Paradigm for Inter-War Race Thinking in Britain', *Patterns of Prejudice*, 42.2 (2008), 151–66. For an account that stresses change, see Barkan, *Retreat of Scientific Racism*, esp. 19.

90. See, for instance, Edwin Embree to David Orme Masson, 27 May 1926, RAC, RF, Record Group 1, FA386, Subseries 410: D, box 3; and RAC, RF, Record Group 1, FA386, Subseries 410, box 3, fol. 29.

91. Chris Renwick, 'Completing the Circle of the Social Sciences? William Beveridge and Social Biology at London School of Economics during the 1930s', *Philosophy of the Social Sciences*, 44.4 (2014), 478–96, esp. 480–81.

92. George W. Stocking Jr, 'Philanthropoids and Vanishing Cultures', in *Objects and Others: Essays on Museums and Material Culture*, ed. by George W. Stocking Jr (Madison: University of Wisconsin Press, 1985), 117.

93. Stocking, *After Tylor*, 368–69.

94. Mark Lamont, 'Malinowski and the "Native Question"', in *Anthropologists and Their Traditions across National Borders*, ed. by Regna Darnell and Frederic W. Gleach (Lincoln: University of Nebraska Press, 2014); and Freddy Foks, 'Bronislaw Malinowski, "Indirect Rule," and the Colonial Politics of Functionalist Anthropology, ca. 1925–1940', *Comparative Studies in Society and History*, 60.1 (2018), 35–57.

CHAPTER 2. PHILANTHROPISTS AND IMPERIALISTS

1. Karuna Mantena, *Alibis of Empire: Henry Maine and the Ends of Liberal Imperialism* (Princeton, NJ: Princeton University Press, 2010).

2. For the various articles of the League, see The Avalon Project, Lillian Goldman Law Library, Yale Law School <https://avalon.law.yale.edu/20th_century/leagcov.asp>.

For indirect rule as an 'ideology', see Mahmood Mamdani, *Citizen and Subject: Contemporary Africa and the Legacy of Late Colonialism* (Princeton, NJ: University Press, 1996). For a reading of the book as a job proposal, see Susan Pedersen, *Internationalism and Empire: British Dilemmas, 1919–1939*, 22 <https://academiccommons.columbia.edu/doi/10.7916/d8-m672-1p02>. For the Mandates system, see Susan Pedersen, *The Guardians: The League of Nations and the Crisis of Empire* (Oxford: Oxford University Press, 2015).

3. Quoted in Stocking, 'Maclay, Kubary, Malinowski – Archetypes from the Dreamtime of Anthropology', 53.

4. For example in ibid.. John W. Cell, 'Who Ran the British Empire', in *More Adventures with Britannia: Personalities, Politics and Culture in Britain*, ed. by

Wm. Roger Louis (London: I. B. Tauris, 1988), 311; and John W. Cell, 'Colonial Rule', in *The Oxford History of the British Empire, Volume IV, The Twentieth Century*, ed. by Judith Brown and Wm. Roger Louis (Oxford: Oxford University Press, 1999), 246–49.

5. Mantena, *Alibis of Empire*, 88.

6. Susan Pedersen, 'Settler Colonialism at the Bar of the League of Nations', in *Settler Colonialism in the Twentieth Century: Projects, Practices, Legacies*, ed. by Caroline Elkins and Susan Pedersen (London: Routledge, 2005); and Pedersen, *Internationalism and Empire*, lecture 2.

7. On the history of the idea of trusteeship in Africa from the Devonshire Declaration through to the late 1930s, see Ronald Hyam, 'Bureaucracy and "Trusteeship" in the Colonial Empire', in *The Oxford History of the British Empire, Volume 4, The Twentieth Century*, ed. by Judith M. Brown and Wm. Roger Louis (Oxford: Oxford University Press, 1999), 255–79. See also A. D. Roberts, 'The Imperial Mind', in *The Cambridge History of Africa, Volume 7, From 1905 to 1940*, ed. by A. D. Roberts (Cambridge: Cambridge University Press, 1986).

8. Patrick Wolfe, 'Settler Colonialism and the Elimination of the Native', *Journal of Genocide Research*, 8.4 (2006), 387–409.

9. As Talal Asad pointed out fifty years ago in his introduction to *Anthropology & the Colonial Encounter*, imperialism has always been ideologically fissured and internally divided: Asad, 'Introduction', in *Anthropology & the Colonial Encounter*, ed. by Asad, 18. And as Archie Mafeje argued in the same decade, any reconstruction of social anthropology's politics must dwell on the central disputes driving the divergent policies of the colonial state. Mafeje, 'The Problem of Anthropology in Historical Perspective'.

10. For an outline of the debate, see E. A. Brett, *Colonialism and Underdevelopment in East Africa: The Politics of Economic Change, 1919–1939* (London: Heinemann, 1973), esp. 44.

11. 'Memorandum for the Rockefeller Foundation written for Mr Embree in March 1926', draft, Malinowski Papers, 9/3.

12. 'Accounting 1928', in RAC, Rockefeller Foundations Archives, Record Group 3, FA112, Subgroup 1, Series 910, box 2, fol. 11, f12; and Bronislaw Malinowski to Elsie Masson, 28 May 1926, in *The Story of a Marriage: The Letters of Bronislaw Malinowski and Elsie Masson*, ed. by Helena Wayne (London: Routledge, 1995), vol. 2, 71.

13. 'Contact Lecture – Lecture II', Malinowski Papers, 14/10.

14. Diana Wylie, 'Confrontation over Kenya: The Colonial Office and Its Critics 1918–1940', *The Journal of African History*, 18.3 (1977), 427–47.

15. Robert G. Gregory, *Sidney Webb and East Africa: Labour's Experiment with the Doctrine of Native Paramountcy* (Berkeley: University of California Press, 1962); and Wylie, 'Confrontation', 427.

16. Roberts, 'Imperial Mind', 43–44; and Brett, *Colonialism and Underdevelopment*, 44.

17. 'Memorandum for the Rockefeller Foundation written for Mr Embree in March 1926', draft, Malinowski Papers, 9/3.

18. Philip Williamson, *National Crisis and National Government: British Politics, the Economy and Empire, 1926–1932* (Cambridge: Cambridge University Press, 1992), 48; Wm. Roger Louis, *In the Name of God, Go! Leo Amery and the British Empire in the Age of Churchill* (New York: W. W. Norton, 1992), 94–98. Leo Amery to Stanley Baldwin, 24 July 1928, document 80 in *Imperial Policy and Colonial Practice, 1925–1945, Part II, Economic Policy, Social Policies and Colonial Research*, ed. by S. R. Ashton and S. E. Stockwell (London: HMSO, 1996), vol. 2, 7–11, at 8.

19. A. G. Hopkins and P. J. Cain, *British Imperialism: 1688–2015*, 3rd edn (London: Routledge, Taylor & Francis Group, 2016), 619.

20. Keith Clements, *Faith on the Frontier: A Life of J. H. Oldham* (London: T&T Clark, 1999), 185–88.

21. John W. Cell, 'Introduction', in *By Kenya Possessed: The Correspondence of Norman Leys and J.H. Oldham, 1918–1926* (Chicago: University of Chicago Press, 1976), 60–61.

22. Ibid., 43–44.

23. On the League, the Mandates, and the 'East Africa question', see Pedersen, *The Guardians*, 222–32; Pedersen, *Internationalism and Empire*, 53–58; and Daniel Gorman, 'Organic Union or Aggressive Altruism: Imperial Internationalism in East Africa in the 1920s', *The Journal of Imperial and Commonwealth History*, 42.2 (2014), 258–85.

24. Pedersen, 'Settler Colonialism', 122–23.

25. Donald Cameron to Lord Lugard, 6 April 1926, Bodleian Library, MSS Lugard, L9/1/20.

26. Pedersen, 'Settler Colonialism', 119.

27. Penelope Hetherington, *British Paternalism in Africa, 1920–1970* (London: Frank Cass, 1978), ch. 5.

28. Pedersen, *Internationalism and Empire*, 50–53.

29. On the history of the idea of trusteeship in East Africa from the Devonshire Declaration through to the late 1930s, see Hyam, 'Bureaucracy and "Trusteeship"', 255–79.

30. Susan Pedersen, 'National Bodies, Unspeakable Acts: The Sexual Politics of Colonial Policy-Making', *The Journal of Modern History*, 63.4 (1991), 647–80, at 647.

31. B. Malinowski, 'Review of Report of the Commission on Closer Union of the Dependencies in Eastern and Central Africa', *Africa*, 2.3 (1929), 317–20, at 317–18.

32. Wylie, 'Confrontation', 427. For a report on parliamentary business and extra-parliamentary pressure group activity on questions of land and labour, see, for instance, 'The Native in Parliament', *The Anti-Slavery Reporter and Aborigines' Friend*, 15.3 (1925), 109–21, esp. 109–11.

33. Bronislaw Malinowski, 'Practical Anthropology', *Africa: Journal of the International African Institute*, 2.1 (1929), 22–38; and Bronislaw Malinowski, 'The Rationalization of Anthropology and Administration', *Africa: Journal of the International African Institute*, 3.4 (1930), 405–30.

34. Malinowski, 'Practical Anthropology', 24.

35. Jan Christiaan Smuts, *Africa and Some World Problems, Including the Rhodes Memorial Lectures Delivered in Michaelmas Term, 1929* (Oxford: Oxford University Press, 1930), 49.

36. L. S. Amery, *The Leo Amery Diaries*, ed. by John Barnes and David Nicholson (London: Hutchinson, 1980), vol. 2, 53.

37. J. H. Oldham, *White and Black in Africa: A Critical Examination of the Rhodes Lectures of General Smuts* (New York: Longmans, Green, 1930).

38. Bronislaw Malinowski, 'Race and Labour', *The Listener*, 16 July 1930, suppl 8, i.

39. Ibid. ii.

40. Ibid., v.

41. For correspondence about the piece, see B. E. Nicolls to Bronislaw Malinowski, 20 June 1930, Malinowski Papers, 12/1.

42. Wylie, 'Confrontation over Kenya', 436.

43. Lord Lugard to Donald Cameron, 4 October 1929, Bodleian Library, Oxford, MSS Lugard, 9/1/39.

44. Frederick Madden and John Darwin, *The Dependent Empire, 1900–1948: Colonies, Protectorates and Mandates* (London: Greenwood Press, 1994), 26.

45. Van Sickle Diaries, RAC, Rockefeller Foundation, Record Group 12, box 482, FA394, 39. On Webb's support for anthropology, see Basu, 'N. W. Thomas and Colonial Anthropology', 88.

46. I rely here on the account given in Gregory, *Sidney Webb and East Africa*.

47. Ibid., 133.

48. *Joint Committee on Closer Union in East Africa 1930–31*, vol. 1, 34.

49. Gregory, *Sidney Webb and East Africa*, 101.

50. Bronislaw Malinowski, 'A Plea for an Effective Colour Bar', *The Spectator*, 27 June 1931, 999–1001, at 1000. This proposal was not without some precedent. In 1923 W. D Ellis and Viscount Peel both proposed buying the settlers out and urging them to leave. Hyam, 'Bureaucracy and "Trusteeship"', 271.

51. For an introduction to some of the debates on the left about internationalism and empire in these years, see John Saville, 'Britain: Internationalism and the Labour Movement between the Wars', in *Internationalism in the Labour Movement, 1830–1940*, ed. by F. L. van Holthoon and Marcel van der Linden (Leiden: E .J. Brill, 1988), vol 2., 565–83.

52. Matera, *Black London*, 322.

53. Bruce Berman and John Lonsdale, 'Custom, Modernity, and the Search for *Kihooto*: Kenyatta, Malinowski, and the Making of *Facing Mount Kenya*', in *Ordering Africa*, ed. by Helen Tilley and Robert Gordon; Matera, *Black London*, ch. 6; and Z. K. Matthews, 'An African View of Indirect Rule in Africa', *Journal of the Royal African Society*, 36.145 (1937), 433–37.

54. Matera, *Black London*, 325.

55. On this count, my argument contradicts the consensual analysis of the dispute given in Tilley, *Africa as a Living Laboratory*, 75–83.

56. Ronald Hyam, *The Failure of South African Expansion, 1908–1948* (London: Macmillan, 1972), 24.

57. Cell, 'Introduction', in Cell, *By Kenya Possessed*.

58. A different explanation for the institute's failure, which stresses the intellectual over-ambition of the Oxford pitch, is offered in Tilley, *Africa as a Living Laboratory*, 96. John Davis supports my reading but this was, in fact, a political nix, describing opposition from within the Colonial Office, in John Davis, 'How All Souls Got Its Anthropologist', in *A History of Oxford Anthropology*, ed. by Peter Rivière (New York: Berghahn Books, 2007), 64.

59. Raymond Buell to Edmund Day, 8 May 1930, RAC, RF, Record Group 1.1, Series 400 F, box 51, fol. 673]

60. Edmund Day to Raymond Buell, 13 May 1930, RAC, RF, Record Group 1.1, Series 400 F, box 51, fol. 673; Excerpt from letter from Day to Selskar Gunn, 21 August 1930, RAC, RF, Record Group 1.1, Series 400 F, box 51, fol. 673.

61. Fisher, 'American Philanthropy and the Social Sciences in Britain, 1919–1939'.

62. Arghiri Emmanuel, 'White-Settler Colonialism and the Myth of Investment Imperialism', *New Left Review*, 73 (1972), 35–57.

63. Fisher, 'American Philanthropy'.

64. Cain and Hopkins in *Imperialism* have followed Ian Drummond in seeing the settler colonial ideal as the paradigm of colonial exploitation in interwar Africa. Ian M. Drummond, *Imperial Economic Policy 1917–1939: Studies in Expansion and Protection* (Toronto: University of Toronto Press, 1974).

65. Raymond Buell to Edmund Day, 8 May 1930. See also Vitalis, *White World Order, Black Power Politics*, 62.

66. Kuklick, *Savage Within*, 203. For a history of comparisons between East Africa and the American South in these years, see Kenneth King, *Pan-Africanism and Education: A Study of Race Philanthropy and Education in the Southern States of America and East Africa* (Oxford: Oxford University Press, 1971).

67. Tilley, 'Introduction', in *Ordering Africa*, 6.

68. 'Colonial Administration class: Discussion of Miss Perham's Paper, 9 May 1933', Malinowski Papers, 6/8.

69. Linstrum, *Ruling Minds*.

70. Mills, *Difficult Folk*, 49.

71. The Kamba are sometimes referred to as Wakamba, Akamba, or Uakamba; I use Kamba throughout.

72. *Rex v. Kumwaka wa Mulumbi & 69 Others*, Kenya Supreme Court, *Law Reports of Kenya – 1932*, XIV (Nairobi), 1933, 139. The case is discussed in Tilley, *Africa as a Living Laboratory*, 261–63; and Katherine Luongo, *Witchcraft and Colonial Rule in Kenya, 1900–1955* (Cambridge: Cambridge University Press, 2011).

73. '60 Sentenced to Death: Murder of "Witch" "Moved Only Half of Spell" African Village Tragedy'; *The Manchester Guardian*, 6 February 1932, 15.

74. 'Witch-Burning Prevented', *New York Times*, 31 January 1932; 'Village Tragedy Sixty Sentenced to Death Murdered a Witch', *Newcastle Morning Herald and Miners' Advocate*, NSW, 26 March 1932, 4; and 'Murder of a "Witch": Death Sentence Confirmed', *The Times of India*, 9 May 1932.

75. Frank Melland, 'A Shadow over Africa.' *The Times*, 13 April 1932, 13.

76. Frederick Lugard, 'Witchcraft In Africa', *The Times*, 20 April 1932, 15.

77. Lugard to Melland, 22 April 1932, Lugard Papers, 12/4 f18.

78. Draft, 'Memorandum for the Rockefeller Foundation written for Mr Embree,' 3, 4, Malinowski Papers, 9/3.

79. 'Memorandum on Colonial Research – Christmas 1927,' 14, Malinowski Papers, 9/3.

80. Law lecture dated 'Tuesday Oct. 17' (no year given), Malinowski Papers, 21/11.

81. Bronislaw Malinowski, *Crime and Custom in Savage Society* (Totowa, NJ: Littlefield, Adams, 1926; repr. 1967), 2.

82. Here the epithet 'primitive' is used in its historical, rather than contemporary sense. For a discussion about interwar anthropologists' use of the concept 'primitive', see James Ferguson, 'Anthropology and Its Evil Twin – "Development" in the Constitution of the Discipline', in *International Development and the Social Sciences: Essays on the History and Politics of Knowledge*, ed. by Frederick Cooper and Randall M. Packard (Berkeley: University of California Press, 1997), 170n4; and Kuper, *Reinvention of Primitive Society*. Malinowski, *Argonauts*, 10.

83. Malinowski, *Crime and Custom*, 54.

84. Malinowski, *Argonauts*, 116; and Malinowski, *Crime and Custom*, 60–61. For the fullest expression of Malinowski's theories about magic see appendix 1 in Bronislaw Malinowski, *Coral Gardens and Their Magic: A Study of the Methods of Tilling the Soil and of Agricultural Rites in the Trobriand Islands* (London: Allen & Unwin, 1935), vol. 1.

85. 'Lecture IV, on Institutions, Law', Malinowski Papers 6/10.

86. 'Excerpts from and Comments on Law in the Making C. K. Allen', 25 June 1938, Malinowski Papers, 21/5.

87. Ibid.

88. C. Clifton-Roberts, 'Witchcraft and Colonial Legislation', *Africa: Journal of the International African Institute*, 8.4 (October 1935), 488–94, at 490.

89. Ibid., 418.

90. Richard D. Waller, 'Witchcraft and Colonial Law in Kenya,' *Past & Present* 180 (August 2003), 241–75. The common response to witchcraft was, as Martin Chanock writes, to follow the English acts of 1736 and 1824 and to treat it as 'pretence'. Martin Chanock, *Law, Custom and Social Order: The Colonial Experience in Malawi and Zambia* (Cambridge: Cambridge University Press, 1985), 326. On the construction of colonial courts in Tanganyika and the contradictory nature of their defense of 'native custom', see Sally Falk Moore, 'Treating Law as Knowledge: Telling Colonial Officers What to Say to Africans about Running "Their Own" Native Courts', *Law & Society Review*, 26.1 (1992), 11–46.

91. Bonny Ibahwoh, *Imperial Justice: Africans in Empire's Court* (Oxford: Oxford University Press, 2013), 56–57.

92. Meyer Fortes to Bronislaw Malinowski, 25 August 1936, University Library, Cambridge, Meyer Fortes Papers (Fortes Papers), 8405/1/45.

93. *Law Reports of Kenya*, 1932, XIV, 139.

94. F. D. Lugard, *The Dual Mandate in Tropical Africa* (Edinburgh: William Blackwood and Sons, 1922), 564.

95. Ira Bashkow, '"The Stakes for Which We Play Are Too High to Allow of Experiments": Colonial Administrators of Papua on Their Anthropological Training by Radcliffe-Brown', *History of Anthropology Newsletter*, 22.2 (1995), 3–14, at 11–12.

96. Bronislaw Malinowski, *The Dynamics of Culture Change: An Inquiry into Race Relations in Africa*, ed. by M. Kaberry, (Oxford: Oxford University Press, 1945), 141.

97. Ibid., 94.

98. Malinowski, 'Practical Anthropology', 24.

99. Malinowski, 'Primitive Economics', 15.

100. Raymond Firth, *Primitive Economics of the New Zealand Maori* (London: G. Routledge, 1929), 25 and 6.

101. Ibid., 11.

102. J. W. Burrow, *Evolution and Society: A Study in Victorian Social Theory* (Cambridge: Cambridge University Press, 1966), 260.

103. Firth, *Primitive Economics*, 25.

104. Lectures on Primitive Economics 1932–33, Malinowski Papers, 6/9.

105. Lionel Robbins, *An Essay on the Nature and Significance of Economic Science* (London: Macmillan, 1932), 15.

106. Ibid., 140 and 141.

107. Ibid., 18–19.

108. Ibid., 19.

109. Richard Thurnwald, *Economics in Primitive Communities* (Oxford: Oxford University Press, 1932), 68–69.

110. Ibid., 297.

111. 'Seminar on Primitive Economics 6 × 1932', 4, Malinowski Papers, 6/9.

112. Robbins, *Essay*, 55.

113. Quotations are from Malinowski, *Argonauts*, 175.

114. Margaret Read, *Native Standards of Living and African Culture Change* (Oxford: Oxford University Press, 1938), 56.

115. Ibid., 12.

116. Ibid., 9.

117. Ibid., 9.

118. Ibid., 6.

119. Ibid., 7.

120. Ibid., 10.

121. Ibid., 11.

122. Ibid., 13.

123. Ibid., 53.

124. Ibid., 47 and 50.

125. Raymond Firth, *Primitive Polynesian Economy* (London: Routledge, 1939), 5.

126. Ibid., 5.

127. Ibid., 2.

128. Raymond Firth, 'Anthropology Looks at Economics', *Science and Society: A Journal of Human Progress*, 1.2 (1937), 48–55, at 55.

129. Philip Pettit makes this argument about functionalist explanations in general in 'Functional Explanation and Virtual Selection', *The British Journal for the Philosophy of Science*, 47.2 (1996), 291–302.

130. Firth, *Primitive Economics*, 456.

131. Ibid., 444.

132. Stocking, 'Maclay, Kubary, Malinowski', 65.

133. 'Dynamics of Contemporary Diffusion,' B. Malinowski pamphlet, n.d., corrected in pencil, Malinowski Papers, 11/5.

134. As argued, for instance, in Carlo Rossetti, 'B. Malinowski, the Sociology of "Modern Problems" in Africa and the Colonial Situation,' *Cahiers d'études africaines* 25.100 (1985): 477–503, 478.

135. On paternalism, see James Ferguson, 'Formalities of Poverty: Thinking about Social Assistance in Neoliberal South Africa,' *African Studies Review* 50.2 (2007): 71–86, 73–74. I thank Jacob Dlamini for pointing out this reference to me. See also Hetherington, *British Paternalism in Africa*, ch. 5. In his final publication, given first as a talk at the historically African American Fisk University, Malinowski maintained race as a component of his analysis, not as a biological fact, but as a sociological construction: Bronislaw Malinowski, 'The Pan-African Problem of Culture Contact,' *American Journal of Sociology* 48, 6 (1943): 649–65, 653. For a discussion of anthropology's contributions to the dissociation of race from biology in this period, see Barkan, *Retreat of Scientific Racism*.

136. Matera, *Black London*, 261.

137. Mantena, *Alibis of Empire*.

CHAPTER 3. PENCILS, SCHEMES AND LETTERS

1. Audrey Richards in conversation with Jack Goody, 3 May 1982, University of Cambridge, https://sms.cam.ac.uk/media/1129889 (retrieved 10 April 2019).

2. For an account of Richards's early fieldwork see Jo Gladstone, 'Significant Sister: Autonomy and Obligation in Audrey Richards' Early Fieldwork', *American Ethnologist*, 13.2 (1986), 338–62.

3. Audrey Richards to Bronsilaw Malinowski, 5 November 1930, Sterling Memorial Library, New Haven, Bronislaw Malinowski Papers (Malinowski Yale Papers), 7/534.

4. Audrey Richards in conversation with Jack Goody, 3 May 1982.

5. Jack Goody, *The Expansive Moment: The Rise of Social Anthropology in Britain and Africa, 1918–1970* (Cambridge: Cambridge University Press, 1995), 33.

6. Thanks to John Arnold for suggesting this car maintenance metaphor.

7. Patricia Owens, 'Lucy Philip Mair – Leading Writer on Colonial Administration, Early International Relations Scholar, and Anthropologist', <https://blogs.lse.ac.uk/lsehistory/2018/10/03/lucy-mair/> (accessed 16 April 2019).

8. Lucy Mair to Audrey Richards, 21 November 1931, Malinowski Papers, 7/16. On paternalist ideas about African societies in this era see Hetherington, *British Paternalism in Africa*.

9. Lucy Mair to Audrey Richards, 21 November 1931.

10. B. Malinowski, 'Introductory Essay on the Anthropology of Changing African Cultures', in *Methods of Study of Culture Contact in Africa*, ed. by Lucy Mair (Oxford: Oxford University Press, 1938).

11. Bronisław Średniawa, "The Anthropologist as a Young Physicist: Bronisław Malinowski's Apprenticeship," *Isis*, 72 (1981), :613–20; and Young, *Malinowski*, ch. 5. On the influence of developments in European science and culture, see *Malinowski between Two Worlds: The Polish Roots of an Anthropological Tradition*, ed. by Roy F. Ellen et al. (Cambridge: Cambridge University Press, 1988); and Manganaro, *Culture, 1922*.

12. Lecture notes, Malinowski Papers, 6/4.

13. 'Lectures on Primitive Economics – Session 1932/33', Malinowski Papers, 6/9.

14. Ibid.

15. Ibid. For an account of 'diffusionism' in British anthropology, see Stocking, *After Tylor*, 179–232.

16. 'Lectures on Primitive Economics – Session 1932/33'.

17. My thanks to Richard Staley for pointing out the difference between Malinowski's *Argonauts* and his pedagogy.

18. 'Primitive Economics Lecture 12 January 1933', Malinowski Papers, 6/9.

19. Lucy Mair to Bronislaw Malinowski, 18 May 1932, Malinowski Papers, 7/16.

20. Lucy Mair to Bronislaw Malinowski, 20 June 1932, Malinowski Papers, 7/16.

21. See Malinowski, *Argonauts*, and for a pithy formulation of the argument, see Malinowski, 'Primitive Economics of the Trobriand Islanders'.

22. Lucy Mair to Bronislaw Malinowski, 24 February 1932, Malinowski Papers, 7/16.

23. Bronislaw Malinowski to Margaret Read, 24 January 1935, Malinowski Papers, 7/12.

24. Margaret Read to Bronislaw Malinowski, 23 March 1935, Malinowski Papers, 7/12.

25. My thanks to Lorraine Daston for pointing this out.

26. Średniawa, 'Anthropologist as a Young Physicist', 620.

27. Urry, *Before Social Anthropology*, 29; and on *Notes & Queries*, see ibid., ch. 1.

28. On the early history of fieldwork setting these developments in context see ibid.; Kuklick, 'Personal Equations'; and George W. Stocking Jr, 'The Ethnographer's Magic' in Stocking, *The Ethnographer's Magic and Other Essays in the History of Anthropology* (Madison: University of Wisconsin Press, 1992).

29. 'Scheme of Culture, Chart 1', Malinowski Papers, 23/24.

30. Kuklick, 'British Tradition', 65.

31. Ursula Klein, 'Paper Tools in Experimental Cultures', *Studies in the History and Philosophy of Science Part A*, 32.2 (2001), 265–302, at 292.

32. Boris Jardine, 'State of the Field: Paper Tools', *Studies in History and Philosophy of Science Part A*, 64 (2017), 53–63, at 56.

33. Robert E. Kohler, 'Place and Practice in Field Biology', *History of Science*, 40.2 (2002), 189–210.

34. Lorraine Daston, 'Objectivity and the Escape from Perspective', *Social Studies of Science*, 22.4 (1992), 597–618, 608–9.

35. Kohler, 'Place and Practice in Field Biology', 202.

36. Bronislaw Malinowski to Margaret Read, 24 January 1935, Malinowski Papers, 7/12.

37. Bronislaw Malinowski to Margaret Read, n.d. (after 7 April 1935), Malinowski Papers, 7/12.

38. Peter Ewer, 'A Gentlemen's Club in the Clouds: Reassessing the Empire Air Mail Scheme, 1933-1939', *The Journal of Transport History*, 28.1 (2007), 75–92.

39. Bronislaw Malinowski to Margaret Read, 24 January 1935, Malinowski Papers, 7/12.

40. Lucy Mair to Bronislaw Malinowski, 24 February 1932, Malinowski Papers, 7/16.

41. Margaret Read to Bronislaw Malinowski, 23 March 1935, Malinowski Papers, 7/12.

42. Margaret Read to Bronislaw Malinowski, 28 February 1935, Malinowski Yale Papers, 7/527.

43. I take this notion of acts of the 'self upon the self' from Joel Isaac, 'Tangled Loops: Theory, History, and the Human Sciences in Modern America', *Modern Intellectual History*, 6.2 (2009), 397–424. Kuklick explains that the myth of the fieldworker as a heroic individual has entered into the mythology of the discipline in 'Personal Equations', 30–31.

44. Kuklick, 'Personal Equations', 16–17.

45. Margaret Read to Bronislaw Malinowski, 28 February 1935, Malinowski Papers, 7/12.

46. On Malinowski's mythic self-presentation in his research, see Stocking, *After Tylor*, 273–74; Stocking, 'Ethnographer's Magic', 58; and James Clifford, *The Predicament of Culture* (Cambridge, MA: Harvard University Press, 1988), 30. On scientific personae see Lorraine Daston and H. Otto Sibum, 'Introduction: Scientific Personae and Their Histories', *Science in Context*, 16.1-2 (2003), 1–8.

47. See, for instance, the recollections of Hortense Powdermaker quoted in Kuper, *Anthropology and Anthropologists*, 44.

48. Lucy Mair to Bronislaw Malinowski, 24 February 1932, Malinowski Papers, 7/16.

49. Lucy Mair to Bronislaw Malinowski, 6 April 1932, Malinowski Papers, 7/16.

50. Margaret Read, 'Third Report on Field Work During Second Tour, December 1936, January and February 1937', Malinowski Papers, 7/12.

51. Margaret Read to Bronislaw Malinowski, 23 March 1935, Malinowski Papers, 7/12.

52. Archie Mafeje, 'Who Are the Makers and Objects of Anthropology? A Critical Comment on Sally Falk Moore's "Anthropology and Africa"', *African Sociological Review/Revue Africaine de Sociologie*, 1.1 (1997), 1–15, at 5.

53. By living in a hut, rather than 'under canvas', her attitude differed from the practice reconstructed by Lyn Schumaker of the Rhodes-Livingstone researchers. Lynette Schumaker, 'A Tent with a View: Colonial Officers, Anthropologists, and the Making of the Field in Northern Rhodesia, 1937-1960', *Osiris*, 11 (1996), 237-58.

54. Margaret Read to Bronislaw Malinwoski, 7 April 1935, Malinowski Papers, 7/12.

55. Lucy Mair to Bronislaw Malinowski, 24 February 1932, Malinowski Papers, 7/16.

56. Lucy Mair to Bronislaw Malinowski, 6 April 1932, Malinowski Papers, 7/16.

57. Ibid.

58. For some contemporary references see G. St. J. Orde Browne, 'Witchcraft and British Colonial Law', *Africa*, 8.04 (1935), 481-87; and Clifton Roberts, 'Witchcraft and Colonial Legislation', 488-94. And for historical reflections on British rule and witchraft in Africa, see Foks, 'Bronislaw Malinowski', 41-46; Bonny Ibhawoh, *Imperial Justice: Africans in Empire's Court* (Oxford: Oxford University Press, 2013); Luongo, *Witchcraft and Colonial Rule in Kenya*; and Waller, 'Witchcraft and Colonial Law in Kenya'.

59. Lucy Mair to Bronislaw Malinowski, 3 May 1932, Malinowski Papers, 7/16. This episode was written up in Lucy Mair, *An African People in the Twentieth Century* (London: George Routledge & Sons, 1934), 269-72.

60. Margaret Read, 'Third Quarterly Report on Fellowship, June-August 1935', Malinowski Papers, 7/12.

61. Schumaker, 'A Tent with a View'.

62. Margaret Read to Bronislaw Malinowski, 7 June 1935, Malinowski Yale Papers, 7/527.

63. Margaret Read to Bronislaw Malinowski, 6 July 1935, Malinowski Yale Papers, 7/527.

64. Margaret Read 'Brief Report on Field Work 1934-35, December 1935', Malinowski Papers, 7/12.

65. Schumaker, 'A Tent with a View', 244.

66. Margaret Read, *Native Standards of Living and African Culture Change* (Oxford: Oxford University Press, 1938), 13.

67. Archie Mafeje, 'The Ideology of "Tribalism"', *The Journal of Modern African Studies*, 9.2 (1971), 253-61.

68. For a compelling reconstruction of the politics of anthropological fieldwork in this period, see John Parker, 'The Dynamics of Fieldwork Among the Talensi: Meyer Fortes in Northern Ghana, 1934-7', *Africa*, 83.4 (2013), 623-45.

69. Andrew Warwick and David Kaiser, 'Conclusion: Kuhn, Foucault, and the Power of Pedagogy', in *Pedagogy and the Practice of Science, Historical and Contemporary Perspectives*, ed. by David Kaiser (Cambridge, MA: MIT Press, 2005), 394.

70. Bronislaw Malinowski to Godfrey Wilson, 22 November 1934, Malinowski Papers, 7/19.

71. Bronislaw Malinowski to Meyer Fortes, 8 May 1934, Cambridge, Fortes Papers, MSS add. 8405, 1/45.

72. Bronislaw Malinowski to Meyer Fortes, 23 January 1935, Fortes Papers, 1/45.

73. Bronislaw Malinowski to Meyer Fortes, 8 May 1934, Fortes Papers, 1/45.

74. Bronislaw Malinowski to Joseph Oldham, 13 September 1931, Malinowski Papers, 9/12. See also the exchange of letters from 1931 and 1932 in Fortes Papers, 1/45.

75. Margaret Read to Bronislaw Malinowski, 7 June 1935.

76. Alfred Radcliffe-Brown to Bronislaw Malinowski, 6 November 1922, Malinowski Yale Papers, box 7, fol. 521.

77. Stocking, 'Radcliffe-Brown and British Social Anthropology', 169.

78. Audrey Richards to Bronislaw Malinowski, 21 September 1931, Malinowski Papers, 9/12.

79. Bronislaw Malinowski to Joseph Oldham, 20 December 1931, Malinowski Papers, 9/12; and Stocking, 'Radcliffe-Brown and British Social Anthropology', 166–67.

80. Audrey Richards to Bronislaw Malinowski, 21 September 1931, Malinowski Papers, 9/12.

81. Meyer Fortes to Edward Evans-Pritchard, 2 September 1934, Fortes Papers, 8405/1/17.

82. Christopher Morton, 'Evans-Pritchard and Malinowski: The Roots of a Complex Relationship', *History of Anthropology Newsletter*, 34.2 (2007), 10–14.

83. Quoted in ibid., 13.

84. Edward Evans-Pritchard to Meyer Fortes, 7 May 1934, Fortes Papers, 8405/1/17.

85. Meyer Fortes to Edward Evans-Pritchard, 2 September 1934.

86. Kuper, *Anthropology and Anthropologists*, 37.

87. Stocking, 'Radlcliffe-Brown and British Social Anthropology'.

88. For a clear account of these differences see A. R. Radcliffe-Brown, 'Applied Anthropology', and B. Malinowski, 'Culture Change in Theory and Practice', both in *Oxford University Summer School on Colonial Administration: Second Session, 1938* (Oxford: Oxford University Press, 1938).

89. On the emergence of the heroic, masculine observer in modern science, see Hevly, 'Heroic Science of Glacier Motion', and on theorising and gender, see Oreskes, 'Objectivity or Heroism?' My thanks to Lorraine Daston for sending me this latter citation.

90. Adam Kuper, 'No Place for a Woman', *Times Literary Supplement*, 9 June 2017 <https://www.the-tls.co.uk/articles/no-place-for-a-woman/> (accessed 28 May 2021). On applied anthropology and the gendered division of labour between 'theory' and 'applied research', I have taken inspiration from Sophie Scott-Brown, 'Women in the (Grass)Field: Phyllis Kaberry and Applied Anthropology in Post-war Africa' (paper delivered at Histories of Anthropology: Transforming Knowledge and Power (1870–1970), Gonville and Caius College, Cambridge, 18 September 2017).

91. Meyer Fortes to Edward Evans-Pritchard, 2 September 1934, Fortes Papers, 8405/1/17.

92. Edward Evans-Pritchard to Meyer Fortes, 25 November 1934, Fortes Papers, 8405/1/17.

93. Ibid. Needless to say, these works have been subject to much the same critique that Evans-Pritchard leveled at Malinowski: too much deduction from prior prejudice and a lack of sensitivity to politics: Clifford, *Predicament of Culture*, 32–34; and Kuper, *Anthropology and Anthropologists*, 58–60.

94. Edward Evans Pritchard to Meyer Fortes, n.d., Fortes Papers 8405/1/17, fol. p. 9.

95. Kuper, *Anthropology and Anthropologists*, 54–62; and Mills, *Difficult Folk*, ch. 3.

96. On Evans-Pritchard's late rapprochement, see John W. Burton, 'The Ghost of Malinowski in the Southern Sudan: Evans-Pritchard and Ethnographic Fieldwork', *Proceedings of the American Philosophical Society*, 127.4 (1983), 278–89, at 286.

97. Ibid.

98. Christopher Morton, *The Anthropological Lens: Rethinking E. E. Evans-Pritchard* (Oxford: Oxford University Press, 2020), 73, 75, 77. The connection between Evans-Pritchard's photography and his rejection of the charts favoured by Malinowski is a topic in need of further research.

99. Stocking, 'Radcliffe-Brown and British Social Anthropology'.

100. Collins, 'On the Acrimoniousness of Intellectual Disputes'.

101. Goody, *Expansive Moment*, 33. For an introduction to the institutional history of post-war social anthropology in Britain, see Spencer, 'British Social Anthropology'; and Kuper, *Anthropology and Anthropologists*, chs. 5, 6, 7.

CHAPTER 4. POPULARISING THE FIELD

1. Bronislaw Malinowski to Elsie Masson, 9 March 1929, *The Story of a Marriage*, 143–44.

2. 'Foreword to the Third Edition', in Bronislaw Malinowski, *The Sexual Life of Savages in North-Western Melanesia*, 3rd edn (London: Routledge & Kegan Paul, 1932), xx.

3. Ibid., xx–xi.

4. Kuklick, *Savage Within*, 12.

5. Anderson, 'Components', 47.

6. Handler, *Critics Against Culture*; Mandler, *Return from the Natives;* and King, *Reinvention of Humanity*.

7. MacClancy, *Anthropology in the Public Arena*, 40–41.

8. Paul A. Robinson, *The Modernization of Sex: Havelock Ellis, Alfred Kinsley, William Masters, and Virginia Johnson* (London: Elek, 1976); Marcus Collins, *Modern Love: Personal Relationships in Twentieth-Century Britain* (Newark: University of Delaware Press, 2006); and Lucy Delap, Ben Griffin, and Abigail Wills, eds., *The Politics of Domestic Authority in Britain since 1800* (Basingstoke: Palgrave Macmillan, 2009), 10.

9. George Robb, 'Marriage and Reproduction', in *Palgrave Advances in the Modern History of Sexuality*, ed. by H. G. Cocks and Matt Houlbrook (Basingstoke: Palgrave Macmillan, 2006), 96.

10. Dagmar Herzog, *Sexuality in Europe: A Twentieth-Century History* (Cambridge: Cambridge University Press, 2012), 6.

11. For a contextualisation of economic debates about feminism, welfare, work and the family in the Edwardian and interwar periods, see Cléo Chassonnery-Zaïgouche, 'Is Equal Pay Worth It?' (OSF Preprints, 2019) <https://doi.org/10.31219/osf.io/8cq9j>.

12. R. J. Overy, *The Morbid Age: Britain and the Crisis of Civilization* (London: Penguin, 2010). On the impact of the First World War see also Richard Allen Soloway, *Birth Control and the Population Question in England 1877–1930* (Chapel Hill: North Carolina University Press, 1982), 160.

13. Herzog, *Sexuality in Europe*, 17; and Lucy Bland and Laura Doan, 'Introduction', in *Sexology Uncensored: The Documents of Sexual Science*, ed. by Lucy Bland and Laura L. Doan (Cambridge: Polity Press, 1998), 3.

14. Teri Chettiar, '"More Than a Contract": The Emergence of a State-Supported Marriage Welfare Service and the Politics of Emotional Life in Post-1945 Britain', *Journal of British Studies*, 55.3 (2016), 566–91, esp. 571 and 581. Lucy Delap and Valerie Sanders, 'Introduction', in *Victorian and Edwardian Anti-Feminism*, ed. by Lucy Delap and Valerie Sanders (London: Routledge, 2010), xxxvii.

15. On the plurality of actors seeking to reimagine marriage, see Herzog, *Sexuality in Europe*, 18.

16. The now classic, argument about the emergence of modern sexuality is found in Michel Foucault, *The History of Sexuality, Volume 1, The Will to Knowledge*, trans. by Robert Hurley (London: Penguin, 1998).

17. H. G. Cocks and Matt Houlbrook, 'Introduction', in *Palgrave Advances in the Modern History of Sexuality*, ed. by H. G. Cocks and Matt Houlbrook (Basingstoke: Palgrave Macmillan, 2006), 4; and Elazar Barkan, 'Victorian Promiscuity: Greek Ethics and Primitive Exemplars', in *Prehistories of the Future: The Primitivist Project and the Culture of Modernism*, ed. by Elazar Barkan and Ronald Bush (Stanford, CA: Stanford University Press, 1995).

18. Joanne Meyerowitz, '"How Common Culture Shapes the Separate Lives": Sexuality, Race, and Mid-Twentieth-Century Social Constructionist Thought', *The Journal of American History*, 96.4 (2010), 1057–84, at 1072; and Collins, *Modern Love*, 4.

19. Kuper, *Reinvention of Primitive Society*, xi.

20. Ibid., 74–75.

21. Ibid., 69–74.

22. Ibid., 107–9 and 105–6.

23. Quoted in Jeremy MacClancy, 'Anthropology: "The Latest Form of Evening Entertainment"', in *A Concise Companion to Modernism*, ed. by David Bradshaw (Oxford: Blackwell, 2003), 78.

24. Kuper, *Reinvention of Primitive Society*, 148–51 and 157–60.

25. Margaret Mead to Bronislaw Malinowski, 9 August 1928, Malinowski Papers, 29/11.

26. Bronislaw Malinowski to Margaret Mead, 29 March 1930, Malinowski Papers, 29/11.

27. 'Preface', in Bronislaw Malinowski, *The Sexual Life of Savages in North-Western Melanesia*, 3rd edn (London: Routledge & Kegan Paul, 1932), x.

28. Andrew P. Lyons and Harriet D. Lyons, *Irregular Connections: A History of Anthropology and Sexuality* (Lincoln: University of Nebraska Press, 2004), 130.

29. Stephen Brooke, *Sexual Politics: Sexuality, Family Planning, and the British Left from the 1880s to the Present Day* (Oxford: Oxford University Press, 2011), 40; Kate Fisher, *Birth Control, Sex and Marriage in Britain, 1918–1960* (Oxford: Oxford University Press, 2006); and Simon Szreter and Kate Fisher, *Sex Before the Sexual Revolution: Intimate Life in England 1918–1963* (Cambridge: Cambridge University Press, 2010).

30. While Arthur Marwick did not talk of marriage reform in his article on 'middle opinion', the milieu is much the same as those collectivist scientists he discusses. Arthur Marwick, 'Middle Opinion in the Thirties: Planning, Progress and Political "Agreement"', *The English Historical Review*, 79.311 (1964), 285–98.

31. For an important overview of Malinowski's theories in light of contemporary post-Freudian psychology, see Shaul Bar-Haim, *The Maternalists: Psychoanalysis, Motherhood, and the British Welfare State* (Philadelphia: University of Pennsylvania Press, 2021), ch. 3.

32. Bronislaw Malinowski, *Sex and Repression in Savage Society* (London: Routledge and Kegan Paul, 1927; repr. 1960), 3 (emphasis in original).

33. Ibid., 4.

34. Ibid., 22.

35. Ibid., 23.

36. Rosalind Coward, 'On the Universality of the Oedipus Complex: Debates on Sexual Divisions in Psychoanalysis and Anthropology', *Critique of Anthropology*, 4.15 (1980), 5–28; George Stocking Jr, 'Anthropology and the Irrational – Malinowski's Encounter with Freudian Psychoanalysis', in *Malinowski, Rivers, Benedict and Others: Essays on Culture and Personality*, ed. by George W. Stocking Jr (Madison: University of Wisconsin Press, 1986), 13–49.

37. Rosalind Coward, *Patriarchal Precedents: Sexuality and Social Relations* (London: Routledge & Kegan Paul, 1983), 103.

38. Meyerowitz, '"How Common Culture Shapes the Separate Lives"', 1072.

39. Barkan, *Retreat of Scientific Racism*, ch. 2.

40. Sigmund Freud, *On Sexuality: Three Essays on the Theory of Sexuality and Other Works*, ed. by James Strachey and Angela Richards (Harmondsworth: Penguin Books, 1977), 40.

41. Yale University Manuscript Collections, Sterling Library, Malinowski Papers, MS19 Series 3, box 29.

42. For a history of the connections between 'sociology' and 'biology' in this regard, see Chris Renwick, *British Sociology's Lost Biological Roots: A History of Futures Past* (Basingstoke: Palgrave Macmillan, 2012).

43. Beardsley Ruml to Bronislaw Malinowski, 15 February 1927, Malinowski Papers, 8/2.

44. Renwick, 'Completing the Circle'.

45. Malinowski, 'Foreword to the Third Edition', in *Sexual Life of Savages*, xx.

46. Mari Jo Buhle, *Feminism and Its Discontents: A Century of Struggle with Psychoanalysis* (Cambridge, MA: Harvard University Press, 2009), 95.

47. Bronislaw Malinowski, 'Parenthood – The Basis of Social Structure', in *The New Generation: The Intimate Problems of Modern Parents and Children*, ed. by V. F. Calverton and Samuel Schmalhausen (New York: The Macaulay Company, 1930), 115.

48. Ibid., 168.

49. Bronislaw Malinowski to Mr Pike, 5 December 1930, Malinowski Papers, 29/15.

50. Naomi Mitchison, *Comments on Birth Control* (London: Faber & Faber, 1930), 25.

51. For an early example, see B. Malinowski, 'Review of Les Formes Élémentaires de La Vie Religieuse: Le Système Totémique en Australie (Bibliothèque de Philosophie Contemporaine) by E. Durkheim', *Folklore*, 24.4 (1913), 525–31.

52. Mitchison, *Comments on Birth Control*, quotes from 27, 28, 30.

53. Bronislaw Malinowski to Elsie Masson, 11 November 1926, *The Story of a Marriage,* vol. 2, 87.

54. Ibid., 172.

55. Ibid., 117.

56. Bertrand Russell to Bronislaw Malinowski, 8 Nov 1928, Yale, Malinowski Papers, box 7, fol. 551; and Bertrand Russell, *Marriage and Morals* (London: George Allen & Unwin, 1929), 20.

57. Russell, *Marriage and Morals*, 173.

58. Aldous Huxley to Norman Douglas, 7 January 1930, in *Letters of Aldous Huxley*, ed. by Grover Smith (London: Chatto & Windus, 1969), 326.

59. Aldous Huxley to Mrs Kethevan Evans, 28 November 1930, in *Letters of Aldous Huxley*, ed. by Grover Smith, 343; and Debra A. Moddelmog, 'Modernism and Sexology', *Literature Compass*, 11.4 (2014), 267–78, 271.

60. Jerome Meckier, '*Brave New World* and the Anthropologists: Primitivism in A. F. 632', in *Aldous Huxley: Modern Satirical Novelist of Ideas – a Collection of Essays by Jerome Mechier*, ed. by Peter Edgerly Firchow and Bernfried Nugel (Münster: LIT Verlag, 2006).

61. Aldous Huxley to Mary Hutchinson, 5 July 1929, in *Aldous Huxley – Selected Letters*, ed. by James Sexton (Chicago: Ivan R. Dee, 2007), 219.

62. Gavin Miller, 'Political Repression and Sexual Freedom in Brave New World and 1984', in *Huxley's Brave New World: Essays*, ed. by David Garrett Izzo and Kim Kirkpatrick (Jefferson, NC: McFarland, 2008), 19; and Peter Edgerly Firchow, *The End of Utopia: A Study of Aldous Huxley's Brave New World* (London: Associated University Presses, 1984), 90.

63. On Huxley's pessimism about scientific planning and the limits of education, see Jerome Meckier, 'A Neglected Huxley "Preface": His Earliest Synopsis of Brave New World', *Twentieth Century Literature*, 25.1 (1979), 1–20.

64. Aldous Huxley, *Music at Night and Other Essays Including 'Vulgarity in Literature'* (London: Chatto & Windus, 1970), 146.

65. Ibid., 147.

66. Meckier, '*Brave New World* and the Anthropologists', 227.
67. Firchow, *End of Utopia*, 90.
68. Ibid., 73, 91; and Meckier, 'Brave New World and the Anthropologists', 225.
69. For a class-based critique of Huxley's writing, see Mark R. Hillegas, *The Future as Nightmare: H.G. Wells and the Anti-Utopians* (Oxford: Oxford University Press, 1967), 120–21.
70. David Cardiff, 'The Serious and the Popular: Aspects of the Evolution of Style in the Radio Talk 1928–1939', in *Radio*, ed. by Andrew Crisell (London: Routledge, 2009), vol. 2, 121.
71. Paddy Scannell and David Cardiff, *A Social History of British Broadcasting, Volume 1, 1922–1939: Serving the Nation* (Oxford: Basil Blackwell, 1990), 153.
72. For the connections between technology, tone and talks see Hugh Chignell, *Public Issue Radio: Talks, News and Current Affairs in the Twentieth Century* (Basingstoke: Palgrave Macmillan, 2011), 11–12.
73. *Marriage, Past and Present – A Debate Between Robert Briffault and Bronislaw Malinowski*, ed. by Ashley Montagu (Boston: Porter Sargent, 1956), 22–23.
74. Ibid., 22.
75. Ibid., 30.
76. Ibid., 31.
77. Ibid., 37.
78. Ibid., 38.
79. Ibid., 41.
80. Ibid., 43.
81. Ibid., 45.
82. Ibid., 50.
83. Ibid., 51.
84. Bronsilaw Malinowski to John Reith, 9 February 1931, Malinowski Papers, 12/1.
85. Ibid.
86. Charles Siepmann to Bronislaw Malinowski, 18 February 1931, Malinowski Papers, 12/1.
87. Sophie Munn-Rankin to Bronislaw Malinowski, 11 February 1931, Malinowski Papers, 14/2. On Engels, see Kuper, *Reinvention of Primitive Society*, 79–80.
88. Ibid.
89. Ibid.
90. Bronislaw Malinowski to Sophie Munn-Rankin, 21 February 1931, Malinowski Papers, 14/2.
91. On radio listening groups, see David Goodman, 'A Transnational History of Radio Listening Groups I: The United Kingdom and United States', *Historical Journal of Film, Radio and Television*, 36.3 (2016), 436–65.
92. Ibid.
93. BBC Talks pamphlet, Malinowski Papers, 12/3.
94. These letters are in Malinowski Papers, 14/2.
95. 'A. G. Hammond to Bronislaw Malinowski, Jan. 30 1930' [*sic*; Hammond must have meant '31], Malinowski Papers, 14/2.

96. Bronislaw Malinowski to A. G. Hammond, 21 Feb 1931, Malinowski Papers, 14/2.
97. Ibid.
98. Meyerowitz, '"How Common Culture Shapes the Separate Lives"'; and Buhle, *Feminism and Its Discontents*.
99. Denise Riley, *War in the Nursery: Theories of the Child and Mother* (London: Virago, 1983).
100. Coward, *Patriarchal Precedents*, 13.
101. Anne Karpf, 'Constructing and Addressing the "Ordinary Devoted Mother"', *History Workshop Journal*, 78.1 (2014), 82–106.
102. Karpf, 'Constructing and Addressing'; Michal Shapira, *The War Inside* (Cambridge: Cambridge University Press, 2013); and Mathew Thomson, *Lost Freedom: The Landscape of the Child and the British Post-War Settlement* (Oxford: Oxford University Press, 2013).
103. Since the writing of this chapter, Shaul Bar Haim's *The Maternalists* has been published in support of this view.
104. Jeremy MacClancy has written about the popularization of anthropology during this era but has put his focus on non-academic figures, and often those explicitly opposed to the Malinowskian project in the discipline. See his *Anthropology in the Public Arena*.
105. On the emergence of 'romance' amongst working-class young people at precisely this moment, see Claire Langhamer, *The English in Love: The Intimate Story of an Emotional Revolution* (Oxford: Oxford University Press, 2013).
106. Szreter and Fisher, *Sex Before the Sexual Revolution*.
107. *Marriage Past and Present*, 81–82.
108. Lucy Delap, Ben Griffin and Abigail Wills, 'Introduction', in *The Politics of Domestic Authority*, ed. by Lucy Delap, Ben Griffin, and Abigail Wills, 10. There are obvious problems with this 'secularisation thesis'. Certainly the Catholic Church under Pius XI forbade the use of contraception and criticised ideas of population control; see the encyclical Casti Connubii <http://www.papalencyclicals.net/Pius11/P11CASTI.HTM>. But the Anglican Church, as Malinowski pointed out, took a different view in resolution 15 of the 1930 Lambeth Conference <www.anglicancommunion.org/media/127734/1930.pdf>. There is also the problem of confusing official doctrine and popular practise. On this note see Matthew Connely's autobiographical introduction to the theme of population control in light of his Catholic grandmother's worries about his parents' lack of family planning: Matthew James Connelly, *Fatal Misconception: The Struggle to Control World Population* (Cambridge, MA: Harvard University Press, 2008), ix.
109. See MacClancy, *Anthropology in the Public Arena*.

CHAPTER 5. FROM KINSHIP STUDIES TO COMMUNITY STUDIES

1. Stuart Middleton, '"Affluence" and the Left in Britain, c. 1958–1974', *The English Historical Review*, 129.536 (2014), 107–38.

2. Jordanna Bailkin, *The Afterlife of Empire* (Berkeley: University of California Press, 2012); Camilla Schofield and Ben Jones, '"Whatever Community Is, This Is Not It": Notting Hill and the Reconstruction of "Race" in Britain after 1958', *Journal of British Studies*, 58.1 (2019), 142–73; and Robbie Shilliam, *Race and the Undeserving Poor: From Abolition to Brexit* (Newcastle upon Tyne: Agenda Publishing, 2018), chs. 5 and 6.

3. Helen McCarthy, *Double Lives: A History of Working Motherhood*. (London: Bloomsbury, 2020), ch. 6.

4. Savage, *Identities and Social Change*.

5. Judith R. Walkowitz, *City of Dreadful Delight: Narratives of Sexual Danger in Late-Victorian London* (Chicago: University of Chicago Press, 1992), ch. 1.

6. A marked trend especially in the work of Ross McKibbin; see Ross McKibbin, *Classes and Cultures, England 1918–1951* (Oxford: Oxford University Press, 1998).

7. See, for two important examples, Lise Butler, 'Michael Young, the Institute of Community Studies, and the Politics of Kinship', *Twentieth Century British History*, 26.2 (2015), 203–24; and Lawrence, 'Inventing the "Traditional Working Class"'.

8. 'Primitive Economics Lecture 12th January 1933', Malinowski Papers, 6/9.

9. J. A. Banks, 'The British Sociological Association—The First Fifteen Years', *Sociology*, 1.1 (1967), 1–9, at 1.

10. Savage, *Identities and Social Change*, 107.

11. As pointed out in Bulmer, 'Introduction', in *Essays on the History of British Sociological Research*, 13.

12. Quoted in Butler, *Michael Young*, 139. Thanks to Lise Butler for this information.

13. Spencer, 'British Social Anthropology', 4–5; and Mills, *Difficult Folk*, ch. 9.

14. Anthony P. Cohen, 'The Social Anthropology of Britain, and the Question of "Otherness"', *Anthropology Today*, 2.6 (1986), 3.

15. Collini, '"Discipline History" and "Intellectual History"'. Jordanna Bailkin notes this trend of siloed disciplinary history in *Afterlife of Empire*, 29–30; see also Savage, *Identities*. J. D. Y. Peel has offered some minimal revision of this trend in 'Not Really a View from Without', and David Mills discusses their relationship in *Difficult Folk*. See also the reflections on the career of Ronnie Frankenberg in Sharon Macdonald, Jeanette Edwards, and Mike Savage, 'Introduction', *The Sociological Review*, 53.4 (2005), 587–602, as well as the other articles in this special issue. Older histories of the disciplines persistently narrated their separation. See Bulmer, *Essays on the History of British Sociological Research*; Halsey, *History of Sociology in Britain*; and Platt, *British Sociological Association*. This is mirrored in the general lack of interest in histories of sociology in the main monographs on anthropology's history: Kuklick, *Savage Within*; Kuper, *Anthropology and Anthropologists*; and Stocking, *After Tylor*.

16. Jenny Bourne and A. Sivanandan, 'Cheerleaders and Ombudsmen', *Race & Class*, 21.4 (1980), 331–52; and Bob Carter and Satnam Virdee, 'Racism and the Sociological Imagination', *The British Journal of Sociology*, 59.4 (2008), 661–79.

17. Lawrence, 'Inventing the "Traditional Working Class"'; and Jon Lawrence, *Me, Me, Me? Individualism and the Search for Community in Post-War England* (Oxford: Oxford University Press, 2019).

18. Butler, 'Michael Young', at 222–23.

19. Alexandre Campsie, 'Mass-Observation, Left Intellectuals and the Politics of Everyday Life', *The English Historical Review*, 131.548 (2016), 92–121.

20. James Hinton, *The Mass Observers: A History, 1937–1949* (Oxford: Oxford University Press, 2013); Boris Jardine, 'Mass-Observation, Surrealist Sociology, and the Bathos of Paperwork', *History of the Human Sciences*, 31.5 (2018), 52–79; and Liz Stanley, 'Mass-Observation's Fieldwork Methods', in *Handbook of Ethnography*, ed. by Paul Atkinson et al. (London: Sage Publications, 2001), 92–108.

21. Stanley, 'Mass-Observation's Fieldwork Methods'.

22. Hinton, *Mass Observers*, 70.

23. Ibid., 71.

24. Ibid., 84.

25. C. Madge and T. Harrisson, eds., *First Year's Work 1937–38 by Mass-Observation* (London: Lindsay Drummond, 1938), 103.

26. Goody, *Expansive Moment*, 74.

27. Raymond Firth, 'An Anthropologist's View of Mass-Observation', *The Sociological Review*, a31.2 (1939), 166–93, at 193.

28. Ibid., 192.

29. Ibid., 167.

30. For a rich account of the study's findings set in the context of post-war London, see Lawrence, *Me, Me, Me?*, ch. 2.

31. Raymond Firth, *We, the Tikopia: A Sociological Study of Kinship in Primitive Polynesia* (London: G. Allen & Unwin, 1936), 56.

32. Ibid.

33. Ibid., 575.

34. Lawrence, 'Inventing the "Traditional Working Class"', 591.

35. 'Report on Initial Stages of an Anthropological Study of Kinship Systems in a Contemporary English Community', British Library for Political and Economic Science, London School of Economics, Raymond Firth Papers, 3/1/14.

36. 'An Inquiry into Contemporary Kinship', 5, Firth Papers, 3/1/8.

37. Ibid., 1.

38. Raymond Firth, 'Introduction', in Raymond Firth, Judith Djamour, and Philip Garigue, *Two Studies of Kinship in London* (London: Athlone Press, 1956), 12.

39. Ibid., 12–13.

40. Ibid., 16.

41. Ibid., 22.

42. Ibid.

43. Ibid., 14

44. Ibid., 18

45. Lawrence, *Me, Me, Me?*, 42.

46. Christian Topalov, '"Traditional Working-Class Neighborhoods": An Inquiry into the Emergence of a Sociological Model in the 1950s and 1960s', *Osiris*, 18 (2003), 212–33.

47. For numbers see Mike Savage, 'Elizabeth Bott and the Formation of Modern British Sociology', *The Sociological Review*, 56.4 (2008), 579–605, 602n2.

48. Roslyn Dubler, '"The Smallest Institute of All": Sociology, Class and the Politics of Knowledge in Postwar Britain' (unpublished honours thesis, University of Sydney, 2013), 44–45 <http://hdl.handle.net/2123/10254>; and Mandler, 'Good Reading for the Million'.

49. Quoted in Butler, *Michael Young*, 135.

50. Peter Willmott and Michael Dunlop Young, *Family and Kinship in East London* (Glencoe, IL: Free Press, 1957), 3 and 3n1.

51. Richard Titmuss, 'Foreword', in ibid., xii.

52. Michael Young and Peter Willmott, *Family and Kinship in East London*, rev edn (Harmondsworth: Penguin, 1962), 36. Where I discuss the first edition specifically it will be cited as such.

53. Ibid., 42.

54. Ibid., 103.

55. Ibid., 56.

56. Butler, 'Michael Young', 6.

57. Ibid.; and Lawrence, 'Inventing the "Traditional Working Class"'.

58. Butler, *Michael Young*, ch. 2.

59. Dubler, '"Smallest Institute of All"', 44–45.

60. Willmott and Young, *Family and Kinship*, 38.

61. Ibid., 199.

62. Firth et al., *Two Studies of Kinship in London*, 22.

63. Topalov, '"Traditional Working-Class Neighborhoods"'.

64. '26th November 1954, Mr Young's Anthropological Study of Bethnal Green', Firth Papers, 3/1/16.

65. For an account of 'race relations' sociology in Britain and its anthropological debts, see Bailkin, *Afterlife of Empire*, ch. 1. On Jephcott as working in a different tradition to Little, Banton, and others, see Helen McCarthy, 'Pearl Jephcott and the Politics of Gender, Class and Race in Post-War Britain', *Women's History Review*, 28.5 (2019), 779–93.

66. Mark Clapson, 'The American Contribution to the Urban Sociology of Race Relations in Britain from the 1940s to the Early 1970s', *Urban History*, 33.2 (2006), 253–73, at 257.

67. Chris Waters, '"Dark Strangers" in Our Midst: Discourses of Race and Nation in Britain, 1947–1963', *Journal of British Studies*, 36.2 (1997), 207–38, at 221–22.

68. Ibid., pp. 226–67; McCarthy, 'Pearl Jephcott', 780; Asa Briggs, *Victorian Cities* (London: Penguin, 1968), 313–15; and Shilliam, *Race and the Undeserving Poor*, 46–55.

69. Robbie Shilliam, 'Behind the Rhodes Statue: Black Competency and the Imperial Academy', *History of the Human Sciences*, 32.5 (2019), 3–27, 14.

70. Ibid., 13; and Bailkin, *Afterlife of Empire*, ch. 1.

71. Lawrence, *Me, Me, Me?*, 56.
72. Bourne and Sivanandan, 'Cheerleaders and Ombudsmen', 332.
73. *Edinburgh University Calendar 1951–52* (Edinburgh: James Thin, 1951), 233–34.
74. Mills, *Difficult Folk*, 135.
75. 'Colonial Students' Political Problems', Edinburgh University Special Collections, Kenneth Little Papers, fol. 12a, and 'Working Group on Diminution of Prejudice – Report of Second Conference on the Problems of Prejudice and Discrimination – Royal Empire Society, June 15 and 16 1957', fol. 12g. He had already done an investigation of racism amongst landlords in K. L. Little, '84. A Note on Colour Prejudice Amongst the English "Middle Class"', *Man*, 43 (1943), 104–7.
76. K. L. Little, 'The Study of Racial Mixture in the British Commonwealth', *The Eugenics Review*, 32.4 (1941), 114–20, 117.
77. K. L. Little, *Negroes in Britain: A Study of Racial Relations in English Society* (London: Kegan Paul, Trench, Trubner, 1947), xii.
78. Ibid., xii.
79. Ibid., 3
80. Ibid, 4.
81. Ibid., 5
82. Ibid., 7.
83. Bourne and Sivanandan, 'Cheerleaders and Ombudsmen', 332.
84. Waters, '"Dark Strangers" in Our Midst', 233, 237.
85. Little, *Negroes in Britain*, xi.
86. Mica Nava, 'Sometimes Antagonistic, Sometimes Ardently Sympathetic: Contradictory Responses to Migrants in Postwar Britain', *Ethnicities*, 14.3 (2014), 458–80, esp. 470.
87. Mills, *Difficult Folk*, 140.
88. Bourne and Sivanandan, 'Cheerleaders and Ombudsmen', 332.
89. Mills, *Difficult Folk*, 143.
90. Ibid., 139.
91. Ibid., 143.
92. Savage, 'Elizabeth Bott and the Formation of Modern British Sociology'.
93. Willmott and Young, *Family and Kinship*, 1st edn, 3 and 3n1.
94. Ibid., 204.
95. 'Seminar notes, 19 November 1954', Firth Papers, 3/1/16.
96. 'Plan for thesis: Elizabeth Bott. 1.10.53', 3, Firth Papers, 8/1/10.
97. Elizabeth Bott, 'Urban Families: Conjugal Roles and Social Networks', *Human Relations*, 8.4 (1955), 345–84, 373.
98. Elizabeth Spillius, *Encounters with Melanie Klein: Selected Papers of Elizabeth Spillius* (Routledge: London, 2007), 10.
99. J. A. Barnes, 'Class and Committees in a Norwegian Island Parish', *Human Relations*, 7.1 (1954), 39–58, at 44.
100. Bott, 'Urban Families', 349.
101. Lawrence, 'Inventing the "Traditional Working Class"'.
102. Ibid., 356.
103. Ibid., 359.

104. Ibid., 365.
105. Savage, 'Elizabeth Bott', 602.
106. Elizabeth Bott to Max Gluckman, 11 February 1952, British Library for Political and Economic Science, London School of Economics, Association of Social Anthropologists Papers, A 1.1a (M2063).
107. Bott to Firth, undated (likely pre-1953), Firth Papers, 8/1/10.
108. Max Gluckman, 'Preface', in Elizabeth Bott, *Family and Social Network: Roles, Norms, and External Relationships in Ordinary Urban Families*, 2nd edn (New York: The Free Press, 1971).
109. Raymond Williams, 'Culture Is Ordinary' (1958), in *Raymond Williams on Culture & Society : Essential Writings*, ed. by Jim McGuigan (Thousand Oaks, CA: Sage Publications, 2014), 1–18.
110. On the context of British ideas of culture and society between the nineteenth and twentieth centuries, see Lepenies, *Between Literature and Science*, 158–63.

CHAPTER 6. THE DEVELOPMENT DECADES

1. For an analysis of the *Survey* and its historical context, see Tilley, *Africa as a Living Laboratory*. See also John W. Cell, 'Lord Hailey and the Making of the African Survey', *African Affairs*, 88.353 (1989), 481–505; and John W. Cell, *Hailey: A Study in British Imperialism, 1872–1969* (Cambridge: Cambridge University Press, 1992). The literature on colonial development in the 1930s and 1940s is large. For some key interventions, see Christophe Bonneuil, 'Development as Experiment: Science and State Building in Late Colonial and Postcolonial Africa, 1930–1970', *Osiris*, 15.1 (2000), 258–81; Cooper, 'Development, Modernization, and the Social Sciences'; Tilley, *Africa as a Living Laboratory*; and Hodge, *Triumph of the Expert*.
2. Linstrum, *Ruling Minds*.
3. H. W. Arndt, *Economic Development: The History of an Idea* (Chicago: University of Chicago Press, 1987).
4. Marc Matera, 'Colonial Subjects: Black Intellectuals and the Development of Colonial Studies in Britain', *Journal of British Studies*, 49.2 (2010), 388–418.
5. John Darwin, *The Empire Project: The Rise and Fall of the British World-System, 1830–1970* (Cambridge: Cambridge University Press, 2009), 518–19.
6. Saul Dubow, 'The Commonwealth and South Africa: From Smuts to Mandela', *The Journal of Imperial and Commonwealth History*, 45.2 (2017), 284–314.
7. Sarah Stockwell, 'Britain and Decolonization in an Era of Global Change', in *The Oxford Handbook of the Ends of Empire*, ed. by Martin Thomas and Andrew S. Thompson (Oxford: Oxford University Press, 2018).
8. 'Political Officer as an Anthropologist' [dated 2 May], Bodleian Library, Oxford, Margery Perham Papers, 229/4, 5.
9. 'Colonial Administration class: Discussion of Miss Perham's Paper, 9 May 1933', Malinowski Papers, 6/8.
10. Ibid.
11. Matera, *Black London*, ch. 6.

12. 'Colonial Administration class: Discussion of Miss Perham's Paper, 9 May 1933'. Malinowski Papers, 6/8; and Matera, 'Colonial Subjects'.

13. Cell, *Hailey*, 222.

14. William Malcolm Hailey, *An African Survey: A Study of Problems Arising in Africa South of the Sahara* (Oxford: Oxford University Press, 1938), 712.

15. Ibid., 713.

16. Gladstone, 'Significant Sister', 346.

17. Malinowski to Zimmern, 23 April 1930, and Malinowski to Zimmern, 13 May 1931, Malinowski Papers, 29/21.

18. Pedersen, 'Settler Colonialism at the Bar of the League of Nations'; and Pedersen, *Guardians*, esp. 29, 124, 131, 258, 198, 403.

19. For a statement of Malinowski's internationalism and theorising of international law, see Bronislaw Malinowski, 'A New Instrument for the Interpretation of Law: Especially Primitive', *The Yale Law Journal*, 51.8 (1942), 1237–54.

20. Cell, *Hailey*, 245.

21. Stefan Collini, *English Pasts: Essays in History and Culture* (Oxford: Oxford University Press, 1999), 280–81.

22. *Oxford University Summer School on Colonial Administration: Second Session, 1938* (Oxford: University Press, 1938), 3–4.

23. Ibid., 6–7.

24. Ibid., 8.

25. Ibid., 51.

26. Ibid., v.

27. Lord Lugard to Margery Perham, n.d., Bodleian Library, Oxford, MSS Perham, 22/1.

28. *Oxford University Summer School*, 68 and 70–71.

29. David Mills, 'Anthropology at the End of Empire: The Rise and Fall of the Colonial Social Sciences Research Council, 1944–1962', in *Empires, Nations, and Natives: Anthropology and State-Making*, ed. by Benoit de L'Estoile, Federico G. Neiburg, and Lygia Sigaud (Durham, NC: Duke University Press, 2005), 149.

30. Charlotte Lydia Riley, '"The Winds of Change Are Blowing Economically": The Labour Party and British Overseas Development, 1940s–1960s', in *Britain, France and the Decolonization of Africa*, ed. by Andrew W. M. Smith and Chris Jeppesen (London: UCL Press, 2017), 49

31. David Mills, 'How Not to Be a "Government House Pet": Audrey Richards and the East African Institute for Social Research', in *African Anthropologies: History, Critique and Practice*, ed. by David Mills, Mwenda Ntarangwi, and Mustafa Babiker (New York: Zed Books, 2006), 81.

32. *Oxford University Summer School*, 19.

33. '30th March 1948 – 1st Meeting at CO', Colonial Research Papers, British Library for Political and Economic Science, London School of Economics, 2/1.

34. OGR Williams comments dated 8 April 1940, on 'Research into problems of political organisation under indirect rule in Africa by Dr E.E. Evans [sic]', TNA, CO 847/20/8.

35. R. D. Grillo, 'Applied Anthropology in the 1980s: Retrospect and Prospect', in *Social Anthropology and Development Policy*, ed. by R. D. Grillo and Alan Rew (London: Tavistock, 1985), 13.
36. Quoted in Mills, *Difficult Folk*, 77 (emphasis in original).
37. Steinmetz, 'Child of the Empire', 368.
38. 'Evans Pritchard's memorandum 15th July 1946', London School of Economics (LSE), ASA papers, box A, folder 1.1.
39. Geoffrey Gorer, for example; see MacClancy, *Anthropology in the Public Arena*, 44.
40. 'A meeting held on Tuesday and Wednesday 23–24 July 1946', ASA Papers, box A, folder 1.1.
41. David Mills, 'Professionalizing or Popularizing Anthropology? A Brief History of Anthropology's Scholarly Associations in the UK', *Anthropology Today*, 19.5 (2003), 8–13, at 12.
42. Mills, *Difficult Folk*, ch. 3; and Mills, 'Anthropology at the End of Empire', 151.
43. Ibid., 149.
44. Mills, 'How Not to Be'.
45. Quoted in ibid., 86.
46. A. I. Richards, ed., *Economic Development and Tribal Change: A Study of Immigrant Labour in Buganda* by (Cambridge: Heffer, 1951), 6.
47. Ibid., 7. For commentary on this subject see Bailkin, *Afterlife of Empire*, ch. 1.
48. Richards, *Economic Development*, 7.
49. Mills, 'How Not to Be', 89.
50. Ibid., 89–90.
51. Ibid., 92–93.
52. David Mills, 'A Major Disaster for Anthropology? Oxford and Alfred Reginald Radcliffe-Brown', in *A History of Oxford Anthropology*, ed. by Peter Rivière (New York: Berghahn Books, 2007).
53. A. R. Radcliffe-Brown, 'On Social Structure', *The Journal of the Royal Anthropological Institute of Great Britain and Ireland*, 70.1 (1940), 1–12, at 5.
54. Ibid., 6.
55. Mills, *Difficult Folk*, 43; Foreman, 'Horizons of Modernity', 44; and Stocking, *After Tylor*, 425–26.
56. Raymond Firth, ed., *Man and Culture – an Evaluation of the Work of Bronislaw Malinowski* (London: Routledge & Kegan Paul, 1957).
57. Mills, 'Anthropology at the End of Empire', 155.
58. E. E. Evans-Pritchard, 'Applied Anthropology', *Africa: Journal of the International African Institute*, 16.2 (1946), 92–98, at 94.
59. E. E. Evans-Pritchard, '198. Social Anthropology: Past and Present the Marett Lecture, 1950', *Man*, 50 (1950), 118–24, at 122.
60. Ibid., 122 and 120.
61. Evans-Pritchard, '198. Social Anthropology', 123.
62. E. E. Evans-Pritchard, *Social Anthropology* (London: Cohen & West, 1951), 9.

63. Ibid.

64. Daryll Forde, '254. Anthropology, Science and History', *Man*, 50 (1950), 155–56; A. L. Kroeber, '33. Social Anthropology: Past and Present', *Man*, 51 (1951), 18; A. R. Radcliffe-Brown, '14. Social Anthropology: Past and Present', *Man*, 52 (1952), 13–14; and E. R. Leach, '199. Social Anthropology: Past and Present', *Man*, 51 (1951), 114–15.

65. I. Schapera, 'Should Anthropologists Be Historians?', *The Journal of the Royal Anthropological Institute of Great Britain and Ireland*, 92.2 (1962), 143–56, at 153.

66. Leach, '199. Social Anthropology'.

67. Mills, 'Anthropology at the End of Empire', 156.

68. Richard Brown, 'Anthropology and Colonial Rule: The Case of Godfrey Wilson and the Rhodes-Livingstone Institute, Northern Rhodesia', in *Anthropology & The Colonial Encounter*, ed. Talal Asad; and Lynette Schumaker, *Africanizing Anthropology: Fieldwork, Networks, and the Making of Cultural Knowledge in Central Africa* (Durham, NC: Duke University Press, 2001), 55–65.

69. Gordon, *Enigma of Max Gluckman*, 330–32.

70. Ibid., 190–91.

71. Marian Kempny, 'History of the Manchester "School" and the Extended-Case Method', in *The Manchester School: Practice and Ethnographic Praxis in Anthropology*, ed. by T. M. S. Evens and Don Handelman (New York: Berghahn Books, 2006). Gordon, *Enigma of Max Gluckman*, 150–51, gives an overview of the critiques of the 1942 paper and its relative lack of influence outside the circle of researchers at the RLI.

72. Schumaker, *Africanizing Anthropology*, 78–79.

73. Paul Cocks, 'Max Gluckman and the Critique of Segregation in South African Anthropology, 1921–1940', *Journal of Southern African Studies*, 27.4 (2001), 739–56; Hugh Macmillan, 'Return to the Malungwana Drift – Max Gluckman, the Zulu Nation and the Common Society', *African Affairs*, 94.374 (1995), 39–65; and Foreman, 'Horizons of Modernity'. Although David Mills is rather sceptical of these claims to originality in 'Made in Manchester? Methods and Myths in Disciplinary History', in *The Manchester School*, 168.

74. Kuper, *Anthropology and Anthropologists*, 32.

75. Malinowski, 'Introductory Essay', in *Methods of Study of Culture Contact*, xiii, xiv–xv.

76. Macmillan, 'Return to the Malungwana Drift', 46–47.

77. Cocks, 'Max Gluckman'.

78. As discussed in ibid.' 742.

79. Ibid., 754.

80. Gordon, *Enigma of Max Gluckman*, 190; and Godfrey Wilson and Monica Wilson, *The Analysis of Social Change: Based on Observations in Central Africa* (Cambridge: Cambridge University Press, 1945).

81. Schumaker, *Africanizing Anthropology*, 42.

82. Richard Werbner, *Anthropology after Gluckman: The Manchester School, Colonial and Postcolonial Transformations* (Manchester: Manchester University Press, 2020).

83. For one particularly influential version of this argument, see V. W. Turner, *Schism and Continuity in an African Society: A Study of Ndembu Village Life*, 2nd edn (Manchester: Manchester University Press, 1957; repr. 1968), esp. 90–93. See also Max Gluckman, 'The Peace in the Feud', *Past & Present*, 18 (1955), 1–14.

84. Foreman, 'Horizons of Modernity', ch. 4.
85. Mills, 'Anthropology at the End of Empire', 158.
86. Schumaker, *Africanizing Anthropology*, 174–80.
87. Foreman, 'Horizons of Modernity', 80–87.
88. Ibid., 99.
89. Adam Kuper, 'Alternative Histories of British Social Anthropology', *Social Anthropology*, 13.1 (2005), 47–64, at 54.
90. Mills, 'Anthropology at the End of Empire'.

CHAPTER 7. FROM DEVELOPMENT ECONOMICS TO THE 'MORAL ECONOMY'

1. A. I. Richards, 'Anthropology on the Scrap-Heap?', *Journal of African Administration*, 13.1 (1961), 3–10.
2. Ibid., 4.
3. Ibid., 5
4. Hetherington, *British Paternalism*, 20; and Frederick Cooper, 'Writing the History of Development', *Journal of Modern European History*, 8.1 (2010), 5–23.
5. Cooper, 'Development, Modernization, and the Social Sciences'; Satish Deshpande, 'Disciplinary Predicaments: Sociology and Anthropology in Postcolonial India', *Inter-Asia Cultural Studies*, 2.2 (2001), 247–60; Ferguson, 'Anthropology and Its Evil Twin'; and Nils Gilman, *Mandarins of the Future: Modernization Theory in Cold War America* (Baltimore, MD: Johns Hopkins University Press, 2003).
6. Charles P. Oman and Ganeshan Wignaraja, *The Postwar Evolution of Development Thinking* (Houndmills, Basingstoke: Macmillan, 1991), 12; and Charlotte Lydia Riley, '"Tropical Allsorts": The Transnational Flavor of British Development Policies in Africa', *Journal of World History*, 26.4 (2016), 839–64.
7. Alden Young, *Transforming Sudan: Decolonization, Economic Development, and State Formation* (Cambridge: Cambridge University Press, 2017), ch. 3; and Daniel Speich, 'The Use of Global Abstractions: National Income Accounting in the Period of Imperial Decline', *Journal of Global History*, 6.1 (2011), 7–28.
8. Matthias Schmelzer, 'The Growth Paradigm: History, Hegemony, and the Contested Making of Economic Growthmanship', *Ecological Economics*, 118 (2015), 262–71; Mauro Boianovsky and Kevin D. Hoover, 'In the Kingdom of Solovia: The Rise of Growth Economics at MIT, 1956–70', *History of Political Economy*, 46.suppl 1 (2014), 198–228; Amartya Sen, 'Introduction', in *Growth Economics: Selected Readings* (Harmondsworth: Penguin, 1970), 9; Cooper and Packard, 'Introduction', 17–18; and Speich, 'The Use', 19.
9. Arndt, *Economic Development*.

10. Ibid.

11. Timothy Mitchell, 'Fixing the Economy', *Cultural Studies*, 12.1 (1998), 82–101. A different chronology is given in Manu Goswami, *Producing India: From Colonial Economy to National Space* (Chicago: University of Chicago Press, 2004), who argues that it was in the 1870s and 1880s that the idea of a national economy arose in the context of Indian anti-colonialism. Daniel Abramson Hirschman, 'Inventing the Economy Or: How We Learned to Stop Worrying and Love the GDP' (unpublished PhD thesis, University of Michigan, 2016), 42–43, 48–49, also casts some doubt on Mitchell's chronology with relation to GDP. Here, though, I am interested in a particular method of national income accounting and with development economics applied by economists in the metropole to areas outside America and Europe, where Mitchell's dating of a transformation in political economy in the 1930s does hold more water.

12. Asad, 'Ethnographic Representation, Statistics, and Modern Power', 82.

13. This is nicely captured in Barbara Bush, 'Colonial Research and the Social Sciences at the End of Empire: The West Indian Social Survey, 1944–57', *The Journal of Imperial and Commonwealth History*, 41.3 (2013), 451–74.

14. Williams, *Culture and Society*, 157.

15. I take this term from James C. Scott, *Seeing Like a State: How Certain Schemes to Improve the Human Condition Have Failed* (New Haven, CT: Yale University Press, 1998). In the case of American social science and development, Daniel Immerwahr has made the point that community development always coexisted with 'high modernist' planning in *Thinking Small: The United States and the Lure of Community Development* (Cambridge, MA: Harvard University Press, 2015).

16. W. Arthur Lewis, 'Review of Primitive Polynesian Economy: Land, Labour and Diet in Northern Rhodesia', *Economica*, 8.29 (1941), 114–16, at 114.

17. Ibid., 115, 116.

18. W. Arthur Lewis, *Theory of Economic Growth* (London: George Allen & Unwin, 1955), 9.

19. Although Lewis's later thoughts on industrial development were perhaps more muted than that; see Mark Figueroa, 'W. Arthur Lewis Versus the Lewis Model: Agricultural or Industrial Development?', *The Manchester School*, 72.6 (2004), 736–50.

20. For a survey of Lewis's ideas, see Robert L. Tignor, *W. Arthur Lewis and the Birth of Development Economics* (Princeton, NJ: Princeton University Press, 2006).

21. Heath Pearson has measured citations in economics journals to show that Lewis's article was by far the most referenced and discussed article on development economics in the period. Heath Pearson, 'Primitive Economics: A Reply', *History of Political Economy*, 34.1 (2002), 273–81, at 275.

22. W. Arthur Lewis, 'Economic Development with Unlimited Supplies of Labour', *The Manchester School*, 22.2 (1954), 139–91, at 142.

23. Ibid., 145.

24. Ibid., 147.

25. Godfrey Wilson, 'An Essay on the Economics of Detrabilalization in Northern Rhodesia', *The Rhodes-Livingstone Papers*, 5 (1941), 17.

26. W. Arthur Lewis, 'The Colonial Problem', *The Student Movement*, 47 (1945), 88.

27. Ibid.

28. Paul R. Krugman, *Development, Geography, and Economic Theory* (Cambridge, MA: MIT Press, 1995), ch. 1.

29. Yoichi Mine, 'The Political Element in the Works of W. Arthur Lewis: The 1954 Lewis Model and African Development', *The Developing Economies*, 44.3 (2006), 329–55; and Barbara Ingham and Paul Mosley, '"Marvellous Intellectual Feasts": Arthur Lewis at the London School of Economics, 1933–48', *History of Political Economy*, 45.2 (2013), 187–221.

30. Deane's research is discussed in Schumaker, *Africanizing Anthropology*; and Mary S. Morgan, 'Seeking Parts, Looking for Wholes', in *Histories of Scientific Observation*, ed. by Lorraine Daston and Elizabeth Lunbeck (Chicago: University of Chicago Press, 2011).

31. Schumaker, *Africanizing Anthropology*, 104–5.

32. Phyllis Deane, 'National Income: Problems of Social Accounting in Central Africa', *The Rhodes-Livingstone Journal*, 5 (1947), 25–43, at 38.

33. Ibid, 39.

34. Schumaker, *Africanizing Anthropology*, 105.

35. Morgan, 'Seeking Parts', 313.

36. Phyllis Deane, 'Problems of Studying Village Economies', *The Rhodes-Livingstone Journal*, 8 (1949), 42–49, at 46–47.

37. Ibid.

38. Luke Messac, 'Outside the Economy: Women's Work and Feminist Economics in the Construction and Critique of National Income Accounting', *The Journal of Imperial and Commonwealth History*, 46.3 (2018), 552–78, at 560–61.

39. Phyllis Deane, *Colonial Social Accounting* (Cambridge: Cambridge University Press, 1953), 209.

40. Quoted in Morgan, 'Seeking Parts', 310

41. Deane, 'Problems', 46.

42. Deane, *Colonial Social Accounting*, xiv.

43. Messac, 'Outside the Economy', 565.

44. For an account of postwar social science that stresses the tool-like nature of research, see Joel Isaac, 'Tool Shock: Technique and Epistemology in the Postwar Social Sciences', *History of Political Economy*, 42.suppl 1 (2010), 133–64. Deane herself used this metaphor: 'These social accounts are essentially practical in origin and intention and the tool-users as well as the tool-makers have a part to play in their design'. Deane, 'National Income', 32.

45. Michele Alacevich, 'The World Bank and the Politics of Productivity: The Debate on Economic Growth, Poverty, and Living Standards in the 1950s', *Journal of Global History*, 6.1 (2011), 53–74.

46. Phyllis Deane, 'The Industrial Revolution and Economic Growth: The Evidence of Early British National Income Estimates', *Economic Development and Cultural Change*, 5.2 (1957), 159–74.

47. Jane Humphries, 'Phyllis Deane', in *Oxford Dictionary of National Biography*, <https://doi.org/10.1093/ref:odnb/105668>.

48. Deane would apply the notion of the Industrial Revolution to Central Africa in the early 1960s, closing the loop, as it were, between economic history and development economics. Phyllis Deane, 'The Industrial Revolution in British Central Africa', *Civilisations*, 12.3 (1962), 331–55.

49. For an exploration of some of these themes, see David Cannadine, 'The Present and the Past in the English Industrial Revolution 1880–1980', *Past & Present*, 103 (1984), 131–72; and Guy Ortolano, 'The Typicalities of the English? Walt Rostow, The Stages of Economic Growth, and Modern British History', *Modern Intellectual History*, 12.3 (2015), 657–84.

50. Gerardo Serra, 'Pleas for Fieldwork: Polly Hill on Observation and Induction, 1966–1982', *Research in the History of Economic Thought and Methodology*, 36 (2018), 93–108.

51. Ibid., 9.

52. For a study of women in the economics profession in the postwar decades, although in America, see Cleo Chassonnery-Zaïgouche, Beatrice Cherrier, and John D. Singleton, '"Economics Is Not a Man's Field": CSWEP and the First Gender Reckoning in Economics (1971-1991)', SSRN, December 28, 2019, <http://dx.doi.org/10.2139/ssrn.3510857>.

53. For one history of this phenomenon, see Philip Mirowski, 'Exploring the Fault Lines: Introduction to the Minisymposium on the History of Economic Anthropology', *History of Political Economy*, 32.4 (2000), 919–32.

54. Foreman, 'Horizons of Modernity', 99.

55. Pearson, 'Primitive Economics: A Reply', 275.

56. W. M. Hailey, *An African Survey, Revised 1956: A Study of Problems Arising in Africa South of the Sahara* (Oxford: Oxford University Press, 1957), 60.

57. Mafeje, 'Problem of Anthropology in Historical Perspective'; and Steinmetz, 'Child of the Empire', 362-63.

58. Kuper, *Anthropology and Anthropologists*, 64.

59. Although Lewis did not stay long in his role, quitting over differences of policy with Nkrumah after fifteen months. Adom Getachew, *Worldmaking After Empire, The Rise and Fall of Self-Determination* (Princeton, NJ: Princeton University Press, 2019), 148.

60. Ibid., ch. 5.

61. Collins, 'On the Acrimoniousness'.

62. See the recollections of Adam Kuper in 'Deconstructing Anthropology: First Annual Stephen F. Gudeman Lecture', *HAU: Journal of Ethnographic Theory*, 9.1 (2019), 10–22.

63. For an overview see Kuper, *Anthropology and Anthropologists*, 93–97.

64. For an exploration of the concept of embeddedness, see Gareth Dale, 'Lineages of Embeddedness: On the Antecedents and Successors of a Polanyian Concept', *American Journal of Economics and Sociology*, 70.2 (2011), 306–39.

65. Karl Polanyi, *The Great Transformation: The Political and Economic Origins of Our Time* (Boston: Beacon Press, 1944; repr. 2001).

66. For some discussion of these terms in the wake of decades of debate, see the introduction to Stuart Plattner, *Economic Anthropology* (Stanford, CA: Stanford University Press, 1989); and Thomas Hylland Eriksen and Finn Sivert Nielsen, *A History of Anthropology*, 2nd edn (London: Pluto Press, 2013), 104–6.

For recent attempts to historicize the prehistory of these debates, see Scott Cook and Michael W. Young, 'Malinowski, Herskovits, and the Controversy over Economics in Anthropology', *History of Political Economy*, 48.4 (2016), 657–79; and Scott Cook, 'Malinowski in Oaxaca: Implications of an Unfinished Project in Economic Anthropology, Part I', *Critique of Anthropology*, 37.2 (2017), 132–59.

67. "Workshop in Economic Anthropology, list of participants," Firth Papers, 5/17.

68. 'Minutes of Workshop', 22 [12?] September 1959, 2, Firth Papers, 5/17.

69. Ibid., 3.

70. Ibid., 7 and 8.

71. Robbins Burling, 'Maximization Theories and the Study of Economic Anthropology', *American Anthropologist*, 64.4 (1962), 802–21; George Dalton, 'Economic Theory and Primitive Society', *American Anthropologist*, 63.1 (1961), 1–25; and Marshall Sahlins, *Stone Age Economics* (Chicago: Aldine-Atherton, 1972). Plattner, *Economic Anthropology*, offers an introduction to the terms.

72. Pearson, 'Primitive Economics: A Reply'. This process carried on throughout the following decades as economics became more and more a self-referential discipline. For an argument using citations, see Marion Fourcade, Etienne Ollion, and Yann Algan, 'The Superiority of Economists', *Journal of Economic Perspectives*, 29.1 (2015), 89–114.

73. 'Minutes of Workshop', 23.

74. This view was exemplified by Alfred Radcliffe-Brown in his presidential address to the Royal Anthropological Institute in 1940. To the anthropologist, he wrote, the 'economic machinery of a society appears in quite a new light if it is studied in relation to the social structure.' 'The exchange of goods and services', he went on, 'is dependent upon, is the result of, and at the same time is a means of maintaining a certain structure, a network of relations between persons and collections of persons.' Radcliffe-Brown, 'On Social Structure', 7 and 8.

75. Karl Polanyi, 'The Economy as Instituted Process', in *Trade and Market in the Early Empires: Economies in History and Theory*, ed. by Karl Polanyi, Conrad M. Arensberg, and H. W. Pearson (Glencoe, IL: Free Press, 1957), 243.

76. Raymond Firth, 'Methodological Issues in Economic Anthropology', *Journal of the Royal Anthropological Institute*, 7.3 (1972), 467–75, at 469. In fact, Firth used the terms 'formal' and 'substantive' in his book *Primitive Polynesian Economy* (1939), in turn crediting the distinction to the Keynesian economist John Hicks in an essay in *Social Sciences, Their Relations in Theory and Teaching* (1936). Firth, *Primitive Polynesian Economy*, 27.

77. Polanyi, *Great Transformation*, 276–80. The references are to Thurnwald (15 refs); Malinowski (8 refs); Firth (5 refs); Radcliffe-Brown (1 ref); the American anthropologists Robert Lowie (2 refs), Ruth Benedict (1 ref), Robert Linton (1 ref), Melville Herskovits (1 ref), Alexander Goldenweiser (1 ref); and the German economist and sociologist Carl Brinkmann (1 ref). On Polanyi and anthropology see S. C. Humphreys, 'History, Economics, and Anthropology: The Work of Karl Polanyi', *History and Theory*, 8 (1969), 165–212. In a report to the Rockefeller Foundation, which funded the leave to write his book *The Great Transformation* (1944), Polanyi wrote of having 'surveyed' 'some of the literature on the economics of primitive peoples in an

endeavour to clarify the concept of the institutional unity of society.' 'Report on Progress', RAC, Rockefeller Foundation, Record Group 1.1, Series 200, box 310, folder 3694.

78. Karl Polanyi, 'Aristotle Discovers the Economy', in *Trade and Market in the Early Empires*, 69.

79. Raymond Firth, 'The Place of Malinowski in the History of Economic Anthropology', in *Man and Culture – an Evaluation of the Work of Bronislaw Malinowski*, ed. by Raymond Firth (London: Routledge & Kegan Paul, 1957), 209.

80. Firth, 'Methodological Issues', 472.

81. Richards, 'Anthropology on the Scrap-Heap?', 7.

82. Keith Thomas, 'Should Historians Be Anthropologists?', *The Oxford Magazine*, n.s., 1.22 (June 1961), 387–88, at 388.

83. Ibid., 387.

84. Ibid., 388.

85. Peter Burke, Brian Harrison, and Paul Slack, 'Keith Thomas', in *Civil Histories: Essays Presented to Sir Keith Thomas*, ed. by Peter Burke, Brian Harrison, and Paul Slack (Oxford: Oxford University Press, 2000).

86. Keith Thomas, 'History and Anthropology', *Past & Present*, 24 (April 1963), 3–24, at 7.

87. Ibid., 11.

88. Ibid., 16.

89. Keith Thomas, 'The Tools and the Job', *Times Literary Supplement*, no. 3345 (7 April 1966), 275–76, at 276.

90. Lawrence Stone, *The Past and the Present Revisited*, Rev. edn (London: Routledge & Kegan Paul, 1987), 12.

91. Peter Mandler, *History and National Life* (London: Profile Books, 2002), 113–16.

92. Alan Macfarlane, *The Family Life of Ralph Josselin, a Seventeenth-Century Clergyman* (Cambridge: Cambridge University Press, 1970); and Alan Macfarlane, *Witchcraft in Tudor and Stuart England: A Regional and Comparative Study* (London: Routledge & Kegan Paul, 1970).

93. Stone, *Past and the Present*, 15.

94. Ibid., 11.

95. Keith Thomas, *Religion and the Decline of Magic: Studies in Popular Beliefs in Sixteenth and Seventeenth Century England* (Harmondsworth: Penguin, 1971), 3.

96. Maria Lúcia G. Pallares-Burke, *The New History: Confessions and Conversations* (Oxford: Wiley, 2002), 91.

97. E. P. Thompson, 'Folklore, Anthropology, and Social History', *The Indian Historical Review*, 3.2 (1977), 247–66, at 260.

98. E. P. Thompson, 'The Peculiarities of the English', *Socialist Register*, 2.2 (1965), 311–62, at 354.

99. E. P. Thompson, 'History from Below', *Times Literary Supplement*, no. 3345 (7 April 1966), 279–80.

100. E. P. Thompson, 'The Moral Economy of the English Crowd in the Eighteenth Century', *Past & Present*, no. 50 (February 1971), 76–136, at 135.

101. Ibid., 78.

102. Ibid., 78.
103. E. P. Thompson, 'Time, Work-Discipline, and Industrial Capitalism', *Past & Present*, 38 (1967), 56–97, at 93, 94, 97.
104. Ibid., 96.
105. Thompson, 'Moral Economy', 131.
106. Tim Rogan, *The Moral Economists: R.H. Tawney, Karl Polanyi, E.P. Thompson, and the Critique of Capitalism* (Princeton, NJ: Princeton University Press, 2017), does not link Polanyi and Thompson and social anthropology, which I am arguing were central planks of their sensitivity to social change. Tawney, too, read his anthropologist colleagues; see his preface in Firth, *Primitive Economics* and his call for economic history to be done with the 'same detachment and objectivity as anthropologists bring to the investigation of similar phenomena in more primitive societies.' R. H. Tawney, 'The Study of Economic History', *Economica*, 39 (1933), 1–21, at 20.
107. Miles Taylor, 'The Beginnings of Modern British Social History?', *History Workshop Journal*, 43 (1997), 155–76, at 158.
108. Guy Ortolano, 'Human Science or a Human Face? Social History and the "Two Cultures" Controversy', *Journal of British Studies*, 43.4 (2004), 482–505, at 487.
109. Peter Laslett, *The World We Have Lost* (London: Methuen, 1965) 235; and E. J. Hobsbawm, *Primitive Rebels: Studies in the Archaic Forms of Social Movement in the 19th and 20th Centuries* (Manchester: Manchester University Press, 1959).
110. Joel Isaac argues that in the case of Clifford Geertz, his later interest in 'culture' as a symbolic system derives from his earlier interest in questions of economic development, thus confirming that the later 'crisis' in fact, deepened existing fault lines, rather than creating new ones. Joel Isaac, 'The Intensification of Social Forms: Economy and Culture in the Thought of Clifford Geertz', *Critical Historical Studies*, 5.2 (2018), 237–66. Lewis blames Geertz for the destruction of anthropology's 'universalist' pretensions in *In Defense of Anthropology*, 12.
111. Anderson, 'Components of the National Culture', 48.
112. Thomas, 'Should Historians Be Anthropologists?', 388.
113. Kerwin Lee Klein, *From History to Theory* (Berkeley: University of California Press, 2011).
114. Collini, '"Discipline History" and "Intellectual History",'as discussed in this book's introduction.

EPILOGUE

1. Anderson, 'Components of the National Culture', 48.
2. 'Professor Sir Raymond Firth,' *Independent*, 5 March 2002 <https://www.independent.co.uk/news/obituaries/professor-sir-raymond-firth-9169738.html>.
3. Talal Asad, 'Anthropology and the Colonial Encounter', reprinted in *The Politics of Anthropology: From Colonialism and Sexism toward a View from Below*, ed. by Gerrit Huizer and Bruce Mannheim (The Hague: Mouton, 1979), 89.

4. Ibid., 91.

5. Leach's life is well told in Stanley Jeyaraja Tambiah, *Edmund Leach: An Anthropological Life* (Cambridge: Cambridge University Press, 2002).

6. On Douglas, Leach, and Levi-Strauss, see Kuper, *Anthropology and Anthropologists*, ch. 6. For the Marxist turn, see the contemporary collection Maurice Bloch, ed., *Marxist Analyses and Social Anthropology* (London: Malaby Press, 1975).

7. T. M. S. Evens and Don Handelman, eds., *The Manchester School: Practice and Ethnographic Praxis in Anthropology* (New York: Berghahn Books, 2006); and Werbner, *Anthropology after Gluckman*.

8. Marian Kempny, 'History of the Manchester "School" and the Extended-Case Method', *Social Analysis*, 49.3 (2005), 144–65, at 155–60.

9. Foreman, 'Horizons of Modernity', 99.

10. Mafeje, 'Who Are the Makers and Objects of Anthropology?', at 5.

11. Peter Forster, 'Empiricism and Imperialism: A Review of the New Left Critique of Social Anthropology', in *Anthropology & the Colonial Encounter*, ed. by Talal Asad, 24.

12. Ibid., 31.

13. Ibid., 24.

14. Mafeje, 'Problem of Anthropology', 318; on the critique of functionalism and structural-functionalism in American sociology, see Robert C. Bannister, 'Sociology', in *The Cambridge History of Science: The Modern Social Sciences, Volume 7*, ed. by Dorothy Ross and Theodore M. Porter (Cambridge: Cambridge University Press, 2003), 352; and Norbert Wiley, 'The Current Interregnum in American Sociology', *Social Research*, 52.1 (1985), 179–207, at 179–80.

15. Joel Isaac, *Working Knowledge: Making the Human Sciences from Parsons to Kuhn* (Cambridge, MA: Harvard University Press, 2012), 8; for a discussion of the links between philosophical critique in the social sciences and purported connections to 'the intellectual culture of modernity', see Forster, 'Empiricism and Imperialism', 24–25; and Asad, 'Introduction', 13n16.

16. Matti Bunzl, 'Anthropology Beyond Crisis', *Anthropology and Humanism*, 30.2 (2005), 187–95, at 189.

17. James Clifford, 'Feeling Historical', *Cultural Anthropology*, 27.3 (2012), 417–26, at 419. I found this quote in a forthcoming review by Rodrigo Moulinié in *History of Anthropology Review*.

18. Spencer, 'British Social Anthropology', 4.

19. Ibid., 4.

20. Ibid., 4.

21. Ibid., 10.

22. Peter Mandler, 'Educating the Nation: IV. Subject Choice', *Transactions of the Royal Historical Society*, 27 (2017), 1–27.

23. Spencer, 'British Social Anthropology', 5, 6.

24. Peter Mandler, 'The Rise and Fall of the Social Sciences in the British Educational System, 1960–2016', in *The History of Sociology in Britain: New Research and Revaluation*, ed. by Plamena Panayotova (London: Palgrave Macmillan, 2019), 282, and for a comparison of student numbers with sociology and psychology, p. 287, fig. 10.2.

25. Spencer, 'British Social Anthropology', 6.
26. Lewis, *In Defense of Anthropology*, 12.
27. For instance, George E. Marcus and James Clifford, eds., *Writing Culture: The Poetics and Politics of Ethnography* (Berkeley: University of California Press, 1986); Bloch, *Marxist Analyses and Social Anthropology*; Michelle Zimbalist Rosaldo, Louise Lamphere, and Joan Bamberger, eds., *Woman, Culture, and Society* (Stanford, CA: Stanford University Press, 1974); Carol MacCormack and Marilyn Strathern, eds., *Nature, Culture and Gender* (Cambridge: Cambridge University Press, 1980). And for an overview of the terrain by the mid-1980s, see Sherry B. Ortner, 'Theory in Anthropology since the Sixties', *Comparative Studies in Society and History*, 26.1 (1984), 126–66. For other helpful summaries of these moves in anthropological theory that took place after the 1960s, see Caroline Humphrey, 'Marxism and neo-Marxism', and Jessica Johnson, 'Feminist Anthropology and the Question of Gender', in *Schools and Styles of Anthropological Theory*, ed. by Matei Candea (Abingdon: Routledge, 2018).
28. William Hamilton Sewell, *Logics of History: Social Theory and Social Transformation* (Chicago: University of Chicago Press, 2005), 17; and Peter Burke, *History and Social Theory*, 2nd edn (Cambridge: Polity, 2005).
29. For reflections about perceived differences between American and British anthropology at this time, see Kuper, 'Deconstructing Anthropology'. For a critique by an anthropologist of one historian's (Keith Thomas) smorgasbord approach to anthropological theory, see Hildred Geertz, 'An Anthropology of Religion and Magic, I', *The Journal of Interdisciplinary History*, 6.1 (1975), 71–89, and the reply, Keith Thomas, 'An Anthropology of Religion and Magic, II', *The Journal of Interdisciplinary History*, 6.1 (1975), 91–109.
30. Natalie Zemon Davis, 'The Reasons of Misrule: Youth Groups and Charivaris in Sixteenth-Century France', *Past & Present*, 50 (1971), 41–75; and Natalie Zemon Davis, 'The Rites of Violence: Religious Riot in Sixteenth-Century France', *Past & Present*, 59, (1973), 51–91. See also Alexandra Walsham, 'Rough Music and Charivari: Letters Between Natalie Zemon Davis and Edward Thompson, 1970–1972', *Past & Present*, 235.1 (2017), 243–62; Robert Darnton, *The Great Cat Massacre and Other Episodes in French Cultural History* (New York: Basic Books, 2009); and Carlo Ginzburg, *The Cheese and the Worms: The Cosmos of a Sixteenth-Century Miller* (Baltimore, MD: Johns Hopkins University Press, 2013). Ginzburg has published in the history of anthropology also, an essay on Malinowski and Robert Louis Stevenson: *No Island Is an Island: Four Glances at English Literature in a World Perspective* (New York: Columbia University Press, 2000). For a history of this interdisciplinary moment, see Klein, *From History to Theory*, and for a retrospective overview of the 1970s from another angle, see David I. Kertzer, 'Social Anthropology and Social Science History', *Social Science History*, 33.1 (2009), 1–16.
31. See, for instance, the classic collection of essays Bryan R. Wilson, *Rationality* (Oxford: Basil Blackwell, 1970); and on postmodernism, Trouillot, 'Anthropology and the Savage Slot'.
32. Adam Kuper, 'Anthropology and Anthropologists Forty Years On', *Anthropology of This Century* 11 (2014) <http://aotcpress.com/articles/anthropology-anthropologists-forty-years/>.

33. Keith Thomas, 'Should Historians Be Anthropologists?', *The Oxford Magazine*, n.s., 1.22 (June 1961), 387; and Jean-Christophe Agnew, 'History and Anthropology: Scenes from a Marriage', *The Yale Journal of Criticism*, 3.2 (1990), 29–50.

34. Firth, *Primitive Economics*, 484.

35. Anna Lowenhaupt Tsing, *The Mushroom at the End of the World: On the Possibility of Life in Capitalist Ruins* (Princeton, NJ: Princeton University Press, 2015); and Ursula K. Le Guin, *The Word for World Is Forest* (London: Gollancz, 1977), 32.

36. Matthew P. Fitzpatrick, 'Indigenous Australians and German Anthropology in the Era of "Decolonization"', *The Historical Journal*, 63.3 (2019), 686–709; Jason Gibson and Helen Gardner, "Conversations on the Frontier: Finding the Dialogic in Nineteenth-Century Anthropological Archives," *History Workshop Journal*, 88 (2019), 47–65; Parker, 'The Dynamics of Fieldwork Among the Talensi'; and Lawrence, 'Inventing the "Traditional Working Class"'.

Bibliography

ARCHIVES

Bodleian Library, Oxford
    Frederick Lugard Papers
    Margery Perham Papers
British Library for Political and Economic Science, London School of Economics
    Association of Social Anthropologists Papers
    Audrey Richards Papers
    Bronislaw Malinowski Papers
    Colonial Research Papers
    Raymond Firth Papers
    Unregistered School Archive Files
Edinburgh University Library
    Kenneth Little Papers
Rockefeller Archive Center, Sleepy Hollow, NY
    Rockefeller Foundation Papers
    Social Science Research Council Papers
Sterling Memorial Library, Yale University, New Haven, CT
    Bronislaw Malinowski Papers,
The National Archives, Kew
    Colonial Office Files
University Library, Cambridge
    Meyer Fortes Papers

NEWSPAPERS

The Manchester Guardian
New York Times
Newcastle Morning Herald and Miners' Advocate
The Spectator
The Times
The Times of India

THESES

Dubler, Roslyn, '"The Smallest Institute of All": Sociology, Class and the Politics of Knowledge in Postwar Britain' (unpublished honours thesis, University of Sydney, 2013) <http://hdl.handle.net/2123/10254>

Fisher, Donald, 'The Impact of American Foundations on the Development of British University Education, 1900–1939' (unpublished PhD thesis, University of California, Berkeley, 1977)

Foreman, Grahame, 'Horizons of Modernity: British Anthropology and the End of Empire' (unpublished PhD thesis, University of California, Berkeley, 2013)

Hirschman, Daniel Abramson, 'Inventing the Economy Or: How We Learned to Stop Worrying and Love the GDP' (unpublished PhD thesis, University of Michigan, 2016)

CONFERENCE PAPERS

Scott-Brown, Sophie, 'Women in the (Grass)Field: Phyllis Kaberry and Applied Anthropology in Post-war Africa' (paper delivered at Histories of Anthropology: Transforming Knowledge and Power (1870–1970), Gonville and Caius College, Cambridge, 18 September 2017)

PRIMARY SOURCES

Amery, L. S., *The Leo Amery Diaries*, ed. by John Barnes and David Nicholson (London: Hutchinson, 1980), vol. 2

Anon, 'The Native in Parliament', *The Anti-Slavery Reporter and Aborigines' Friend*, 15.3 (1925), 109–21

Barnes, J. A. 'Class and Committees in a Norwegian Island Parish', *Human Relations*, 7.1 (1954), 39–58

Bloch, Maurice, ed., *Marxist Analyses and Social Anthropology* (London: Malaby Press, 1975)

Bott, Elizabeth, 'Urban Families: Conjugal Roles and Social Networks', *Human Relations*, 8.4 (1955), 345–84

———, *Family and Social Network: Roles, Norms, and External Relationships in Ordinary Urban Families*, 2nd edn (New York: The Free Press, 1971)

British and Australian Trade in the South Pacific (Melbourne: A. J. Mullett, 1918)

Burling, Robbins, 'Maximization Theories and the Study of Economic Anthropology', *American Anthropologist*, 64.4 (1962), 802–21

Chambers' Twentieth Century Dictionary of the English Language (Edinburgh: W. & R. Chambers, 1908) <https://www.gutenberg.org/files/37683/37683-h/37683-h.htm>

Clifton-Roberts, C. 'Witchcraft and Colonial Legislation', *Africa: Journal of the International African Institute*, 8.4 (October 1935), 488–94

Dalton, George, 'Economic Theory and Primitive Society', *American Anthropologist*, 63.1 (1961), 1–25

Darnton, Robert, *The Great Cat Massacre and Other Episodes in French Cultural History* (New York: Basic Books, 2009)

Davis, Natalie Zemon, 'The Reasons of Misrule: Youth Groups and Charivaris in Sixteenth-Century France', *Past & Present*, 50 (1971), 41–75

———, 'The Rites of Violence: Religious Riot in Sixteenth-Century France', *Past & Present*, 59, (1973), 51–91

Deane, Phyllis, 'National Income: Problems of Social Accounting in Central Africa', *The Rhodes-Livingstone Journal*, 5 (1947), 25–43

———, 'Problems of Studying Village Economies', *The Rhodes-Livingstone Journal*, 8 (1949), 42–49

———, *Colonial Social Accounting* (Cambridge: Cambridge University Press, 1953)

———, 'The Industrial Revolution and Economic Growth: The Evidence of Early British National Income Estimates', *Economic Development and Cultural Change*, 5.2 (1957), 159–74

———, 'The Industrial Revolution in British Central Africa', *Civilisations*, 12.3 (1962), 331–55

Edinburgh University Calendar 1951–52 (Edinburgh: James Thin, 1951)

Evans-Pritchard, Edward, *Witchcraft, Oracles and Magic among the Azande* (Oxford: Clarendon Press, 1937)

———, 'Applied Anthropology', *Africa: Journal of the International African Institute*, 16.2 (1946), 92–98

———, '198. Social Anthropology: Past and Present the Marett Lecture, 1950', *Man*, 50 (1950)

———, *Social Anthropology* (London: Cohen & West, 1951)

Firth, Raymond, *Primitive Economics of the New Zealand Maori* (London: G. Routledge, 1929)

———, *We, the Tikopia: A Sociological Study of Kinship in Primitive Polynesia* (London: G. Allen & Unwin, 1936)

———, 'Anthropology Looks at Economics', *Science and Society: A Journal of Human Progress*, 1.2 (1937), 48–55

———, 'An Anthropologist's View of Mass-Observation', *The Sociological Review*, a31.2 (1939), 166–93

———, *Primitive Polynesian Economy* (London: Routledge, 1939)

———, 'Introduction', in Raymond Firth, Judith Djamour, and Philip Garigue, *Two Studies of Kinship in London* (London: Athlone Press, 1956)

———, ed., *Man and Culture – an Evaluation of the Work of Bronislaw Malinowski* (London: Routledge & Kegan Paul, 1957)

———, 'The Place of Malinowski in the History of Economic Anthropology', in *Man and Culture – an Evaluation of the Work of Bronislaw Malinowski*, ed. by Raymond Firth (London: Routledge & Kegan Paul, 1957)

———, 'Methodological Issues in Economic Anthropology', *Journal of the Royal Anthropological Institute*, 7.3 (1972), 467–75

Forde, Daryll, '254. Anthropology, Science and History', *Man*, 50 (1950), 155–56

Freud, Sigmund, *On Sexuality: Three Essays on the Theory of Sexuality and Other Works*, ed. by James Strachey and Angela Richards (Harmondsworth: Penguin Books, 1977)

Ginzburg, Carlo, *The Cheese and the Worms: The Cosmos of a Sixteenth-Century Miller* (Baltimore, MD: Johns Hopkins University Press, 2013)

Gluckman, Max, 'The Peace in the Feud', *Past & Present*, 18 (1955), 1–14

Hailey, William Malcolm, *An African Survey: A Study of Problems Arising in Africa South of the Sahara* (Oxford: Oxford University Press, 1938)

———, *An African Survey, Revised 1956: A Study of Problems Arising in Africa South of the Sahara* (Oxford: Oxford University Press, 1957)

Hobsbawm, E. J. *Primitive Rebels: Studies in the Archaic Forms of Social Movement in the 19th and 20th Centuries* (Manchester: Manchester University Press, 1959)

Huxley, Aldous, *Music at Night and Other Essays Including 'Vulgarity in Literature'* (London: Chatto & Windus, 1970)

Jarvie, I. C. *The Revolution in Anthropology* (London: Routledge & Kegan Paul, 1964)

Joint Committee on Closer Union in East Africa 1930–31 (London: H.M.S.O., 1931), vol. 1

Kroeber, A. L., '33. Social Anthropology: Past and Present', *Man*, 51 (1951), 18

Laslett, Peter, *The World We Have Lost* (London: Methuen, 1965)

Law Reports of Kenya – 1932 (Nairobi, 1933), vol. 14

Le Guin, Ursula K., *The Word for World Is Forest* (London: Gollancz, 1977)

Leach, E. R., '199. Social Anthropology: Past and Present', *Man*, 51 (1951), 114–15

Lewis, W. Arthur, 'Review of Primitive Polynesian Economy; Land, Labour and Diet in Northern Rhodesia', *Economica*, 8.29 (1941), 114–16

———, 'The Colonial Problem', *The Student Movement*, 47 (1945)

———, 'Economic Development with Unlimited Supplies of Labour', *The Manchester School*, 22.2 (1954), 139–91

———, *Theory of Economic Growth* (London: George Allen & Unwin, 1955)

Little, K. L., 'The Study of Racial Mixture in the British Commonwealth', *The Eugenics Review*, 32.4 (1941), 114–20

———, '84. A Note on Colour Prejudice Amongst the English "Middle Class"', *Man*, 43 (1943), 104–7

———, *Negroes in Britain: A Study of Racial Relations in English Society* (London: Kegan Paul, Trench, Trubner, 1947)

Lugard, F. D., *The Dual Mandate in Tropical Africa* (Edinburgh: William Blackwood and Sons, 1922)

Macfarlane, Alan, *The Family Life of Ralph Josselin, A Seventeenth-Century Clergyman* (Cambridge: Cambridge University Press, 1970)
———, *Witchcraft in Tudor and Stuart England: A Regional and Comparative Study* (London: Routledge & Kegan Paul, 1970)
Madden, Frederick, and John Darwin, eds., *The Dependent Empire, 1900–1948, Colonies, Protectorates and Mandates* (London: Greenwood Press, 1994)
Madge, C., and T. Harrisson, eds., *First Year's Work 1937–38 by Mass-Observation* (London: Lindsay Drummond, 1938)
Mair, Lucy, *An African People in the Twentieth Century* (London: George Routledge & Sons, 1934)
Malinowski, Bronislaw, 'Review of Les Formes Élémentaires de La Vie Religieuse: Le Système Totémique en Australie (Bibliothèque de Philosophie Contemporaine) by E. Durkheim', *Folklore*, 24.4 (1913), 525–31
———, 'The Primitive Economics of the Trobriand Islanders', *The Economic Journal*, 31.121 (1921), 1–16
———, *Argonauts of the Western Pacific: An Account of Native Enterprise and Adventure in the Archipelagoes of Melanesian New Guinea* (London: Routledge & Kegan Paul, 1922; repr. 1978)
———, *Crime and Custom in Savage Society* (Totowa, NJ: Littlefield, Adams, 1926; repr. 1967)
———, *Sex and Repression in Savage Society* (London: Routledge and Kegan Paul, 1927; repr. 1960)
———, 'Practical Anthropology', *Africa: Journal of the International African Institute*, 2.1 (1929), 22–38
———, 'Review of Report of the Commission on Closer Union of the Dependencies in Eastern and Central Africa', *Africa*, 2.3 (1929), 317–20
———, *The Sexual Life of Savages in North-Western Melanesia*, 3rd edn (London: Routledge & Kegan Paul, 1929; repr. 1932)
———, 'The Rationalization of Anthropology and Administration', *Africa: Journal of the International African Institute*, 3.4 (1930), 405–30
———, 'Race and Labour', *The Listener*, 16 July 1930, Supplement 8 i-v
———, 'Parenthood – The Basis of Social Structure', in *The New Generation: The Intimate Problems of Modern Parents and Children*, ed. by V. F. Calverton and Samuel Schmalhausen (New York: The Macaulay Company, 1930)
———, 'A Plea for an Effective Colour Bar', *The Spectator*, 27 June 1931, 999–1001
———, *Coral Gardens and Their Magic: A Study of the Methods of Tilling the Soil and of Agricultural Rites in the Trobriand Islands* (London: Allen & Unwin, 1935)
———, 'Introductory Essay on the Anthropology of Changing African Cultures', in *Methods of Study of Culture Contact in Africa*, ed. by Lucy Mair (Oxford: Oxford University Press, 1938)
———, 'Culture Change in Theory and Practice', in *Oxford University Summer School on Colonial Administration: Second Session, 1938* (Oxford: Oxford University Press, 1938)

———, 'A New Instrument for the Interpretation of Law: Especially Primitive', *The Yale Law Journal*, 51.8 (1942), 1237–54
———, 'The Pan-African Problem of Culture Contact,' *American Journal of Sociology* 48, 6 (1943), 649–65
———, *The Dynamics of Culture Change: An Inquiry into Race Relations in Africa*, ed. by M. Kaberry (Oxford: Oxford University Press, 1945)
Matthews, Z. K., 'An African View of Indirect Rule in Africa', *Journal of the Royal African Society*, 36.145 (1937), 433–37.
Mitchison, Naomi, *Comments on Birth Control* (London: Faber & Faber, 1930)
Montagu, Ashley, ed., *Marriage, Past and Present – A Debate Between Robert Briffault and Bronislaw Malinowski* (Boston: Porter Sargent, 1956)
Oldham, J. H., *White and Black in Africa; a Critical Examination of the Rhodes Lectures of General Smuts* (New York: Longmans, Green, 1930)
Orde Browne, G. St. J., 'Witchcraft and British Colonial Law', *Africa*, 8.4 (1935), 481–487
Oxford University Summer School on Colonial Administration: Second Session, 1938 (Oxford: Oxford University Press, 1938)
Pettit, Philip, 'Functional Explanation and Virtual Selection', *The British Journal for the Philosophy of Science*, 47.2 (1996), 291–302
Polanyi, Karl *The Great Transformation: The Political and Economic Origins of Our Time* (Boston: Beacon Press, 1944; repr. 2001)
———, 'The Economy as Instituted Process', in *Trade and Market in the Early Empires: Economies in History and Theory*, ed. by Karl Polanyi, Conrad M. Arensberg, and H. W. Pearson (Glencoe, Ill.: Free Press, 1957)
———, 'Aristotle Discovers the Economy', in *Trade and Market in the Early Empires: Economies in History and Theory*, ed. by Karl Polanyi, Conrad M. Arensberg, and H. W. Pearson (Glencoe, Ill.: Free Press, 1957)
Radcliffe-Brown, A. R., 'Applied Anthropology', in *Oxford University Summer School on Colonial Administration: Second Session, 1938* (Oxford: Oxford University Press, 1938)
———, 'On Social Structure', *The Journal of the Royal Anthropological Institute of Great Britain and Ireland*, 70.1 (1940), 1–12
———, '14. Social Anthropology: Past and Present', *Man*, 52 (1952), 13–14
Read, Margaret *Native Standards of Living and African Culture Change* (Oxford: Oxford University Press, 1938)
Report of the Eighty-Fourth Meeting of the British Association for the Advancement of Science (London: John Murray, 1915)
Richards, A. I., ed., *Economic Development and Tribal Change: A Study of Immigrant Labour in Buganda* (Cambridge: Heffer, 1951)
———, 'Anthropology on the Scrap-Heap?', *Journal of African Administration*, 13.1 (1961), 3–10
Robbins, Lionel, *An Essay on the Nature and Significance of Economic Science* (London: Macmillan, 1932)
Russell, Bertrand, *Marriage and Morals* (London: George Allen & Unwin, 1929)
Sahlins, Marshall, *Stone Age Economics* (Chicago: Aldine-Atherton, 1972)
Schapera, I., 'Should Anthropologists Be Historians?', *The Journal of the Royal Anthropological Institute of Great Britain and Ireland*, 92.2 (1962), 143–56

Sexton, James, ed., *Selected Letters of Aldous Huxley* (Chicago: Ivan R. Dee, 2007)
Smith, G. Elliot, *The Evolution of Man* (Oxford: Oxford University Press, 1924)
Smith, Grover, ed., *Letters of Aldous Huxley* (London: Chatto & Windus, 1969)
Smuts, Jan Christiaan, *Africa and Some World Problems, Including the Rhodes Memorial Lectures Delivered in Michaelmas Term, 1929* (Oxford: Oxford University Press, 1930)
Tawney, R. H., 'The Study of Economic History', *Economica*, 39 (1933), 1–21
Thomas, Keith, 'Should Historians Be Anthropologists?', *The Oxford Magazine*, n.s., 1.22 (June 1961), 387–88
——, 'History and Anthropology', *Past & Present*, 24 (April 1963), 3–24
——, 'The Tools and the Job', *Times Literary Supplement*, no. 3345 (7 April 1966), 275–76
——, *Religion and the Decline of Magic: Studies in Popular Beliefs in Sixteenth and Seventeenth Century England* (Harmondsworth: Penguin, 1971)
Thompson, E. P., 'The Peculiarities of the English', *Socialist Register*, 2.2 (1965), 311–62
——, 'History from Below', *Times Literary Supplement*, no. 3345 (7 April 1966), 279–80
——, 'Time, Work-Discipline, and Industrial Capitalism', *Past & Present*, 38 (1967), 56–97
——, 'The Moral Economy of the English Crowd in the Eighteenth Century', *Past & Present*, no. 50 (February 1971), 76–136
——, 'Folklore, Anthropology, and Social History', *The Indian Historical Review*, 3.2 (1977), 247–66
Thurnwald, Richard, *Economics in Primitive Communities* (Oxford: Oxford University Press, 1932)
Turner, V. W., *Schism and Continuity in an African Society: A Study of Ndembu Village Life*, 2nd edn (Manchester: Manchester University Press, 1957; repr. 1968)
Walsham, Alexandra, 'Rough Music and Charivari: Letters Between Natalie Zemon Davis and Edward Thompson, 1970–1972', *Past & Present*, 235.1 (2017), 243–62
Wayne, Helena, ed., *The Story of a Marriage: The Letters of Bronislaw Malinowski and Elsie Masson*, 2 vols. (London: Routledge, 1995)
Williams, Raymond, *Culture and Society* (London: Vintage Digital, 1958; repr. 2015)
——, 'Culture Is Ordinary' (1958), in *Raymond Williams on Culture & Society : Essential Writings*, ed. by Jim McGuigan (Thousand Oaks, CA: Sage Publications, 2014)
Wilson, Bryan R., *Rationality* (Oxford: Basil Blackwell, 1970)
Wilson, Godfrey, 'An Essay on the Economics of Detribalization in Northern Rhodesia', *The Rhodes-Livingstone Papers*, 5 (1941)
Wilson, Godfrey, and Monica Wilson, *The Analysis of Social Change: Based on Observations in Central Africa* (Cambridge: Cambridge University Press, 1945)
Young, Michael Dunlop, and Peter Willmott. *Family and Kinship in East London* (Glencoe, IL: The Free Press, 1957)

Young, Michael, and Peter Willmott, *Family and Kinship in East London*, rev edn (Harmondsworth: Penguin, 1962)

SECONDARY SOURCES

Alacevich, Michele, 'The World Bank and the Politics of Productivity: The Debate on Economic Growth, Poverty, and Living Standards in the 1950s', *Journal of Global History*, 6.1 (2011), 53–74

Adelman, Jeremy, ed., *Empire and the Social Sciences: Global Histories of Knowledge* (London: Bloomsbury Publishing, 2019)

Agnew, Jean-Christophe, 'History and Anthropology: Scenes from a Marriage', *The Yale Journal of Criticism*, 3.2 (1990), 29–50

Ahmad, Salma, 'American Foundations and the Development of the Social Sciences between the Wars: Comment on the Debate between Martin Bulmer and Donald Fisher', *Sociology*, 25.3 (1991), 511–20.

Alberti Samuel J. M. M., 'Museum Nature,' in *Worlds of Natural History*, ed. by Helen Anne Curry et al. (Cambridge: Cambridge University Press, 2018)

Anderson, Perry, 'Components of the National Culture', *New Left Review*, series I, 50 (1968), 3–57

Arndt, H. W., *Economic Development: The History of an Idea* (Chicago: University of Chicago Press, 1987)

Asad, Talal, 'Introduction,' in *Anthropology & the Colonial Encounter*, ed. Talal Asad (Amherst, NY: Humanity Books, 1973; repr. 1998)

——, 'Anthropology and the Colonial Encounter,' reprinted in *The Politics of Anthropology: From Colonialism and Sexism toward a View from Below*, ed. by Gerrit Huizer and Bruce Mannheim (The Hague: Mouton, 1979)

——, 'Ethnographic Representation, Statistics, and Modern Power',' in *From the Margins: Historical Anthropology and Its Futures*, ed. by Brian Keith Axel (Durham, NC: Duke University Press, 2002)

Ashton, S. R., and S. E. Stockwell, eds., *Imperial Policy and Colonial Practice, 1925–1945: Part II, Economic Policy, Social Policies and Colonial Research* (London: HMSO, 1996)

Bailkin, Jordanna, *The Afterlife of Empire* (Berkeley, CA: University of California Press, 2012)

Bank, Andrew, *Pioneers of the Field: South Africa's Women Anthropologists* (Cambridge: Cambridge University Press, 2016)

Banks, J. A., 'The British Sociological Association—The First Fifteen Years', *Sociology*, 1.1 (1967), 1–9

Bannister, Robert C., 'Sociology', in *The Cambridge History of Science: The Modern Social Sciences*, vol. 7, ed. by Dorothy Ross and Theodore M. Porter (Cambridge: Cambridge University Press, 2003)

Bar-Haim, Shaul, *The Maternalists: Psychoanalysis, Motherhood, and the British Welfare State*, (Philadelphia: University of Pennsylvania Press, 2021)

Barkan, Elazar, *The Retreat of Scientific Racism: Changing Concepts of Race in Britain and the United States between the World Wars* (Cambridge: Cambridge University Press, 1992)

Barkan, Elazar, and Ronald Bush, eds., *Prehistories of the Future: The Primitivist Project and the Culture of Modernism* (Stanford, CA: Stanford University Press, 1995)

Barth, Fredrik, et al., *One Discipline, Four Ways: British, German, French, and American Anthropology* (Chicago: University of Chicago Press, 2005)

Bashkow, Ira, '"The Stakes for Which We Play Are Too High to Allow of Experiments": Colonial Administrators of Papua on Their Anthropological Training by Radcliffe-Brown', *History of Anthropology Newsletter* 22.2 (1995), 3–14

Basu, Paul, "N. W. Thomas and Colonial Anthropology in British West Africa: Reappraising a Cautionary Tale," *Journal of the Royal Anthropological Institute*, 22.1 (2016), 84–107

Bayly, C. A., *The Birth of the Modern World, 1780–1914: Global Connections and Comparisons*, (Malden, MA: Blackwell Pub, 2004)

Bennett, Brett M., and Joseph Morgan Hodge, eds., *Science and Empire: Knowledge and Networks of Science across the British Empire, 1800–1970* (Basingstoke: Palgrave Macmillan, 2011)

Berman, Bruce, and John Lonsdale, 'Custom, Modernity, and the Search for *Kihooto*: Kenyatta, Malinowski, and the Making of *Facing Mount Kenya*', in *Ordering Africa*, ed. by Helen Tilley and Robert Gordon (Manchester: Manchester University Press, 2010)

Bland, Lucy, and Laura Doan, 'Introduction,' in *Sexology Uncensored: The Documents of Sexual Science*, ed. by Lucy Bland and Laura L. Doan (Cambridge: Polity Press, 1998)

Boianovsky, Mauro, and Kevin D. Hoover, 'In the Kingdom of Solovia: The Rise of Growth Economics at MIT, 1956–70', *History of Political Economy*, 46.suppl 1 (2014), 198–228

Bonneuil, Christophe, 'Development as Experiment: Science and State Building in Late Colonial and Postcolonial Africa, 1930–1970', *Osiris*, 15.1 (2000), 258–81

Bourne, Jenny, and A. Sivanandan, 'Cheerleaders and Ombudsmen', *Race & Class*, 21.4 (1980), 331–52

Brett, E. A. *Colonialism and Underdevelopment in East Africa: The Politics of Economic Change, 1919–1939* (London: Heinemann, 1973)

Briggs, Asa, *Victorian Cities* (London: Penguin, 1968)

Brooke, Stephen, *Sexual Politics: Sexuality, Family Planning, and the British Left from the 1880s to the Present Day* (Oxford: Oxford University Press, 2011)

Brown, Richard, 'Anthropology and Colonial Rule: The Case of Godfrey Wilson and the Rhodes-Livingstone Institute, Northern Rhodesia', in *Anthropology & The Colonial Encounter*, ed. Talal Asad (Amherst, NY: Humanity Books, 1973; repr. 1998)

Buhle, Mari Jo, *Feminism and Its Discontents: A Century of Struggle with Psychoanalysis* (Cambridge, MA: Harvard University Press, 2009)

Bulmer, Martin, "Introduction,' in *Essays on the History of British Sociological Research*, ed. Martin Bulmer (Cambridge: Cambridge University Press, 1985)

Bunzl, Matti, 'Anthropology Beyond Crisis', *Anthropology and Humanism*, 30.2 (2005), 187–95
Burke, Peter, *History and Social Theory*, 2nd edn (Cambridge: Polity, 2005)
Burke, Peter, Brian Harrison, and Paul Slack, 'Keith Thomas,' in *Civil Histories: Essays Presented to Sir Keith Thomas*, ed. by Peter Burke, Brian Harrison, and Paul Slack (Oxford: Oxford University Press, 2000)
Burrow, J. W., *Evolution and Society: A Study in Victorian Social Theory* (Cambridge: Cambridge University Press, 1966),
Burton, Antoinette M., *The Trouble with Empire: Challenges to Modern British Imperialism* (Oxford: Oxford University Press, 2015)
Burton, John W., 'The Ghost of Malinowski in the Southern Sudan: Evans-Pritchard and Ethnographic Fieldwork', *Proceedings of the American Philosophical Society*, 127.4 (1983), 278–89
Bush, Barbara, *Imperialism, Race and Resistance: Africa and Britain, 1919–1945* (London: Routledge, 1999)
———, 'Colonial Research and the Social Sciences at the End of Empire: The West Indian Social Survey, 1944–57', *The Journal of Imperial and Commonwealth History*, 41.3 (2013), 451–74
Butler, Lise, 'Michael Young, the Institute of Community Studies, and the Politics of Kinship', *Twentieth Century British History*, 26.2 (2015), 203–24
———, *Michael Young, Social Science and the British Left, 1945–70* (Oxford: Oxford University Press, 2020)
Callon, Michel, 'Some Elements of a Sociology of Translation: Domestication of the Scallops and the Fishermen of St Brieuc Bay', *The Sociological Review*, 32.S1 (1984), 196–233
Campsie, Alexandre, 'Mass-Observation, Left Intellectuals and the Politics of Everyday Life', *The English Historical Review*, 131.548 (2016), 92–121
Cannadine, David, 'The Present and the Past in the English Industrial Revolution 1880–1980', *Past & Present*, 103 (1984), 131–72
Cardiff, David, 'The Serious and the Popular: Aspects of the Evolution of Style in the Radio Talk 1928–1939', in *Radio*, ed. by Andrew Crisell (London: Routledge, 2009)
Carter, Bob, and Satnam Virdee, 'Racism and the Sociological Imagination', *The British Journal of Sociology*, 59.4 (2008), 661–79
Cell, John W., 'Introduction,' in *By Kenya Possessed: The Correspondence of Norman Leys and J.H. Oldham, 1918–1926* (Chicago University of Chicago Press, 1976), 60–61.
———, 'Who Ran the British Empire', in *More Adventures with Britannia: Personalities, Politics and Culture in Britain*, ed. by Wm. Roger Louis (London: I. B. Tauris, 1988)
———, 'Lord Hailey and the Making of the African Survey', *African Affairs*, 88.353 (1989), 481–505
———, *Hailey: A Study in British Imperialism, 1872–1969* (Cambridge: Cambridge University Press, 1992)
———, 'Colonial Rule', in *The Oxford History of the British Empire, Volume IV, The Twentieth Century*, ed. by Judith Brown and Wm. Roger Louis (Oxford: Oxford University Press, 1999)

Chanock, Martin, *Law, Custom and Social Order: The Colonial Experience in Malawi and Zambia* (Cambridge: Cambridge University Press, 1985)

Chassonnery-Zaïgouche, Cléo, 'Is Equal Pay Worth It?' (OSF Preprints, 2019) <https://doi.org/10.31219/osf.io/8cq9j>

Chassonnery-Zaïgouche, Cleo, Beatrice Cherrier, and John D. Singleton, '"Economics Is Not a Man's Field": CSWEP and the First Gender Reckoning in Economics (1971–1991)' (28 December 2019). Available at SSRN <http://dx.doi.org/10.2139/ssrn.3510857>

Chettiar, Teri, '"More than a Contract": The Emergence of a State-Supported Marriage Welfare Service and the Politics of Emotional Life in Post-1945 Britain', *Journal of British Studies*, 55.3 (2016), 566–91

Chignell, Hugh, *Public Issue Radio: Talks, News and Current Affairs in the Twentieth Century* (Basingstoke: Palgrave Macmillan, 2011)

Clapson, Mark, 'The American Contribution to the Urban Sociology of Race Relations in Britain from the 1940s to the Early 1970s', *Urban History*, 33.2 (2006), 253–73

Clements, Keith, *Faith on the Frontier: A Life of J. H. Oldham* (London: T&T Clark, 1999)

Clifford, James, *The Predicament of Culture* (Cambridge, MA: Harvard University Press, 1988)

———, 'Feeling Historical', *Cultural Anthropology*, 27.3 (2012), 417–26

Cocks, H. G., and Matt Houlbrook, eds., *Palgrave Advances in the Modern History of Sexuality* (Basingstoke: Palgrave Macmillan, 2006)

Cocks, Paul, 'Max Gluckman and the Critique of Segregation in South African Anthropology, 1921–1940', *Journal of Southern African Studies*, 27.4 (2001), 739–56

Cohen, Anthony P., 'The Social Anthropology of Britain, and the Question of "Otherness"', *Anthropology Today*, 2.6 (1986), 3.

Cohn, Bernard S., *Colonialism and Its Forms of Knowledge: The British in India* (Princeton, NJ: Princeton University Press, 1996)

Collini, Stefan, '"Discipline History" and "Intellectual History": Reflections on the Historiography of the Social Sciences in Britain and France', *Revue de Synthèse*, 109.3–4 (1988), 387–99

———, *English Pasts: Essays in History and Culture* (Oxford: Oxford University Press, 1999)

Collini, Stefan, John A. Burrow, and Donald Winch, *That Noble Science of Politics: A Study in Nineteenth-Century Intellectual History* (Cambridge: Cambridge University Press, 1983)

Collins, Marcus, *Modern Love: Personal Relationships in Twentieth-Century Britain* (Newark, DE: University of Delaware Press, 2006)

Collins, Randall, 'Toward a Theory of Intellectual Change: The Social Causes of Philosophies', *Science, Technology & Human Values*, 14.2 (1989), 107–40

———, 'On the Acrimoniousness of Intellectual Disputes', *Common Knowledge*, 8.1 (2002), 47–70

Connelly, Matthew James, *Fatal Misconception: The Struggle to Control World Population* (Cambridge, MA: Harvard University Press, 2008)

Cook, Scott, 'Malinowski in Oaxaca: Implications of an Unfinished Project in Economic Anthropology, Part I', *Critique of Anthropology*, 37.2 (2017), 132–59

Cook, Scott, and Michael W. Young, 'Malinowski, Herskovits, and the Controversy over Economics in Anthropology', *History of Political Economy*, 48.4 (2016), 657–79

Cook, Simon, 'The Tragedy of Cambridge Anthropology: Edwardian Historical Thought and the Contact of Peoples', *History of European Ideas*, 42.4 (2016), 541–53

Cooper, Frederick, 'Development, Modernization, and the Social Sciences in the Era of Decolonization: The Examples of British and French Africa', *Revue d'Histoire des Sciences Humaines*, 10.1 (2004), 9–3

———, 'Writing the History of Development', *Journal of Modern European History*, 8.1 (2010), 5–23

Cooper, Frederick, and Randall M. Packard, eds., *International Development and the Social Sciences: Essays on the History and Politics of Knowledge* (Berkeley: University of California Press, 1997)

Coward, Rosalind, 'On the Universality of the Oedipus Complex: Debates on Sexual Divisions in Psychoanalysis and Anthropology', *Critique of Anthropology*, 4.15 (1980), 5–28

———, *Patriarchal Precedents: Sexuality and Social Relations* (London: Routledge & Kegan Paul, 1983)

Dale, Gareth, 'Lineages of Embeddedness: On the Antecedents and Successors of a Polanyian Concept', *American Journal of Economics and Sociology*, 70.2 (2011), 306–39.

Darnell, Regna, 'North American Traditions in Anthropology: The Historiographic Baseline', in *A New History of Anthropology*, ed. by Henrika Kuklick (Oxford: Blackwell, 2008)

Darwin, John, *The Empire Project: The Rise and Fall of the British World-System, 1830–1970* (Cambridge: Cambridge University Press, 2009)

Daston, Lorraine, 'Objectivity and the Escape from Perspective', *Social Studies of Science*, 22.4 (1992), 597–618

Daston, Lorraine, and H. Otto Sibum, 'Introduction: Scientific Personae and Their Histories', *Science in Context*, 16.1–2 (2003), 1–8

Davis, John, 'How All Souls Got Its Anthropologist', in *A History of Oxford Anthropology*, ed. by Peter Rivière (New York: Berghahn Books, 2007)

Davis, Nile A., 'Empire of Abstraction: British Social Anthropology in the "Dependencies"' <https://jhiblog.org/2020/06/29/empire-of-abstraction-british-social-anthropology-in-the-dependencies>

de L'Estoile, Benoît, 'The "Natural Preserve of Anthropologists": Social Anthropology, Scientific Planning and Development', *Social Science Information*, 36.2 (1997), 343–76

Delap, Lucy, Ben Griffin, and Abigail Wills, eds., *The Politics of Domestic Authority in Britain since 1800* (Basingstoke: Palgrave Macmillan, 2009)

Delap, Lucy, and Valerie Sanders, 'Introduction'. in *Victorian and Edwardian Anti-Feminism*, ed. by Lucy Delap and Valerie Sanders (London: Routledge, 2010)

Deshpande, Satish, 'Disciplinary Predicaments: Sociology and Anthropology in Postcolonial India', *Inter-Asia Cultural Studies*, 2.2 (2001), 247–60

Dirks, Nicholas B., *Castes of Mind: Colonialism and the Making of Modern India* (Princeton, NJ: Princeton University Press, 2001)

Drayton, Richard, 'Where Does the World Historian Write From? Objectivity, Moral Conscience and the Past and Present of Imperialism', *Journal of Contemporary History*, 46.3 (2011), 671–85

Drummond, Ian M., *Imperial Economic Policy 1917–1939: Studies in Expansion and Protection* (Toronto: University of Toronto Press, 1974)

Dubow, Saul, 'The Commonwealth and South Africa: From Smuts to Mandela', *The Journal of Imperial and Commonwealth History*, 45.2 (2017), 284–314

Ellen, Roy F., et al., eds., *Malinowski between Two Worlds: The Polish Roots of an Anthropological Tradition* (Cambridge: Cambridge University Press, 1988)

Emmanuel, Arghiri, 'White-Settler Colonialism and the Myth of Investment Imperialism', *New Left Review*, 73 (1972), 35–57

Esty, Jed, *A Shrinking Island: Modernism and National Culture in England* (Princeton, NJ: Princeton University Press, 2004)

Evens, T. M. S., and Don Handelman, eds., *The Manchester School: Practice and Ethnographic Praxis in Anthropology* (New York: Berghahn Books, 2006)

Ewer, Peter, 'A Gentlemen's Club in the Clouds: Reassessing the Empire Air Mail Scheme, 1933–1939', *The Journal of Transport History*, 28.1 (2007), 75–92

Falk Moore, Sally, 'Treating Law as Knowledge: Telling Colonial Officers What to Say to Africans about Running "Their Own" Native Courts', *Law & Society Review*, 26.1 (1992), 11–46

Ferguson, James, 'Anthropology and Its Evil Twin – "Development" in the Constitution of the Discipline', in *International Development and the Social Sciences: Essays on the History and Politics of Knowledge*, ed. by Frederick Cooper and Randall M. Packard (Berkeley: University of California Press, 1997)

———, 'Formalities of Poverty: Thinking about Social Assistance in Neoliberal South Africa,' *African Studies Review*, 50.2 (2007): 71–86

Figueroa, Mark, 'W. Arthur Lewis Versus the Lewis Model: Agricultural or Industrial Development?', *The Manchester School*, 72.6 (2004), 736–50

Firchow, Peter Edgerly, *The End of Utopia: A Study of Aldous Huxley's Brave New World* (London: Associated University Presses, 1984)

Fisher, Donald, 'American Philanthropy and the Social Sciences in Britain, 1919–1939; the Reproduction of a Conservative Ideology', *The Sociological Review*, 28.2 (1980), 277–315

———, 'The Role of Philanthropic Foundations in the Reproduction and Production of Hegemony: Rockefeller Foundations and the Social Sciences', *Sociology*, 17.2 (1983), 206–33

Fisher, Kate, *Birth Control, Sex and Marriage in Britain, 1918–1960* (Oxford: Oxford University Press, 2006)

Fitzpatrick, Matthew P., 'Indigenous Australians and German Anthropology in the Era of "Decolonization"', *The Historical Journal*, 63.3 (2019), 686–709

Foks, Freddy, 'Bronislaw Malinowski, "Indirect Rule," and the Colonial Politics of Functionalist Anthropology, ca. 1925–1940', *Comparative Studies in Society and History*, 60.1 (2018), 35–57

Forrester, John, and Laura Cameron, *Freud in Cambridge* (Cambridge: Cambridge University Press, 2017)

Forster, Peter, 'Empiricism and Imperialism: A Review of the New Left Critique of Social Anthropology', in *Anthropology & the Colonial Encounter*, ed. Talal Asad (Amherst, NY: Humanity Books, 1973; repr. 1998)

Foucault, Michel, *The History of Sexuality, Volume 1, The Will to Knowledge*, trans. by Robert Hurley (London: Penguin, 1998)

Fourcade, Marion, *Economists and Societies: Discipline and Profession in the United States, Britain, and France, 1890s to 1990s* (Princeton, NJ: Princeton University Press, 2009)

Fourcade, Marion, Etienne Ollion, and Yann Algan, 'The Superiority of Economists', *Journal of Economic Perspectives*, 29.1 (2015), 89–114

Fuller, C. J., 'History, Anthropology, Colonialism, and the Study of India', *History and Theory*, 55.3 (2016), 452–64

———, 'Ethnographic Inquiry in Colonial India: Herbert Risley, William Crooke, and the Study of Tribes and Castes', *Journal of the Royal Anthropological Institute*, 23.3 (2017), 603–21

Fulton, Joe B., 'The "Enviable Detachment" of the Anthropologist: Barbara Pym's Anthropological Aesthetic', *Papers on Language & Literature*, 39.1 (2003), 91–108

Geertz, Hildred, 'An Anthropology of Religion and Magic, I', *The Journal of Interdisciplinary History*, 6.1 (1975), 71–89

Gell, Alfred, 'Introduction, Notes on Seminar Culture and Some Other Influences,' in *The Art of Anthropology: Essays and Diagrams*, by Alfred Gell and Eric Hirsch (London: Athlone Press, 1999)

Getachew, Adom, *Worldmaking After Empire: The Rise and Fall of Self-Determination* (Princeton, NJ: Princeton University Press, 2019)

Gibson, Jason, and Helen Gardner, 'Conversations on the Frontier: Finding the Dialogic in Nineteenth-Century Anthropological Archives', *History Workshop Journal*, 88 (2019), 47–65

Gilman, Nils, *Mandarins of the Future: Modernization Theory in Cold War America* (Baltimore, MD: Johns Hopkins University Press, 2003)

Ginzburg, Carlo, *No Island Is an Island: Four Glances at English Literature in a World Perspective* (New York: Columbia University Press, 2000)

Gladstone, Jo, 'Significant Sister: Autonomy and Obligation in Audrey Richards' Early Fieldwork', *American Ethnologist*, 13.2 (1986), 338–62

Goldstein, Doris S., 'The Organizational Development of the British Historical Profession, 1884–1921', *Historical Research*, 55.132 (1982), 180–93

Goodman, David, 'A Transnational History of Radio Listening Groups I: The United Kingdom and United States', *Historical Journal of Film, Radio and Television*, 36.3 (2016), 436–65

Goody, Jack, *The Expansive Moment: The Rise of Social Anthropology in Britain and Africa, 1918–1970* (Cambridge: Cambridge University Press, 1995)

Gordon, Robert J., *The Enigma of Max Gluckman, The Ethnographic Life of a 'Luckyman' in Africa* (Lincoln: University of Nebraska Press, 2018)

Gorman, Daniel, 'Organic Union or Aggressive Altruism: Imperial Internationalism in East Africa in the 1920s', *The Journal of Imperial and Commonwealth History*, 42.2 (2014), 258–85

Goswami, Manu, *Producing India: From Colonial Economy to National Space* (Chicago: University of Chicago Press, 2004)

Gray, Geoffrey, *A Cautious Silence: The Politics of Australian Anthropology* (Canberra: Aboriginal Studies Press, 2007)

Gregory, Robert G., *Sidney Webb and East Africa: Labour's Experiment with the Doctrine of Native Paramountcy* (Berkeley: University of California Press, 1962)

Grillo, R. D., 'Applied Anthropology in the 1980s: Retrospect and Prospect', in *Social Anthropology and Development Policy*, ed. by R. D. Grillo and Alan Rew (London: Tavistock, 1985)

Hall, Catherine, and Sonya O. Rose, (eds., *At Home with the Empire: Metropolitan Culture and the Imperial World* (Cambridge: Cambridge University Press, 2006

Halsey, A. H. *A History of Sociology in Britain: Science, Literature, and Society* (Oxford: Oxford University Press, 2004)

Halsey, A. H., and M. A. Trow, *The British Academics* (London: Faber & Faber, 1971)

Handler, Richard, *Critics Against Culture: Anthropological Observers of Mass Society* (Madison: University of Wisconsin Press, 2005)

Hann, C. M., and Keith Hart, *Economic Anthropology: History, Ethnography, Critique* (Cambridge: Polity, 2011)

Herzog, Dagmar, *Sexuality in Europe: A Twentieth-Century History* (Cambridge: Cambridge University Press, 2012)

Hetherington, Penelope, *British Paternalism in Africa, 1920–1970* (London: Frank Cass, 1978)

Hevly, Bruce, 'The Heroic Science of Glacier Motion', *Osiris*, 11 (1996), 66–86

Hillegas, Mark R., *The Future as Nightmare: H.G. Wells and the Anti-Utopians* (Oxford: Oxford University Press, 1967)

Hilliard, Christopher, *English as a Vocation: The Scrutiny Movement* (Oxford: Oxford University Press, 2012)

Hinton, James, *The Mass Observers: A History, 1937–1949* (Oxford: Oxford University Press, 2013)

Hodge, Joseph Morgan, *Triumph of the Expert: Agrarian Doctrines of Development and the Legacies of British Colonialism* (Athens: Ohio University Press, 2007)

Hopkins, A. G., and P. J. Cain, *British Imperialism: 1688–2015*, 3rd edn (London: Routledge, Taylor & Francis Group, 2016)

Humphrey, Caroline, 'Marxism and Neo-Marxism', in *Schools and Styles of Anthropological Theory*, ed. by Matei Candea (Abingdon: Routledge, 2018)

Humphreys, S. C., 'History, Economics, and Anthropology: The Work of Karl Polanyi', *History and Theory*, 8 (1969), 165–212

Humphries, Jane, 'Phyllis Deane', in *Oxford Dictionary of National Biography* <https://doi.org/10.1093/ref:odnb/105668>

Hyam, Ronald, *The Failure of South African Expansion, 1908–1948* (London: Macmillan, 1972)

———, 'Bureaucracy and "Trusteeship" in the Colonial Empire', in *The Oxford History of the British Empire, Volume 4, The Twentieth Century*, ed. by Judith M. Brown and Wm. Roger Louis (Oxford: Oxford University Press, 1999)

Hylland Eriksen, Thomas, and Finn Sivert Nielsen, *A History of Anthropology*, 2nd edn (London: Pluto Press, 2013)

Ibahwoh, Bonny, *Imperial Justice: Africans in Empire's Court* (Oxford: Oxford University Press, 2013)

Immerwahr, Daniel, *Thinking Small: The United States and the Lure of Community Development* (Cambridge, MA: Harvard University Press, 2015)

Ingham, Barbara, and Paul Mosley, '"Marvellous Intellectual Feasts": Arthur Lewis at the London School of Economics, 1933–48', *History of Political Economy*, 45.2 (2013), 187–221

Isaac, Joel, 'Tangled Loops: Theory, History, and The Human Sciences in Modern America', *Modern Intellectual History*, 6.2 (2009), 397–424

———, 'Tool Shock: Technique and Epistemology in the Postwar Social Sciences', *History of Political Economy*, 42.suppl 1(2010), 133–64.

———, *Working Knowledge: Making the Human Sciences from Parsons to Kuhn* (Cambridge, MA: Harvard University Press, 2012)

———, 'The Intensification of Social Forms: Economy and Culture in the Thought of Clifford Geertz', *Critical Historical Studies*, 5.2 (2018), 237–66

James, Wendy, 'The Anthropologist as Reluctant Imperialist', in *Anthropology & the Colonial Encounter*, ed. Talal Asad (Amherst, NY: Humanity Books, 1973; repr. 1998)

Jardine, Boris, 'State of the Field: Paper Tools', *Studies in History and Philosophy of Science Part A*, 64 (2017), 53–63

———, 'Mass-Observation, Surrealist Sociology, and the Bathos of Paperwork', *History of the Human Sciences*, 31.5 (2018), 52–79

Johnson, Jessica, 'Feminist Anthropology and the Question of Gender', in *Schools and Styles of Anthropological Theory*, ed. Matei Candea (Abingdon: Routledge, 2018)

Jones, Ross L., and Warwick Anderson, 'Wandering Anatomists and Itinerant Anthropologists: The Antipodean Sciences of Race in Britain between the Wars', *The British Journal for the History of Science*, 48.01 (2015), 1–16

Karpf, Anne, 'Constructing and Addressing the 'Ordinary Devoted Mother"', *History Workshop Journal*, 78.1 (2014), 82–106

Kempny, Marian, 'History of the Manchester "School" and the Extended-Case Method', *Social Analysis*, 49.3 (2005), 144–65

———, 'History of the Manchester "School" and the Extended-Case Method', in *The Manchester School: Practice and Ethnographic Praxis in Anthropology*, ed, by T. M. S. Evens and Don Handelman (New York: Berghahn Books, 2006)

Kertzer, David I., 'Social Anthropology and Social Science History', *Social Science History*, 33.1 (2009), 1–16

King, Charles, *The Reinvention of Humanity: A Story of Race, Sex, Gender and the Discovery of Culture* (London: Penguin, 2019)
King, Kenneth, *Pan-Africanism and Education: A Study of Race Philanthropy and Education in the Southern States of America and East Africa* (Oxford: Oxford University Press, 1971)
Klein, Kerwin Lee, *From History to Theory* (Berkeley: University of California Press, 2011)
Klein, Ursula, 'Paper Tools in Experimental Cultures', *Studies in the History and Philosophy of Science Part A*, 32.2 (2001), 265–302
Kohler, Robert E., 'Place and Practice in Field Biology', *History of Science*, 40.2 (2002), 189–210
——, *Inside Science: Stories from the Field in Human and Animal Science* (Chicago: University of Chicago Press, 2019)
Krugman, Paul R., *Development, Geography, and Economic Theory* (Cambridge, MA: MIT Press, 1995)
Kuklick, Henrika, *The Savage Within: The Social History of British Anthropology, 1885–1945* (Cambridge: Cambridge University Press, 1991)
——, 'Islands in the Pacific: Darwinian Biogeography and British Anthropology', *American Ethnologist*, 23.3 (1996), 611–38
——, 'Personal Equations: Reflections on the History of Fieldwork, with Special Reference to Sociocultural Anthropology', *Isis*, 102.1 (2011), 1–33
——, 'After Ishmael: The Fieldwork Tradition and Its Future', in *Anthropological Locations, Boundaries and Grounds of a Field Science*, ed. by Akhil Gupta and James Ferguson (Berkeley: University of California Press, 1997)
——, 'The British Tradition', in *A New History of Anthropology*, ed. by Henrika Kuklick (Oxford: Blackwell, 2008)
Kuper, Adam, *The Reinvention of Primitive Society: Transformations of a Myth*, 2nd edn (London: Routledge, 2005)
——, 'Alternative Histories of British Social Anthropology', *Social Anthropology*, 13.1 (2005), 47–64
——, 'Anthropology and Anthropologists Forty Years On', *Anthropology of This Century*, 11 (2014) <http://aotcpress.com/articles/anthropology-anthropologists-forty-years/>
——, *Anthropology and Anthropologists: The British School in the Twentieth Century*, 4th edn (London: Routledge, 2015)
——, 'No Place for a Woman', *Times Literary Supplement*, 9 June 2017 <https://www.the-tls.co.uk/articles/no-place-for-a-woman/> [accessed 28 May 2021]
——, 'Deconstructing Anthropology: First Annual Stephen F. Gudeman Lecture', *HAU: Journal of Ethnographic Theory*, 9.1 (2019), 10–22
Kushner, Tony, 'H. J. Fleure: A Paradigm for Inter-War Race Thinking in Britain', *Patterns of Prejudice*, 42.2 (2008), 151–66
Lamont, Mark, 'Malinowski and the "Native Question"', in *Anthropologists and Their Traditions across National Borders*, ed. by Regna Darnell and Frederic W. Gleach (Lincoln: University of Nebraska Press, 2014)
Langham, Ian, *The Building of British Social Anthropology: W.H.R. Rivers and His Cambridge Disciples in the Development of Kinship Studies, 1898–1931* (Dordrecht, Holland: D. Reidel, 1981)

Langhamer, Claire, *The English in Love: The Intimate Story of an Emotional Revolution* (Oxford: Oxford University Press, 2013)
Larsen, Timothy, *The Slain God: Anthropologists and the Christian Faith* (Oxford: Oxford University Press, 2014)
Larson, Frances, *Undreamed Shores: The Hidden Heroines of British Anthropology* (London: Granta, 2021)
Lawrence, Jon, 'Inventing the "Traditional Working Class": A Re-Analysis of Interview Notes from Young and Willmott's Family and Kinship in East London', *The Historical Journal*, 59.2 (2016), 567–93
———, *Me, Me, Me? Individualism and the Search for Community in Post-War England* (Oxford: Oxford University Press, 2019)
Lepenies, Wolf, *Between Literature and Science: The Rise of Sociology* (Cambridge: Cambridge University Press, 1988)
Lewis, Herbert S., *In Defense of Anthropology: An Investigation of the Critique of Anthropology* (London: Transaction Publishers, 2014)
Liebersohn, Harry, *The Return of the Gift: European History of a Global Idea* (Cambridge: Cambridge University Press, 2011)
Linstrum, Erik, *Ruling Minds: Psychology in the British Empire* (Cambridge, MA: Harvard University Press, 2016)
Louis, Wm. Roger, *In the Name of God, Go! Leo Amery and the British Empire in the Age of Churchill* (New York: W. W. Norton, 1992)
Luongo, Katherine, *Witchcraft and Colonial Rule in Kenya, 1900–1955* (Cambridge: Cambridge University Press, 2011)
Lyons, Andrew P., and Harriet D. Lyons, *Irregular Connections: A History of Anthropology and Sexuality* (Lincoln: University of Nebraska Press, 2004)
MacClancy, Jeremy, 'Anthropology: "The Latest Form of Evening Entertainment"', in *A Concise Companion to Modernism*, ed. by David Bradshaw (Oxford: Blackwell, 2003)
———, *Anthropology in the Public Arena: Historical and Contemporary Contexts* (Chichester: Wiley-Blackwell, 2013)
MacCormack, Carol, and Marilyn Strathern, eds., *Nature, Culture and Gender* (Cambridge: Cambridge University Press, 1980)
Macdonald, Sharon, Jeanette Edwards, and Mike Savage, 'Introduction', *The Sociological Review*, 53.4 (2005), 587–602
Macmillan, Hugh, 'Return to the Malungwana Drift – Max Gluckman, the Zulu Nation and the Common Society', *African Affairs*, 94.374 (1995), 39–65
Maddock, Kenneth, 'Brown, Alfred Reginald Radcliffe (1881–1955)', *Oxford Dictionary of National Biography* <https://doi.org/10.1093/ref:odnb/37877>
Mafeje, Archie, 'The Ideology of "Tribalism"', *The Journal of Modern African Studies*, 9.2 (1971), 253–61
———, 'The Problem of Anthropology in Historical Perspective: An Inquiry into the Growth of the Social Sciences', *Canadian Journal of African Studies/Revue Canadienne des Études Africaines*, 10.2 (1976), 307–33
———, 'Who Are the Makers and Objects of Anthropology? A Critical Comment on Sally Falk Moore's "Anthropology and Africa"', *African Sociological Review/Revue Africaine de Sociologie*, 1.1 (1997), 1–15

Mamdani, Mahmood, *Citizen and Subject: Contemporary Africa and the Legacy of Late Colonialism* (Princeton, NJ: University Press, 1996)

Mandler, Peter, *History and National Life* (London: Profile Books, 2002)

——, *Return from the Natives: How Margaret Mead Won the Second World War and Lost the Cold War* (New Haven, CT: Yale University Press, 2013)

——, 'Educating the Nation: IV. Subject Choice', *Transactions of the Royal Historical Society*, 27 (2017), 1–27

——, 'The Language of Social Science in Everyday Life', *History of the Human Sciences*, 32.1 (2019), 66–82

——, 'Good Reading for the Million: The "Paperback Revolution" and the Co-Production of Academic Knowledge in Mid Twentieth-Century Britain and America', *Past & Present*, 244.1 (2019), 235–6

——, 'The Rise and Fall of the Social Sciences in the British Educational System, 1960–2016', in *The History of Sociology in Britain: New Research and Revaluation*, ed. by Plamena Panayotova (London: Palgrave Macmillan, 2019)

Manganaro, Marc, *Culture, 1922: The Emergence of a Concept* (Princeton, NJ: Princeton University Press, 2002)

Mantena, Karuna, *Alibis of Empire: Henry Maine and the Ends of Liberal Imperialism* (Princeton, NJ: Princeton University Press, 2010)

Marchand, Suzanne, 'Has the History of the Disciplines Had Its Day?', in *Rethinking Modern European Intellectual History*, ed. by Samuel Moyn and Darrin M. McMahon (Oxford: Oxford University Press, 2014)

Marcus, George E., and James Clifford, eds., *Writing Culture: The Poetics and Politics of Ethnography* (Berkeley: University of California Press, 1986)

Marwick, Arthur, 'Middle Opinion in the Thirties: Planning, Progress and Political "Agreement"', *The English Historical Review*, 79.311 (1964), 285–98

Matera, Marc, 'Colonial Subjects: Black Intellectuals and the Development of Colonial Studies in Britain', *Journal of British Studies*, 49.2 (2010), 388–418

——, *Black London: The Imperial Metropolis and Decolonization in the Twentieth Century* (Berkeley: University of California Press, 2015)

McCarthy, Helen, 'Social Science and Married Women's Employment in Post-War Britain', *Past & Present*, 233.1 (2016), 269–305

——, 'Pearl Jephcott and the Politics of Gender, Class and Race in Post-War Britain', *Women's History Review*, 28.5 (2019), 779–93

——, *Double Lives: A History of Working Motherhood* (London: Bloomsbury, 2020)

McKibbin, Ross, *Classes and Cultures, England 1918–1951* (Oxford: Oxford University Press, 1998)

Meckier, Jerome, 'A Neglected Huxley "Preface": His Earliest Synopsis of *Brave New World*', *Twentieth Century Literature*, 25.1 (1979), 1–20

——, '*Brave New World* and the Anthropologists: Primitivism in A.F. 632', in *Aldous Huxley: Modern Satirical Novelist of Ideas – a Collection of Essays by Jerome Mechier*, ed. by Peter Edgerly Firchow and Bernfried Nugel (Münster: LIT Verlag, 2006)

Meloni, Maurizio, 'The Transcendence of the Social: Durkheim, Weismann, and the Purification of Sociology', *Frontiers in Sociology*, 1 (2016) <http://dx.doi.org/10.3389/fsoc.2016.00011>

Messac, Luke, 'Outside the Economy: Women's Work and Feminist Economics in the Construction and Critique of National Income Accounting', *The Journal of Imperial and Commonwealth History*, 46.3 (2018), 552–78

Meyerowitz, Joanne, '"How Common Culture Shapes the Separate Lives": Sexuality, Race, and Mid-Twentieth-Century Social Constructionist Thought', *The Journal of American History*, 96.4 (2010), 1057–84

Middleton, Stuart, '"Affluence" and the Left in Britain, c. 1958–1974', *The English Historical Review*, 129.536 (2014), 107–38

Miller, Gavin, 'Political Repression and Sexual Freedom in Brave New World and 1984', in *Huxley's Brave New World: Essays*, ed. by David Garrett Izzo and Kim Kirkpatrick (Jefferson, NC: McFarland, 2008)

Mills, David, 'Professionalizing or Popularizing Anthropology? A Brief History of Anthropology's Scholarly Associations in the UK', *Anthropology Today*, 19.5 (2003), 8–13

——, 'Anthropology at the End of Empire: The Rise and Fall of the Colonial Social Sciences Research Council, 1944–1962', in *Empires, Nations, and Natives: Anthropology and State-Making*, ed. by Benoit de L'Estoile, Federico G. Neiburg, and Lygia Sigaud (Durham, NC: Duke University Press, 2005)

——, 'How Not to Be a "Government House Pet", Audrey Richards and the East African Institute for Social Research', in *African Anthropologies: History, Critique and Practice*, ed. by David Mills, Mwenda Ntarangwi, and Mustafa Babiker (New York: Zed Books, 2006)

——, 'Made in Manchester? Methods and Myths in Disciplinary History', in *The Manchester School: Practice and Ethnographic Praxis in Anthropology*, ed, by T. M. S. Evens and Don Handelman (New York: Berghahn Books, 2006)

——, 'A Major Disaster for Anthropology? Oxford and Alfred Reginald Radcliffe-Brown', in *A History of Oxford Anthropology*, ed. by Peter Rivière (New York: Berghahn Books, 2007).

——, *Difficult Folk? A Political History of Social Anthropology* (New York: Berghahn Books, 2008).

Mine, Yoichi, 'The Political Element in the Works of W. Arthur Lewis: The 1954 Lewis Model and African Development', *The Developing Economies*, 44.3 (2006), 329–55

Mirowski, Philip, 'Exploring the Fault Lines: Introduction to the Minisymposium on the History of Economic Anthropology', *History of Political Economy*, 32.4 (2000), 919–32.

Mitchell, Timothy, 'Fixing the Economy', *Cultural Studies*, 12.1 (1998), 82–101

Moddelmog, Debra A., 'Modernism and Sexology', *Literature Compass*, 11.4 (2014), 267–78

Morgan, Mary S., 'Seeking Parts, Looking for Wholes', in *Histories of Scientific Observation*, ed. by Lorraine Daston and Elizabeth Lunbeck (Chicago: University of Chicago Press, 2011)

Morton, Christopher, 'Evans-Pritchard and Malinowski: The Roots of a Complex Relationship', *History of Anthropology Newsletter*, 34.2 (2007), 10–14

——, *The Anthropological Lens: Rethinking E. E. Evans-Pritchard* (Oxford: Oxford University Press, 2020)

Murdock, George Peter, 'British Social Anthropology', *American Anthropologist*, 53.4 (1951), 465–73

Nava, Mica, 'Sometimes Antagonistic, Sometimes Ardently Sympathetic: Contradictory Responses to Migrants in Postwar Britain', *Ethnicities*, 14.3 (2014), 458–80

Niehaus, Isak, 'Anthropology at the Dawn of Apartheid: Radcliffe-Brown and Malinowski's South African Engagements, 1918–1934', *Focaal European Journal of Anthropology*, 76.3 (2017), 103–17

O'Brien, Patricia, 'Remaking Australia's Colonial Culture? White Australia and Its Papuan Frontier 1901–1940', *Australian Historical Studies*, 40.1 (2009), 96–112.

Ogan, Eugene, 'Copra Came Before Copper: The Nasioi of Bougainville and Plantation Colonialism, 1902–1964', *Pacific Studies*, 19.1 (1996), 31–51

Oman, Charles P., and Ganeshan Wignaraja, *The Postwar Evolution of Development Thinking* (Houndmills, Basingstoke: Macmillan, 1991)

Oreskes, Naomi, 'Objectivity or Heroism? On the Invisibility of Women in Science', *Osiris*, 11 (1996), 87–113.

Ortner, Sherry B., 'Theory in Anthropology since the Sixties', *Comparative Studies in Society and History*, 26.1 (1984), 126–166

Ortolano, Guy, 'Human Science or a Human Face? Social History and the "Two Cultures" Controversy', *Journal of British Studies*, 43.4 (2004), 482–505

———, *The Two Cultures Controversy: Science, Literature and Cultural Politics in Postwar Britain* (Cambridge: Cambridge University Press, 2009)

———, 'The Typicalities of the English? Walt Rostow, the Stages of Economic Growth, and Modern British History', *Modern Intellectual History*, 12.3 (2015), 657–84.

Overy, R. J., *The Morbid Age: Britain and the Crisis of Civilization* (London: Penguin, 2010)

Owens, Patricia, 'Lucy Philip Mair – Leading Writer on Colonial Administration, Early International Relations Scholar, and anthropologist', <https://blogs.lse.ac.uk/lsehistory/2018/10/03/lucy-mair/>

Pallares-Burke, Maria Lúcia G., *The New History: Confessions and Conversations* (Oxford: Wiley, 2002)

Parker, John, 'The Dynamics of Fieldwork Among the Talensi: Meyer Fortes in Northern Ghana, 1934–7', *Africa*, 83.4 (2013), 623–45

Parmar, Inderjeet, 'American Foundations and the Development of International Knowledge Networks', *Global Networks*, 2.1 (2002), 13–30

Pearson, Heath, 'Primitive Economics: A Reply', *History of Political Economy*, 34.1 (2002), 273–81.

Pedersen Susan, 'National Bodies, Unspeakable Acts: The Sexual Politics of Colonial Policy-Making', *The Journal of Modern History*, 63.4 (1991), 647–80

———, 'Settler Colonialism at the Bar of the League of Nations', in *Settler Colonialism in the Twentieth Century: Projects, Practices, Legacies*, ed. by Caroline Elkins and Susan Pedersen (London: Routledge, 2005)

———, *Internationalism and Empire: British Dilemmas, 1919–1939* (2014) <https://academiccommons.columbia.edu/doi/10.7916/d8-m672-1p02>

———, *The Guardians: The League of Nations and the Crisis of Empire* (Oxford: Oxford University Press, 2015).

Peel, J. D. Y., 'Not Really a View from Without: The Relations of Social Anthropology and Sociology', in *British Sociology Seen from Without and Within*, ed. by A. H. Halsey and W. G. Runciman (Oxford: Oxford University Press, 2005)

Pellew, Jill, 'A Metropolitan University Fit for Empire: The Role of Private Benefaction in the Early History of the London School of Economics and Political Science and Imperial College of Science and Technology, 1895–1930', *History of Universities* 46 (2012), 202–45

Pels, Peter, 'Global "Experts" and "African" Minds: Tanganyika Anthropology as Public and Secret Service, 1925–61', *Journal of the Royal Anthropological Institute* 17, 4 (2011): 788–810

Pietsch, Tamson, *Empire of Scholars: Universities, Networks and the British Academic World, 1850–1939* (Manchester: Manchester University Press, 2013)

Platt, Jennifer, *The British Sociological Association: A Sociological History* (Durham, NC: Sociologypress, 2003)

Plattner, Stuart, *Economic Anthropology* (Stanford, CA: Stanford University Press, 1989)

Pocock, J. G. A., *Barbarism and Religion, Volume 4, Barbarians, Savages and Empires* (Cambridge: Cambridge University Press, 2005)

Qureshi, Sadiah, *Peoples on Parade: Exhibitions, Empire and Anthropology in Nineteenth-Century Britain* (Chicago: University of Chicago Press, 2011)

———, 'Peopling Natural History', in *Worlds of Natural History*, ed. by Helen Anne Curry et al. (Cambridge: Cambridge University Press, 2018)

Ranger, T. O., 'From Humanism to the Science of Man: Colonialism in Africa and the Understanding of Alien Societies', *Transactions of the Royal Historical Society*, 5th ser., 26 (1976), 115–41

Reed, Isaac Ariail, and Mayer N. Zald, 'The Unsettlement of Communities of Inquiry', in *Theorizing in Social Science: The Context of Discovery*, ed. by Richard Swedberg (Stanford, CA: Stanford University Press, 2014)

Renwick, Chris, *British Sociology's Lost Biological Roots: A History of Futures Past* (Basingstoke: Palgrave Macmillan, 2012)

———, 'Completing the Circle of the Social Sciences? William Beveridge and Social Biology at London School of Economics during the 1930s', *Philosophy of the Social Sciences*, 44.4 (2014), 478–96

Rich, Paul, 'The Long Victorian Sunset: Anthropology, Eugenics and Race in Britain, c. 1900–48', *Patterns of Prejudice*, 18.3 (1984), 3–17

Riley, Charlotte Lydia, '"Tropical Allsorts": The Transnational Flavor of British Development Policies in Africa', *Journal of World History*, 26.4 (2016), 839–64

———, '"The Winds of Change Are Blowing Economically": The Labour Party and British Overseas Development, 1940s–1960s', in *Britain, France and the Decolonization of Africa*, ed. by Andrew W.M. Smith and Chris Jeppesen (London: UCL Press, 2017)

Riley, Denise, *War in the Nursery: Theories of the Child and Mother* (London: Virago, 1983)

Roberts, A. D., 'The Imperial Mind', in *The Cambridge History of Africa, Volume 7, From 1905 to 1940*, ed. by A. D. Roberts (Cambridge: Cambridge University Press, 1986)

Robinson, Paul A., *The Modernization of Sex: Havelock Ellis, Alfred Kinsley, William Masters, and Virginia Johnson* (London: Elek, 1976)

Rodgers, Daniel T. 'Paths in the Social History of Ideas', in *The Worlds of American Intellectual History*, ed. by Joel Isaac et al. (Oxford: Oxford University Press, 2016)

Rogan, Tim, *The Moral Economists: R.H. Tawney, Karl Polanyi, E.P. Thompson, and the Critique of Capitalism* (Princeton, NJ: Princeton University Press, 2017)

Rosaldo, Michelle Zimbalist, Louise Lamphere, and Joan Bamberger, *Woman, Culture, and Society* (Stanford, CA: Stanford University Press, 1974)

Rossetti, Carlo, 'B. Malinowski, the Sociology of "Modern Problems" in Africa and the Colonial Situation,' *Cahiers d'études africaines* 25.100 (1985): 477–503

Rouse, Sandra, 'Expedition and Institution: A. C. Haddon and Anthropology at Cambridge', in *Cambridge and the Torres Strait*, ed. by Anita Herle and Sandra Rouse (Cambridge: Cambridge University Press, 1998)

Said, Edward W., 'Representing the Colonized: Anthropology's Interlocutors', *Critical Inquiry*, 15.2 (1989), 205–25

Savage, Mike, 'Elizabeth Bott and the Formation of Modern British Sociology', *The Sociological Review*, 56.4 (2008), 579–605

——, *Identities and Social Change in Britain since 1940: The Politics of Method* (Oxford: Oxford University Press, 2010)

Saville, John, 'Britain: Internationalism and the Labour Movement between the Wars', in *Internationalism in the Labour Movement, 1830–1940*, ed. by F. L. van Holthoon and Marcel van der Linden (Leiden: E. J. Brill, 1988), vol. 2, 565–83

Scannell, Paddy, and David Cardiff, *A Social History of British Broadcasting, Volume 1, 1922–1939: Serving the Nation* (Oxford: Basil Blackwell, 1990)

Schaffer, Simon, *From Physics to Anthropology and Back Again* (Chicago: Prickly Pear, 1994)

Schmelzer, Matthias, 'The Growth Paradigm: History, Hegemony, and the Contested Making of Economic Growthmanship', *Ecological Economics*, 118 (2015), 262–71

Schofield, Camilla, and Ben Jones, '"Whatever Community Is, This Is Not It": Notting Hill and the Reconstruction of "Race" in Britain after 1958', *Journal of British Studies*, 58.1 (2019), 142–73

Schumaker, Lynette, 'A Tent with a View: Colonial Officers, Anthropologists, and the Making of the Field in Northern Rhodesia, 1937–1960', *Osiris*, 11 (1996), 237–58.

——, *Africanizing Anthropology: Fieldwork, Networks, and the Making of Cultural Knowledge in Central Africa* (Durham, NC: Duke University Press, 2001).

Scott, James C., *Seeing Like a State: How Certain Schemes to Improve the Human Condition Have Failed* (New Haven, CT: Yale University Press, 1998)

Sebastiani, Silvia, *The Scottish Enlightenment: Race, Gender, and the Limits of Progress* (London: Palgrave Macmillan, 2013)

Segal, ,'Robert A., 'Durkheim in Britain: The Work of Radcliffe-Brown', *Journal of the Anthropological Society of Oxford*, 30.2 (1999), 131–62

Seim, David L., *Rockefeller Philanthropy and Modern Social Science* (London: Pickering & Chatto, 2013)

Sen, Amartya, 'Introduction', in *Growth Economics: Selected Readings* (Harmondsworth: Penguin, 1970)

Serra, Gerardo, 'Pleas for Fieldwork: Polly Hill on Observation and Induction, 1966–1982', *Research in the History of Economic Thought and Methodology*, 36 (2018), 93–108

Sewell, William Hamilton, *Logics of History: Social Theory and Social Transformation* (Chicago: University of Chicago Press, 2005)

Shapira, Michal, *The War Inside* (Cambridge: Cambridge University Press, 2013)

Shilliam, Robbie, *Race and the Undeserving Poor: From Abolition to Brexit* (Newcastle upon Tyne: Agenda Publishing, 2018)

——, 'Behind the Rhodes Statue: Black Competency and the Imperial Academy', *History of the Human Sciences*, 32.5 (2019), 3–27

Sillitoe, Paul, 'The Role of Section H at the British Association for the Advancement of Science in the History of Anthropology', *Durham Anthropology Journal*, 13.2 (2005) <https://citeseerx.ist.psu.edu/viewdoc/summary?doi=10.1.1.123.9527>

Sivasundaram, Sujit, 'The Animal and Human in the Idea of Race', *Comparative Studies of South Asia, Africa and the Middle East*, 35.1 (2015), 156–72

Soffer, Reba N., 'The Development of Disciplines in the Modern English University', *The Historical Journal*, 31.4 (1988), 933–46

——, 'The Modern University and National Values, 1850–1930', *Historical Research*, 60.142 (1987), 166–87.

Soloway, Richard Allen, *Birth Control and the Population Question in England 1877–1930*. (Chapel Hill: North Carolina University Press, 1982)

Speich, Daniel, 'The Use of Global Abstractions: National Income Accounting in the Period of Imperial Decline', *Journal of Global History*, 6.1 (2011), 7–28.

Spencer, Jonathan, 'British Social Anthropology: A Retrospective', *Annual Review of Anthropology*, 29 (2000), 1–24.

Spillius, Elizabeth, *Encounters with Melanie Klein: Selected Papers of Elizabeth Spillius* (Routledge: London, 2007)

Średniawa, Bronisław "The Anthropologist as a Young Physicist: Bronisław Malinowski's Apprenticeship," *Isis*, 72 (1981), 613–20

Stanley, Liz, 'Mass-Observation's Fieldwork Methods', in *Handbook of Ethnography*, ed. by Paul Atkinson et al. (London: Sage Publications, 2001)

Steinmetz, George, 'A Child of the Empire: British Sociology and Colonialism, 1940s–1960s', *Journal of the History of the Behavioral Sciences*, 49.4 (2013), 353–78

——, 'Defensive Anthropology', *Postcolonial Studies*, 17.4 (2014), 436–50, 443

——, 'Sociology and Colonialism in the British and French Empires, 1945–1965', *Journal of Modern History*, 89.3 (2017), 601–48
Stocking, George W., Jr, 'Radcliffe-Brown and British Social Anthropology', in *Functionalism Historicized: Essays on British Social Anthropology*, ed. by George W. Stocking Jr. (Madison: University of Wisconsin Press, 1984)
——, 'Philanthropoids and Vanishing Cultures', in *Objects and Others: Essays on Museums and Material Culture*, ed. by George W. Stocking Jr. (Madison: University of Wisconsin Press, 1985)
——, 'Anthropology and the Irrational – Malinowski's Encounter with Freudian Psychoanalysis', in *Malinowski, Rivers, Benedict and Others: Essays on Culture and Personality*, ed. by George W. Stocking Jr (Madison: University of Wisconsin Press, 1986)
——, *Victorian Anthropology* (New York: Free Press, 1987)
——, 'Maclay, Kubary, Malinowski – Archetypes from the Dreamtime of Anthropology', in George W. Stocking Jr, *The Ethnographer's Magic and Other Essays in the History of Anthropology* (Madison: University of Wisconsin Press, 1992), 253–55
——, *The Ethnographer's Magic and Other Essays in the History of Anthropology* (Madison: University of Wisconsin Press, 1992)
——, *After Tylor: British Social Anthropology, 1888–1951* (Madison: University of Wisconsin Press, 1995)
Stockwell, Sarah, 'Britain and Decolonization in an Era of Global Change', in *The Oxford Handbook of the Ends of Empire*, ed. by Martin Thomas and Andrew S. Thompson (Oxford: Oxford University Press, 2018)
Stone, Lawrence, *The Past and the Present Revisited*, rev. edn (London: Routledge & Kegan Paul, 1987)
Storr, Cait, '"Imperium in Imperio": Sub-Imperialism and the Formation of Australia as a Subject of International Law', *Melbourne Journal of International Law*, 19.1 (2018), 335–68.
Szreter, Simon, and Kate Fisher, *Sex Before the Sexual Revolution: Intimate Life in England 1918–1963* (Cambridge: Cambridge University Press, 2010)
Tambiah, Stanley Jeyaraja, *Edmund Leach: An Anthropological Life* (Cambridge: Cambridge University Press, 2002)
Taylor, Miles, 'The Beginnings of Modern British Social History?', *History Workshop Journal*, 43 (1997), 155–76
Thomas, Keith, 'An Anthropology of Religion and Magic, II', *The Journal of Interdisciplinary History*, 6.1 (1975), 91–109
Thomson, Mathew, *Lost Freedom: The Landscape of the Child and the British Post-War Settlement* (Oxford: Oxford University Press, 2013)
Tignor, Robert L., *W. Arthur Lewis and the Birth of Development Economics* (Princeton, NJ: Princeton University Press, 2006).
Tilley, Helen, 'Introduction: Africa, Imperialism, and Anthropology', in *Ordering Africa: Anthropology, European Imperialism and the Politics of Knowledge*, ed. by Helen Tilley and Robert Gordon (Manchester: Manchester University Press, 2010)
——, *Africa as a Living Laboratory: Empire, Development, and the Problem of Scientific Knowledge, 1870–1950* (Chicago: University of Chicago Press, 2011)

Topalov, Christian, 'Traditional Working-Class Neighborhoods': An Inquiry into the Emergence of a Sociological Model in the 1950s and 1960s', *Osiris*, 18 (2003), 212–33

Trouillot, Michel-Rolph, 'Anthropology and the Savage Slot: The Poetics and Politics of Otherness', in *Recapturing Anthropology: Working in the Present*, ed. by Richard G. Fox (Santa Fe, NM: School of American Research Press, 1991)

Tsing, Anna Lowenhaupt, *The Mushroom at the End of the World: On the Possibility of Life in Capitalist Ruins* (Princeton, NJ: Princeton University Press, 2015)

Tuhiwai Smith, Linda, *Decolonizing Methodologies: Research and Indigenous Peoples* (London: Zed Books, 2012)

Urry, James, *Before Social Anthropology: Essays on the History of British Anthropology* (Philadelphia: Harwood Academic Publishers, 1993)

———, 'Making Sense of Diversity and Complexity: The Ethnological Context and Consequences of the Torres Strait Expedition and the Oceanic Phase in British Anthropology, 1890–1935', in *Cambridge and the Torres Strait: Centenary Essays on the 1898 Anthropological Expedition*, ed. by Anita Herle and Sandra Rouse (Cambridge: Cambridge University Press, 1998).

Vitalis, Robert, *White World Order, Black Power Politics: The Birth of American International Relations* (Ithaca, NY: Cornell University Press, 2015)

Walkowitz, Judith R., *City of Dreadful Delight: Narratives of Sexual Danger in Late-Victorian London* (Chicago: University of Chicago Press, 1992)

Waller, Richard D., 'Witchcraft and Colonial Law in Kenya,' *Past & Present* 180 (August 2003), 241–75

Warwick, Andrew, and David Kaiser, 'Conclusion: Kuhn, Foucault, and the Power of Pedagogy', in *Pedagogy and the Practice of Science, Historical and Contemporary Perspectives*, ed. by David Kaiser (Cambridge, MA: MIT Press, 2005)

Waters, Chris, '"Dark Strangers" in Our Midst: Discourses of Race and Nation in Britain, 1947–1963', *Journal of British Studies*, 36.2 (1997), 207–38

Werbner, Richard, *Anthropology after Gluckman: The Manchester School, Colonial and Postcolonial Transformations* (Manchester: Manchester University Press, 2020)

Wetherell, D., and C. Carr-Gregg, *Camilla: C.H. Wedgwood 1901–1955, a Life* (Sydney: New South Wales University Press, 1990), 24-28

Wiley, Norbert, 'The Current Interregnum in American Sociology', *Social Research*, 52.1 (1985), 179–207

Williamson, Philip, *National Crisis and National Government: British Politics, the Economy and Empire, 1926–1932* (Cambridge: Cambridge University Press, 1992)

Wolfe, Patrick, *Settler Colonialism and the Transformation of Anthropology: The Politics and Poetics of an Ethnographic Event* (London: Cassell, 1999)

———, 'Settler Colonialism and the Elimination of the Native', *Journal of Genocide Research*, 8.4 (2006), 387–409.

Wylie, Diana, 'Confrontation over Kenya: The Colonial Office and Its Critics 1918–1940', *The Journal of African History*, 18.3 (1977), 427–47

Young, Alden, *Transforming Sudan: Decolonization, Economic Development, and State Formation*, (Cambridge: Cambridge University Press, 2017)

Young, Michael W., *Malinowski: Odyssey of an Anthropologist, 1884–1920* (New Haven, CT: Yale University Press, 2004)

Index

Abraham, R. C., 28
African People in the Twentieth Century, An (1934), 71
African Political Systems (1940), 143, 163
African Survey (1938), 130, 133–35, 138. See also Hailey, Malcolm
Amery, Leo, 35, 38, 131, 136; and colonial policy in East Africa, 35
Analysis of Social Change, The (1945), 149
Anderson, Perry, 7, 173
Andeyera (surname unknown, prophet and ritual expert), 70
Annales: Economies, sociétiés, civilisations, 172
Arensberg, Conrad, 118
Argonauts of the Western Pacific (1922), 3, 13, 23–25, 46, 49, 52, 62: as source for E. P. Thompson, 171
Asad, Talal: and *Anthropology & the Colonial Encounter*, 7, 176, 194n9
Assa (surname unknown, Lucy Mair's research assistant), 70
Association of Social Anthropologists (ASA), 139, 144, 179
Australia, 22–23, 26, 83; Australian National University, 140; British Association for the Advancement of Science in, 19; inquiry into Pacific trade, 22–23, 33; Mandate of New Guinea, 22, 28; Radcliffe-Brown's time in, 28
Azikwe, Nnamdi, 42

Bailey, F. G., 176
Balfour, Henry, 143
Banton, Michael, 117, 118, 120
Barnes, John, 124, 158
Barth, Fredrick, 176
Barth, Sir Jacob, 45
Bassey N'Dem, Eyo, 118, 121
Beemer, Hilda, 132
Benedict, Ruth, 2
Bermondsey. *See* London
Bethnal Green. *See* London
Beveridge, William, 31, 87
Boas, Franz, 2, 119
Bourdieu, Pierre, 180
Bowlby, John, 99
Bott, Elizabeth, 2, 122–28
Bremnes, Norway, 124
Briffault, Robert, 92, 93–95
British Association for the Advancement of Science (BAAS), its 1914 meeting in Australia, 19
British Broadcasting Corporation (BBC), 92
Bücher, Karl, 50
Buell, Raymond, 42

257

258 | Index

Bunche, Ralph, 133
Buxton, Leonard, 143

Cabinet Office, 138
Caine, Sydney, 138
Cameron, Donald, 36, 136
Cardiff, 118
Carnegie Corporation, 135
Central Intelligence Agency (CIA), as sponsor of Cold War social science, 7, 178
Christianity: and contraception, 100; missionary work in the British Empire, 36, 70–71; as a research subject during fieldwork, 62, 71–72, 149
Clifton-Roberts, C., 47
Cohen, Andrew, 141
Cohen, Anthony, 103
Cold War, 153, 157
Collins, Sydney, 117, 118, 121
colonial cadets, training of, 10
Colonial Economic and Development Council (CDC), 138
Colonial Office, as sponsor of anthropology, 11, 27–28, 138
Colonial Social Science Research Council (CSSRC), 131–32, 138–40, 142, 143, 143, 150
Colson, Elizabeth, 176
Commonwealth Development and Welfare Act (CDWA), 131, 137
"companionate marriage," 100
comparative method, 15
communism, 81, 88, 96
community studies: as drawing on anthropological theories, 113, 116, 118; as methodologically similar to social anthropology, 102–3
Crime and Custom in Savage Society (1926), 46
cultural relativism, 2, 57–58

Darnton, Robert, 180
Darwin, Charles, 83
Deane, Phyllis, 157
decolonisation, 131, 152, 173
Delamere, Lord (Hugh Cholmondley), 49
development (as policy), 131, 138, 143, 150, 152, 167–68; and the League of Nations, 135. *See also* economics
"diffusionism," 14; and its supercession by functionalism, 30
disciplinary history, 3, 6, 78–79; Collini's "lateral" and "vertical" views of, 3, 4, 104, 174

Dobbs, C. M., 40
Douglas, Mary, 176, 180
Driberg, Jack, 35
Dual Mandate in Tropical Africa, The, 32
Durkheim, Émile, 19, 22, 27, 83

East African Institute of Social Research (EAISR), 140, 142, 146
economic anthropology. *See* economics
economic development. *See* economics
Economic Development and Tribal Change (1954), 141, 156
economic history, as having similar origins to development economics, 161
economics, 130; anthropologists' critiques of neoclassical economics, 51–52, 54, 165–66; arguments about the need to combine economic and anthropological expertise, 53–55, 160, 167; comparing evolutionism and functionalism in its study, 50; and economic development, 138, 141, 152–63, 168; and "economic dualism," 49–50, 156; and gift/non-monetary exchange, 24, 52, 159–60, 165–66, 172; Lionel Robbins' definition of, 51; Malinowski's interest in researching economic life, 22–23; Margaret Read's research in the field, 72; Phyllis Deane's research, 157–63; "substantivism" and "formalism," 163–68. *See also* Malinowski, Bronislaw; moral economy
Edinburgh, 117–19, 121
Elliot Smith, Grafton, 12, 19, 26; and "diffusionism," 13–16; as having relatively more prestige than Malinowski in mid 1920s, 13; and the Rockefeller Foundations, 30
Ellis, Havelock, 81, 85
Elton, Geoffrey, 170
Empire Air Mail, as facilitator of exchange between field and seminar, 66–67
Engels, Friedrich, 83, 96
Epstein, A. L., 176
Essay on the Economics of Detribalization in Northern Rhodesia, An (1941, 1942), 146
Essay on the Nature and Significance of Economic Science, An (1932), 51
eugenics, 82, 119
Evans-Pritchard, Edward, 3, 75–78, 103, 106, 135, 139, 141, 172, 176; and witchcraft, 47
evolutionism (in anthropology), 50, 86, 94

expertise: in comparison to amateurism, 9–11; its growth in the British Empire, 10–11; the politics of, 42–44, 132–33, 189nn18,19; and the Rockefeller Foundation, 29–30

Fabian Colonial Bureau, 157
family. *See* kinship
Family and Kinship in East London (1957), 105, 112–17, 122
Father in Primitive Society, The (1927), 85
feminism, 89, 92, 98–99, 180
fieldwork: colonial context of, 22, 69, 72, 177; by contrast to other types of field science, 65, 68; as core method of social anthropology, 13, 63–64, 68, 75; and economic anthropology, 158–60, 162; and gender, 17, 72–73; histories of, 17; as opposed to "armchair anthropology," 17–18, 64–65; before Malinowski, 18; marking out the boundary between professionals and amateurs, 10, 17
Firth, Raymond, 50, 139, 146, 176, 178, 181; and community studies, 103; and economic anthropology 54–56, 79, 165–68; his research about kinship, 107–12; on Mass Observation, 107
Fison, Lorimer, 83
Forde, Daryll, 139
Ford Foundation, 113, 153
Fortes, Meyer, 5, 48, 73–78, 103, 135, 139, 143
Frankenberg, Ronald, 150
Frazer, J. G., 84
Freud, Sigmund, 22, 83, 85–86
Freudians/Freudianism, 81, 83–84, 88, 98–99
functionalism, 3, 114, 124, 174; its attraction to midcentury intellectuals, 5, 169, 173; criticisms of, 177–78; as a method, 58–60, 62–63
Fustel de Coulanges, 144

Geertz, Clifford, 180
Ghana (Gold Coast), 28, 98, 162
Gillen, Frank, 83
Ginsberg, Morris, 103
Ginzburg, Carlo, 180
Glass, David, 139
Glass, Ruth, 117
Gluckman, Max, 5, 78, 121, 127, 139, 143, 156, 176; economics research, 158; his directorship of the RLI, 146–49, 158; his time at Oxford, 147; his views of Phyllis Deane's; at Manchester, 176–77. *See also* Manchester School
Godelier, Maurice 176
Goody, Jack, 59
Gough, Kathleen, 166
government anthropology, 28
Great Transformation, The (1944), 164, 167; and its anthropological citations, 223n77
Gunn, Selkar, 29

Haddon, A. C., 14, 16, 20, 25
Hailey, Malcolm, 130, 133–35, 136, 163
Haldane, J. B. S., 89
Hall, Radclyffe, 80
Harris, Frank, 80
Harrison, Tom, 105–6
Herero and Nama genocide, 23
Hill, Polly, 162
historiography of social anthropology: apparently declining in popular relevance by 1930s, 80–81; as British, 5; caught between histories of literary criticism and sociology, 3; by comparison to American anthropology, 2, 81; by comparison to other national traditions, 6; and gender, 79, 162; going back to Renaissance and/or Enlightenment, 3; the necessity of taking an imperial and international approach to, 6; and policy in the British Empire, 41, 186n30; as related to sociology via community studies, 102–4; as response to Victorian "crisis of faith," 3; in terms of the history of the science of "race," 9; and this book's criticism of the former argument, 99–100; statement of this book's approach to, 4, 8, 175
history (academic discipline): Evans-Pritchard's comments about its similarity to social anthropology, 144–46; social history and social anthropology, 168–72
Hobhouse, Leonard, 103
Hobsbawm, Eric, 172
Hoernlé, Winnifred, 5, 27, 147
Hogbin, Ian, 146
"homo economicus," 51
Hoselitz, Bert, 165–66
Huxley, Aldous, 2, 90–92
Huxley, Julian, 89

India, 131
indirect rule (ideology of colonial rule), 32, 42; and economics, 53, 156; and

indirect rule (*continued*)
    Malinowski's ideas about it, 32–33, 49, 56; and the rule of law, 47–48
Institute of Race Relations, 104
International Bank for Reconstruction and Development, 153
International Institute of African Languages and Cultures (IIALC), 30, 42–44, 45, 60
International Monetary Fund, 153

Jamaica, 141, 157
James (surname unknown, employed as Margaret Read's research assistant), 69
Jephcott, Pearl, 117
Jonathan (surname unknown, employed as Margaret Read's cook), 69
Joseph, Keith, 116
Junod, Violaine, 118

Kaldor, Nicholas, 162
Keith, Arthur, 13
Kenya, 34, 37, 44–45, 138, 141
Kenyatta, Jomo, 42, 133
kinship, 80, 93–95, 107–8, 120, 139, 143; amidst context of demographic and cultural change in western Europe, 81–82; Bott's research about social networks and family, 122–28; Firth's research in London, 107–12; history of research about, 83–84; Malinowski's theories of, 87–88, 93–95
Kiriwina (one of the Trobriand Islands), 22, 23
Klein, Melanie, 99
Kula, 23
Kumwaka (surname unknown), 45
Kuper, Hilda, 146

Land, Labour and Diet in Northern Rhodesia (1939), 155
land tenure, 35, 37–38, 134–35
Laski, Harold, 89
Laslett, Peter, 172
Latour, Bruno, 180
Lawrence, D. H., 80, 91
Laura Spelman Rockefeller Memorial (LSRM). *See* Rockefeller Foundation
law and legal anthropology, 45–49
Leach, Edmund, 79, 139, 146, 176
League of Nations, 134–35; and colonial development, 135; and Permanent Mandates Commission, 32, 134; and the question of sovereignty in Tanganyika, 36
Leavis, F. R., 2

Le Clair, Edward, 166
Lévi-Strauss, Claude, 176, 180
Lewis, Arthur W., 138, 153, 163, 165; "Economic Development with Unlimited Supplies of Labour" (1954), 155–56; reviews books by Firth and Richards, 155
Leys, Norman, 35
literary criticism, as "concealed sociology," 2
Little, Kenneth, 117–22
London: Firth's research in Bermondsey, 108–12; Young and Willmott in Bethnal Green, 112–17. *See also* London School of Economics (LSE)
London School of Economics (LSE), 5, 10, 26, 28, 30–31, 35, 41, 44, 46, 50–52, 58, 60, 119, 122, 123, 139, 140–42
Lowie, Robert, 118
Lugard, Frederick Lord, 32, 40–41, 136; his politics, 36, 39–40; his views on magic and witchcraft, 45–46, 48
Lynd, Helen and Robert, 118

Macdonald, Malcolm, 135, 137
MacDonald, Ramsay, 40
Macfarlane, Alan, 170
Macmillan, Harold, 152
Madge, Charles, 105–6
Mafeje, Archie, as critic and historian of anthropology, 7, 177–78
magic. *See* witchcraft
Mailu (island in West Pacific), 20
Maine, Henry, 32, 94
Mair, Lucy, 60, 62, 67, 79, 134–35, 139, 176
Maitland, Frederic William
Malawi (Nyasaland), 157
Malinowski, Bronislaw, 5, 103, 135; accounts of him as originator of social anthropology in Britain, 3, 13; comments on Mass Observation, 106; as inspiration for community studies research, 113; his interventions in contemporary colonial political debate, 37–39, 132–33, 137; his liberalism, 89; his methodological differences with contemporaries, 12–13, 20, 64–65; his methodology, 3, 13, 20, 58, 61–62, 64; and the Rockefeller Foundation, 30; his support for the League of Nations, 134; in the Trobriand Islands, 19–25. *See also* economics; fieldwork; historiography of social anthropology; kinship; seminar, Malinowski's, at the LSE
Man and Culture (1957), 143

Manchester School, 146, 149, 150, 177–78. *See also* Gluckman, Max
Marett, Ranulph, 143
market, the, 165–67. *See also* economics; Polanyi, Karl
Marxism, 149, 169, 176, 180
Mass Observation, 105–7
Matheson, Hilda, 92–93, 133
Matthews, H. F. 28
Matthews, Z. K., 41, 133
McLennan, John, 83
Mead, Margaret, 2, 84, 108
Meade, James, 157
Meek, C., 28
Melland, Frank, 45
Mitchell, Clyde, 141, 176
Mitchison, Naomi, 89
Mnyoki (surname unknown), 45
moral economy, 24, 171–72, 180, 225n106
Morgan, Lewis Henry, 83, 96
motherhood. *See* kinship
Mumambwe (surname unknown, employed as Margaret Read's interpreter), 69
Munn-Rankin, Sophie, 96
Murdock, George Peter, 6
Murray, Hubert, 48
Murray, Keith, 138
museums, as spaces for displaying and constructing anthropological expertise, 9–10, 26, 142
Mwaiki (surname unknown), 45
Myers, John, 143

Nadel, Siegfried, 79, 139, 140
Namier, Lewis, 172
National Institute of Economic and Social Research (NIESR), 157
Negroes in Britain: A Study of Racial Relations in English Society (1947), 117, 119–20
Nigeria, 28, 32, 132, 136, 141
Nkrumah, Kwame, 152, 162, 163
Notes & Queries, 18, 64–65
Nuer (1940), 78
Nyerere, Julius, 152

Oedipus complex, 86
Oldham, J. H., 36
Oxford, University of. *See* University of Oxford

Parsons, Talcott, 108
participant observation, 22
Patterson, Sheila, 117

Perham, Margery, 132, 137
Perry, William, 14, 26
Piddington, Ralph, 118
Pirenne, Henri, 144
Pitt-Rivers Museum, 142
plantations, 22–23, 49–50
Polanyi, Karl, 154, 164, 166–67. *See also* economics
Power, Frederick, 144
"primitive, the," 22, 83, 156
Primitive Economics of the New Zealand Maori (1929), 50
Primitive Polynesian Economy (1939), 54, 155
Primitive Rebels (1959), 172
professionalisation, in the social sciences, 9–10, 26
psychology, 130
Pym, Barbara, 1

race. *See* racism
"race relations sociology," 104, 117–22
racism: of anthropologists, 61; and assumptions guiding "trusteeship," 37, 56, 200n135; and British univeristies, 56; in European natural science, 9; as inspiration for anthropological research, 14–15, 34, 193n89; as justification for anthropological research, 12, 34, 193n88; and justifications for East African settler supremacy, 35; and Rockefeller philanthropy, 31, 34; and segregation, 41. *See also* "race relations sociology"
Radcliffe-Brown, Alfred, 5, 19; as cited in sociology journals, 103; his early career, 26–28; the challenge he posed to Malinowski's authority in 1930s, 74, 75, 78; and economics, 223n74; his relationship with colonial research, 135, 137, 139, 141, 144; his teaching at Oxford, 142–43
radio: and cultures of listening 92–93, 97; listening groups, 96–97. *See also* BBC
Rattray, R. S., 28
Read, Margaret: her career, 79, 140, 176; her fieldwork methods and experiences, 64, 66–67, 74; her research on economics, 52–54, 72; and the postwar institutionalisation of social anthropology, 139
Rees-Williams, David, 138
Reith, John, 95
Religion and the Decline of Magic (1971), 170
Rhodes, Cecil, 49

Rhodes-Livingstone Institute (RLI), 140, 141, 146–49, 158, 160
Richards, Audrey, 139, 140, 141–42, 144, 146; and the challenge to social anthropology posed by development economics, 152, 155, 156, 164, 168; her fieldwork and methodology, 58–60; sexism and advancement in the profession, 79, 141
Rivers, W. H. R., 16–17, 18, 25
Robbins, Lionel, 51
Robeson, Eslanda, 133
Rockefeller Foundation, 28–31, 34, 87, 153, 165; and the politics of expertise in eastern Africa, 42–43. *See also* racism
Rosenstein-Rodan, Paul
Rostow, Walt, 153
Royal Anthropological Institute (RAI), 64
Ruml, Beardsley, 87
Russell, Bertrand, 90
Russell, Dora, 84, 90

Said, Edward, 178
Salter, Arthur, 138
Schapera, Isaac, 140, 146, 160
Seligman, Brenda, 139
Seligman, Charles, 13, 18, 26
seminar, Malinowski's, at the LSE, 44, 50–51, 132–33, 139; as "collective apprenticeship," 59; and importance of sending letters back and forth between field and seminar, 66–67, 71, 73–74; as "obligatory passage point" in discipline's history, 6; as a vehicle for creating an "ordinary science," 73
settler colonialism, 33, 34–36, 55–56, 135
"settler question." *See* settler colonialism
Sex and Repression in Savage Society (1927), 85
sexology, 81, 85
Sexual Life of Savages in Northwestern Melanesia, The (1929), 58, 80, 85, 87
Siepmann, Charles, 96
Smuts, Jan, 38, 131
social network. *See* kinship
Social Science Research Council, 165. *See also* Rockefeller Foundation
sociology: and community studies, 102–3; contemporary differences/similarities with biology, 87; as "gentlemanly social science," 2, 128; historiography of, 2–3, 102–3, 127–28, 184n9, 211n15
Solanke, Ladipo, 42

South Africa, 5, 26; University of Cape Town, 26–27, 140, 147
Stanner, William, 141
statistics: and economics, 160; and ethnographic research, 154; and the study of kinship, 111, 116
Stone, Lawrence, 169
Stone, Richard, 157, 160
Stopes, Marie, 81, 90
structural-functionalism, 78, 143
System of National Accounts and Supporting Tables (1953), 154

Tanzania (Tanganyika), 36, 136
Tavistock Institute, 122–23, 127
Terray, Emmanuel, 176
Theory of Economic Growth (1955), 155
Thomas, Keith, 2, 169–70. *See also* history
Thompson, E. P., 2, 170–72; his criticisms of economic growth, 172. *See also* history; moral economy
Thurnwald, Richard, 52
Tikopia, 108
Titmuss, Richard, 113
Torres Straits, anthropological expedition to, 16–18
Touluwa (Trobriand chief), 22
Treasury, 138
Trobriand Islands, 22, 52, 86
trusteeship (colonial ideology), 33, 35, 135, 136, 156; and "paramountcy," 37. *See also* racism
Turner, Victor, 176, 180
Two Studies of Kinship in London (1956), 108
Tylor, E. B., 10, 83

Uganda, 62, 68, 140, 141
United Nations (UN), 164
universities: and expansion of funding after Second World War, 178–79; as growing in importance as sites of knowledge production, 10, 25, 27; and the influence of Rockefeller money, 29–30; number of anthropologists working at, 10, 179; as teaching different kinds of anthropology in the 1920s, 28; where you could study anthropology in the early twentieth century, 26; where you could study anthropology in postwar Britain, 179
University College, London (UCL), 16, 139
University of Cambridge, 10, 14, 16, 17, 25, 26, 27, 28, 79, 119, 121 139, 142, 164

University of Chicago, 142, 165–68
University of Manchester, 79, 121, 139, 145, 149, 150, 172. *See also* Gluckman, Max
University of Oxford, 10, 26, 28, 38, 79, 121, 130, 140; as centre of postwar research in anthropology, 142–46, 147, 163–64; Colonial Administration Summer School (1938), 135–37; failure of opening a rival anthropological institute to LSE (1931), 42–44

van de Velde, Theodoor, 81
Vinogradoff, Paul, 144

We, The Tikopia (1936), 108
Webb, Sidney, 40
Wells, H. G., 91
Westermarck, Edward, 87, 97

Williams, O. G. R., 138
Williams, Raymond, 1, 128, 154
Willmott, Peter, 105, 112–17
Wilson, Godfrey, 73, 146, 148, 156
Wilson, Monica, 146, 148
Winnicott, Donald, 99
witchcraft, 44–49
Witchcraft, Oracles, and Magic among the Azande (1937), 3
World Bank, 164
World We Have Lost, The (1965), 172
Worsley, Peter, 150

Young, Hubert, 146
Young, Michael, 2, 103, 112–17

Zambia (Northern Rhodesia), 68, 140, 146, 157–59
Zemon Davis, Natalie, 180

Founded in 1893,
UNIVERSITY OF CALIFORNIA PRESS
publishes bold, progressive books and journals
on topics in the arts, humanities, social sciences,
and natural sciences—with a focus on social
justice issues—that inspire thought and action
among readers worldwide.

The UC PRESS FOUNDATION
raises funds to uphold the press's vital role
as an independent, nonprofit publisher, and
receives philanthropic support from a wide
range of individuals and institutions—and from
committed readers like you. To learn more, visit
ucpress.edu/supportus.

www.ingramcontent.com/pod-product-compliance
Lightning Source LLC
Chambersburg PA
CBHW030531230426
43665CB00010B/850